Need to Know

NEED TO KNOW

Vocation as the Heart of
Christian Epistemology

John G. Stackhouse, Jr.

OXFORD
UNIVERSITY PRESS

OXFORD

UNIVERSITY PRESS

Oxford University Press is a department of the
University of Oxford. It furthers the University's objective
of excellence in research, scholarship, and education
by publishing worldwide.

Oxford   New York
Auckland   Cape Town   Dar es Salaam   Hong Kong   Karachi
Kuala Lumpur   Madrid   Melbourne   Mexico City   Nairobi
New Delhi   Shanghai   Taipei   Toronto

With offices in
Argentina   Austria   Brazil   Chile   Czech Republic   France   Greece
Guatemala   Hungary   Italy   Japan   Poland   Portugal   Singapore
South Korea   Switzerland   Thailand   Turkey   Ukraine   Vietnam

Oxford is a registered trade mark of Oxford University Press
in the UK and certain other countries.

Published in the United States of America by
Oxford University Press
198 Madison Avenue, New York, NY 10016

© Oxford University Press 2014

Library of Congress Cataloging-in-Publication Data
Stackhouse, John G. (John Gordon), 1960–
Need to know : vocation as the heart of Christian epistemology / by John G. Stackhouse, Jr. 1 [edition].
pages   cm
ISBN 978-0-19-979064-7 (hardcover : alk. paper)—ISBN 978-0-19-979073-9 (updf)—
ISBN 978-0-19-937697-1 (epub)—ISBN 978-0-19-937698-8 (online content)
1. Thought and thinking—Religious aspects—Christianity.
2. Knowledge, Theory of (Religion)   I. Title.
BV4598.4.S73   2014
230.01—dc23   2013043903

9 8 7 6 5 4 3 2 1

Printed in the United States of America
on acid-free paper

To Nick

The fear of Yhwh is the beginning of knowledge.

Proverbs 1:7

In times of doubtings and questionings, when our belief is perplexed by new learning, new teaching, new thought, when our faith is strained by creeds, by doctrines, by mysteries beyond our understanding, give us the faithfulness of learners and the courage of believers in thee; give us boldness to examine and faith to trust all truth; patience and insight to master difficulties; stability to hold fast our tradition with enlightened interpretation to admit all fresh truth made known to us, and in times of trouble, to grasp new knowledge readily and to combine it loyally and honestly with the old; alike from stubborn rejection of new revelations, and from hasty assurance that we are wiser than our fathers,

Save us and help us, we humbly beseech thee, O Lord.

Bp. George Ridding

CONTENTS

PREFACE

A work is never completed except by some accident such as weariness, satisfaction, the need to deliver, or death: for, in relation to who or what is making it, it can only be one stage in a series of inner transformations.

Paul Valéry

There is something inescapably comical in offering a book to the world on how to think properly: "There, now, everyone. Think like this." One leaves oneself vulnerable to jibes regarding both one's intelligence and one's modesty from any wag in one's acquaintance—and my circle of acquaintance is positively wag-full. Furthermore, over the pleasant prefatorial custom of crediting people who have helped one write one's book, to which I shall proceed presently, there looms the shadow of implicating all those good people in whatever disappointment the reader will presently feel.

I press on regardless, for surely one of the commonplaces of contemporary scholarship is that none of us know it all and we each instead must contribute to the Great Conversation what we can, at whatever point in our lives we find that we must deliver ourselves of our opinions. After more than thirty years of thinking about thinking, that time for me has come at last.

One might think that after all that time I would have read more on the various subjects involved in this project. I do regret that I have failed to read nearly as much as I would like to have read. I hope that readers, and especially those who are authors of books and articles on relevant matters, will appreciate that I have tried to read responsibly, to learn *enough* to do *what I am called to do*. Thus the very theme of this book is exemplified in this apologia and apology: I am genuinely sorry for not citing, because I have not read, so many writings that doubtless have made valuable contributions to epistemological reflection. And if that work would make a substantial difference to the model I am setting out here, I look forward to its improvement by someone who has read better than have I.

At the same time, I don't want to disqualify myself in an unseemly paroxysm of humility. I know the difference between a Zeno's paradox and a Gettier problem, and having spent years studying and teaching Western intellectual history, I have a nodding acquaintance with the syllabus of epistemological "Greats." The project at hand, however, is not an exhaustive catalogue of epistemological literature, but an attempt to respond to some of the basic and perennial problems of philosophy— and, indeed, of human life in general. So I have had to remain focused on the constructive task, referring to whatever literature I think most pertinent and trusting the reader to appreciate that it would be tedious to note every connection I can think of between what I am doing and what Someone Else has done.

Two suggestions, if I may, about reading strategy. First, the book is meant to be read sequentially and entirely, as most books are. But the chapter on "The Current Situation" offers an intellectual history of the modern period that readers already conversant with such matters may skip. The argument of the book will remain nicely intact. Readers who are not entirely sure, however, about terms such as "Enlightenment," "Romanticism," "modernism," "postmodernism," and the like are invited to take this whirlwind tour to set the stage for all that follows.

Second, the book comes in two versions, so to speak, within the same covers. I have reserved a considerable amount of material for the notes so that general readers can follow the line of my argument in the main text as cleanly as possible. Those who seek more interaction with at least some of the questions raised herein can then easily glance down at the notes for the "extended version."

Now, about genealogy—the book's, not mine. My parents were my first teachers. My mother, a schoolteacher and later university instructor, insisted that I learn to read early on and that I start school precociously—which I did, starting at age three. My father had extraordinarily wide curiosity, a sticky mind for what we used to call "general knowledge," and a humility utterly blind to class, despite his income and status as a successful surgeon, so I learned to be open to learning from any and every source, rather than attending only to favorite disciplines and conventional authorities.

A Bible school instructor, who was also my Uncle Nelson Annan, was the first person other than my parents to combine piety with scholarship. He enjoyed both apologetics and preaching, both debating theological concepts and leading fervent worship. He set me a wholistic example that encouraged me to settle for nothing less in what was to follow.

What followed were ten years of university training, during which Mark Noll, Martin Marty, and Brian Gerrish in particular taught me directly (and George Marsden taught me via his writings) how to think and write historically. Their integration of ideas, political developments, economic realities, spiritual dimensions, and even geographical facts introduced me to thinking in a very broad place while insisting on plain evidence, plain reasoning, and plain exposition to justify whatever I might wish to aver. I note that this is not the typical training of someone venturing into the realm of epistemology, and it will help explain the unusual approach taken in this book.

In thinking about thinking, however, the main influence upon me was the group of American philosophers whose school was sometimes, and not quite accurately, termed "Reformed epistemology." William Alston, George Mavrodes, Alvin Plantinga, Nicholas Wolterstorff and others set out an epistemological vision that captured my interest and, soon, loyalty. In what I do epistemologically I gladly follow in their train.

Penultimately, I thank students in courses and seminars I have offered on "Christian thinking" in churches across North America and in classes at Tyndale Theological Seminary, the University of Manitoba, and especially Regent College. In no intellectual project I have undertaken have student suggestions been more helpful, truly formative and reformative, than in this one. I thank Regent also for the research leave (which we still charmingly refer to as a "sabbatical") that provided me the sustained, focused time to write a coherent first draft of a book that threatened always to sprawl. I have been assisted by a number (by now a large number) of superb research assistants over the thirty years I have been attending to this project, most recently by Abigail Woolley and Megan Ramsay. Alvin Plantinga has kindly tutored me along the way in some of the more abstruse elements of his crucial work. My revision of the manuscript itself was aided by the judicious comments of Paul Helm, Edwin Hui, David Martin, Charles Taylor, and Abigail Woolley. And my hat is off and my bow is low toward Cynthia Read, who inexplicably has consented once again to edit and publish my work, now for the fourth time. (A few readers might note passages that seem familiar from previous OUP books of mine. I do apologize that I could not think of alternative ways of putting certain matters, so I have borrowed from those books here and there.)

Finally, I dedicate this book to Nicholas Wolterstoff for several reasons. First, it was his book *Reason within the Bounds of Religion* that introduced me as a very young graduate student to a new way of thinking about thinking to which I was immediately converted. Second, Nick's scholarly versatility, from the history of philosophy to aesthetics and from political ethics to the grounds of scriptural revelation, has offered abundant demonstrations of what his epistemological works have taught about how a Christian mind might carefully and fruitfully work. Third, Nick has played a key role in my career: from consenting to read the manuscripts of several of my books to vouching for those books to the press and the public, and from writing letters of reference hither and yon to rendering wise personal counsel to me at various turns in the road of my career. In particular, he encouraged me to write this book, and that encouragement came at a *kairos*, for which I am especially grateful.

Need to Know

Introduction

Christians are supposed to think. Despite the overheated rhetoric of the (not-so-) New Atheists who characterize all theists as *ipso facto* anti-intellectual, if not actually mad, and despite the fact that many people of various ideological stripes have indeed been forbidden from thinking in any critical and constructive way by their parents, their religious leaders, or their political masters—let alone by their putative deities—we might better say three wonderful things:

- Christians are *free* to think,
- Christians are *invited* to think, and
- Christians are *expected* to think.[1]

In this regard, one recalls the familiar dominical saying:

And one of them, a lawyer, asked [Jesus] a question to test him. "Teacher, which commandment in the law is the greatest?"

He said to him, "You shall love the Lord your God with all your heart, and with all your soul, and with all your *mind*. This is the greatest and first commandment." (Matt. 22:35 38; emphasis added)

Christians are not to exercise blind faith—as if anyone does. (More—much more—on that point later.) Christians do not have a universal Guide to Life that covers every situation for Christians to follow such that we can dispense with analysis, reflection, and decision. (Some assert that the Bible is such a guide, but it is not. Some claim that the Holy Spirit infallibly provides such particular direction,

---

1. Doug Frank gave a lecture in 1997 at a conference of the Evangelical Scholarship Initiative and the Institute for the Study of American Evangelicals at Wheaton College in which he made this point powerfully: thinking is not just an obligation, but a privilege granted us by God (author's notes).

but that is not true, either. Much more will follow on these contentions, also.) Christians do not know it all already, however confident some appear to be that they do. Instead, Christians are called by our Lord to think.

Jesus locates his command to think, of course, within the broader commandment to devote all that we are to God and to God's service. The clear implication is that we are to think, yes, and in a way conducive to that concern—in short, to think *Christianly*.

Many authors in our time have called on Christians to think Christianly. In doing so, they generally have deplored the way many Christians in fact do think.[2] The usual target of this criticism is *compartmentalization*. In this mode, which is characteristic especially of modernity and its differentiation of social sectors into autonomous regions of value and practice (business, politics, education, leisure, family, health care, religion, and so on), Christians think in a differentiated, or compartmentalized, way. They retain their traditional Christian beliefs about a range of so-called spiritual things, whether doctrines about God and Christ, rituals such as baptism and the Lord's Supper, ethics such as telling the truth and refusing to steal, and the like. There is a compartment in their minds marked "Christian," and within that dedicated space they think Christian thoughts about Christian things in a Christian way.[3]

The remaining parts of their minds, however, are devoted to pursuits that such Christians do not count as "Christian." Again, business, politics, education, leisure, and so on—all of these areas of life are viewed as not specifically Christian. To be sure, such an attitude *prima facie* makes a certain amount of sense. It seems odd to think of filling out a requisition for new office supplies "Christianly," or deciding what would be the most Christian option for effective water metering in one's city, or teaching the periodic table of elements in a discernibly Christian way. But because such Christians cannot think of specifically Christian ways to consider these matters, by default they must decide about them—*and* matters of much more

---

2. I have in mind such books as Harry Blamires, *The Christian Mind: How Should a Christian Think?* (Ann Arbor, MI: Servant Books, 1980 [1963]); and Mark A. Noll, *The Scandal of the Evangelical Mind* (Grand Rapids, MI: Eerdmans, 1994).

3. By the term "compartmentalization" I do not mean to imply that those who engage in it are stupidly or even dishonestly unreflective. Even, and sometimes especially, highly reflective Christians engage in compartmentalization as a way of coping with the imperial demands of two or more conflicting intellectual domains. Leslie Woodcock Tentler, a professor of history at the Catholic University of America, disarmingly confesses, "Like most believers today, I do a lot of compartmentalizing: theological concepts rest in one mental box, secular notions about causality and motivation in another. In certain moods, I am almost persuaded that my work as a historian proceeds independently of my 'religious self'" ("One Historian's Sundays," in *Religious Advocacy and American History*, ed. Bruce Kuklick and D. G. Hart (Grand Rapids, MI: Eerdmans, 1997), 211. This volume of unusually strong essays indicates how strong is the temptation to compartmentalize among first-rate Christian historians. On ethical dimensions of this phenomenon, see Steven M. Tipton, "Social Differentiation and Moral Pluralism," in *Meaning and Modernity: Religion, Polity, and Self*, ed. Richard Madsen, William M. Sullivan, Ann Swidler, and Steven M. Tipton (Berkeley: University of California Press, 2002), 15–40.

obvious ideological significance—instead according to the reigning convictions of the respective social sphere.[4]

- Compartmentalized Christian executives, for example, seek as their company's highest goal *not* a way to extend the kingdom of God, *but* the maximization of financial return to their shareholders.
- Compartmentalized Christian professors seek as their scholarship's highest goal *not* the investigation of God's universe according to guidelines furnished by God's revelation, *but* the discovery of new knowledge according to their discipline's predominant school of thought.
- Compartmentalized Christian politicians seek as their office's highest goal *not* the realization of Biblical ideals for human flourishing and the redemption of the earth, *but* the achievement of their party's platform and its perpetuation in power.
- And compartmentalized Christian entertainers seek as their career's highest goal *not* the edification of the people of God, the evangelization of others, and the bringing of delight to their fellow human beings *but* simply the largest possible audience over the longest possible time.

Furthermore, this compartmentalization affects *all of us* in *each* of these areas, not just those whose occupations lie in one or another sphere. Compartmentalized Christians make all of their *commercial* decisions according to the values of the marketplace; their *intellectual* decisions according to whatever ideology currently holds sway in their schools or favorite media; their *political* decisions according to the dictates of their preferred party, philosopher, or pundit; and their *entertainment* decisions according merely to what gives them the most pleasure. There is no intentional and important connection between their Christian convictions, on the one hand, and their thinking about most of their lives, on the other. Christian ideas, terms, and values instead reside only in the compartment devoted to Sunday morning worship, midweek Bible studies, individual prayers, and (perhaps) family life—although family life itself is typically overrun by the imperatives of other spheres, whether sports leagues, dance lessons, musical ensembles, and the like. Christian convictions are relegated to the private and individual spheres of life. Other zones—the public ones—are ruled by other convictions, and so are the Christians themselves when within them.

Other forms of Christian thinking are much more wholistic, but they, too, have their drawbacks. A common form of Christian thought has been radically *conservative*.

---

4. The implicit atheism of much modern life due, in part, to differentiation and compartmentalization is explored in detail in Peter L. Berger, *The Sacred Canopy: Elements of a Sociological Theory of Religion* (Garden City, NY: Anchor, 1969); Craig M. Gay, *The Way of the (Modern) World, or, Why It's Tempting to Live as If God Doesn't Exist* (Grand Rapids, MI/Carlisle, Cumbria/Vancouver: Eerdmans/Paternoster Press/Regent College Publishing, 1998); and Charles Taylor, *A Secular Age* (Cambridge, MA: Belknap, 2007).

In this taxonomy of Christian thought, conservative thinking seeks primarily to maintain the constant, unchanging truth against the challenges of time. As Clark Pinnock writes, "Its favorite verse might be Paul's word to Timothy: 'Guard the truth that has been entrusted to you' (2 Tim. 1:14)."[5] Pinnock in fact sets out a helpful scheme in his book, *Tracking the Maze*, upon which the following discussion builds.

Whether in Roman Catholic, Orthodox, or Protestant varieties, conservative thinking has the same three-part structure of authority in practice—whatever a particular community or individual might claim otherwise. The first level is an authoritative text. For conservative Christians, this text is the Bible. Protestants will disagree with Orthodox and Catholic Christians about the status of the Apocrypha, but within the particular conservative community in question, the Bible in the accepted form is revered as the utterly authoritative text to be believed, obeyed, and cherished.

There are many Protestants who believe that *sola scriptura* is all there is to their conservatism: fidelity to the Bible alone. But conservative thinking is not so simple in practice, however much a group will protest that it is "non-creedal." The second level of such thinking comprises an authoritative tradition. "Tradition" in this case means quite strictly "what is passed on" (Latin *traditio*)—to the next generation of believers. This bundle can include official creeds and other summaries of doctrine, including the so-called "statements of faith" of evangelical communities and institutions. It can also include liturgies, whether explicit like those in a Catholic mass or Anglican service, or implicit like the "order of service" and all of the "expected" actions in a Baptist or Mennonite meeting. Authoritative tradition also lionizes favorite theologians, such that disputes are settled by the right quotation from Cyril, Thomas Aquinas, Martin Luther, John Calvin, or Menno Simons. Even devotional practices can be absolutely authoritative, whether the use of a rosary in one community or the discipline of the "daily quiet time" in another.

The Bible, however, is a complex book. And the multiplied complexities of tradition in a group older than a decade require the third level in conservative thought, authoritative interpreters. In Roman Catholicism, the pope, aided by the leading minds of the Church, officially constitutes the teaching office of the Church, while in practice the local bishop or even parish priest is understood to speak infallibly on behalf of the Church, and therefore of Christ. In Orthodoxy, the patriarchs and councils give guidance but, again, in practice the local authority is understood to be beyond question. In many forms of Protestantism, the apposite synod or council or conference provides the authoritative answer to vexing questions, while local bishops or pastors rule without brooking any dispute. Conservative congregations that are not bound by the judgments of higher courts and officers have authoritative interpreters in pastors, "Bible teachers," revered authors, and so on. Once more, a conservative mentality can

---

5. Clark H. Pinnock, *Tracking the Maze: Finding Our Way through Modern Theology from an Evangelical Perspective* (San Francisco: Harper & Row, 1990), 33.

be discerned easily enough if a point is made merely by reference to what the pope says, or what the local pastor decrees, or even what a popular media figure broadcasts.

Christian thought in the conservative mode therefore amounts to this: learning, as correctly and comprehensively as possible, what your community says is true, and then believing and acting accordingly. Every idea, every experience, every suggestion, every doubt is referred back to the tradition and there it is placed, albeit sometimes with considerable strain, within that tradition's absolute, unchanging categories. Anything new is by definition deviant and dangerous.[6]

Before we go on to consider alternative modes of thought, we must pause to underline that this conservative method can be found right across the varieties of Christianity, not only from "high" to "low" (as in Catholic to Baptist), but also in theological traditions as various as Pentecostalism and liberalism. For in those latter traditions, however much the claim might be made that Christians are to be "Spirit-led" or "free to think," there are conservative versions of them in which no one would dare question a longstanding congregational practice nor the prophecies of the local "apostle," or would express doubt about the political strategy of a mainline denomination or disavow Paul Tillich, Rosemary Ruether, Hans Küng, James H. Cone, or the latest spiritual guru. (My own tribe does not emerge from this discussion untouched, for many are the circles in which invoking C. S. Lewis or N. T. Wright suffices to squelch all dissent.)

Conservative Christians look back for reassurance while other Christians, as we shall see, typically look forward to new discoveries—those I will call "liberals" in this scheme. Still others, classical Protestants, Roman Catholics, and Orthodox, dwell in a creative tension of past, present, and future as they draw on Scripture, tradition, reason and experience with the help of the church's teachers. The Christians we encounter under the rubric of *mysticism*, however, seek to escape the limitations in all of these attitudes and resources. Scripture, tradition, reason, the magisterium and so on, they say, are only bridges, only ladders, toward what really counts, namely, encounter with God.

What Christian could disagree with this priority? Of course all Christians yearn for greater connection with God. Yet mystical Christians go much further to load their epistemological eggs decisively into the basket of experience as the one key source in determining all of their lives. As Rudolph Otto puts it, "essentially mysticism is the stressing to a very high degree, indeed the overstressing, of the non-rational or supra-rational elements in religion."[7]

---

6. For a survey of religious communities that tend to manifest this sort of mentality, albeit in quite diverse varieties, see Martin E. Marty and R. Scott Appleby, eds., *Fundamentalisms Observed* (Chicago: University of Chicago Press 1991).

7. Rudolf Otto, *The Idea of the Holy*, trans. John W. Harvey, 2nd ed. (New York and Oxford: Oxford University Press, 1950 [1923]), 22.

Some of these mystical Christians are erudite and articulate, schooled in the great writings of spiritual adepts past and present. They undertake a disciplined life that leads them, they believe, into a close communion with God that is basically ineffable but also decisive in every area of their lives. Their traditions and texts—and, in most cases, their spiritual directors (we can note how fundamental elements so often resurface in various contexts)—authoritatively guide them toward self-validating experiences that provide a basis upon which they make all of the important decisions of their lives. And, customarily, this mentality is then identified with the much more generic Christian posture of faith, such that those who live by dependence upon God for specific intuitions in each circumstance are truly living the apostolic ideal versus their benighted brothers and sisters who are bound to yokes of textual interpretation, rational reflection, and the like.

The more popular version appears in some Pentecostal-charismatic circles and in certain other Protestant sects—the Society of Friends (Quakers) is one of long-standing prominence. In such groups, the "inner light," the "testimony of the Spirit," "a word of knowledge," or a "still, small voice" gives direct, authoritative guidance to the individual or the group. (The question of whether divine guidance should be sought by the individual or the group is an important difference among mystics.) When a Christian decides to quit school because "I just felt God wanted me to" or when another decides to buy an expensive car "because I believe the Lord wants me to have it"—both of which claims were rendered in my hearing—one is dealing with this extreme understanding of the epistemic import of immediate experience.

Again, it must be recognized that all Christians properly aspire to developing due recognition of "the Master's voice." And church history is full of stories of dramatic inclinations to action, key words coming to mind, Scripture texts shining on the page, and full-blown visions that provided guidance in extreme moments for Christians who then evidently went about honouring God in this or that endeavor. But when mystical Christians believe that God routinely renders highly specific teaching or advice in a way that leaves reason, tradition, and Scripture behind, other Christians look askance.[8] In particular, they wonder about what check there is among mystics upon rationalization, self-delusion, psychosis, or even demonic influence in individual cases, and upon demagoguery or mass hysteria in corporate ones.[9]

---

8. Perhaps the leading recent philosophical defender of the epistemological status of mystical experience has been William Alston, and he is quite clear that mystical perception must be subject to the checks provided by "the Bible, the ecumenical councils of the undivided church, Christian experience through the ages, Christian thought, and more generally the Christian tradition" (*Perceiving God: The Epistemology of Religious Experience* [Ithaca, NY: Cornell University Press, 1991], 193).

9. An extraordinary and perplexing modern example is supplied by Basilea Schlink, one of the founders of the Evangelical Sisterhood of Mary after World War II in Germany. Herself highly educated and from a well educated family, her intuitive sense of God's quite specific guidance in all manner of decisions affecting herself and many others—including questions even of

Dietrich Bonhoeffer quotes Romans 12:2 ("Do not be conformed to this world, but be transformed by the renewing of your minds, so that you may discern what is the will of God"), Philippians 1:9–10 ("And this is my prayer, that your love may overflow more and more with knowledge and full insight to help you to determine what is best"), and Ephesians 5:9 ("Try to find out what is pleasing to the Lord") and then offers this pastoral counsel:

> These verses thoroughly correct the notion that a single-minded discerning of the will of God must occur in the form of intuition, by abandoning all reflection, by naïvely grasping the first thought or feeling that insinuates itself, that is, any psychologizing misunderstanding of the simplicity of the new life that has begun in Jesus. It cannot be taken for granted that the will of God, laden with the accent of eternity, would naturally impress itself upon the human heart, that it would be clearly self-evident and identical with what the heart itself imagines. The will of God may lie very deeply hidden among many competing possibilities. It is also not a system of rules that are fixed from the outset, but always new and different in each different life circumstance. This is why it is necessary to discern again and again what the will of God is. Heart, intellect, observation, and experience must work together in this discernment. This discernment of the will of God is such a serious matter precisely because it is no longer our own knowledge of good and evil that is at issue here, but the living will of God; because knowing the will of God is not at our human disposal, but dependent entirely on God's grace.... The will of God can now no longer be confused with the voice of the heart, nor with any kind of inspiration, nor with any kind of absolute principle, since it reveals itself anew only to those discerning it in each particular case.[10]

Many Christians in centuries past have mused upon both the narrow question of establishing the authenticity of spiritual experiences and the broader issue of the correct place of spiritual experience in a Christian epistemology. And it certainly would be wrong to characterize all mystically-oriented Christians as despising the deliverances of reason, tradition, and Scripture—just as not all those who would call themselves "conservative" belong under the previous heading. What the present heading denotes is the distinctive cognitive style of focusing centrally upon

---

the seeking of medical care and the provision of food—have baffled or thrilled thousands of readers. See Basilea Schlink, *Realities: The Miracles of God Experienced Today*, trans. Larry Christenson and William Castell (Grand Rapids, MI: Zondervan, 1966). For perceptive and learned comments on mysticism, see Sir Norman Anderson, *Christianity and World Religions: The Challenge of Pluralism* (Leicester, UK and Downers Grove, IL: InterVarsity, 1984), 37–45.

10. Dietrich Bonhoeffer, *Ethics*, ed. Clifford J. Green, trans. Reinhard Krauss, Charles C. West, and Douglas W. Stott (Minneapolis, MN: Fortress, 2005 [1949]), 321. David Martin agrees: "The long struggle between Christianity and mysticism is not due to a rejection of mystical experience in itself. It is based rather on a rejection of mystical experience as providing the exclusive definition of religion. Man does not retire to the interior castle or live by illumination. He lives by the Word: *logos*, reason, embodiment" (*The Breaking of the Image: A Sociology of Christian Theory and Practice* [Vancouver: Regent College, 2006 (1979)], 116).

mystical experience to the denigration and even exclusion of other resources God has given us to shape and guard our thinking.

The form of Christian thinking that has characterized orthodox Protestantism and its leading theologians draws on the Bible, tradition, reason, and experience. Sometimes identified with John Wesley and the tradition that bears his name (so the "Wesleyan Quadrilateral"), this *Protestant Quadrilateral* can be discerned broadly in the writings of his Protestant predecessors, even though it is not affirmed as a four-resource method as such, and in most orthodox non-Wesleyans after him.[11]

Each of the four resources is valued by this model as a God-given source of truth. Human beings characteristically misuse and misunderstand these resources because of sin or ignorance, but they are worthy vehicles nonetheless. Scripture is special among these four, however, as it both provides a foundation for the others and judges the others. Classical Protestantism asserts that Christian thinking proceeds best by presupposing the truth of Scripture and thus adopting a worldview informed particularly and fundamentally by Biblical ideas. From this foundation one moves out to consider what reason, experience, and tradition have further to say. Following consultation of these three secondary resources, one returns to Scripture again as the adjudicator to determine what of the deliverances of reason, experience, and tradition is in fact true—since the Bible alone can divine what is only partially revealed, let alone what has been distorted by sin, in these other three worthy sources.

Even as many Protestants would put the matter this way, Luther, Calvin, and many others would insist on a key refinement of its terminology. For they would assert that it is not the Bible that does the divining, for a mere text—however glorious be its inspiration and luminous its meaning—cannot act. Instead, it is the Holy Spirit of God who interprets the Bible to the believer and the believing community, and thus helps them understand also what is true in the composite portrait of reality to be garnered from all four resources.

Roman Catholic and Orthodox churches elaborate on this scheme in two respects. First, in at least some main streams of thought in both forms of Christianity, tradition is understood as revelation of the same value as the Bible—for the same Holy Spirit inspired both and intends them to function in the church as authoritative resources. (To be sure, other Catholics and Orthodox have placed the highest priority on Scripture, particularly by defining the relationship of Scripture and tradition so as to make the latter in some respect derivative of or dependent upon the authority of the former.) Second, the Roman Catholic Church has made it clear that Christ's church is properly taught and led by Christ's vicar, the pope. Popes are

---

11. For the coining of "Wesleyan quadrilateral," see Albert C. Outler, *The Wesleyan Theological Heritage: Essays of Albert C. Outler*, ed. Thomas C. Oden and Leicester R. Longden (Grand Rapids, MI: Zondervan, 1991). For a more recent statement of its use and usefulness, see Donald A. D. Thorsen, *The Wesleyan Quadrilateral: Scripture, Tradition, Reason and Experience as a Model of Evangelical Theology* (Grand Rapids, MI: Zondervan, 1990).

not infallible except in the extraordinary and rare instances of pronouncements *ex cathedra*. But popes are indeed "fathers" whose authority must be respected by those they serve as such. And Orthodox churches typically revere their patriarchs similarly, even as they officially decide the most crucial matters in ecumenical councils. (The question of how church councils figure in the authoritative formulation and declaration of doctrine is a vexed one in Roman Catholic history.)

As we have seen in the case of *conservative* thinking, some Protestants can act just like certain Catholics and Orthodox, despite their claims to be deeply different. And in the present mode, most Protestants also typically respect senior teachers of one sort or another, whether those of high church office, or those gathered in legitimate assemblies of leaders, or those occupying distinguished academic positions, or those of charisma made evident in powerful preaching, teaching, writing, or broadcasting. Respecting such teachers, however, does not entail abject agreement—as it does in the conservative cognitive style. And in the scheme I will lay out soon, I will discuss the question of how authorities are to be discerned and responded to. So, odd as it is to lump together Catholic and Orthodox Christians with Protestants in a cognitive style whose name derives from Wesley (although Wesley, as a grateful reader of Catholic and Orthodox divines, would likely be delighted), I trust that the common denominator is evident: Scripture, tradition, reason, and experience as God-given resources, with Scripture supreme as both framework and judge.

What I am calling the *liberal* Christian cognitive style gets its name from the Latin *liber*, or "free." Liberals are free from what they see to be authoritarian constraint upon their thought to consider all options and believe what is (really) true. Rather than looking backward, as conservatives do, or inward/upward in the moment as mystics do, liberals look forward as human beings accumulate and refine more and more knowledge according to the best intellectual disciplines of today and tomorrow.

Conservative Christians sometimes use "liberal" as a synonym for "heresy," and with some reason, since from the conservative point of view to choose (Greek *hairesis*) for oneself what to believe, rather than merely and strictly to receive what has been handed down, is precisely the root error of all such thought. The particular tradition known as "liberal theology," originating with F. D. E. Schleiermacher (1768–1834), has indeed departed from orthodox doctrine in various respects throughout its career, but in our consideration of *methods* of Christian thought, it is helpful to set aside the *conclusions* of particular liberal theologians and schools in order to look instead at what this "free" thinking means as a mode.

The four elements of reason, experience, tradition, and scripture that form the quadrilateral of resources in classical Protestant thought here metamorphose into a "Liberal Triangle." Reason and experience remain as full partners, with the category of (authoritative) Scripture now collapsing under the heading of tradition as the Bible is regarded as simply more-or-less respected early Christian literature. Indeed, the Bible becomes just one conversation partner among others at best, and to that of an actual opponent to be overcome or a useless artifact to be ignored at worst. For their part, reason and experience predominate over tradition, and especially *contemporary* reason and experience—the best of what we know and sense now. The key attitude, then, is of free investigation of the world while retaining some connection with Christian identity without any obligation to Christian authorities. Thus, of course, as scholarship proceeds and the experiences of the church change in some respects, so each generation will have to produce its own theology to reflect its current apprehension of religious matters.[12]

In some varieties of liberal thinking, reason predominates over experience. Process theology, for instance, depends upon the highly speculative process philosophy of Alfred North Whitehead (1861–1947). Other forms of liberal thought are deeply postmodern, reveling in the endless play of indeterminate texts, including the Bible's, rather than submitting to the strictures of any particular governing ontology.[13]

Yet many thinkers attracted to a liberal outlook have adopted it at least partly motivated by experience. John Cobb, for instance, has confessed to a deep revulsion to the doctrine of predestination and therefore to any view of a God sovereignly governing the cosmos, thus finding in the "open-ended" universe and "evolving" God of process theology a more congenial model.[14] Other liberal Christian thought emerges fundamentally from experience, such as forms of liberation theology provoked by

---

12. A classic example of liberal methodology is provided by Sallie McFague: "I begin with the assumption that what we can say with any assurance about the character of Christian faith is very little and that even that will be highly contested. Christian faith is, it seems to me, most basically a claim that the universe is neither indifferent nor malevolent but that there is a power (and a personal power at that) which is on the side of life and its fulfillment. Moreover, the Christian believes that we have some clues for fleshing out this claim in the life, death, and appearances of Jesus of Nazareth. Nevertheless, each generation must venture, through an analysis of what fulfillment could and must mean for its own time, the best way to express that claim. A critical dimension of this expression is the imaginative picture, the metaphors and models, the underlying conceptual systems of theology. One cannot hope to interpret Christian faith for one's own time if one remains indifferent to the basic images that are the lifeblood of interpretation and that greatly influence people's perceptions and behavior. One of the serious deficiencies in contemporary theology is that though theologians have attempted to interpret the faith in new concepts appropriate to our time, the basic metaphors and models have remained relatively constant: they are triumphalist, monarchical, patriarchal. Much *deconstruction* of the traditional imagery has taken place, but little *construction*. If, however, metaphor and concept are, as I believe, inextricably and symbiotically related in theology, there is no way to do theology for our time with outmoded or oppressive metaphors and models.... In this situation, one thing that is needed—and which I attempt in these pages—is a *remythologizing* of the relationship between God and the world. I will experiment with the models of God as mother, lover, and friend of the world, and with the image of the world as God's body" (*Models of God: Theology for an Ecological, Nuclear Age* [Philadelphia: Fortress Press, 1987], x–xi.

13. For examples, see Elizabeth Castelli et al., eds., *The Postmodern Bible: The Bible and Culture Collective* (New Haven, CT: Yale University Press, 1997). For an astringent assessment of such an approach to Scripture, see Leland Ryken, "Bible Stories for Derrida's Children," *Books & Culture* 3 (January 1998): 38–41.

14. Cobb made this point to me following a lecture held at the Wheaton College Graduate School, Illinois, in 1985.

the oppression of the poor in Latin America, or feminist (including womanist, *mujerista*, and similar) theologies responding to the patriarchalist oppression of women. Yet these experience-based theologies are often pursued with considerable intellectual rigor, especially with attention to sociology, history, linguistics, and so on. (It must also be noted that liberation and feminist theology have been pursued by Christians in modes other than the liberal, including classical Protestant and Catholic modes, as well as in the mode I will recommend later.)

However it may lean toward one source or the other, however, the Liberal Triangle is based on reason and experience, with whatever guidance from Christian tradition any particular Christians deem useful as they freely discern—unencumbered by inherited traditions or current authorities—what they believe to be truth for today. A typical liberal response to a criticism that a congregation had departed from traditional doctrine or ethics sounds like this: "We would repent only if we felt that we could do so with complete integrity…if we could be shown [to be wrong] through experience, or the example of Jesus, or the stories of the people who are living with us."[15]

It is important to keep clear that one can be using a liberal method whether or not one arrives at so-called liberal conclusions. Many Christians believe things about God, the world, and so on because of their reliance upon inherited church tradition (including a few snippets of Scripture) as confirmed by their reason and experience. One thinks, for example, of many people who hold conservative views regarding the ordination of women who have never investigated the issue by way of careful exegesis of Scripture. Other Christians clearly rely primarily upon religious experience in concert with their church's tradition and a certain amount of rational argument without seriously examining the teachings of Scripture as authoritative revelation per se. One thinks of those who believe that speaking in tongues is the mark of the baptism of the Holy Spirit, a dubious teaching finally undergoing serious scrutiny among Pentecostal and charismatic theologians just in our own time.

We can also pause to note the irony of two false freedoms of liberalism. G. K. Chesterton a century ago said that those who have jettisoned the authority of Scripture and tradition now must submit to the "oligarchy" of one's leading contemporaries and whatever is *bien-pensée* among one's peers.[16] (One thinks of Richard Rorty's oft-cited remark that truth is whatever your peers will let you get away with saying.) Note also that in so-called liberal circles the strength of *recent* tradition can be quite strong—say, the tradition of the civil rights movement, the tradition of feminism, or the tradition of democratic socialism. If tradition is in fact unquestionable in such circles, we do not now have a liberal *cognitive style*, but are actually thinking in a *conservative* mode.

---

15. Pastor Anneli Braul of South Calgary Inter-Mennonite Church, quoted in Les Sillars, "Pro-Gay Church Asked to Repent," *Faith Today* (January 1999): 38; interpolation in original.

16. G. K. Chesterton, *Orthodoxy* (Garden City, NY: Image, 1959 [1908]), 48.

The option most rued by defenders of sound Christian thinking is of course the most extreme: complete *capitulation* to current culture, or to some subculture within it. Some Christians practice an intentional form of this mode, consciously trying to adapt the Christian tradition to a contemporary ideology of some kind, usually in the interest of "updating" the faith to make it "relevant" to their non-Christian peers. One finds such people typically in the most avant-garde liberal churches or in the murky realms of "spirituality"—although many evangelical churches in North America and elsewhere now seem almost entirely to operate in this mode as well.

More commonly, Christian individuals simply discard whatever parts of the faith are challenged by alternative convictions in the culture they inhabit. Teenagers dispense with the inhibitions of Christian teaching on sexual purity. Adults cheat on their highly inconvenient tax returns. Reincarnation seems more just, or at least more hopeful, than the Christian doctrine of just one life and then eternal judgment, so now many westerners avow it even as they self-identify as Christians.[17] As some sociologists have memorably put it, more and more moderns are opting for "religion à la carte," picking from the smorgasbord of religious varieties what happens to suit them at the time, and leaving the rest alone.

This pattern resembles compartmentalization in that some bits of authentic Christianity may well remain in a person's worldview. But in compartmentalization there is a genuine, if severely restricted, Christianity in operation. In capitulation, Christianity is dissected and parts of it blended with other things under the sovereignty of the individual self, not of Jesus Christ. It thus ceases to be Christianity at all.[18]

CRITIQUE

The options of compartmentalization and capitulation hardly need further notice here. As for the others, I have already implied that Christians ought to criticize the *liberal* option as sitting far too loose both to Scripture's teaching and authority, primarily, as well as to tradition's value, secondarily. The liberal method reduces the communication from God to humanity far too much, and runs the grave risk of leaving us religious people talking to ourselves and *about* ourselves—as Ludwig Feuerbach scoffed years before Sigmund Freud did. Yet let us value the liberal concern for appropriate freedom from the limitations of human authorities past and present, even as we must not limit, let alone jettison, the revelation given to us

---

17. See the polling reported regularly in the *oeuvre* of sociologist Reginald Bibby on these trends in Canada, beginning with *Fragmented Gods: The Poverty and Potential of Religion in Canada* (Toronto: Irwin, 1987).

18. See Rodney Clapp, ed., *The Consuming Passion: Christianity and the Consumer Culture* (Downers Grove, IL: InterVarsity Press, 1998); and Charles Taylor, *Sources of the Self: The Making of Modern Identity* (Cambridge, MA: Harvard University Press, 1989).

God's written Word and the wisdom of Christians accumulated through the centuries.

The attraction of *conservative* theology is obvious: Who does *not* want to know the truth, plain and simple, and especially in our epistemologically troubled times? Conservatism gives one pause, however, by the wide and contradictory varieties of conservative Christian thought: conservative Lutherans (of a mutually recriminatory sort), conservative Calvinists (ditto), conservative Methodists—and Baptists and Catholics and Orthodox and Restorationists and Mennonites and on and on. Who is right? Some? A compromise or synthesis of several? Any? And how would one tell?

One also cannot endorse the conservative option when it is manifestly so cautious about, even closed-off toward, knowledge gained from other areas of human inquiry. This bifurcation of knowledge makes for useless and costly battles in the mind (and in the church and in the larger culture), whether the putative divide between special and general revelation, creation and evolution, theology and social science, and so on. We will explore important zones of tension among the various resources God has given us, including science, art, spiritual experience, and so on, alongside the Bible and tradition. But we will also see that to simply rule out these resources is not only unhelpful but impossible.

Surely respecting the legacy of the past, moreover, does not entail insisting on its comprehensive perpetuation in each new generation and in every circumstance. Historical study, in fact, shows us that there *was* no "golden age," no actual time T at which a particular tradition—let alone the Christian church at large—achieved a perfect state from which any departure would be a decline. This fact ought to warn people unhappy with the current state of Christianity away from the temptation to seek refuge in a happy past, whether the early days of their denomination, or eras of renewal such as the Evangelical Revivals or the Reformation, or upwellings of spiritual energy as in the high middle ages, or the misty times of the church fathers, or even the New Testament church(es)—perhaps *especially* the fractious, compromising, apostle-frustrating New Testament churches! Conservative individuals, congregations and denominations, however, act as if there were such a perfect time and it is their job to repristinate it in every generation.

Indeed, as George Lindbeck warns, "the meaning of rites and utterances depends on contexts. To replicate the old forms in new situations frequently betrays the original meaning, the original spirit."[19] What was once a gesture of blessing can look in another time and place as a sign of condescension, even oppression. For example, what once was understood as a Biblical teaching meant to ameliorate a harmful social arrangement between slaves and slaveholders became a justification for the perpetuation of that arrangement by ministers who defended slavery from their pulpits.

---

19. George A. Lindbeck, *The Nature of Doctrine: Religion and Theology in a Postliberal Age* (Philadelphia: Westminster Press, 1984), 79.

It occurs to me that the conservative/liberal dichotomy reflects two poles of our fundamental experience as human beings. Conservatism is a natural inclination when one senses danger: surely it's best to stick with what has worked in the past. Liberalism reflects a safe situation in which challenges can be faced as opportunities, not threats. Anxiety over vulnerability and scarcity will prompt conservative feelings; confidence in security and abundance might prompt much more initiative. The conservative impulse is toward authority and particularly the recovery of tradition, while the liberal impulse is toward autonomy, discovery, and innovation.

The cognitive styles I have labeled "conservative" and "liberal" here clearly are extremes that cannot be commended. As we proceed, however, we will want sympathetically to retain what is clearly sensible and valuable about the natural inclination behind each. We also ought to recognize how our perception of our situation might influence us, perhaps strongly, toward one or the other cognitive style regardless of any serious analysis we might have undertaken about its actual merits.

Mysticism seems to transcend the backward/forward tension between conservative and liberal to go *upward* or, perhaps, *inward*. It certainly seems to be well motivated toward the laudable goal of a deep, personal relationship with God. In pursuing that end, however, mysticism unnecessarily abandons good gifts from God. It foolishly cuts itself loose from both protections and resources God has wisely offered us in Scripture, tradition, reason, and various kinds of experience. Life in the world, after all, is not merely spiritual, and mysticism of this extreme sort ultimately disparages the flesh, the physical, the natural world that God himself created and pronounced "very good" (Genesis 1). Indeed, mysticism tends finally to disobey the divine imperatives to love God, to love one's neighbor as oneself, and to care for the world as it abandons them in its quest for the transcendent joy of a constant beatific vision.

It seems, then, that we ought to return to the Protestant Quadrilateral—really, a *Christian* Quadrilateral. This model draws upon all four elements. Yet it does so, as I will now show, in a way that no longer meets the needs of thoughtful Christians in our time.

THE NEED FOR A NEW MODEL

In the Christian Quadrilateral, the Bible is both foundation and adjudicator, the infallible guide to truth against which all other knowledge claims would be corrected. Yet a chain of observations unreels from this conviction in the light of the history of the church and particularly in the face of the pluralism and postmodernity of our time.

First, when we Christians do our thinking, we do not in fact draw our thinking directly from "Scripture alone"—even if we're the sorts of Protestants that like to say we do. We must *interpret* the Bible. This task entails, at a minimum, selecting what we judge to be the passages relevant to our question (rather than reading through and reflecting upon the entire Bible each time), a process that can give us both more and less than we ought to have, as we mistakenly include what are in fact irrelevancies while overlooking what is truly germane. We then must compose some sort of coherent account of their teaching for us on the present matter, both principles and practices. We cannot and do not simply consult an index of the Bible's contents and read out what we ought to think or feel or do about any matter at hand.

Second, it is clear that Christians disagree in significant respects about *how* to interpret the Bible (hermeneutics). Therefore Christians have notoriously, and from the beginning, disagreed in many respects about *what* the Bible says—both to its original audiences and to audiences today.

Third, the situation is exacerbated as we observe that not only have Christians disagreed about interpreting the Bible's teaching—an observation that itself is not necessarily troublesome, as plenty of ignorant people maintain mistaken views of physics or economics while experts know better—but Christians of evident good-will and intelligence and skill have disagreed, and deeply, about the interpretation of the Bible. (One thinks now of disagreements, and deep ones, among physicists and economists.) So the many and important disagreements about how to interpret the Bible and therefore what the Bible says are not simply matters of disparate levels of godliness or ability. They will not disappear, and certainly have not so far disappeared, simply with the addition of more holiness and better hermeneutics.

Fourth, it seems evident that reason, experience, and tradition all affect our interpretation of Scripture, from the very reading of it forward through all subsequent reflection upon it. (Augustine offers considerable teaching on how wide must be the correlative learning of the skilled exegete for him or her to rightly understand the Scripture in De doctrina christiana.) None of us can help the automatic functions of our minds in construing sentences to make them make sense—that is, to make them cohere with what else we think we know. And these are functions that draw on our idiosyncratic reservoirs of what we have learned via experience, tradition, and learning of other sorts, all arranged in categories and relationships according to what we have come to think is reasonable. So with all this interaction among various mental resources and faculties going on, it is not obvious how our interpretation of Scripture can act as a pure, infallible corrective to them in return.[20]

Finally, however, we might consider an even more radical possibility that drastically qualifies the whole enterprise of Christian thinking: the possibility that God might just be content with this state of affairs. That is, the foregoing may not be *problems to be solved* at all, but may instead be signs pointing us toward a better paradigm that takes for granted these, and other, significant characteristics of our thinking. It is time, in fact, for us to turn to such an alternative, beginning with a

---

20. It is sobering that the president of a major American theological seminary can still declare, "Science is on a journey; revelation is a destination. We begin and end with revelation at RTS" (Michael Milton, interim president of Reformed Theological Seminary; quoted in Charles Honey, "Adamant on Adam," *Christianity Today* [June 2010]: 14).

series of modifications of the Christian Quadrilateral that will respond to the post-modern challenges we have encountered. Moreover, we need an alternative that will respond also to the proper concerns of premodern and modern thinking, whether about the validity of tradition and the value of authorities, or about the actual reliability of experience and reason and the confidence we ought to have, or not have, in our thought.

Is there another alternative available, therefore? Can Christians remain faithful to the Christian tradition while also learning from contemporary culture—and other cultures, past and present? Indeed, can both faithfulness to the past and open-ness to new ideas combine to produce an enriched Christian mind?

Christian thought is supposed to be responsive to God and responsive to the world God created, sustains, loves, and redeems. Christian thinking is, in this sense, supposed to be *responsible*. Christian thought also is supposed to assist Christians in *serving* God and God's world. In this sense, too, it is to be *responsible*.

The rest of this book considers how such thought might proceed. This book is not simply another rallying cry, not yet another call for comprehensive Christian thinking. Such calls have been sounded well by others in our time.[21] Indeed, every Christian college or university worthy of the adjective "Christian" summons students to think Christianly about all of life, as do student fellowships on secular campuses, such as the InterVarsity Christian Fellowship in which I first encountered such a challenge.

This book is an answer to that call. It offers an epistemology: an outline of just how Christians ought to think about whatever they are called to think about. It is thus a kind of a recipe, a generic method, if not quite an algorithm, that Christians can use to consider whatever lies before us.

Currently, intelligent Christians must each cobble together an epistemology for himself or herself. Such Christians know that the Bible ought to be important in Christian thought in some way or another, as should church tradition—or at least *our own* church's tradition.... We know that reason has a place, of course, as has human experience. We appreciate the help of others, whether venerable authorities or trusted friends. Perhaps we also realize that spiritual health affects our intellectual integrity in some way, so we pray and worship, and try to avoid sin and repent when we don't. If we have our priorities straight, we recognize that the point of all of our thinking is to honor God and serve God's kingdom.

But how can we be sure that we have explored all of the necessary resources in a given instance? How should we make proper use of each one? How ought we then to gather these resources together and coordinate them properly? Is there any way to be sure we aren't simply coming to conclusions dictated by our particular social

---

21. Blamires, *The Christian Mind* is perhaps the best known of such clarion calls for Christians to resist especially compartmentalization and capitulation, and to think Christianly about all of life. See also Nicholas Wolterstorff, *Reason within the Bounds of Religion* (Grand Rapids, MI: Eerdmans, 1976).

location or psychological make-up? And how can we do all this in the press of real life? If we do not have a workable, portable epistemology that includes and orders all of these resources, we will settle for what *is* workable and portable. If the Bible seems too foreign and theology too abstruse, if philosophy seems too arcane and science too complex, then we will think what we *can* think and decide on the basis of what we *do* think we understand. And such thinking will generally not be strongly and richly Christian. Responding to this fundamental challenge—of thinking Christianly all the time about everything—is the burden of this book.

At the heart of this project are two fundamental convictions and their corollaries, concepts that will surprise and perhaps dismay some readers. I hope that once the shock subsides, however, these convictions will be seen as both sound and helpful in framing the task and joy of Christian thinking.

Both of these convictions emerge from the idea of *vocation*. I will explain what I mean by that in the next chapter. For now, however, I will simply set out these two convictions as crucial to my conception of Christian thinking.

1. God calls human beings to be a particular kind of creature and to live a particular kind of life. Since it makes no sense to believe God would commission us and then under-resource us, God instead can be relied upon to provide the knowledge we need—among all the other resources we need—in order to fulfill that calling. We need to know whatever it is we need to know in order to be who God wants us to be and to do what God wants us to do. So we can trust God to provide us what we need to know in order to succeed in our vocation.[22]

2. God calls particular human beings to particular vocations. God therefore can be relied upon to provide the particular knowledge we need—among all the other particular resources we need—to fulfill those particular callings. We need to know particularly whatever it is we particularly need to know in order to be particularly who God wants us to be to do particularly what God wants us to do. So we can trust God to provide us particularly what we need to know. Christian thinking properly undertaken is therefore to be undertaken in ways particular to our particular identity and activity. We are not all philosophers or theologians, and so a truly Christian epistemology has to work also for engineers and entertainers, homemakers and hotel managers, pilots and parents, governors and garbage collectors. So we can trust God to provide us what we need to know in order to succeed in our vocation.

The corollaries of these principles, however, also obtain. Yes, we can count on God to give us what we need in order to be and to do as God intends. That principle

---

22. This axiom immediately liberates human thought from the chains of mere physical causation, as if our thought is nothing more than a biochemical reaction to stimuli along pathways established by evolutionary survival toward no end greater than the propagation of our genetic material. I refute naturalism/materialism thus.

implies, though, that God will not necessarily grant us knowledge about matters that are not pertinent to our particular vocations. Christian epistemology is not guaranteed to provide assured knowledge on every subject for everyone. In fact, as I will argue, a vocational understanding of epistemology helps to explain why God allows Christians to think wrong thoughts and why God aids non-Christians to think right ones. Furthermore, much of this book is devoted to considering the assertions that any person's thinking about *anything* is importantly in doubt; that traditional or modern claims—including *Christian* claims—to infallibility are unfounded; and that if we do not therefore reside on an epistemological Gibraltar, we need nonetheless *some* way of justifiably standing our ground or else be swept off the beach into a raging chaos of directionless, groundless confusion. The epistemology of this book inhabits this middle space between radical, unobtainable certainty and radical, unendurable doubt.

Consider, then, the idea that God is not interested in giving us knowledge for its own sake. I realize that epistemology, and Christian epistemology in particular, generally takes for granted that a nonnegotiable desideratum of thinking is to find out truths and to be able to recognize and, yes, justify them as such. Yet I counter that the point of the Christian life, and of human life, is not to arrive at correct ideas. The *telos* of the world is *shalom*: flourishing, fruitfulness, peace. Given that our current world is obviously in need of more shalom, the point of life here and now is to make as much shalom as possible. As gaining knowledge helps us to do that, God can be counted on to provide it as we seek it properly. As gaining knowledge will *not* help us to do that, Christian epistemology acknowledges that God will not give us what is, in this respect, gratuitous or even counterproductive knowledge. In fact, I will suggest that God's purposes are sometimes fulfilled by people holding wrong ideas, including nontrivial ideas, even if they are earnest seekers after truth.[23]

Thus, beyond its first task of outlining the structure of a Christian epistemology ("How do we know?"), this book addresses the other major question of epistemol-

---

23. I throw down the gauntlet here. John Frame speaks for many when he affirms as an axiom that "the Holy Spirit does not cause us to believe lies. He is the God of truth, and so he makes us believe what is true, what is in accord with all evidence and logic" ("Presuppositional Apologetics," in *Five Views on Apologetics*, ed. Steven B. Cowan [Grand Rapids, MI: Zondervan 2000], 210). How is it, then, that Christians believe things that seem not to be true, or fully true, or comprehensively true—about even religious matters, let alone cosmology, politics, and so on? To remark on the noetic effects of sin on the unredeemed is irrelevant, of course. To suggest instead that sanctification is an ongoing process and thus Christians continue to believe untrue things because of the grip of sin on their lives is, I believe, accurate so far as it goes—but why does the Holy Spirit not always and everywhere compensate for our continuing frailty and fallenness when we are at least mostly sincere in our epistemic quests? I suggest that the answer does not lie in any lack of teaching ability on the part of God nor entirely on the side of our recalcitrant sinfulness, but in God's providence such that God allows us, even directs us (I don't think that distinction is important in this context), to believe things that are not true in order to make us most useful in his service. So, scandalous as it seems *prima facie* to say that the Holy Spirit does not invariably teach us the truth, the whole truth, and nothing but the truth, I place the rock of stumbling squarely in the way, and will try to justify it in what follows.

ogy as its second: "How do we know we know?" What are the grounds on which we can have any sort of confidence in our apprehensions and conceptualizations? I will be saying for the next two hundred pages or so that we need to know particular things well enough and confidently enough to fulfill our callings. God can be counted on to tell us what we need to know in order to be and do what we are mandated to be and do. (This radical connection of vocation and epistemology, which lies at the heart of this proposal, is not one I have encountered elsewhere: the reader is thus cordially encouraged to be on his or her guard.[24]) But we can count on God granting us knowledge *only* according to our vocation—only, as the saying goes, on a "need to know" basis.

God will be (epistemically) faithful so that we can be (vocationally) faithful. That is the central contention of this book.

---

24. George Steiner properly points to Book IX of Augustine's *Confessions* as a *locus classicus* for all discussions of how verbal truth is rooted in the Word who is the Way, the Truth, and the Life (*Lessons of the Masters* [Cambridge, MA and London: Harvard University Press, 2003], 43–46). I also want to signal my debt to Clark H. Pinnock for an essay that prodded me toward some of the conclusions offered here: "The Work of the Holy Spirit in Hermeneutics," *Journal of Pentecostal Theology* 2 (1993): 3–23.

1

The Current Situation

Cognitive Pluralism

THREE DEFINITIONS OF PLURALISM

"Pluralism" is a word we encounter all the time, but few speakers or writers pause to define what they mean by it. Pluralism has at least three definitions and defining the term is crucial, since someone might well *recognize* pluralism in the first sense, *endorse* some kinds of pluralism in the second while rejecting others, and then perhaps endorse or reject this or that form of pluralism in the third. Thoroughly exploring what we mean by "pluralism" will help us clarify the epistemological challenges we face in contemporary life.

Pluralism as Mere Plurality

At the most elementary level, pluralism means the state of being "more than one." The typical supermarket confronts a shopper with thirty kinds of breakfast cereal—just one instance of a bewildering pluralism of choices. Sociologists suggest that such proliferation of varieties of goods, services, and even ideologies is characteristic of modernizing societies—a process they call *pluralization*.[1] So pluralism in this first sense is a condition, a state of affairs, a matter of value-free description. Is there more than one? Then there is pluralism.

---

1. Helpful introductions to these subjects with special attention to religion are the following: Peter L. Berger, *The Sacred Canopy: Elements of a Sociological Theory of Religion* (Garden City, NY: Anchor Books, 1969); Os Guinness, *The Gravedigger File: Papers on the Subversion of the Modern Church* (Downers Grove, IL: InterVarsity Press, 1983); David Lyon, *The Steeple's Shadow: On the Myths and Realities of Secularization* (Grand Rapids, MI: Eerdmans, 1985).

When it comes to issues of epistemology, the countries I know best, Canada and the United States, have long been characterized by diversity. Each of the peoples already inhabiting North America had a distinctive culture that included a particular way of understanding the world. When European traders, soldiers, and colonists arrived, they brought several alien forms of thinking, whether religions such as Christianity and Judaism or modes of thinking appropriate to European commerce and modern warfare.[2]

Since that time, pluralism has increased dramatically, especially in our own era. Changes in immigration policy since the Second World War have welcomed greater immigration to North America and, indeed, to Europe and Australasia from areas outside the North-West of Europe, thus drawing in the much different outlooks of southern and eastern Europe, Asia, Africa, and Latin America. This has meant the rise of Islam, Hinduism, Buddhism, and less well known religions in cities and towns across the modern world. So-called New Religions, whether the indigenous faiths of the Mormons and Jehovah's Witnesses or imports such as Hare Krishna and *Santería*, have been widely reported. Diverse understandings of such basic features of life as marriage and family, ethnic loyalty, political power, and the complex relationship of religion and society have radically pluralized most modern and modernizing societies around the globe. So when someone remarks on religious or ideological pluralism nowadays, he probably does not mean to remark merely that "there is more than one option." More likely, he means to note the huge number and wide diversity of options now present on the local intellectual landscape.

Pluralism as Preference

This second definition goes beyond mere recognition that "there is more than one" to affirm that "*it is good* that there is more than one." Here pluralism moves from sociological description to ideological prescription, from "what is" to "what ought to be."

This preference can apply to a wide range of things. I prefer candy shops that offer more than one flavor of treat, for example, because sometimes I feel like enjoying chocolate and other times I prefer, well, chocolate in combination with something else. When I moved to a small town in Iowa for a few years, I learned quickly that everyone wisely patronized *both* grocery stores, *both* service stations, *both* pharmacies, and so on, in order to keep both in business. Economic pluralism meant preferring competition to monopoly. Pluralism can be expressed even about

---

2. See Jon Butler, *Awash in a Sea of Faith: Christianizing the American People* (Cambridge, MA: Harvard University Press, 1990); John Webster Grant, *Moon of Wintertime: Missionaries and the Indians of Canada in Encounter since 1534* (Toronto: University of Toronto Press, 1984); Terrence Murphy and Roberto Perlin, ed., *A Concise History of Christianity in Canada* (Toronto: Oxford University Press, 1996).

ultimate questions of life and death. Someone might prefer her society to include more than one philosophy, more than one ideology, and more than one religion because she believes that the presence of competing alternatives prevents any individual or any group from asserting unchallenged claims to truth, justice, and power. Such pluralism, on this understanding, also can lead to mutually enriching instruction among the various sets of convictions.

Each of us therefore is almost certainly a "pluralist" in one or another respect. Preferring plurality in some instances does not, of course, commit one to preferring it in all instances. Someone who held to every one of the pluralist views in the previous illustration still might resist, say, "matrimonial pluralism," as she strongly prefers monogamy to polygamy. Someone else might well prefer private property to communal ownership, or the rule of law to anarchy, and so on. We must therefore resist the aura of correctness that in some circles nowadays attends the word "pluralism" as if it is always good to be pluralist. Most of us are pluralistic in only some matters and definitely not in others.

An aura of correctness around the word extends to the third level of definition as well, the level of most importance for our epistemological considerations.

Pluralism as Relativism

Someone might recognize a situation as pluralism: "There is more than one." Someone might actually prefer a situation to be pluralistic: "It is good that there is more than one." But this third level of pluralism goes beyond both of these to declare that no single option among the available varieties in a pluralistic situation can be judged superior to the others.

It is worth pointing out that in a situation of intellectual diversity that included many alternatives but only one that seemed appealing, there would be no problem. But frequently we are faced with more than one highly plausible option—even several apparently equally attractive but mutually exclusive alternatives. How, we ask ourselves, can patently good and intelligent people believe such different things? "Pluralism as relativism" is an understandable response. And there are several varieties of it.

"Everything Is Beautiful." This is the attitude that every option is good. Vanilla is good and so is chocolate, and so opting for one or the other is a matter of mere subjective preference, not objective judgment. What is said of flavors is true of choices in other spheres as well. All have their merits, and all should be affirmed. This attitude surfaces especially when one encounters the bewildering variety of religions. Hinduism, Buddhism, Christianity, Native religion, New Age varieties, Wicca—all are good and simply different from each other, not better or worse than each other. They all ought to be affirmed as valid spiritual paths.

I recall students in my university courses on world religions who introduced themselves as having a particular religious outlook. Some were Jews, some Sikhs, some Buddhists or Hindus or Jains or Muslims or Christians of various sorts. Many were, as lifelong believers in their traditions, convinced that his or her religion was in fact the best of all. But many of them confessed that they felt that they *shouldn't* think that way. Somehow, they had received the notion that sophisticated people saw the world's religions as equally good. I have heard the same testimony many times from journalists who belong to a particular religion but who say they feel obliged by their profession to treat all religions as equally good. To be sure, this attitude is commercially advantageous: Avoid offending people with value judgments and you'll keep more readers, listeners, and viewers. But this attitude also seemed to be part of an ethos of proper, not merely profitable, journalism in a pluralistic society.

Before analyzing the next form of pluralism, let's pause to note how this one can be easily challenged by referring to extremes. Do you really believe, one might ask such a pluralist-as-relativist, that Nazism is just as good as the Judaism it tried to exterminate? Do you really not distinguish morally between the rites of infant baptism in this religion and infant sacrifice in that one? Does offering widows social and economic support in their bereavement make the same sense to you as expecting them to be immolated on their husbands' funeral pyres? This naïve relativism rarely stands up to a question of this sort—and it is much less commonly found nowadays, particularly after 9/11 and similar outbreaks of religiously associated violence elsewhere.

"All the Good Options Are Good—and We Say Which Ones." An apparently more nuanced version of pluralism-as-relativism says that all of the options in a particular sphere are *partially* good and *partially* bad: They all can be appreciated as more-or-less approximate versions of ultimate reality. An élite, moreover, can see through these various alternatives to the truth that transcends them all. This truth points to ultimate reality itself, and it is recognizable to those who have the panoramic and critical ability to see it.

Such an outlook, whether it shows up as a particular approach to literary criticism, or politics, or religion, should be recognized as being actually pseudo-relativistic and not finally pluralistic at all. For it maintains that there is indeed one "best" position among those available, and it is the position held by those who possess this ultimate insight.

In the spheres of religion and spirituality, this outlook abounds. Whether it be the New Age celebrity who is happy to bless all religion/faith/spirituality in some vague and sweeping way while maintaining that his particular philosophy is the very key to life, or a professor of religion who articulates what he believes to be the core truths of Ultimate Reality that lie behind the world's (confused) faiths, the claim to affirm all spiritual paths finally amounts to a limited and condescending approval of what the claimant sees as merely various approximations of the final and supreme truth that is recognized by those "in the know."[3] This view, in short, pretends to pluralism while

---

3. I have in mind people such as Eckhard Tolle in the former category and John Hick in the latter. See Eckhard Tolle, *The Power of Now: A Guide to Spiritual Enlightenment* (New York: New

offering one version as in fact the best of the lot. Let's pass on, then, to other forms of pluralism that are truly pluralistic—that actually do not privilege one viewpoint as better than all others.

There Are No Grounds for Judgment. The more sophisticated, and rarer, forms of pluralism-as-relativism assert that whatever one's own revulsion toward this or that idea or practice, one possesses no universal, objective standard against which to assess it as good or evil, true or false, beautiful or ugly, helpful or harmful. Indeed, one cannot even affirm that "one option is as good as another" because there is no standard of *good* that is not itself the product of one or another option.

Allan Bloom complained that most students—at least at schools such as his beloved University of Chicago—claim to believe that everything is relative:

> There is one thing a professor can be absolutely certain of: almost every student entering the university believes, or says he believes, that truth is relative.... The students' backgrounds are as various as America can provide. Some are religious, some atheists; some are to the Left, some to the Right; some intend to be scientists, some humanists or professionals or businessmen; some are poor, some rich. They are unified only in their relativism and in their allegiance to equality....
>
> Relativism is necessary to openness; and this is the virtue, the only virtue, which all primary education for more than fifty years has dedicated itself to inculcating. Openness... is the great insight of our times. The true believer is the real danger. The study of history and of culture teaches that all the world was mad in the past; men always thought they were right, and that led to wars, persecutions, slavery, xenophobia, racism, and chauvinism. The point is not to correct the mistakes and really be right; rather it is not to think you are right at all.[4]

Pluralism here runs well beyond the recognition of different moral codes and even the preference for the presence of different ethics. Here pluralism becomes radical: There is no final judgment to be made among competing systems of ethics.

Many of my own university students have displayed a deep ambivalence about ethics other than their own. In introductory religion courses, for example, many opine that the way this or that religion treats women appalls them. Yet in the very next paragraph of an essay, such students commonly revert to what they intend to

---

World, 1999); John Hick, *A Christian Theology of Religions: The Rainbow of Faiths* (Louisville, KY: Westminster John Knox Press, 1995).

4. Allan Bloom, *The Closing of the American Mind: How Higher Education Has Failed Democracy and Impoverished The Souls of Today's Students* (New York: Simon and Schuster, 1987), 25–26. Having lectured to a variety of Canadian, American, and British students in the years since Bloom's book was published, I believe his judgment to be as true today as it was then... in *élite, secular* universities such as the University of Chicago, where he taught. In more provincial and parochial schools, where I have spent my career as a teacher with only the occasional lectures given to the Harvards, Yales, Edinburghs, and the like, I daresay one more frequently encounters solid ideological conviction, including plenty of dogmatism, of various sorts.

be a relativistic judgment, namely, that they would probably agree with that religion's understanding of gender if they had been raised in that faith. This latter admission seems to imply that the students' disgust toward what they judge to be sexist violence is nothing more than an effect of their particular upbringing. Morality, in sum, is merely a social construction, an artifact of this or that culture, and not reflective of any objective moral order that lies beyond any person's or any civilization's preference. This reduction of values to mere historical happenstance ("I was raised in Canada by Christians and not in Yemen by Muslims") pervades the discussion of ethics in our time.

Let's notice in passing, however, that such a remark can reflect nothing more than a banal belief about how ethical convictions are formed. *Of course* we learn our ethics primarily from our society, as we do most of the culture we learn. To remark on this fact as if it says something important about the *validity* of this or that ethical conviction is clearly just a version of the genetic fallacy. By discrediting the origin (or "genesis") of an idea, we supposedly discredit the idea itself: Because cultures generate at least some convictions that aren't universally valid, we cannot accept any of their convictions as being universally valid. Yet, as David Martin reminds us, "we do not say of an artist's vision that its quality, specificity, 'truth,' uniqueness, and intensity are invalidated by the constraints exerted by his social time, place, and biography. He works within a 'school' and a culture just as *homo religiosus* works within a particular scheme of discipleship and of culture."[5]

Or perhaps the mistake is a version of another common, but fallacious, belief: Because various people hold various opinions on this matter, then none of those opinions can be taken as finally true—as if everyone has an equal claim to authority on disputed matters and thus the mere existence of disagreement means no judgment can be made. Just because students in a mathematics course disagree about the correct answer to a problem, however, does not mean that one answer is not in fact correct and the others wrong. Just because people disagree about the best way to build an automobile doesn't mean that some cars are not in fact superior to others.

Despite this widespread relativism, however, we should also note that few people in our culture seem prepared to endorse sheer relativism, particularly in ethical questions. Leaving aside the colossal social and political implications of such anarchy (implications that seem not to occur to people who easily mouth such relativistic sentiments), many of our neighbors do place limits even on private morality. They might claim to affirm "whatever makes you happy/spiritual/enlightened," but they immediately draw lines when certain versions of happiness/spirituality/enlightenment cross their paths. Usually these limits are little more than sentimental altruism ("X is okay if and only if it is a loving thing to do") or truncated liberalism ("X is okay if it does not hurt anyone else"), but they are indeed limits. And such people normally share the common moral outlook of their

---

5. David Martin, *Reflections on Sociology and Theology* (Oxford: Clarendon, 1997), 100.

culture, despite whatever independence of mind they might advertise: They, too, simply *know* that child molestation is wrong, and so are genocide, and rape, and so on. So, despite students' testimony that they are relativists, I must testify that I have encountered very few students who do, in fact, consistently believe in sheer moral or ideological relativism.

There remain, however, two intellectually serious versions of this pluralism-as-relativism that warrant attention.

There Is No "Good" or "Evil." Nihilism (from *nihil*, "nothing") asserts that there simply is no universal standard: no God or gods; no *karma, dao, brahman, tian*, or *logos*; no structuring principle of the universe in terms of right or wrong, better or worse. We can indeed make judgments about true or false. Nihilism itself is a firm belief that things are a certain way and not otherwise. But statements of moral and aesthetic judgment must be recognized for what they are: mere statements of individual or group preference—and, usually, individual or group *interest*. (We can look to Feuerbach, Schopenhauer, Freud, Nietzsche, Sartre, Kafka, Beckett, Cage, and Foucault for variations on this theme.) The universe is devoid of such standards beyond what we invent for ourselves and what some among us are pleased to call (in their delusion, or perhaps in their desire to manipulate others) anything other than our own preferences.

Such confidence that the cosmos is of this sort may be found in the New Atheism, as it is in most communism, secular humanism, and other forms of convinced secularism. Far more prevalent, however, is a *lack* of epistemic confidence in the form of the following version of relativism.

There Is No Way to Tell Good from Evil. This view is sometimes called simply *skepticism*, and in its most extreme and hopeless form, *cynicism*. It suggests that whether or not there does exist an objective standard by which to adjudicate things—whether there really are metaphysical, moral, and aesthetic *facts* in the cosmos—we human beings can't know those facts as such or, at least, we can't know them for certain. To be sure, we might stumble upon this or that truth, even a truth in some absolute form, such as a mathematical or physical formula that exactly describes some sort of relationship in the real world. But even in such cases, we still could not know for certain, without any qualification or doubt, that what we *think* we know as true is in fact true. We cannot escape our limitations to see things correctly from a universal perspective. Thus it is more accurate and more helpful to describe our so-called conclusions as provisional. We should say that *A* or *B* is our conviction "as far as we know—and we could very well be wrong." We must not claim that our views are certainly right—even our most important views, including our religions.

It might surprise some readers to find that I think that there is much to say in favor of at least a mild form of this skepticism, even from (and even particularly from) a Christian point of view, although the previous chapter dropped plenty of hints in this regard. Let me just register this opinion for now, and defend it below once we discuss the various ways of thinking (that is, the "cognitive styles") of our time. And what we will find in what follows is an interweaving of the various sorts of pluralism, from a situation of remarkable diversity to more-or-less plausible endorsements of plurality to various forms of relativism.

THE CONTEMPORARY VARIETY OF COGNITIVE STYLES

In what follows, there are several patterns to notice. First, there are key tensions in play in intellectual life that serve to blur sharp distinctions between the categories of "traditional" and "modern." The degree to which a culture prizes conservation versus innovation depends on whether a society experiences scarcity versus abundance, vulnerability versus security, and therefore anxiety versus confidence. Is the current situation fraught with dangerous threats or brimming with challenging opportunities? To the extent that society tends toward the former outlook, intellectual life—like the rest of culture—will tend to resort to authority and spend its energies in the recovery and conservation of tradition. If society is of the latter outlook, then intellectual life will tend toward a confident autonomy and devote itself to the discovery and accumulation of new knowledge.

Since in the career of any given civilization these tensions will be in flux, we can expect to discern within it currents of both conservation and innovation, and then witness occasional upwellings of one or the other depending on that society's sense of the world and its place in it. We can also expect variations within the same society, notably the intellectual culture of relatively secure and prosperous elites versus the culture of contemporaries who experience life as precarious subsistence. We therefore should not settle for the common stereotypes of expecting all premodern societies to be uniformly conservative (for how then could they, and did they, discover things—as they clearly did?) and all modern societies to be relentlessly innovative (for how then to explain recurring modern references to this or that "golden age"?).

Second, cognitive styles emerge consecutively in history, but later styles do not everywhere and always supplant earlier ones. Instead, in many situations cognitive styles accumulate, sometimes constituting the characteristic outlook of respective individuals and communities within a pluralized society and sometimes providing alternative resources for the same individuals or communities—just as some cultures around the world access one religious tradition for certain needs while retaining another for other occasions. (The common example, seen on every continent, is of a tribe converting to Christianity and adopting a panoply of Christian devotional practices while retaining some of its tribal lore to deal with outbreaks of disease or demon possession, worries about fertility, and so on.) By the time we reach the twentieth century in this survey of western intellectual history, we will find that there are several major, and many minor, different cognitive styles in play in our culture.

Finally, in recent decades this multiplicity of cognitive styles has become more evident than ever *within* the minds of individuals and communities, so that someone might well think in a particular way about some things in her life while deploying different cognitive styles for other things. This widespread and complex multiplicity, fragmentation, and versatility is characteristic of advanced modern societies and their inhabitants—it is, in fact, at the heart of what some call the "postmodern" or "hypermodern" condition.

To begin, then, we turn to the first modern cognitive style, that of the Enlightenment, contrasting it with what I will generalize as the "traditional" cognitive style that was, and is, typical of premodern cultures.[6]

The Enlightenment

This movement in western thought arose out of the Scientific Revolution of the seventeenth century and came into its own in the eighteenth. It was called the "Age of Reason," or, as the French put it, *le siècle des lumières* ("the century of lights"). Like any major development in civilization, the Enlightenment is a complex phenomenon, whose nature and effects are perhaps infinitely debatable.[7] But standard descriptions of it include the following emphases.

First, when it came to matters of epistemology the Enlightenment characteristically put its confidence in reason and experience. Rationalists might follow René Descartes's lead and emphasize the former; empiricists might follow John Locke instead and emphasize the latter. But both sorts believed that the surest route to knowledge of the world lay in the appropriate use of what the senses said, what people learned from inward examination, and what disciplined reflection made of it all.

According to the most enthusiastic proponents of the Enlightenment, here was human emancipation from superstition and tradition, from a view of knowledge that privileged the lore of the tribe and the teaching office of an élite cadre presiding by conventional right rather than intrinsic intellectual prowess. No more would

---

6. The following are widely used introductions to medieval and modern intellectual history: David Knowles, *The Evolution of Medieval Thought* (New York: Vintage, 1962); Marcia L. Colish, *Medieval Foundations of the Western Intellectual Tradition* (New Haven, CT: Yale University Press, 1999); Steven Ozment, *The Age of Reform, 1250–1550: An Intellectual and Religious History of Late Medieval and Reformation Europe* (New Haven, CT and London: Yale University Press, 1980); Franklin L. Baumer, *Modern European Thought: Continuity and Change in Ideas, 1600–1950* (New York: Macmillan, 1977); and Roland N. Stromberg, *European Intellectual History Since 1789* [many editions] (Englewood Cliffs, NJ: Prentice-Hall, 1966). See also Colin Brown, *Christianity and Western Thought A History of Philosophers, Ideas & Movements*, vol. 1 (Downers Grove, IL: InterVarsity Press, 1990); and Alan G. Padgett and Steve Wilkens, *Faith & Reason in the Nineteenth Century: Christianity & Western Thought*, Vol. 2 (Downers Grove, IL: InterVarsity Press, 2000).

7. Henry F. May, for example, traces no fewer than five "enlightenments" in America alone: *The Enlightenment in America* (New York: Oxford University Press, 1976).

knowledge be construed as learning what the established authorities had taught and, when it wasn't clear just how they were agreeing, taking the pains necessary to reconcile them into a harmonious account of the truth. Now human beings were free to think for themselves, looking forward to new discovery rather than backward to the glories of the past.

This change of outlook was not as stark as the propagandists of Enlightenment tended to suggest. Socrates, Plato, and Aristotle, after all, did some original thinking of their own—as did the pre-Socratic philosophers before them. Jesus and his apostles could properly be understood to have introduced a few new ideas into the world. Augustine, Anselm, Aquinas—just to sample the first letter of the medieval alphabet—did not merely parrot the past. Yes, the Renaissance was self-consciously the "rebirth" of the best of the classical tradition, but its leading proponents were innovative as well as conservative, whether one considers the revolution of perspective (pioneered by Ghiberti and Brunelleschi, developing Arab precedents) or pretty much the whole of Leonardo da Vinci's astonishing output. And the so-called Reformation was, in fact, a massive reconception and reconstruction of Christianity, however much its early figures originally understood their project as merely trying to turn the clock back a few centuries behind late medieval extravagances.

So when Immanuel Kant declared breathlessly that humanity was now "come of age," we can recognize something of an overstatement born of the delight of freeing oneself from the domination of what one despises of one's heritage. A south German idiom relates a young man's first sexual experience as constituting his "enlightenment" (*Aufklärung*), implying his passage from dependent childhood into independent adulthood. He has, as the English idiom puts it, "become a man." Humanity enjoyed now a new status and responsibility, inspired by the widening global cultural horizon of the European Age of Discovery every bit as much as by the widening scientific horizon of the Scientific Revolution. Kant thus famously encouraged his civilization to "dare to know," *sapere aude*![8]

In their extreme enthusiasm, atheists discarded divine revelation as a source of knowledge, while more moderate intellectual revolutionaries reduced the God of the Bible to a deistic Clockmaker. The prestige of Voltaire, Diderot, Jefferson, Franklin, and others have given the Enlightenment an "anti-Christian" or at least an "anti-orthodox" taint such that people today—particularly both reactionary Christians and militant atheists—believe that the Enlightenment as a whole was antagonistic to the Christian religion. But this view is wrong. Christian thinkers as orthodox as John Wesley and Jonathan Edwards took the basic Enlightenment themes for granted as they examined the world by way of experience and reason for signs of God's gracious providence.[9] They, too, saw science as a reliable means of

---

8. See Kant's famous essay "What Is Enlightenment?" reprinted many times.

9. For the influence of the Enlightenment on British evangelicals, see the pertinent chapters of David W. Bebbington, *Evangelicalism in Modern Britain: A History from the 1730s to the 1980s* (London: Unwin Hyman, 1989). The vast literature on Jonathan Edwards agrees at least on

understanding the natural world. They, too, saw reason and experience as unlocking secrets of human life as well, even probing the depths of the human psyche and spiritual matters such as conversion, sanctification, and the nature of true revival. They shared the confidence of most of the scientists of the preceding century—that is, the paragons of the Scientific Revolution that inspired the Enlightenment—that science explored the divinely-authored Book of Nature while theology explored the divinely authored Book of Scripture. Because the two Books had a single Author, the Books would never ultimately disagree, and the wise person—and civilization—profitably consulted both.

For a second Enlightenment theme—regardless of one's view of God and revelation—was that truth was discoverable and objective. Truth about great, basic matters was not shrouded in mystery, dispensed only on occasion by individual proclamation, whether Delphic oracle or charismatic prophet. Instead, the scientific method asserted that truth was apprehended as the community of scholars investigated the world, gathered data, hypothesized explanations, and then confirmed, modified, or replaced each other's conclusions by going over and over the same ground. Truth was not something revealed arbitrarily by some supernatural power, nor too complicated for humanity to understand. Truth was "out there" to be had.

The third Enlightenment theme spoke to *who* possessed the truth. Truth was not the province of magicians or priests or rulers or other privileged élites. It was open to all through society's scholars. To be sure, specialists (then as now) might well converse in terminology and concepts well above the heads of the general population. But there was, ideally, no deliberate mystification and no secrecy. Anyone with the intelligence and skill to engage in such conversation was welcome. Truth was universal, for the benefit of all. And when someone thought he had discovered truth, he made his investigation public—literally, *published* it—for the rest of the interested world to test it.

The convictions of the Enlightenment are still readily apparent three centuries later. Most day-to-day "bench science" proceeds this way, in physics, chemistry, biology, and geology. This model of data, hypothesis, and trial—all processed according to objective standards—also continues to inform much sociology, psychology, economics, and other social sciences. Perhaps supremely, however, the Enlightenment persists in the applied sciences, notably engineering and medicine. Terms here are univocal: no one is supposed to mistake a 10-centimeter brass flathead Phillips wood screw for anything else. Ambiguity and impulse are dangerous in both airplane construction and surgery. Reason and experience are the reliable routes to knowledge.

---

this, that he was very much a child of the Enlightenment. See, for example, Sang Hyun Lee, *The Philosophical Theology of Jonathan Edwards*, exp. ed. (Princeton, NJ: Princeton University Press, 2000); and Gerald R. McDermott, *Jonathan Edwards Confronts the Gods: Christian Theology, Enlightenment Religion, and Non-Christian Faiths* (Oxford and New York: Oxford University Press, 2000). And for Edwards himself, see *Scientific and Philosophical Writings*, ed. Wallace E. Anderson (New Haven, CT: Yale University Press, 1980).

No one in this cognitive style designs an engine or treats a disease on the basis of a mystical impulse or because an ancient authority says so.

Romanticism

Toward the end of the eighteenth century, and particularly in the wake of the French Revolution, intellectuals in various European centers began to react against Enlightenment ideas.[10] In everyday speech, the word "romantic" now conjures up images of moonlight, soft breezes, hillsides, rippling water, and love. These stereotypes actually are not all that far off the mark in directing us to important themes in the Romantic movement.

Where the Enlightenment had looked to experience-as-data and reason-as-disengaged-reflection, Romanticism looked to feeling as discerned by intuition. The images in Romantic writing are organic, versus the mechanical metaphors of the Enlightenment. The Romantic comprehends the way things are, not by acquiring data through the senses and then rationally processing that information, but by literally feeling the world through one's intuitive union with it—as one simply knows whether one's fingers are cold or hot, or whether a family member beside you is happy or sad. It is direct access to things by organic and mystical union. As even the scientist Humphry Davy felt it, "Every thing seemed alive, and myself part of the series of visible impressions; I should have felt pain in tearing a leaf from one of the trees."[11]

The paragon of Enlightenment virtue was the physicist Isaac Newton. As Alexander Pope so memorably wrote: "Nature and Nature's laws lay hid in night:/ God said, Let Newton be! and all was light."[12] The characteristic Enlightenment thinker was a *philosophe*, a thinker who took in the bits of the world and synthesized them in his brain into general abstract concepts. The leading Romantic authors instead, however, were poets such as William Wordsworth and Alexander Pushkin. They *felt* the way the world was and spoke from the heart.

For, secondly, where the Enlightenment had been coolly objective in its acquisition of truth, Romanticism was warmly subjective. Enlightenment thinking, in the

---

10. I recognize that there is a longstanding debate as to whether the Romantic movement is best understood as a kind of "Counter-Enlightenment." I think it is, but I trust the description of Romanticism that follows will be generic enough to mollify even those who don't.

11. Quoted by David M. Knight, *Humphry Davy: Science and Power* (Cambridge, MA and Oxford: Basil Blackwell, 1992), 36; cited in John Hedley Brooke, "Science and Theology in the Enlightenment," in *Religion and Science: History, Method Dialogue*, ed. W. Mark Richardson and Wesley J. Wildman (New York: Routledge, 1996), 25.

12. "Epitaph intended for Sir Isaac Newton"; quoted in John Bartlett, ed., *Familiar Quotations*, ed. Emily Morison Beck, 14th ed. (Boston and Toronto: Little, Brown, 1968), 412b.

powerful indictment of William Wordsworth, murders to dissect.[13] The object of study is pinned down on a cold, hard surface amid gleaming metal apparatus. Illuminated by harsh, artificial light, it is slowly disintegrated under the probing of scientific instruments. To the contrary, the Romantics argued, knowledge was a matter of being a part of things, not of taking things apart. Reality was the warm-blooded life of individual elements in organisms or communities, not the isolation of monads or the frozen death of abstractions—the movement of dancers, not the fixedness of mannequins and models. The world essentially is flow and freedom, not universal constants and scientific laws. As the Enlightenment patiently separates (the Greek root of "analysis" means "to dissolve") truth, goodness, and beauty, Romanticism enthusiastically melds them into holistic organic flourishing.

Alfred, Lord Tennyson, provides an example of the Romantic view of religious faith:

That which we dare invoke to bless;
    Our dearest faith; our ghastliest doubt;
    He, They, One, All; within, without;
The Power in darkness whom we guess;

I found him not in world or sun,
    Or eagle's wing, or insect's eye;
    Nor through the questions men may try,
The petty cobwebs we have spun:

If e'er when faith had fallen asleep,
    I heard a voice 'believe no more'
    And heard an ever-breaking shore
That tumbled in the Godless deep;

A warmth within the breast would melt
    The freezing reason's colder part,
    And like a man in wrath the heart
Stood up and answered 'I have felt.'[14]

Thirdly, then, if one were to open oneself up to the world in this way, truth was "out there" to be apprehended "in here," in the personal center of one's life. This was not the same sort of public truth as championed by the Enlightenment, the truth of formulaic generalizations verified by a community of scholars. Yet it is a public sort of truth, and in this respect Romanticism is just as modern as the Enlightenment. Anyone who will cultivate the right cognitive attitudes and skills—not scientific

---

13. "The Tables Turned," 1798.
14. Alfred, Lord Tennyson, Canto CXXIII of "In Memoriam."

ones, now, but intuitive, aesthetic ones—will see the way things are. Romanticism, like the Enlightenment, aimed at comprehending the cosmos, but its characteristic expression was the poem, not the equation.[15] The confidence of the Romantics was therefore a sort of reflection of the confidence of the Royal Society itself: If we look at the right things in the right way, we all will come to the same (correct) conclusions.

Modern intellectual life seems to offer little space for Romanticism. Some theories of literary and other artistic interpretation do emphasize intuitive apprehension of the truth. Some university departments of women's studies, aboriginal studies, social work, education, and other departments that emphasize the empowerment of marginalized groups sometimes feature reactions against what they see as objectification by emphasizing Romantic ways of knowing. In such dialogues, intuition, freedom, harmony with nature, and so on are set against rationality, oppression, alienation from nature, and the like.

The presence and importance of this movement lingers in other zones of contemporary life. Perhaps this is most conspicuous with respect to music. Few of us even attempt to justify our preference for this artist or for that composition by objective criteria of aesthetic excellence. We lack the musical and aesthetic vocabulary to champion our favorite song as, say, "polyphonically rich, with subtle echoes of Josquin Des Près and ironic allusions to Tennessee bluegrass chord progressions, that meets all of the harmonic requirements of Paul Hindemith's influential theory." To do so would appear (as perhaps it did just now) impossibly pretentious. Instead, we simply hand over the CD to a friend and say, "Listen to this!" with the confidence that, if our friend is properly oriented to art, he cannot but agree that this song is not just pleasant to his ears, but objectively, intrinsically good.

Romanticism also continues to exert powerful influence in the area of religion: People take on a religion because it simply feels right. Some forms of Wicca or native spirituality purport to offer the wisdom of the ancients despite powerful historical evidence to the contrary—evidence that the beliefs and rituals for latter-day Druid or Iroquois religion go no further back than a century or so. I once encountered on an Internet discussion list the claim that nine million women were executed as witches during the European witch hunts. When I suggested to the group on the basis of authoritative research that this was a preposterously high figure, I was told that no matter what historical scholarship might say, "We know in our bones that nine million of our sisters died." How is such a belief held to be true? It is validated in the Romantic sense: It feels right.

---

15. Daniel Chua helpfully clarifies this point: "Thus the absolute Idea is not a static entity, but a productive *activity* from which all matter is created and in which all things live, move and have their being. The Romantics called this divine process 'poesis,' which is often translated as 'poetry,' but really signifies a kind of absolute *productivity* that is aesthetic in essence and unfolds in all the arts" (Daniel K. L. Chua, *Absolute Music and the Construction of Meaning* [Cambridge, UK and New York: Cambridge University Press, 1999], 173).

Christians inclined toward Enlightenment-style thinking—as many are, despite its reputation in some circles as a synonym for modern atheism—must not, as some do, paint Romanticism only in unflattering colors. Our faith has a strong tradition of valuing such perceptions of the world. Mystical experiences that seem overwhelmingly true, if rationally unverifiable, show up across the Christian spectrum. "You ask me how I know he lives?/He lives within my heart," runs the popular gospel song. The worldwide explosion of Pentecostalism shows that Christian interest in intuitive apprehension of reality has hardly disappeared. From Augustine through Thomas Aquinas to John Calvin and even contemporary Christian philosophers such as William Alston and Alvin Plantinga, Christian intellectuals have sought to preserve a place for feeling and intuition in Christian apprehension of the world.[16] Christianity has room for Romantic themes—as one of the first great Romantics, Samuel Taylor Coleridge, tirelessly maintained. And in what follows, we will make room for them as well.

Process

As the nineteenth century progressed, new currents developed that both carried forward previous elements and added new ones. An increasingly dominant mode of thought saw *process* to be the chief category in which to understand reality. In a kind of reiteration of the Enlightenment, reason and experience were again championed as the high roads to truth. Now, however, these resources were qualified by a third element, *history*. The Enlightenment had hoped to devise universal laws that governed all things past, present, and future. But in the nineteenth century a number of influential thinkers began to see that, while such universal laws might still be discoverable, what they described were processes that could be understood properly only over time—and sometimes very long periods of time indeed.

One needed to look beneath the surface of things and beyond the present moment to understand reality. Truth was still discoverable and objective, but one needed to know where and how to look for it. Thus all could partake of truth, but only as many as would take the long and deep view, the view of Process.

Georg W. F. Hegel thus formulated a sweeping metaphysics that sought to explain the entire cosmos in terms of a vast process of Spirit and Matter interacting over all of time towards a great, final realization of Spirit's self by Itself. In this context, Hegel interpreted human history as a process of continual interaction of new combinations that would produce better results each time—in the process of his so-called dialectic. Karl Marx famously turned Hegel on his head and taught that human history was fundamentally the story of the struggle between economic

16. William P. Alston, *Perceiving God: The Epistemology of Religious Experience* (Ithaca, NY: Cornell University Press, 1991); Alvin Plantinga, *Warranted Christian Belief* (New York: Oxford University Press, 2000).

classes over material power, not the story of Spirit coming to self-realization. His call to revolution was based on the strong sense that he knew precisely where he was in the material dialectic of history and thus (particularly in Lenin's and Mao's versions) what needed to be done at a particular juncture in that story. Charles Darwin joined other scientists in breaking the chains of the static mentality of early nineteenth-century science. He provided a mechanism (natural selection) for the increasingly popular idea of the evolution, rather than the divine direct creation, of species. Finally, Sigmund Freud turned to the study of human psychology and suggested that adult feelings, behaviors, and values were largely the results of childhood experiences—the end-results of lifelong processes. Hegel, Marx, Darwin, and Freud therefore were simply brighter luminaries in a whole constellation of thinkers that decisively introduced process as a fundamental category of thought. This was, so to speak, the Enlightenment in a new mode, the mode of "becoming," not simply "being."[17]

There aren't many Hegelians around anymore, although some recent convergences between Eastern mysticism and science call to mind Hegel's conviction that the cosmos is fundamentally spiritual. In the twentieth and twenty-first centuries, a good deal of social science, history, and other forms of cultural study has been influenced by Marxism of one form or another. Darwin, of course, has provided the reigning paradigm in biology, but also has contributed to the popularity of evolutionary models in geology and cosmology—extending also into sociobiological interpretations of human thought and behavior as well. For at least the last generation, Freud has been under heavy attack for this or that aspect of his theory or his scientific practice (or the lack of the latter, according to some), but the clock cannot be turned back to before his basic recognition of the developmental nature of human psychology. More general "ideas of progress"—ideas which impelled so much of the dynamism of European culture in the nineteenth century and of American culture throughout the twentieth—continue to inform much economic theory as well as certain popular politics around the world. And the recognition that many ideas are merely the results of particular historical circumstances rather than the discovery of timeless truths informs jurisprudence and legislation. They attend to precedents in the past in order only to guide, but certainly not simply to determine, the laws being made and interpreted today and tomorrow.

All three of these currents—Enlightenment, Romanticism, and the fundamental sense of Process—continue to flourish in the intellectual culture of our own time. But none of them dominates, and thus there is no set of "rules of engagement" by which all intellectual disputes can be resolved. In this pluralized situation, in fact, sometimes the only recourse is to alliances, agreements, compromises, and coercions—in short, to one or another *modus vivendi* resolved as a matter of negotiated power. Recognition of this pluralized situation

---

17. This is the dominant motif in Baumer.

has taken intellectual and more broadly cultural forms, forms sometimes identified as "postmodern."

Postmodernity

The heart of postmodernity is *doubt* regarding any claims to having The Truth, the
great explanation, the theory of everything. It is despair about ever arriving at the
utopian Last Days, the end of history, the One Final Best.

As such, however, postmodernity is hardly new. In important respects, it is
merely the latest version of skepticism. The lineage of skepticism in Western civilization goes back at least as far as the ancient Greeks, who produced the first
Skeptics, and also to the world-weary Ecclesiastes of the Hebrew Scriptures, while
the skeptical Daoist tradition in China goes back at least as far.

Centuries later, and also centuries before postmodernity, medieval philosophers argued about how well our view of things correlates with the way things actually are. The argument came to a head in the so-called realist/nominalist controversy
of the later Middle Ages. Realists such as Thomas Aquinas followed the broadly
Socratic tradition and believed that our names for things arise out of our recognition of actual essences in reality. Thus we call this thing a tree and that other thing
a tree because we recognize that they share a similar essence of "tree-ness."
Nominalists such as William of Ockham believed that our names for things are
simply matters of convention and could easily have been otherwise. We call these
two different things trees because from our particular point of view they seem similar. But the similarity isn't essential. The terms or names we devise (hence *nominalism*) are just the labels we happen to stick on things rather than acknowledgments
of the way things are in themselves. Followers of postmodern debates about the
relationship—or lack of one—between the "signifier" and the "signified" will see
antecedents in this dispute.

In the seventeenth century, the great empiricist philosopher John Locke recognized
that our minds do shape the way we perceive and think about things. He is well known
for his suggestion that the human mind is a *tabula rasa*, a "blank slate," on which experiences are simply imprinted. He is less well known, however, for his recognition of some
properties of things as being essential to them (such as their extension in space—their
shape) and some of their properties as being dependent on circumstances (such as
their color, which depends on the light available and the optical apparatus of the be-
holder). In fact, Locke applied his skeptical psychology—in which we could be dead
certain of very little—to politics, encouraging the English, after a century of civil strife,
to hold their convictions more humbly and less violently.[18]

---

18. For a powerful reconsideration of Locke, see Nicholas Wolterstorff, *John Locke and the
Ethics of Belief* (Cambridge: Cambridge University Press, 1996). We will take up Locke again in
the last chapter.

Following the provocations of David Hume, who was Locke's more radical successor, Immanuel Kant roused himself to declare not only a distinction (which was obvious), but an unbridgeable divide (which was troubling), between a thing as it is "in itself" (*an Sich*) and that thing as it appears "to me" (*für mich*). Kant's extensive analysis and argument have been immensely influential on all sorts of later thinkers up to our own day. It is his paradigm, in fact, that has set the terms for most epistemology in the modern era, prompting the radical qualification of empiricism into positivism and pragmatism. These movements were exercises in a kind of "second naïveté" (with apologies to Ricoeur for this different use of his phrase) as thinkers as diverse as Auguste Comte and William James encouraged us to regard the world "as if"—*as if* our knowledge of appearances were knowledge of the things themselves, for *practically* it amounted to the same thing: the successful negotiation of the multiple challenges of life. (Thus, I suggest, in most respects Kant's great noumenal/phenomenal divide became a distinction without a [practical] difference.)

Since the mid-twentieth century, however, these significant qualifications of our claims to knowledge have been carried by a wave of large-scale social change. The result is a cultural situation enough different from what has gone before to warrant a new term, namely, "postmodernity."[19]

Words that begin with "postmodern-" are notoriously hard to define to everyone's satisfaction. That problem is in itself something of a postmodern joke, an irony to be observed with the wry smiles and knowing winks of the postmodern cognoscenti. I shall try to explain the joke by distinguishing between what I call the *condition* or *situation* of "postmodernity" and the characteristic *response* to this condition, for which I will reserve the term "postmodernism."

The postmodern situation is literally "after the modern." So far we have looked at three cognitive styles: Enlightenment, Romanticism, and Process (Enlightenment as qualified by historical consciousness). Each of these is distinctly modern, and it is over against their common modernity that the postmodern attitude defines itself.

Modern thinking was directed at finding the truth, as was premodern thinking also in its own various modes. Characteristic of modernity is the guiding hope that, given enough time and energy, human beings could experience the world, think

---

19. The canon of postmodernity and postmodernism, so to speak, includes the recognized works of Jacques Derrida, Jean-François Lyotard, Jacques Lacan, Emmanuel Levinas, Michel Foucault and their ilk. The literature emergent from and surrounding all things "pomo" is immense, of course. In addition to the works mentioned in the subsequent notes, I have found most informative and suggestive the following books, dealing as they do with much broader aspects of the postmodern condition than deconstruction per se: George Steiner, *Real Presences* (Chicago: University of Chicago Press, 1989); J. Richard Middleton & Brian J. Walsh, *Truth Is Stranger than It Used to Be: Biblical Faith in a Postmodern Age* (Downers Grove, IL: InterVarsity Press, 1995); Terry Eagleton, *The Illusions of Postmodernism* (Oxford: Blackwell, 1996); Robert Hughes, *The Shock of the New*, rev. ed. (New York: Knopf, 1991); Tom Wolfe, *From Bauhaus to Our House* (New York: Farrar Straus Giroux, 1981); and Wolfe, *The Painted Word* (New York: Bantam Books, 1975).

hard, and come up with reliable answers—even *correct* answers—regarding the nature of things (or, at least, things as they appeared to us). Here was a powerful *confidence* that all persons of goodwill, sufficient gifts (whether in intelligence, aesthetic sensibility, and so on) and appropriate skill can examine the pertinent data and come to the same true conclusions.

Critics of modernity often scorn it for its assumption that it had everything figured out. And, to be sure, there are some nice, big targets available for such contempt.[20] The confidence of modernity, though, is in the *project*, not so much in the (provisional) conclusions. However much confidence modern scientists might have placed in Newton's laws, for example, Albert Einstein's challenges to Newton didn't spell the end of the scientific method nor did they shake modern epistemological confidence to the core. Such revisions are typical of the way the project is *supposed* to work. New theories are tested by new experiments and then correlated with what else we think we know. Newton's famous claim that he merely stood on the shoulders of giants applies to him, too, as scientists build on his work, recognizing that Sir Isaac's formulations still work very well for everything that isn't very big, very small, or very fast. Science carries on with the confidence that it is coming to closer and closer *approximations* of reality, even as zealots in every generation have gotten carried away and pronounced this or that idea to be the simple, final truth.

It is important to note that the same kind of confidence, *mutatis mutandis*, is characteristic of the Romantic movement as well. Romanticism also was sure that people of goodwill (that is, those who sincerely sought the truth), sufficient gifts (especially intelligence coupled with aesthetic and spiritual sensibilities), and appropriate training (no technical skills were needed, except for ability in, say, painting or poetry, but the skills of observation, concentration, openness to intuition, and so on, were cultivated) could perceive the way things actually are. The Romantics shared their views with each other, whether informally in conversation and correspondence or formally in works of art, with the twofold confidence that they were in fact perceiving reality and that their companions would perceive it the same way. That is, Romanticism was not a kind of radical individualism, though it is sometimes characterized as such. Like the Enlightenment, Romanticism believed that it was perceiving reality as it is, and that all "right-thinking" people would perceive it similarly.

The nineteenth-century moderns had precisely the same confidence. Look at things in Hegel's way, or Marx's way, or Darwin's way, or Freud's way, or even Nietzsche's way and you would penetrate to the heart of reality. Details might still need to be worked out, evidence still to be gathered to support this or that unsubstantiated conjecture, or even modifications still to be applied to this or that sub-point (Hegelians, Marxists, Darwinists, Freudians, and Nietzscheans

---

20. A highly popular compendium of such folly is Christopher Cerf and Victor Navasky, *The Experts Speak: The Definitive Compendium of Authoritative Misinformation*, rev. ed. (New York: Villard, 1998 [1984]).

have been busy in all three tasks), but the basic scheme was sound. This is the way things are.

Modern confidence in knowledge (sometimes called, in the older, broader sense of the term, "science") was extended throughout society into a confidence in technology (thus, *"applied* science") such that we could shape, and even remake, the world to suit our purposes. *Mastery* and *control* become key implications of the modern mind, whether intellectually (as in "mastering one's field" and "controlling the sources") or much more broadly in all of life via technology ("mastery over disease," "climate control").

Thus whether Voltaire, Wordsworth, or Marx, each conforms to this epitome of the modern project: "We can find out what we need to find out, in order to think what we need to think, in order to do what we need to do, in order to get what we want to get."

It is this confidence that has been lost in postmodernity. Indeed, this confidence has been repudiated. Instead, there is the characteristic postmodern recognition that all human perception and thought is necessarily *perspectival* or *subjective*, and this in two senses: both "from a point of view" (and so *from where*) and also "affected by the one (the subject) doing the viewing" (and so *by whom*).

In the former sense of subjectivity, human knowledge is limited by, restricted to, and characterized by the quality of a particular viewpoint: a certain place, a certain time, a certain light, and so on. There is no absolute viewpoint available to us, no view from everywhere/nowhere. There are only particular vantage places that give angles of vision on only particular things. I see the concert from the cheap seats in the second balcony; you see it from the front row; he sees it from the wings; she sees it from center stage. Our reports on the concert will vary because our points of view vary. In this regard, we recall Einstein's fourth dimension and appreciate that our point of view is qualified also by time: our sense of the concert varies also with how much of the concert has transpired at the point of our report. (What might have seemed a fresh idea the first time has become tiresome on repetition, or what seemed a minor motif the first time has become by its fourth iteration, and in an accumulating musical context, a major factor in the experience.)[21]

In the second place, human knowledge is characterized by the quality of the particular knower—or community of knowers. Gender, age, race, education, physical and mental health, emotional state, prejudices, beliefs, appetites, preferences, and previous knowledge all affect the processes of human perception and interpretation. I see the concert as an envious would-be rock star whose garage band never made it out of the garage. You see the concert as a long-time fan who camped out for two days to get those choice seats. He sees the concert with the gimlet eye and narrow ambition of a jaded manager. And she is having the time of her life playing her first big concert in her

---

21. Jeremy S. Begbie offers seminal suggestions in an entire chapter devoted to repetition: "Repetition and Eucharist," chap. in *Theology, Music, and Time* (Cambridge: Cambridge University Press, 1999), 155–75.

hometown. What happened at the concert and how good was it? It depends whom you ask. To put this more simply, were all four of us to sit together in a box and watch the opening act, we would *still* report on a different concert experience because we are different people, not just because later on that night during the main event we will take up different vantage points around the hall. There is no neutral, disinterested thinking. There are simply angles of vision on things that offer various approximations of the way things are to different people who see things differently.

Notice, however, that this acknowledgment of subjectivity presumes an objective reality that is being observed variously by various people in various situations. Subjectivism can be fully recognized without giving way to utter skepticism or radical relativism.

We can go back now and refine some of what has been said about modernity particularly after the Enlightenment. For in Romanticism and in the subsequent historicized version of the Enlightenment in the nineteenth century, modernity manifested an increasing tension between a universal, cosmopolitan outlook—the Enlightenment was just that: generic enlightenment of generic human beings by the generic rational reflection upon generic experience—and a growing appreciation of the differences, even divisions, among human beings. Nationalism grows up in the wake of the disintegration of Christendom fueled by Romantic recoveries of past (or "past," even ersatz) cultural heritages, whether Sir Walter Scott's novels, Pre-Raphaelite paintings, neo-Gothic civic architecture, or German celebrations of the distinctive Teutonic *Kultur*. Hegel, Marx, Darwin, Freud all seem to push back from the other direction as they offer total explanations for all cosmic/human/biological/psychological history in the "long nineteenth century" of relatively peaceful relations among the European powers, powers interconnected literally in the family connections of the monarchs. With the guns of August 1914, however, tribalism begins to triumph over universal humanity, national interests over the remnants of "Western civilization," the specific over the generic. And the distinctively located, embedded, and related subjectivism of postmodernity emerges in the wake of the fragmentation of Europe—which was, in modern views, simply the leading edge of human culture.

These qualifications and developments lead to the conclusion that human knowledge is therefore not only finite—a quality not disputed by premoderns or moderns—but always *uncertain*, and deeply, importantly so. We cannot know that we know everything we need to know about something in order to know that what we think we know we actually know for certain.[22] Nor can we know that we have properly reflected upon what we perceive such that our conclusions can be held with certainty. Elton Trueblood puts the situation nicely: "Deductive reasoning

---

22. I will try to be sure always to include the obvious exceptions to my "No Certainty" rule, namely, one's own state of mind (one can be certain that one is experiencing happiness or pain) and self-evident propositions such as "2 + 2 = 4." I trust that scrupulous readers will fill in those exceptions if I fail to remember to do so.

cannot have certainty about its premises and...inductive reasoning cannot have certainty about its conclusions."[23]

At its most chaste, the scientific method says the same thing, claiming only that its current conclusions are the best yet, not the best possible. For their part, premodern cultures readily admit the mysteriousness of the cosmos and the severe limits of human knowledge. Yet in both premodern and modern cultures, there is a confidence in basic convictions that amounts to a certainty. *This is the way the world is.* Postmodernity, again, comes *after* modernity (and premodernity) and particularly after the hubris of so many thinkers and communities who sounded and acted as if they did know things for certain—and big, important things, such as the nature of the world, the character or nonexistence of the Deity, the direction of history, and the right thing for each person to do in each circumstance. Postmodernity has retorted with a proclamation of the "end of ideology," a denunciation of the failure of all of the grand schemes and comprehensive systems of past cultural efforts, and particularly those of the modern era.[24]

Postmodernity has no confidence in unifying structures, in the "right way" of doing things, whether writing a poem, building a skyscraper, painting a portrait, or educating a child. The "correct way" of doing things was always part of a Great Story of how the world came about and what our place in it now is. Such Great Stories (what in the terms of French postmodernist theory were termed *grands récits*, translated not-so-happily as "meta-narratives") dominated our lives and our culture as those in authority told them to the rest of us to keep things they way they preferred them to be. Marx, Freud, Nietzsche and others tried to unmask such stories (and particularly the Genesis-to-Revelation story of Christianity) as mere "ideologies" or "rationalizations" of the powerful. Thus are matters of justice intertwined with matters of epistemology and metaphysics. In postmodernity, however, even the metanarratives of the masters of suspicion themselves come under suspicion. As one of the most influential postmodernists puts it, the postmodern attitude most simply is one of "incredulity toward metanarratives"—*all* metanarratives.

Postmodernity thereby deserves its alternate title of *hypermodernity*, for in this respect it is modernity against itself: The modern emphasis upon the critical role of reason and experience is now directed against every scheme of modern conceptualization that had used those very tools to construct this or that *grand récit*. And the doubts about human claims to knowledge that have been present in every generation have blossomed into a general attitude of skepticism as perhaps never before in this civilization.

Furthermore, the additional category of *history* is also at work. Hegel, Marx, Darwin, and Freud believed that the truth could not be found in the analysis of

---

23. D. Elton Trueblood, *The Teacher* (Nashville, TN: Broadman Press, 1980), 38.

24. Anthony Thiselton puts it concisely: "Postmodernism implies a *shattering of innocent confidence in the capacity of the self to control its own destiny*. It signals a loss of trust in global strategies of social planning, and in universal criteria of rationality" (Anthony C. Thiselton, *Interpreting God and the Postmodern Self* [Edinburgh: T. & T. Clark and Grand Rapids, MI: Eerdmans, 1995], 11; emphasis in original).

snapshots of the present, but only in locating present appearances in long historical contexts. So does postmodernity see the narratives of Hegel, Marx, Darwin, and Freud themselves as historically conditioned, as the products of a particular culture at a particular time, not as truths that transcend the ages. Thus postmodernity is inclined to reductionism of a historicist sort: "That's just the sort of thing a white, educated, male, Canadian Christian *would* say!" or, more discreetly, "That's merely the perspective of the ruling class of fifteenth-century Venice, whose mouthpiece this writer clearly was."

Therefore, when someone comes along to say, "Here is the Great Story that explains all the other stories," the postmodern person reflexively responds, "Hmph! I doubt it. How could any of us, or even any group of us, pretend to have figured it out, to have seen it whole, to have come up with the Grand Scheme? And what are you up to, anyway, trying to foist this story on us? What's in it for you?" Francis Bacon's Enlightenment-inspiring dictum that "knowledge is power," by which he meant that understanding the cosmos enabled us to interact with it more effectively, now is subject to an ironic and sinister reversal: "power is 'knowledge.'"

In this mode of thought, then, "truth" is still discoverable. But "truth" represents only the particular convictions of particular individuals or groups who examine reality as best they can and make the best interpretations of it that they can in line with their own values and agenda. In postmodernity, therefore, there is none of the modern confidence that we are heading for a universal utopia built on the grounds of our increasingly accurate knowledge of reality by means of our increasingly effective technology—whether the technology is agricultural, political, or artistic.

Talk of utopias, certainties, and effective technologies points to the broader cultural patterns of postmodernity and to the social changes that have occasioned its widespread influence in our time. It is no coincidence that postmodernity came into vogue in Europe in the middle of the twentieth century and in North America only in the last quarter of it. For the mood of disenchantment with Great Stories descends upon Europe through the trials of the two world wars and the intervening Depression. Here the glorious imperial powers of modern Europe are exposed as no more noble than the most bloodthirsty of their conquered colonial peoples. And no European seriously holds to the blithe "idea of progress" once the camps of Dachau, Treblinka, and Auschwitz come to light, once the saturation bombing of Dresden is reported, and once the smoke of Hiroshima and Nagasaki is seen around the world. Canadians and Americans, whose countries enjoy a rise in economic and political power through the first half of the twentieth century, have a corresponding crisis of confidence only later, when they pass through the turmoil of the Cold War, Vietnam, rapid urbanization and inflation, the energy crisis, and the revolution of mores in the 1960s and 1970s.

Thus the débâcles and confusions of the twentieth century provide many occasions for Western culture to doubt the grounds of its modern confidence. Unsurprisingly, then, the mood shift to anxiety in the face of multiple dangers prompts a cultural deceleration and, indeed, a reflex to look backward. But since postmodernity has undercut the claims of the distant, as well as the immediate, past, what sort of retrieval now makes sense?[25]

Many people, of course, refuse to accept the postmodern critique of modernity, or are oblivious to it, and carry on nicely in modern mode. For all of the post-modern excitement in the academies or art galleries, Wall Street and the World Trade Organization motor along under the aegis of modernity. And so do most of the sciences, the applied sciences, industry, agriculture, and other fixtures of contemporary life. The *mentalité* of postmodernity has not touched them—except, perhaps, in their advertising. As Neil Postman points out, "Amid the conceptual debris, there remained one sure thing to believe in—technology."[26]

Others have found refuge from both modernity and postmodernity in a retreat to premodern ideologies. These refuges usually offer a combination of religion and culture, of both faith and ethnicity. So we see resurgent Islam in various places around the world; nationalist Hindu movements in India; and fundamentalist or Pentecostal-charismatic Christianity in the United States, parts of Africa, Latin America, and elsewhere. To be sure, most of these turns to the premodern are selective. Such movements are often happy to employ up-to-the-minute technologies, whether of persuasion or coercion, in pursuit of their goals, and do not generally long for a return simply to a more primitive society. Instead, they try to blend the premodern and the modern in the interest of resisting what they see to be the evils of the contemporary world and particularly of the United States as the bellwether of modern culture.

Postmodernism is the collective array of responses to postmodernity that accept this view of things and then attempt to construct a way of viewing the world, and perhaps an entire way of life, on that basis. To understand these responses, it is helpful to concentrate again first on the intellectual and cultural élites, among whom we see postmodernism emerging after the early twentieth-century artistic movement known as *modernism*.

Modernism is not mere modernity, of course, but denotes the particular movement that bridged the broad modern project of cultural optimism and the skepticism and even despair of mid-twentieth-century postmodernity.[27] Modernism

---

25. I know just enough about Japan to sense that it is a different, but relevant, case of a modern society dealing with the trauma of massive disillusionment and the stress of rapid social change. The oft-remarked affinity of the Japanese for ritual plurality—Shinto rites for this, Buddhist rites for that, and a Christian (= Western = modern) wedding along the way—points to a deep fragmentation of the national culture, a truly hypermodern situation. I am sorry I cannot offer more to consider in this respect.

26. Neil Postman, *Technopoly: The Surrender of Culture to Technology* (New York: Vintage, 1993 [1992]), 55.

27. So Norman F. Cantor, *Twentieth-Century Culture: Modernism to Deconstruction* (New York: Peter Lang, 1988). I recognize that modernism is one of the most complex episodes in our cultural history, including as it does contradictory tendencies and products on a vast scale. Therefore, helpless to do otherwise, I will focus on what Martha Bayles calls "constructive"

shares some of the traits of postmodernity: cynicism regarding nineteenth-century "grand narratives"; lack of regard for "great truths"; a fear of empires and other "great collectivities"; and a distrust of technology and "mass man." The talented and tenacious individual artist would turn away from the world as given, and especially from the huge intellectual and social structures imposed on him by culture at large, and would create his own spaces and sounds, even his own language. Think of T. S. Eliot's innovation in verse, James Joyce's novelties and neologisms in *Finnegans Wake*, and Piet Mondrian's exploration of pure form and color without regard for representation of the world "out there."

Modernism thus turned away from the past and from the metanarratives of the modern project. Yet it still takes pride in its own products as beautiful, good, and true in an absolute sense. Modernism is really a sort of sequel to Romanticism: Those who have the proper ability can read and look and listen to this or that modernist work, and they will "get it." They, too, will see that this composition or that poem just *is* beautiful (or, perhaps, sublime, to pick up another key Romantic term), good, or true.

It is this last shred of modern confidence that disappears in postmodernity and in the postmodernisms that respond to it. Even the heroism of modernism will not bring us to the Olympus of absolutes.

Postmodernism got its name first from developments in architecture—which is a bit surprising, since architecture is not generally in the vanguard of cultural innovation. (One can spend one's own money and time on experimental poetry or painting, but one has to spend lots of other people's time and money in architecture, and that tends to militate against wild innovation.)

As twentieth-century architecture moved through the modernist Bauhaus and "International" styles, no new style emerged as a clear successor, as the new correct way to design and build. Reflecting the loss of confidence in culture at large, architects turned to the past. But because there was no golden age to repristinate, architects took a new, quite radically modest approach. Rather than confidently proclaim either the New New Thing or the New Old Thing, they began to rummage through the past for bits and pieces they would put together in a *bricolage*. This term was

---

modernism, leaving aside "perverse" modernism (a term Bayles borrows from Jacques Barzun) and then the less constructive aspects of postmodernism as well. (Ironically—and irony is thick in the air in all of this—I mention deconstruction precisely because I take it to be, especially in Derrida's hands, an attempt to accomplish something good, not merely tear things down and apart.) Bayles herself dismisses postmodernism entirely as simply the continuation of characteristics of perverse modernism: "injunctions to break with the past, to attack aesthetic standards, to shock the audience, and to erase the line between art and life" (385). I agree with most of what she writes about perverse modernism per se: I don't agree, however, that this is all there is to say about postmodernism, so I say more.

For Bayles's terminology, see *Hole in Our Soul: The Loss of Beauty and Meaning in American Popular Music* (Chicago, IL: University of Chicago Press, 1996 [1994]), 32–54. For illustrations just from the world of graphic art of how bewilderingly complex modernism is, see Robert Hughes, *The Shock of the New*, rev. ed. (New York: Knopf, 1991 [1981]).

popularized by Claude Lévi-Strauss and was itself a form of ironic self-deprecation as a *bricoleur* is, literally, a handyman or a "do-it-yourselfer," making do with whatever happens to be at hand. Such a conjoining of disparate elements would result in what designers hoped would be a powerful mix. "Eclecticism" became a byword in this new fashion.

Sometimes, to be sure, "eclecticism" was merely a glamorous label used by interior designers desperately trying to make sense of expensive items collected promiscuously by well-heeled clients who insisted on keeping everything they bought—as the pages of *Architectural Digest* amply testified. Often the use of past elements was ironic, as architects reduced or expanded things out of traditional proportions or used surprising materials in their reproduction in what was to some viewers startlingly creative and to others merely silly.[28] Indeed, among the first widely recognized postmodern buildings in America was Philip Johnson and John Burgee's AT&T building (later the Sony Building) in Manhattan, which sported on its roof a Chippendale broken pediment in concrete several storeys high.[29] The objective was not to make art that would speak to the ages (architect Frank Gehry's popular buildings, from Seattle to Bilbao, reminded many of lightly crumpled tinfoil) but to proffer witty allusions. And sometimes it worked, producing a joyful celebration of the art of various times and places, and delightful wonder at the way diverse artistic elements can begin new "conversations" in new contexts.

The collage of diverse images came powerfully to the mass media in music videos, with their rapidly cut scenes that frequently had only a tangential relationship, if any, to the music or lyrics of the song being performed—or even, in more radical versions, to each other. Popular music itself borrowed from the past, from the "covering" of popular songs from the 1950s and 1960s, to the much more radical phenomenon of "sampling" from a variety of sources to construct new musical events, a genre pioneered by hip-hop DJs at black urban dance halls.[30]

Advertising quickly picked up on this trend. In the later 1980s and 1990s, television commercials and print spreads often used images that were apparently unrelated to the product in question but were intended to provoke particular feelings in the viewer that the advertisers hoped would be associated with the product. Since the information came at the viewer so quickly or obliquely, and since there was no actual argument to be assessed (as in "Buy our product because of the following three advantages it offers . . . "), the commercials were literally irrational. They were

---

28. Witold Rybczynski is quietly devastating regarding the literally superficial ornaments of so much slapdash, overwrought building design, even to the point of wryly identifying "the seven implants of postmodern architecture" (see *Looking Around: A Journey through Architecture* [San Francisco: Harper & Row, 1992], 259–69).

29. Rybczynski credits Michael Graves's Portland Building as "the first major building designed by a member of the so-called postmodernist school" *Looking Around*, 154). The Johnson-Burgee building is often recognized as *legitimating* postmodernism as a major corporate client puts a major building in Manhattan.

30. For a helpful introduction to the emergence of hip-hop, see Bayles, 342–46.

sometimes effective nonetheless because of their appeal to other human faculties and drives.

All of these trends, of course, have been turbocharged by the Internet, by hypertext links that provide literal intertextuality, by the accelerating churn of fashion and other trends, by the "glocalization" made possible by almost instant, if also tremendously truncated, exposure to other peoples, places, and practices, and by the constant consumerist appeal to fashion at least your perception of the world according to your own preferences.[31]

This unsystematic, helter-skelter kaleidoscope is one characteristic experience of postmodernity, if an extreme one. Cubism, with its shards floating in weird planes of multiple perspectives, and with hands becoming violins and women becoming monsters in metaphysical as well as epistemological ambiguity, nicely introduces us into the whirl of postmodernity. Wallace Stevens's poem likewise moves us from the consideration of radical subjectivity to a welter of experiential elements:

> Twenty men crossing a bridge,
> Into a village,
> Are twenty men crossing twenty bridges,
> Into twenty villages,
> Or one man
> Crossing a single bridge into a village.
>
> This is old song
> That will not declare itself...
>
> Twenty men crossing a bridge,
> Into a village,
> Are
> Twenty men crossing a bridge
> Into a village.
>
> That will not declare itself
> Yet is certain as meaning...
>
> The boots of the men clump
> On the boards of the bridge.
> The first white wall of the village

---

31. Sven Birkerts combines many of these elements concisely: "For what is postmodernism at root but an aesthetic that rebukes the idea of an historical time line, as well as previously uncontested assumptions of cultural hierarchy. The postmodern artifact manipulates its stylistic signatures like Lego blocks and makes free with combinations from the formerly sequestered spheres of high and popular art. Its combinatory momentum and relentless referencing of the surrounding culture mirror perfectly the associative dynamics of electronic media" (*The Gutenberg Elegies: The Fate of Reading in an Electronic Age* [New York: Ballantine, 1994], 123).

Rises through fruit-trees.
Of what was it I was thinking?
So the meaning escapes.

The first white wall of the village...
The fruit-trees...[32]

More typically, as modern societies have themselves "differentiated" into largely separate spheres and institutions—financial, religious, artistic, commercial, familial, educational, and so on—so have their inhabitants' minds become unabashedly polymorphic. Not only, that is, do some of us (e.g., engineers) think in an Enlightenment mode while others (e.g., composers) think in a Romantic mode, but many of us tend to shift from one mode to another, depending on what sphere of our life we are engaging at the moment. There has always been, of course, a common-sense shifting from one mode to another depending on the situation. Ancient literature, from the venerable Chinese warrior-poet tradition to the career of the warrior-poet David in the Hebrew Scriptures, attests to the universal experience of shifting from one form of comprehension and expression to another depending on the context. In the modern period, however, particular ways of knowing were championed imperialistically, so to speak, as simply the right way to think about serious matters. Scientific method is the key to knowledge. No, no, replied the rationalists: careful deduction from clear and distinct ideas is the royal road to truth. Oh, dear, retorted the Romantics: one needs to reconnect with the cosmos and listen to what the universe will communicate to you via intuition. Hah! said the masters of suspicion: you're kidding yourselves, or your bosses are fooling you, and you ought to wake up and listen to our story about how things got this way and where they are going. The postmodernists suggest instead that reality is often more complex than any one sort of people, any one interest group, in any one situation, can comprehend. Sometimes light acts like a wave, sometimes like a particle. As linguists George Lakoff and Mark Johnson put it,

no one metaphor...will do. Each one gives a certain comprehension of one aspect of the concept and hides others. To operate only in terms of a consistent set of metaphors is to hide many aspects of reality. Successful functioning in our daily lives seems to require a constant shifting of metaphors. The use of many metaphors that are inconsistent with one another seems necessary for us if we are to comprehend the details of our daily existence.[33]

32. Wallace Stevens, "Metaphors of a Magnifico" (1918).

33. George Lakoff and Mark Johnson, *Metaphors We Live by* (Chicago: University of Chicago Press, 1980), 221.

Indeed, as the elites conducted their war of ideas, ordinary people negotiated an increasingly demanding experience of social fragmentation. The typical city-dweller—who was becoming the typical human being by the end of the twentieth century—spent her day moving from home to the workplace to the gym to the spiritual group to social gatherings, with each context imposing a significantly different outlook and expectations. At home values such as relational sensitivity, self-sacrifice, gentleness, and romance might dominate, while the supreme values at work might be efficiency, dependability, and docility. At the gym, physical health is everything, while at the midweek prayer meeting, spiritual concerns reign supreme. Note that in each case the values are not only different, but often mutually antagonistic. And each, on its own turf, insists on total loyalty.

Furthermore, for our purposes we can note that ways of knowing in each situation can be somewhat, or even totally, different. The modern person might well think in a starkly scientific way at her job as an analyst of geological samples, while she comes home to treat her two-year-old with reference to family traditions, her maternal instincts, her memories of her own childhood, and so on. She may never pause to try to draw the various epistemological patterns of her life into a single paradigm, so she cannot help experiencing the stress of cognitive and ideological whiplash. How could she not experience such stress, as she exits and enters such disparate and demanding contexts?

In postmodernity (or hypermodernity), such rapid shifting has come to entail that we take none of these modes as providing what our forebears thought it provided, namely, absolutely truthful and reliable access to reality. More and more of us nowadays do not blink at such locutions as "your truth" and "my reality," even as our forebears would identify such expressions with mental illness. Indeed, it is this easy versatility, this strainless switching among various and even contradictory values and cognitive styles, that is one of the most striking characteristics of the postmodern mind.

The best-known existentialists of the mid-twentieth century brought to wide audiences the idea that the cosmos did not itself have any meaning. As Europe consumed itself in wars of unprecedented destruction, Simone de Beauvoir, Albert Camus, and Jean-Paul Sartre agreed that there was no God, no Order, no universal morality. Instead, it was up to each individual to select the values by which he or she would live. For them (unlike their Christian existentialist counterparts, such as Gabriel Marcel) "existence precedes essence." There is no blueprint already provided for our lives: We choose through our living (existence) who we are (essence).

A generation later, deconstruction emerged in the university literature departments now not through novels and plays, as in existentialism, but in arcane works of literary criticism and history—*commentary* on texts.[34] Jean-François Lyotard, Jacques Lacan, Jean Baudrillard, Roland Barthes, Luce Irigaray, Emmanuel Levinas, and above all Jacques Derrida and Michel Foucault used reason, experience, and

---

34. See George Steiner, *Real Presences*, on commentary.

history to undermine what most people thought were issues already settled by reason, experience, and history. Which authors and which works belonged on the standard reading list (canon) of great literature? What were these works actually saying? Which of society's conventions were truly rooted in the professed ideals of that society and which were merely technologies of repression and exploitation? Who got to decide these things?

By patiently and cleverly exposing the ambiguities of both books and institutions, deconstruction opened up literary criticism and history to new possibilities and new voices. It showed that our accepted interpretations are open to question by others. Indeed (and this was the important political point), such work demonstrated that our accepted interpretations are determined by the powerful in a society, and that those who have been marginalized by the powerful might well read those texts quite differently.

Deconstruction thus dovetailed with the agenda of those seeking liberation and dignity for people who had been silenced or subjugated because of their class, gender, ethnicity, or sexuality. Deconstruction had originated as an intellectual concern to repudiate the *grands récits* not only of traditional interpretation but also of the new orthodoxy of structuralist interpretation that thought it could discern the universal patterns inherent in all language. Thus deconstruction is sometimes identified as poststructuralism. Those who were concerned for oppressed groups, however, saw in deconstruction a tool to level the interpretive playing field, to pull down the canonical authors and privileged institutions: the "Dead White European Males" (DWEMs, as the argot had it) and the all-too-alive white males who perpetuated this regime.

Alas, marginalizing a group of authors, however privileged, in the name of revolution on behalf of the marginalized does seem to increase irony at the expense of integrity.[35] Worse, some activists have rather cynically engaged in what one might call a "pseudo-postmodernist two-step." This is the rhetorical device of first using postmodernist criticism to de-privilege élites and then asserting that the views of one's own group are alone true and good. Notice that this is not the relativistic claim that one's group's views are just as good as anyone else's, for to claim that would be to assume a universal standard of goodness, and that is inconsistent with postmodern doubt about any such standard—or, at least, about human beings' ability to know such a standard and to know it with certainty. Furthermore, such relativism would be politically useless, for if the convictions of privileged white men are just as good as the protesters', why should the former yield any power to the latter?[36]

---

35. Brian Walsh and Sylvia Keesmaat note how certain postmodern interpreters of the Apostle Paul denounce him for insisting on schemes of "norm" and "aberration," thus accomplishing only "a new kind of violence with a new opponent who is deemed to have deviated from another assumed normative stance" (Brian J. Walsh and Sylvia C. Keesmaat, *Colossians Remixed* [Downers Grove, IL: IVP, 2004], 104–05).

36. This problem of political impotence lies at the heart of Alan Sokal and Jean Bricmont's vigorous indictment of some of the doyens of postmodernism, *Fashionable Nonsense: Postmodern Intellectuals' Abuse of Science* (New York: Picador, 1998).

If one were to adjust the claim to align with postmodern pluralism, one might say that one's group's concerns represent just one viewpoint among many, without grounds for any to be preferred to another in any objective sense. But now there is, again, no basis for getting other people to change their minds and do what you want them to do. Instead, there is here simply an exploitation of postmodernism to level the field and then a reversion to modernity (or premodernity) to champion one's own agenda (whether feminist, black, gay, or whatever) as simply better. So-called political correctness has been the most obvious manifestation of this maneuver.[37] If, as La Rochefoucauld said, hypocrisy is the tribute vice pays to virtue, this "two-step" is the curtsey certain kinds of postmodernism render to realism. Political action must be grounded in claims that no one can dismiss as simply "true for you." As feminist philosopher Lorraine Code puts it: "Feminists know, if they know anything at all, that they have to develop the best possible explanations—the 'truest' explanations—of how things are if they are to intervene effectively in social structures and institutions.... They have to be able to produce accurate transformative analyses of things as they *are*."[38]

Truly radical nihilism (the assumption that there is no meaning to the cosmos) isn't actually postmodernist, as nihilism makes categorical assertions quite assuredly—such as "there is no meaning to the cosmos." But what we might call "practical nihilism" is entailed by radical postmodernism, as it cannot arrive at what is true, good, or beautiful, but can ever and only be in permanent revolution.[39] (Perhaps, then, only those at two extreme ends—already comfortable in academe or utterly enraged against the social and political status quo—can engage for long in such attitudes and pursuits.)

Radical skepticism, however, can be truly postmodernist, as it says that whatever truth might be available to, say, the mind of God (whether there is a God or not), it is not available and recognizable as such to us human beings, finite and flawed as we are. There is only "truth" as whatever individuals or groups find "empowering" or "useful" to them. And that's what we should all settle for. Perhaps most surprisingly, such language is not uncommon even in the "hardest" of the sciences, physics, in which the welter of apparent mysteries and even absurdities of

---

37. For examples, see William C. Placher, *Unapologetic Theology: A Christian Voice in a Pluralistic Conversation* (Louisville, KY: Westminster/John Knox Press, 1989), 92–104. Martha Bayles describes this sort of thing as a "fast shuffle" (7–8).

38. Lorraine Code, "Taking Subjectivity into Account," in *Feminist Epistemologies*, ed. Linda Alcoff and Elizabeth Potter (New York: Routledge, 1993), 40. Emphasis in original. It is interesting to note in passing how Code demonstrates her postmodernist discomfort with any strong claims to realism by her use of the scare quotes around "truest," when that word, unironically, is exactly what she seems to intend to say. See also Georg G. Iggers's account of postmodernism's provocative, but ultimately contradictory, effects on the writing of history: *Historiography in the Twentieth Century: From Scientific Objectivity to the Postmodern Challenge* (Hanover, NH and London: Wesleyan University Press, 1997).

39. Peter C. Emberley, *Zero Tolerance: Hot Button Politics in Canada's Universities* (Toronto: Penguin, 1996), 105–6.

quantum theory produces a kind of high-level games-playing. From Niels Bohr ("it is wrong to think that the task of physics is to find out how nature is.... The mathematical formalism of quantum mechanics... merely offers rules of calculations") to Stephen Hawking ("Even if there is only one possible unified theory, it is just a set of rules and equations"), a fundamental, even bizarre, diffidence has suffused the descendants of Isaac Newton.[40]

One can see in many forms of postmodernism, therefore, a genuine struggle to appreciate and cope with the limitations of the human mind—and of particular human minds located in particular places, times, communities, and circumstances.[41] The worry arises, of course, that all this "unmasking," however justified and liberating, nonetheless risks reducing artistic judgments to social scientific and political ones. The meaning and value of a text—and "text" now can mean a painting or a sonata every bit as much as a novel or a poem—is no longer sought in aesthetic categories at all. Art no longer performs any intrinsically valuable function but is of only epiphenomenal or instrumental significance, referring to grim realities of power relations while possessing no intrinsic worth in expressing realities—virtues, vices, aspirations, fears, and other qualities—of the human experience.[42]

Is postmodernism therefore a coherent paradigm that replaces the modern, or is it simply the rubble from the collapse of the old out of which certain brave and creative souls will make what they can? As we acknowledge that various forms of postmodernism aim to construct more than a hodgepodge of old and new simply to entertain, or turn a profit, or win a battle, we wonder if they can possibly succeed. They aim to liberate the mind and improve the human lot while recognizing how little we actually do know—with no certainty that we are heading in the right direction.[43] At least, however, all of this fragmentation, indeterminacy, and pragmatism makes human

---

40. Niels Bohr, *Atomic Theory and the Description of Nature* (Cambridge: Cambridge University Press, 1934), 60; Stephen Hawking, *A Brief History of Time: From the Big Bang to Black Holes* (Toronto: Bantam, 1988), 174; both quoted in Stanley L. Jaki, *Means to Message: A Treatise on Truth* (Grand Rapids, MI: Eerdmans, 1999), 50.

41. I have found it useful at times to construct a taxonomy of postmodernist varieties, such as this one: postmodernisms of subversion (e.g., deconstruction); postmodernisms of play, even decadence (e.g., architecture, advertising); postmodernisms of cynical conservatism (e.g., Rorty); postmodernisms of particularity (e.g., Afrocentrism, radical feminism); postmodernisms of despair (e.g., existentialism); and postmodernisms of provisionality (e.g., Reformed epistemology and the outlook offered here).

42. This critique has been widely made in regard to literature, of course, but it applies across the board to art of all kinds. See, for example, the concerns of Jeremy S. Begbie regarding music in *Theology, Music, and Time* (Cambridge: Cambridge University Press, 2000), 14–15. See also the complex and incisive ruminations on ideology and music in the early Romantic period presented in Daniel K. L. Chua, *Absolute Music and the Construction of Meaning* (Cambridge: Cambridge University Press, 1999).

43. Alvin Plantinga acknowledges numerous areas of overlapping concern between postmodernism and Christianity in *Warranted Christian Belief* (New York: Oxford University Press, 2000), 423–25. The rest of his chapter on "Postmodernism and Pluralism" offers some powerful rebuttals to some common arguments against Christianity offered in the name of those two (425–57).

individuals and groups harder to herd and exploit by the powers that be. It seems, however, that all that can be said is that anarchy is better, to many postmodernists, than totalitarianism.

It is in this context that a prominent feature of modern religion comes into focus. In this movement, known by various terms with overlapping, if not entirely coinciding, fields of reference—implicit religion, informal religion, "Do-It-Yourself" religion, religion "*à la carte*"—and featured by the media in the more extravagant forms of New Age spirituality, postmodern people feel free to pick, from among the elements of the religious and philosophical traditions they happen to encounter, what appeals to them, what they judge will help them achieve their goals in life.[44] For all the wide variety of those elements—from Tantric sex workshops to tarot cards, from love potions to crystals, from yogic meditation techniques to the study of Kabbalah, and from séances to psychotherapy—the common features of this outlook are religious elements being commodified into purchasable technologies or learn-able techniques that can be added (or subtracted) at will by the sovereign self in the interests chosen entirely by that self. "I'm not religious, but I'm spiritual," one says nowadays in a phrase that would have been met with only a blank stare fifty years ago. "Religion" in this context means "formal" or "organized" religion: those religions with proper names and fixed traditions and recognized arbiters. Following the postmodern demolition of all looming authorities—idols and icons alike—there remains only the choosing self, who chooses to be "spiritual"—which means, indeed, "whatever I want it to mean." Thus does postmodernism nicely dovetail with consumerism.[45]

Other kinds of pluralism and postmodernism confront us on every hand: in aesthetics (what is art and what matters in art?), in politics and economics (which way forward—and for whom?), and so on. As we pay attention to how cognitive styles reflect social context, we see that what exacerbates all of this bewilderment in North America, as in some other modern societies, is the ideology and program of multiculturalism.

As I understand it, the policy of multiculturalism was intended to build stronger, richer communities and countries by encouraging various ethnic groups to maintain something of their inherited character and, out of the glories of each tradition, to contribute something to the general project of society. Multiculturalism resists the "melting pot" ideal of assimilation that homogenizes everyone into just one preexisting type of citizen and community, and instead encourages diversity of outlooks, ideas, practices, and products for the benefit of all. "Interculturalism" thus has emerged more recently as a term meant to emphasize the cooperative nature of

---

44. Reginald W. Bibby, *Fragmented Gods: The Poverty and Potential of Religion in Canada* (Toronto: Irwin, 1987); Robert N. Bellah et al., *Habits of the Heart: Individualism and Commitment in American Life* (New York: Harper & Row, 1985).

45. I discuss these themes in *Humble Apologetics: Defending the Faith Today* (New York and Oxford: Oxford University Press, 2002), esp. chs. 2, 3, and 4.

this enterprise, to assert more clearly the importance of the common good vis-à-vis the well-being of each constituent culture.

As has been widely remarked, however, much multiculturalism in both attitude and program has had the effect of encouraging people to concentrate on their own ethnicities, their own differences, and their own communities so as to separate them from the whole. As one observer put it some time ago, "The ideal of diversity—of mixing things up, spreading the wealth, creating a new Us—never happened."[46] Instead of a "multicultural culture," there has emerged a "multiplicity of cultures" that strains the unity of the society that comprises them as each focuses on its own good according to its own lights while demanding its fair share of the tax pie.

Undergirding multiculturalism and then being reinforced by it has been a widespread relativism, especially among the white, nominally Christian population that has held most of the power and status in Canada, the United States, and the European and Australasian countries that also have promoted multiculturalism. A sense of guilt for past sins of chauvinism and exploitation (and much of this sense of guilt surely is justified) has combined with an ignorant sentimentality about the values and practices of other cultures to produce widespread confusion about just how people of different views on fundamental matters truly can live together—and not just sample each other's native costumes, food, and dances, as if multiculturalism means becoming mere tourists in each other's neighborhoods.

Multiculturalism has become a vague slogan under which all sorts of people can march: premodern or modern activists promoting their own group; secular liberal élites who are happy to see their conservative opponents divide into disparate and competing factions; postmodern pluralists who contend that no one group should dominate everyone else; and well-meaning folk who wonder why we can't all just get along. Thus multiculturalism can be seen to be fostering pluralism of all three types. Interestingly, it also simultaneously promotes premodern outlooks within some groups; modern confidence in the governing groups that "manage" multiculturalism; and postmodern doubt among participant-observers who see how superficially multiculturalism has papered over deep differences and how difficult it is to sort through competing claims to truth to know what, if anything, can be seized on as such.

It is in this intellectual and social landscape that contemporary Christian thinking takes place—at least, in modern parts of the world strongly affected by Western culture. We thus turn to the heart of what is *Christian* in order to lay the foundations and framework for *thinking*.

---

46. Holland Carter, "Beyond Multiculturalism, Freedom?" *The New York Times on the Web* (http://www.nytimes.com/2001/07/29/arts/design/20COTT.html). This incisive article focuses particularly on the art world, but its implications touch on most other aspects of multiculturalism. Cf. Reginald W. Bibby, *Mosaic Madness: The Poverty and Potential of Life in Canada* (Toronto: Stoddart, 1990); and Charles Taylor et al., *Multiculturalism* (Princeton, NJ: Princeton University Press, 1994).

2

Vocational Thinking

According to the first Evangelist, Jesus said, "You shall love the Lord your God with all your heart, and with all your soul, and with all your mind" (Matt. 22:37). According to Mark, he said, "You shall love the Lord your God with all your heart, and with all your soul, and with all your mind, and with all your strength" (Mark 12:30). And the third of the Synoptic Gospels gives yet another version: "You shall love the Lord your God with all your heart, and with all your soul, and with all your strength, and with all your mind" (Luke 10:27).

Clearly the main point in these reiterations of the Great Commandment is that we are to love God with all we are and have. Note that Jesus adds the element of "mind" to the Old Testament formulations (cf. Deut. 6:5 and passim). To be sure, we must note also that this term *nous* includes more than "the intellect" or "the capacity for reason" as we tend to understand "mind" today, but can include in some usages the capacity for feeling, for moral judgment, and for spiritual discernment. But including "mind" means nothing *less* than our reason. And its inclusion rounds out the sense that we are, indeed, to love God with all we are and have.

For our purposes, I conclude from these texts that thinking is best understood as a mode of loving God.[1] It is perhaps more obvious that other modes of human life are modes of loving God: trusting God (faith), praising God (worship), conversing with God (prayer), learning from God (discipleship), working with God (mission), and so on. But thinking is not off by itself, as if apprehending and comprehending the world were actions somehow outside the purview of the Great Commandment, along the line of amoral, even automatic, functions of human life such as breathing or feeding. No, the Gospels make clear in their inclusion of "mind"

---

1. My sometime Regent College colleague Bruce Waltke echoes this view in "Honouring Regent's Philosophy of Education," *Crux* (Summer 2007): 8–12. He cites his former student Jerry Pauls's thesis on the wisdom of Agur that "radically reshapes the crisis of knowing...as a crisis of relationship" ("Proverbs 30:1-6: 'The Words of Agur' as Epistemological Statement" [Th.M. thesis, Regent College, 1993], 124).

in all three lists ("strength" doesn't make it onto Matthew's list) that Jesus intends thinking to be understood as an activity of love toward God.

We might then ask what epistemological implications there might be in conceiving of thinking as a mode of love for God, as part of the human being giving of himself or herself entirely to God, of being and doing all one can be or do in order to please God in every respect and to cooperate with God in every aspect of life. This book is, in its entirety, an answer to that question.

To begin the answer, therefore, requires us to pull back and look first at the fundamental questions of what being human is about and what human life is for. Since human history, moreover, has somehow resulted in the emergence of a new class of people, Christians, we must ask what Christians are to be and do vis-à-vis their fellow human beings and in relation to God's calling upon them as this special class.

What we must understand first, then, is the category of *vocation*. We must understand what is God's call upon humanity and upon Christians, such that we can proceed to conceiving of thinking in its proper context, as part of our whole-selved response to our divine vocation. And understanding thinking in terms of vocation provides both the hope and the humility we need to counter both the excessive skepticisms and oppressive dogmatisms of our time.

THE GREAT STORY

The Bible is, overall, a story. It is much more than a story, of course, as it contains a wide range of other genres: poems, laws, prophecies, lyrics, proverbs, letters, apocalypses, and more. Yet the Bible, in both its literary structure and its overarching depiction of the cosmos, is a narrative, with a beginning, a middle, and an end.

The narrative of the Bible, moreover, is told as being true. It does not read as if it were merely "true to life," offering a series of Middle Eastern illustrations of timeless and global moral and spiritual realities, as Aesop's Fables do in Greek literature. The communities that generated the Bible have taken it to be true also as in the narrative sense of "what actually happened, what is happening, and what is going to happen" in *history*, however stylized the depiction may be in a given case. The Bible gives us the Great Story within which we can helpfully locate all other stories, all other histories and schemes and theories and explanations. (If this claim seems to flatly contradict the postmodern distrust of metanarratives, well, it does—and yet it also soothes the worries that fuel that postmodern distrust, as we shall see anon.)

We will understand and live our lives best, therefore, if we see where we are in the great narrative of the Bible and thus understand our parts in God's plan. As the athlete arriving late for a game needs to quickly ascertain what has been happening before he can determine what needs to be done to help his team most, and as the movie hero demands to be briefed on the history of the situation, the current state of the crisis, and the objectives to be reached in the time remaining, so we must ascertain where we are in the narrative of the world. Fundamental errors of all sorts have been made by failing to take seriously the narrative shape of the Biblical scheme of things and also by failing to locate oneself properly within that story. We need to comprehend our context as a condition for deciding properly about how to act in this context.[2]

A common summary of the Biblical narrative runs thus: Creation, Fall, Redemption, and Consummation.[3]

"In the beginning, God created the heavens and the earth" (Gen. 1:1). God creates the world and it is pronounced "very good." We shall have more to say about God's commissioning of human beings in that account. For now, however, we can pause over the quality attributed to creation at that time: "very good."

The world is very good, in all its materiality, temporality, and finitude—qualities that in some philosophies and cultures mark it as *not* good, but as something to be traversed, endured, or even despised and resisted. The Bible revels in the goodness of the world. Animals matter; plants matter; the oceans and rivers and lakes matter; the air matters: God intended them all to exist and he made them good.

Human beings matter, too, and God made us for one express purpose: to garden the rest of the planet. Again, we will explore this commissioning (Gen. 1:26–28) in more detail presently. We should notice here, however, that not only is what we sometimes call "the natural world" good, but human *culture* is created as part of the cosmos God calls "very good." Humans were not meant to stroll through Eden merely picking up fallen fruit to munch on our way to swim or sunbathe or sleep in some truly animalistic paradise. We were meant to take what God created and *work* it, cultivate it, do something with it. And, as I shall detail shortly, such creativity requires, among other resources, thinking.

The Creation story must be understood, however, precisely as the beginning of a larger story that unfolds in the subsequent chapters. Yet some epistemologies have proceeded as if we were still in Eden. No one seriously argues that we dwell in Arcadia, of course. We all know that the world contains lots of evil. What some people do seriously argue, however, and many more of us simply assume, is that our intellectual dealings with the world are simply and unqualifiedly good. WYSIWYG— "What You See Is What You Get"—is how many people think they think. Here is the (relevant, properly interpreted, comprehensively gathered) information and here are the (infallibly induced and accurately articulated) conclusions. This theory is clearly

---

2. I trust that this approach avoids the pitfalls sometimes attributed to Lindbeckian postliberalism (and, to be sure, of Barthianism before it) as a kind of excessive reification, even totalization, of the Biblical narrative: see Miroslav Volf, "Theology, Meaning, and Power," in *The Future of Theology: Essays in Honor of Jürgen Moltmann*, ed. Miroslav Volf, Carmen Krieg, and Thomas Kucharz (Grand Rapids, MI: Eerdmans, 1996), 98–113.

3. Richard Bauckham cautions us that "the Bible itself offers no summary of the whole story from beginning to end" (*Bible and Mission: Christian Witness in a Postmodern World* [Grand Rapids, MI: Eerdmans, 2003], 93), and elaborates on the "profusion and sheer untidiness of the narrative materials" (92). But I expect that he, and at least most Christian readers, would agree on the basic outline offered here.

correct. That politician is obviously an oaf. This car is plainly superior. That claim is patently false. We trust in our thinking implicitly, and in both senses of that word: without reflection and without doubt.

We do not, however, live in a pristine paradise, neither epistemological nor in any other sense. In the Fall, depicted in Genesis 3, humanity disobeys God. Not content to be the image of God, humans decide to be "like God" in some other sense, abandoning moral innocence to gain the knowledge of good and evil—knowledge gained, alas, by experience. Having already known good, they now know evil by committing it and by bearing its consequences.

The consequences of sin show up epistemologically, as we shall detail later. For now, however, we can note some odd details—epistemological details—in the ancient story of the temptation of Eve and the Fall of humanity.

In the woman's conversation with the serpent, God's express words—to refrain from eating of the forbidden fruit else you will surely die—are altered to make them both more severe ("Don't *touch* it") and less definite ("*in case* you *might* die"). In this morality tale, we also see a weird clouding of the cognitive. The woman literally doesn't get God's proscription quite right, as if to leave open an alternative that the serpent is only too happy to provide. Thus does a cognitive move lead to a moral one. (Or is the cognitive move a result of a previous, implicit, moral one?)

Then when God calls the human pair to account, the resulting finger-pointing away from oneself (Adam does it first, and Eve then follows his example) is not only morally wrong, but cognitively wrong: It literally isn't the truth—the *whole* truth—of the matter. I don't mean to press this point about rationality too far, but in Genesis 4, Cain seems to be confused about how to honor God in sacrifice and then, rather than alter his behavior in the light of God's correction, he proceeds to kill Abel—a story so familiar to us that we must not fail to see how *irrational* is Cain's action, quite apart from its being *immoral*. For how can killing Abel possibly improve Cain's situation, which is a situation of God's dissatisfaction with him and his sacrifice? *What was Cain thinking?* we might cry, and we cannot know. From the beginning, sin seems an act of both wickedness and derangement.

We must be careful, however, not to be so impressed by the moral impairment of human reasoning that we live as if our world (and thus our thinking) is utterly fallen, corrupted beyond repair, a valley of the shadow of death through which we must hurry, worriedly and doubtfully, in order to reach the morally and epistemo-logically sunlit highlands of the next life. Even the immediate Biblical context suggests a quite different view of human history after the Fall: an interweaving of the good and the bad. Genesis 4 proceeds from the story of Cain and Abel to show us further ethical decline in the person of Lamech, who marries two wives and then boasts to them of his disproportionate violence, killing a man who had (merely) hurt him. Yet Lamech fathers three sons who pioneer crucial dimensions of civilization: herding, music, and metalwork. Even *this* family, therefore, fathered by a bloodthirsty lout, produces goodness through three creative and productive offspring.

Despite these good developments, however, the world and its human garden-ers clearly are doomed by the spreading plague of sin. Thus the Bible shows us a relatively quick decay of humanity into a state so awful that God wipes them off the face of the earth in the great Flood, sparing only the righteous remnant of Noah and his family to re-start the garden. This narrative takes up only a handful of chapters in Genesis, and then what we might call the "time-lapse" pace of the early narrative slows down to focus on one man, Abram. He and his descendants—both physical and spiritual—take up the rest of the narrative of the Bible until the final apocalypse. And none of those characters, including Noah and Abram them-selves, are depicted as free from sin—except one. Everyone else needs salvation, and so most of the Christian Story focuses on the third stage, Redemption.

This era is ours. But the Bible's richness of narrative about this era leads us to see that it is too simple to say that we live in the era of redemption. For this era divides up into at least three discrete sub-eras, and it makes a crucial difference for ethics which sub-era is the pertinent one. Further subdivisions are important for under-standing how this or that part of the Bible pertains to us, but we ought to begin with the fundamental distinction between the Old Testament and the New, with the earthly career of Jesus as the bridge between them. The question of the relations among these three sub-eras is fundamental to Christian thinking.

If the Old Testament is taken as normative for all believers at all times, then we Christians should be applying it today in all its particulars—ceremonial, civil, litur-gical, and so on.[4] Few Christian groups advocate such a position today. (Christian Reconstructionism, also known as "Theonomy," a deviant form of Calvinism, per-haps comes closest.) But whenever Christians simply draw out a text from the Old Testament and apply it directly to a current question, we are faced with the possi-bility of an important ethical anachronism, a failure to see that "today" is not 1000 B.C., "here" is not the ancient Near East, and "we" are not the people of Israel. The American religious right trades in this sort of prooftexting in its partisanship toward the current State of Israel as if it is directly fulfilling Old Testament prophecy and is entitled to the regard expected of Gentiles for God's chosen people—despite the manifest secularity of the vast majority of Israelis (which would disqualify them as "true Israel," according to the Biblical prophets), quite apart from what one thinks of Israeli policies toward Palestinians. "Prosperity gospel" preachers around the world also claim promises of earthly health and wealth that make sense in an Old Testament situation but do not so obviously fit in the very different economy of the New (Dt. 7:13; 8:7–13; II Chr. 7:14; cf. II Cor. 11:23–28).

---

4. Richard Bauckham writes thus about the Old Testament laws: "They are not sufficient to form a code of law for regular consultation by the judicial authorities. They are *examples* of laws rather than an exhaustive collection.... Neither the Old Testament law as a whole, nor specific parts of it, should be regarded as a statute-book for use in the courts. Rather its purpose is to educate the people of God in the will of God for the whole of their life as his people, to create and develop the conscience of the community" (*The Bible in Politics: How to Read the Bible Politically* [Louisville, KY: Westminster/John Knox, 1989], 26).

To notice the difference between the Old and the New is not to disparage the Old, much less to dismiss it as irrelevant. I myself have already drawn on the first few chapters of Genesis to make some points that I think are crucial in a Christian understanding of things, and I will detail my sense of the proper use of the Bible in Christian thought later on. The correct "use of the Law" is a perennial subject of controversy among Christians, but all of the major traditions of Christian thought affirm *some* use of it as God's abiding Word.

When we come to the career of Jesus, then, many Christians happily set up ethical camp, so to speak, longing to follow Jesus as the first disciples did and intending to "just"—follow Jesus, listen to Jesus, obey Jesus, and the like. Whatever the beguilements of such nostalgia, we must not succumb to them. We are not Jesus (!), and we are not the first disciples listening to him on a Galilean hillside—just as we are not Israel during the Exodus, Conquest, or Monarchy.

Jesus himself is the great bridge between God and creation via the lords of Creation, human beings. Jesus is also the center of God's great plan of Redemption, through his Incarnation, public ministry, Crucifixion, Resurrection, Ascension, and Second Coming. In the light of this great work, the church's earliest and most central confession was that "Jesus is Lord." In the logic of the Story and in the logic of salvation, therefore, the gospels that narrate the life of Jesus are positioned at the beginning of the New Testament.

From these facts, however, some Christians have drawn some improper conclusions that affect Christian thinking both materially and formally. Materially, we must deal with the tradition of *imitatio Christi*, the "imitation of Christ" as the fundamental model for Christian life. Thomas á Kempis's spiritual classic is but the most famous work in a long line of literature commending the life of Christ as the model for our own. In our own culture, this tradition has been popularized in the slogan, "What Would Jesus Do?"—a slogan that is now almost a century old, stemming as it does from Charles Sheldon's bestselling book of 1897, *In His Steps*.[5] And the tradition does have strong Biblical warrant, of course. In his Upper Room Discourse, Jesus says that he is setting his disciples an example of loving service (John 13:15). Indeed, his New Commandment explicitly binds them to imitation: "I give you a new commandment, that you love one another. Just as I have loved you, you also should love one another" (John 13:34). Paul urges his churches to imitate Christ (Eph. 5:1-2; 1 Thess. 1:6)—although often he says instead to imitate more senior Christians who are themselves imitating Christ, such as himself (1 Cor. 4:16; 11:1; Phil. 3:17; 1 Thess. 2:14; 2 Thess. 3:7-9; cf. Heb. 6:12; 13:7). And the Epistle to the Hebrews points to Jesus as the great example—indeed, the "Author and Finisher of our faith" (Heb. 12:2-3, KJV).

It has been an important mistake, however, to construe Christian discipleship to mean following Christ as if "following" meant *simply* "imitating." It is crucial to

---

5. Charles M. Sheldon, *In His Steps: What Would Jesus Do?* (New York and Toronto: Revell, 1897).

recall the truism that we are *not Jesus*, for Jesus was who he was and did what he did in order to accomplish his distinctive mission. We are not called to fulfill the ancient promises to Israel and to inaugurate the Kingdom of God. We are not called to be the Savior of the world and the Lord of Resurrection life. For that matter, we are not all called to be Jewish, or male, or single; no one reading this book has been called to live two thousand years ago, in the Levant, under Roman oppression; and few of us are called to a trade, only to give it up for public religious teaching ministry. There is much about Jesus that we are not called to imitate, for there is much that is particular to his particular identity and vocation.

For another thing, Jesus does not call us to do his work, but to *extend* his work—indeed, to perform "greater works than these" (Jn. 14:12). Imbued with the Spirit of Jesus, yes, and as the Body of Christ, yes, we are to bear witness to Jesus Christ far beyond the extents of his own quite limited preaching tours in Israel—with only the occasion venturing beyond to the Gentiles—and to make disciples of all nations, which the church is in the process of doing today after two thousand years of labor. Beyond this direct extension of his work, furthermore, Christians are called—as we shall see in more detail presently—to continue in the generic human work of gardening the world, albeit with the distinctive mark of those who know the Great Gardener and who work in conscious and delighted cooperation with him.

Thus it is crucial that we see that we are not thinking and living as if Jesus were present now in his earthly ministry, but *after* that: *after* the Crucifixion, the Resurrection, and the Ascension; *after* Pentecost and the giving of the Holy Spirit; *after* the Gospels and the Book of Acts that launches the church's distinctive sub-era and mission. We live *after* the Old Testament *and after* the career of Jesus in a *third* sub-era of redemption, the age of the church before the return of Christ in the consummation of history. "It is for your benefit that I go away," Jesus told his disciples (Jn. 16:7), and we must take him at his word and not think and live as if he hadn't gone away and is present for us now as he was then, to follow in that particular mode of ministry.

"What did Jesus say?" therefore is the wrong question for Christian thought just as "What would Jesus do?" is the wrong question for Christian ethics. "What would Jesus want me or us to think, be, and do, here and now?" is the right question.

Connected with this material issue is a formal issue for Christian thinking. Many Christians, including some quite sophisticated theologians, seem to equate the priority of Christ himself versus other human beings with the priority of the Gospels versus other books of the Bible. But this is an important hermeneutical error, and in at least four respects.

First, even though the Gospels come first in the canon of the New Testament, they are probably not the earliest testimonies to Jesus in the Bible. Paul's early letters, most scholars agree, predate most or all of the four Gospels. So if we are seeking access to the most primitive layer of "Jesus tradition," in terms of whole books (rather than this pericope or that saying or this hymn or that parable), Paul's work would deserve priority.

Second, we should not, in fact, be privileging whatever we guess is the earlier material of the New Testament versus the later, because all of it is inspired by God and therefore has the same status: scripture. Furthermore, any historian knows that sometimes later accounts are better than earlier ones precisely because the later accounts can have benefited from access to several earlier accounts plus perspective that only time can bring. So there is neither theological nor historical ground for preferring "earlier" to "later"—and that goes for pitting Mark's gospel against John's, too.

Third, privileging the Gospels in the name of privileging Jesus would make sense in terms of the relative status of the Lord Jesus versus his disciples, except that the Gospels are not *authored* by Jesus. They are authored by early Christians, just as the other New Testament documents are. So to privilege the Gospels is simply to prefer Matthew to Paul, or Mark to Peter, or John to, well, John (I–III John). Such a preference cannot claim justification on the basis of the supreme dignity of Christ, therefore, but instead reduces to a preference of *genre*, of gospels over epistles, and such a preference hardly has decisive literary or theological merit. (Indeed, the championing of the Gospels over the rest of the New Testament is particularly odd coming from educated Christians, who sound as if they have discovered a "red-letter edition" of the Bible—except that their new version prints *all* of the Gospels in red ink, while the rest of the Bible remains black.[6])

Finally, while the story of Jesus is indeed the key to history, to emphasize the Gospels over the rest of the New Testament is to forget that Jesus is Lord over *all* of history, Jesus is Head of the church that succeeds him in earthly ministry, and Jesus is in fact the Author of the *whole* New Testament via the inspiration of the Holy Spirit—as he is, indeed, the God who inspired the whole Bible. The better hermeneutical path, therefore, is to keep clearly in view what each of the books of the Bible have to offer us and to draw upon them according to their distinctive natures, regarding not only their genre strengths and limitations, but also the place of their subject matter in the Christian Story. We Christians are not to be forever

---

6. This, to me, is one of the most fundamental mistakes typically made in the Anabaptist tradition and thus by such important exemplars of it as John Howard Yoder: "For the radical Protestant there will always be a canon within the canon; namely, that recorded experience of practical moral reasoning in genuine human form that bears the name of Jesus" (*The Priestly Kingdom: Social Ethics as Gospel* [Notre Dame, IN: University of Notre Dame Press, 1985], 37). This error must be exposed as such, particularly because it is frequently accompanied by the overbearing rhetoric of this method being more Christian than thou, as in the following typical phrasing of Yoder: "Since Constantine, one tradition has assumed that it is the duty of Christians to be the chosen organs of God to guide history in the right direction, . . . it has been decided on a priori grounds that the teachings of Jesus with regard to Mammon and Mars were not meant to be obeyed, [and] that we have in 'nature' or 'common sense' or 'culture' or somewhere else a body of ethical rules which outrank the teachings and example of Jesus" (*The Priestly Kingdom*, 119). I believe that Christian thinking should be Christological and Christocentric, but, as I am arguing here, that means neither that the earthly career of Jesus is normative in Yoder's sense nor that the gospels themselves are privileged above other Biblical literature. For affirmation of how Christ ought to figure in theology, see my "Evangelical Theology Should Be Evangelical," in *Evangelical Futures: A Conversation on Theological Method*, ed. John G. Stackhouse, Jr. (Grand Rapids, MI: Baker Academic, 2000), 39–58.

repristinating the experience of the disciples trooping about with Christ in ancient Judea—nor, for that matter, the experience of the disciples in the early chapters of Acts. For there are *more* chapters in Acts, and the very "unfinished" nature of that book has prompted many readers to the conclusion that God intends the rest of the church to *keep writing it*, generation by generation, until the Lord of the church returns, to fulfill the promise made at that book's beginning (Acts 1:11).

Richard Bauckham offers some crucial reflections in this vein that are well worth listening to at length:

> The difference between the testaments might be better expressed in terms of a difference of political context. Much of the Old Testament is addressed to a people of God which was a political entity and for much of its history had at least some degree of political autonomy. The Old Testament is therefore directly concerned with the ordering of Israel's political life, the conduct of political affairs, the formulation of policies, the responsibilities of rulers as well as subjects, and so on. The New Testament is addressed to a politically powerless minority in the Roman Empire. Its overtly political material therefore largely concerns the responsibilities of citizens and subjects who, though they might occasionally hope to impress the governing authorities by prophetic witness (Matt. 10:18), had no ordinary means of political influence....
>
> The difference between the testaments explains why, from the time of Constantine onwards, whenever the political situation of Christians has moved towards more direct political influence and responsibility, the Old Testament has tended to play a larger part in Christian political thinking than the New Testament. This has been the case not only in the classic "Christendom" situation of much of Western Christian history, where the confessedly Christian society bore an obvious resemblance to political Israel. It can also quite often be seen in situations where Christians have supported revolutionary movements and in modern pluralistic democracies.[7]

The proper epistemological aim is to make the best sense of the *whole* Bible for inspired instruction on how to be God's people in the world.

---

7. Bauckham, *The Bible in Politics*, 3–4. Bauckham later adds: "The Bible's political teaching is in some degree *conditioned* by the social and political context in which it arose.... For example, the political wisdom of the book of Proverbs, with its emphasis on the stability of a fixed social order (Prov. 19:10; 30:21–23) and its sometimes deferentially uncritical attitude to the monarchy (Prov. 16:10–15; 25:3), reflects the outlook of the court circles from which it derives. This makes it not a mistaken but a *limited* viewpoint, and therefore one which needs to be balanced by other aspects of biblical teaching" (13). Finally: "The most difficult hermeneutical task is probably that of relating the Bible to the really novel features of the modern world which the Bible does not directly address. All too often Christians who try to see the world in a biblical perspective end up forcing the modern world on to the Procrustean bed of the biblical world (i.e., the world within which and to which the Bible was originally written). Genuinely novel features of the modern world are either reduced to some feature of the biblical world, so that their novelty is not really admitted, or else they are not seen as really important features of the modern world, so that their novelty can be admitted but trivialized" (131).

Indeed, Christian epistemology also takes into account the ongoing work of the Holy Spirit in the life of the church. Jesus promised the Holy Spirit would continue to teach the church after his departure:

> I still have many things to say to you, but you cannot bear them now. When the Spirit of truth comes, he will guide you into all the truth; for he will not speak on his own, but will speak whatever he hears, and he will declare to you the things that are to come. He will glorify me, because he will take what is mine and declare it to you.
>
> (Jn. 16:13–14)

As Oliver O'Donovan writes,

> God has continued to teach the church what it needs to know in each emerging situation. For example, there was no revealed political doctrine in the New Testament, prescribing how the state was to be guided. The early church had simply to proclaim God's Kingdom come in Christ. The political doctrine of Christendom was discovered and elicited from the practical experience of Christian political discipleship.[8]

The Christian therefore has to be suspicious of any form of thought that effectively shrinks the canon to a few, favorite books, whether Gospels, Epistles, Torah, apocalyptic, or what have you. And we wisely pay critical attention to the experiences and reflections of our Christian forebears since the apostolic period, looking for further wisdom from God in the tradition of the church.

I will have much more to say about how we ought best to understand the Bible and tradition and how to coordinate their various elements with each other and with other things we know from other resources. For now, we ought to complete our brief survey of the Christian Story by considering the consummation of the ages in the return of Jesus Christ.

The history of Christian art is replete with instances of the common Christian aspiration to return to the Garden of Eden, a "peaceable kingdom" of rustic tranquility. Yet this vision is more Islamic, in fact, than Christian. It is the Qur'an that speaks of heaven in terms a Bedouin would appreciate: tall trees providing cool shade, endless water, soothing greenery, and the like.

To be sure, the imagery of returning to Eden is importantly truer to the Bible than the even more common Western imagery of our eventually departing the earth to rise to celestial spiritual heights, there to be eternally rapt in mystical union with the divine. It is vital that this "church myth" be exposed as the quasi-Platonic vision it is—a hyper-spiritual vision that nicely separates Christian concern from distracting earthly matters such as justice, compassion, and environmental responsibility, and renders us literally too heavenly minded to be of any earthly good, and especially of any force resistant to the powers that be. Wendell Berry is scathing on this point: "Despite protests to the contrary, modern Christianity has become

---

8. O'Donovan, *Desire*, 219.

willy-nilly the religion of the state and the economic status quo. Because it has been so exclusively dedicated to incanting anemic souls into Heaven, it has been made the tool of much earthly villainy."[9]

We are *not going to Heaven*: Heaven is the abode of God. We are of the earth ("human" from *humus*), and earth is our home, upon which God has been graciously pleased to dwell with us.[10] The apocalyptic vision in both Testaments is decidedly earthy and earthly: a kingdom, with its capital in Jerusalem, that unites all the peoples of the earth around the worship of God. It is an astonishingly rich vision of purification, judgment, health, security, harmony, plenty, celebration, diversity, and fellowship. We do not go *back* to the garden, and we do not go *up* to Heaven. We go *forward* to the *garden city* of the New Jerusalem, pictured best in Revelation 21 and 22. The earth suffers throughout the Book of Revelation. But, like its human inhabitants, it is renewed and made fit for this final, eternal cohabitation of God, humanity, and the rest of earthly creation. We must note that it is not *brand* new, just as its human lords are not *brand* new: there is no second *creatio ex nihilo*. Instead, God resurrects humanity and, so to speak, resurrects the earth as well into a resplendent ecology of vitality and beauty in which all live in mutually beneficial relationship with each other.

Oliver O'Donovan puts it well:

> No destiny can possibly be conceived in the world, or even out of it, other than that of a city. It is the last word of the Gospel, as it is of the New Testament: a city that is the heart of a world, a focus of international peace; a city that is itself a temple rather than possessing a temple, itself a natural environment rather than possessing a natural environment; a city that has overcome the antinomies of nature and culture, worship and politics, under an all-directing regime that needs no mediation; a city that has the universe within it, and yet has an "outside"—not in the sense of an autonomous alternative, but of having all alternatives excluded, a city with a Valley of Hinnom [O'Donovan means "hell"], which does not, therefore, have to carry within it the cheapness and tawdriness that have made all other cities mean.[11]

This vision is our "imagined future," without a clear sense of which no one can resist the relentless conformist pressures of our culture and strive for something different and better.[12] This vision is the hope of *shalom*, the rich Hebrew word that goes far

---

9. Wendell Berry, "Christianity and the Survival of Creation," in *Sex, Economy, Freedom, and Community* (New York: Pantheon, 1992); quoted in Walsh and Keesmaat, 168.

10. Paul Marshall, *Heaven Is Not My Home: Living in the Now of God's Creation* (Nashville, TN: Word, 1998). See also Richard J. Mouw's excellent exposition of Isaiah along these lines: *When the Kings Come Marching In: Isaiah and the New Jerusalem* (Grand Rapids, MI: Eerdmans, 1983).

11. O'Donovan, 285.

12. Anna Fels, *Necessary Dreams: Ambition in Women's Changing Lives* (New York: Pantheon, 2004); see also Barry A. Harvey, "What We've Got Here Is a Failure to Imagine: The Church-Based University in the Tournament of Competing Visions," *Christian Scholar's Review* 34 (Winter 2005): 201–15.

beyond the cessation of hostility and disruption to encompass *flourishing*: each element (human, animal, plant, and so on) flourishing as itself; each element enjoying flourishing relationships with every other element; each *group* or *community* flourishing, and enjoying good relationships with its constituent individuals, other individuals, and other groups; all human beings relating well to all of our fellow creatures and to our ecosystems in general; and everyone and everything joining with all creation in flourishing relationship with God. Thus shalom is truly a global concept, an ideal of universal well-being.[13]

Richard Bauckham writes about *blessing* as God's fundamental mode of relating to his creation, the mode of bringing shalom, and a mode we are to imitate as his image:

> Blessing in the Bible refers to God's characteristically generous and abundant giving of all good to his creatures and his continual renewal of the abundance of created life.... God's blessing of people overflows in their blessing of others and those who experience blessing from God in turn bless God, which means that they give all that creatures really can give to God: thanksgiving and praise.
>
> ....It is in the most comprehensive sense God's purpose for his creation. Wherever human life enjoys the good things of creation and produces the good fruits of human activity, God is pouring out his blessing.[14]

I have dealt elsewhere with many ethical ramifications of this great story.[15] For our present epistemological purposes, however, we must now turn to the concept of vocation. Given this sweeping narrative of original goodness, terrible fall, extensive redemption, and final glory, why did God create us? The answer to that question will provide us with crucial foundations for Christian thinking, as we see it properly as an element of God's calling on our lives.

VOCATION

The word "vocation" comes from the Latin word *vocare*, and thus means "calling." In Christian history, however, this word has become bound up with the category of "work," albeit in three different ways.

First, some Christians have understood that work *is* vocation. Especially in Roman Catholic and Orthodox Christianity, the term "vocation" means the call to a "religious" career and, indeed, life-pattern: monks, nuns, priests, and so on each have a "calling" or a "vocation." This use of "vocation" later was secularized in its application

---

13. Among the best descriptions I have encountered of shalom is the one provided by Nicholas Wolterstorff in *Until Justice and Peace Embrace* (Grand Rapids, MI: Eerdmans, 1983), 69–72.

14. Bauckham, *Bible and Mission*, 34.

15. Particularly in *Making the Best of It: Following Christ in the Real World* (New York: Oxford University Press, 2008).

to other traditional professions—indeed, to what some would call "secular priest-hoods"—so that one still hears of a "calling" to medicine, law, or education.

Second, other Christians have understood vocation to be the call of Christ to *every* Christian, not just the full-time clergy. But this call is to particular, "Christian" activities, not to a full-time job, much less to an entire life-pattern. Thus one's work is typically *not* one's vocation. Our jobs provide for our physical needs, and are thus a necessity in the world as it is, but they are not actually part of our divine calling. Instead, the call of Christ is to evangelism, or charity, or peacemaking, or justice-seeking, or some other work that goes beyond the regular work—and, indeed, the regular life—of any normal human being.[16]

A third view is the one I commend, namely, that work *is part of* vocation. One of the key revisions of Christian life that emerged from the sixteenth-century Protestant Reformation was in this zone. The Reformers declared, contrary to the tradition of medieval orders, that there are no "super-Christians" or "regular Christians," there are just *Christians*. There are not some people who are saints and others who are non-saints. All of us are saints, since the root of that word is "to be set apart for special use," and we are each set apart by God for his service.

With this eradication of the "two-tiered" system, then, came two positive teach-ings: All (legitimate) work is blessed by God *and* vocation is more than work. Vocation is the divine calling *to be a Christian* in every mode of life, whether public as well as private, religious as well as secular, adult as well as juvenile, corporate as well as individual, female as well as male. And thus to be a Christian in every mode of life is to show something of what it means to be a (redeemed and renewed) human being as well.

Indeed, we have now to work backwards even farther, to the very creation of hu-manity. For long before the Bible speaks of any Christians, it speaks on its very first page about God's creation and call of human beings.

Creation and the Permanent Human Vocation

Then God said, "Let us make humankind in our image, according to our likeness; and let them have dominion over the fish of the sea, and over the birds of the air, and over the cattle, and over all the wild animals of the earth, and over every creeping thing that creeps upon the earth."

---

16. I was raised in a typical sectarian Protestant version of this ethic, such that the only instruc-tion we received about work was to avoid sin and evangelize one's workmates and customers all one could. Interestingly, however, even someone as sophisticated as Jacques Ellul "could propose that the Christian find his vocation outside of his occupation—as Amos did his prophesying and Paul his apostleship. 'On this own time' and in the situation where the Christian *can* exercise a bit of freedom, let him find activity that truly can witness to the age that is coming, that truly can be done in response to the call of God, that truly can be seen as a free service in behalf of God and the neighbor. Ellul cites his own volunteer work in a club for juvenile delinquents as an example of such vocation; his writing of Christian books would qualify as well" (Vernard Eller, "A Voice on Vocation: The Contribution of Jacques Ellul," *The Reformed Journal* 29 [May 1979]: 20).

So God created humankind in his image, in the image of God he created them; male and female he created them. God blessed them, and God said to them, "Be fruitful and multiply, and fill the earth and subdue it; and have dominion over the fish of the sea and over the birds of the air and over every living thing that moves upon the earth."
(Genesis 1:26-28)

The first description of human beings in the Bible says that human beings are supposed to be like God and as such are to wield "dominion" over the rest of the world. Despite current ambivalence over the place and role of human beings in regard to the rest of the world, the Bible says that human beings are literally the lords (*dominus*) of creation.

Such language in our society might trigger the outrage most of us feel over the human exploitation and despoliation of the rest of creation. But according to the Bible, human beings are created "in the image of God" and therefore are literally to look like and act like God in regard to the rest of Creation. And how does this Great King act toward the world he made? With care: with sustenance and creativity. David Martin avers, "Providence ... is about God's consistent and persistent sustaining provision, power, and purpose for us and the world."[17] Human beings likewise are the world's *gardeners*, under God's commission, and in that image we see the reciprocity of relation between humans and their fellow creatures. For who benefits from the gardener doing his work well, the gardener or the garden? Clearly they both do. The gardener is "in charge" and in both senses: he gets to decide what is to be done with the garden because he has been mandated by God to make those decisions—precisely in order to benefit both himself and the garden under his care.

The late Pope John Paul II warns us well:

Humankind, which discovers its capacity to transform and in a certain sense create the world through its own work, forgets that this is always based on God's prior and original gift of things that are. People think that they can make arbitrary use of the earth, subjecting it without restraint to their wills, as though the earth did not have its own requisites and a prior God-given purpose, which human beings can indeed develop but must not betray.[18]

In order to accomplish this task (this mission, this calling) of benevolent, symbiotic dominion, God tells the first humans to spread out over the face of the planet: "be fruitful and multiply, and fill the earth . . ."—three mentions of reproduction, each one increasing in magnitude, with the purpose of bringing the whole earth under cultivation: ". . . and subdue it; and have dominion. . . ." The earth is created

---

17. Martin, 139.

18. *Centesimus Annus, Encyclical Letter on the Hundredth Anniversary of Rerum Novarum* (Boston: St. Paul Books, 1991), 54; quoted in Jean Bethke Elshtain, *Who Are We? Critical Reflections and Hopeful Possibilities* (Grand Rapids, MI: Eerdmans, 2000), 53.

"very good," but *not perfect*. It is not, as both Hebrew and Greek words for "perfect" denote, "mature" or "complete." It is, in fact, *wild*, and God gives this good wildness to human beings as a medium in which to create, a good land to cultivate into a better land.

Later Biblical teaching places this primal commandment to garden the world within the context of relationship implied in the very creation of human beings by God and in that creation as male and female:

> "You shall love the Lord your God with all your heart, and with all your soul, and with all your mind." This is the greatest and first commandment. And a second is like it: "You shall love your neighbor as yourself." On these two commandments hang all the law and the prophets.
>
> (Mt. 22:37–40)

We can summarize these three commandments thus: Love God, love your neighbor, love the rest of creation—understanding, of course, that the love for each will be appropriate to its object.

At least three fundamental implications follow from these commandments. First, it is striking that the first commandment given to human beings in the Bible is this one: cultivate the world. In the Bible's account we literally are gardeners first. God has never rescinded this commandment, but rather it is assumed throughout the subsequent narrative of Scripture. It must be noted in this regard, contrary to what has sometimes been affirmed on this question, that the Incarnation of our Lord was not, in fact, necessary to "sanctify the ordinary" or otherwise to validate our everyday work. Indeed, Jesus comes as the Son of Man, the "human one," to remind us, as well as to show us flawlessly, what God had already revealed to us of the dignity of human being and of our work in his world.

Furthermore, it will be our task, and our glory, to carry on this mission of dominion in the immediate presence of our Lord Jesus in the world to come: "If we endure," Paul promises, "we will reign with him" (2 Tim. 2:12). And in the Revelation given to John, the Christian faithful several times are described as reigning with Christ (Rev. 5:10; 20:6; 22:5). Over what or whom is there for resurrected humanity to reign with Christ, all of his enemies having been removed from the scene forever? The answer is clear: a renewed earth, as the dominion commandment continues to articulate our identity and function as "image of God." Dallas Willard writes, in flat contradiction of the ideal of the "beatific vision":

> We will not sit around looking at one another or at God for eternity but will join the eternal Logos, "reign with him," in the endlessly ongoing creative work of God....
>
> Thus, our faithfulness over a "few things" in the present phase of our life develops the kind of character that can be entrusted with "many things."...His plan is for us

to develop, as apprentices to Jesus, to the point where we can take our place in the ongoing creativity of the universe.[19]

Indeed, Jesus himself is not just taking a sabbatical between his First and Second Comings. The Bible shows him continuing to work, ruling the world, helping the church in its mission of disciple-making and blessing the forces of shalom-making in general as, indeed, the Prince of Peace (= shalom). Jesus, moreover, will continue to work to make shalom upon his return, forcibly restoring the world to order, judging all that is awry and amiss, and setting the stage for the glorious era to follow.

Second, all of our fellow human beings share the dignity and responsibility of these commandments. Those who obey them, whether they consciously honor God or not, are doing God's will in this primal respect, and God continues to bless humanity with both a degree of correct orientation to these tasks and the resources to undertake them. Inasmuch as any of our neighbors are, indeed, loving God, loving their neighbors, or cultivating the earth in whatever might be their work, art, leisure, and so on, we Christians ought to recognize it as such, approve it and cooperate with it—again, whether or not the name of God or of Jesus is invoked in the enterprise.[20]

Third, and finally to explicit epistemological matters, we can take as axiomatic that God does not call us to do something we cannot accomplish. Quite the contrary, he delights in supplying our needs to fulfill his will. It follows, therefore, that human beings can rely on God to provide the *knowledge* we need, among the other resources we need, to think what we need to think in order to be what he wants us to be and to do what he wants us to do.

This point is the thrust of the discussion so far. The doctrine of vocation provides grounds that are so conspicuously lacking in so much modern epistemology: grounds for confidence in human apprehension and comprehension of the world. We can rely on our knowledge of the world since without such confidence we could not possibly obey these primal commandments to love God, love our neighbors, and love the rest of Creation.[21]

---

19. Dallas Willard, *The Divine Conspiracy: Rediscovering Our Hidden Life in God* (San Francisco: Harper, 1998), 378.

20. For agreement from a quite different quarter that deep differences in metaphysics and morality do not usually impede useful work in everything from physics to philosophy, see Richard Rorty, "Phony Science Wars," *The Atlantic Monthly* (November 1999): 120–22.

21. Christian philosopher and physicist Stanley Jaki offers a much more general argument for realism and one that does not involve any religious claims, as mine does. He avers that no philosophy is worthy of the name that does not begin with acceptance of the basic givenness, the reality, of objects and of our (reasonably reliable) apprehension of them. The very act of doing philosophy, he points out, assumes the existence of the means by which they articulate it (paper, computers) and those to whom they communicate it, the interlocutors who are themselves *objects* we apprehend. I am impressed by Jaki's vigorous and entertaining argument, even as it seems to me to amount to a sophisticated version of "Oh, come off it! *Of course* we have access to the real world," an appeal that finally either grabs you or it doesn't. (Stanley L. Jaki, *Means to*

Alas, of course, we cannot rest at this level of naïve realism. First, we cannot simply proceed in the blithe confidence that we perceive the world accurately and completely and then interpret it infallibly and comprehensively. We cannot do so because we are limited creatures and the cosmos is complex—in just about every way we can consider. So our *finitude* drastically limits our claim to knowledge.

A second consideration, our *fallenness*, emerges early in the Bible's narrative. Our God-given task of cultivating the world has been made much harder because of sin. The primal commands to form a team of male and female and multiply their influence through offspring in order to cultivate the world become markedly more difficult to obey in the wake of the Fall:

> To the woman [God] said, "I will greatly increase your pangs in childbearing; in pain you shall bring forth children, yet your desire shall be for your husband, and he shall rule over you." And to the man he said, "Because you have listened to the voice of your wife, and have eaten of the tree about which I commanded you, 'You shall not eat of it,' cursed is the ground because of you; in toil you shall eat of it all the days of your life; thorns and thistles it shall bring forth for you; and you shall eat the plants of the field. By the sweat of your face you shall eat bread until you return to the ground, for out of it you were taken; you are dust, and to dust you shall return."
>
> (Gen. 3:16-19)

The obvious results of sin are the multiplied pain of childbirth and the multiplied impediments of farming. But these external difficulties are exacerbated by psychological and sociological derangement: the husband will now dominate the wife while the wife's desire for him compels her to remain in this doubly painful relationship. And it is this internal derangement, this refusal to love God and our neighbor, this confusion as to the direction in which our proper self-interest lies, that marks us epistemically: "They are darkened in their understanding, alienated from the life of God because of their ignorance and hardness of heart" (Eph. 4:18). One hardly has to be a philosopher to note that we all tend to see what we want to see; we tend to hear what suits us to hear; we readily give credence to what interests us—in both senses of "interest."

So now where are we? God gives us a world and commands us to care for it. To do so requires that we have a knowledge of the world and a knowledge of how to care for it at least adequate to that mandate. Yet the world is a place that keeps exceeding our ability to understand it, much less manage it. And our understanding is compromised drastically by our penchant to view reality in the way most conducive to our preferences.

Have we therefore traversed from strong epistemic confidence to abject epistemic despair in the space of a few paragraphs?

Message: A Treatise on Truth [Grand Rapids, MI: Eerdmans, 1999].) For another contemporary Christian philosopher's appreciation of the perennial problem of proving that other people actually do exist, see Alvin Plantinga, *God and Other Minds: A Study of the Rational Justification of Belief in God* (Ithaca, NY: Cornell University Press, 1967).

The problem of knowledge thus intersects with the problem of evil and the story of the Gospel. And the framework within which to set this nexus is the category of God's providential salvation of the world.

The fundamental problem in the Bible, after all, is not epistemological. It is moral and spiritual and relational. Our basic plight is not that we don't yet know enough—enough to sort ourselves out, and run good societies, and administer the planet to the benefit of all its inhabitants. No, while it is true that we certainly do not know enough to accomplish any of those objectives, our fundamental problem is not what we think: it is what and whom we love. We don't love God above all else, we don't love our neighbors as ourselves, and we don't love the planet to maximize its flourishing. Instead, we pursue what we confusedly think is in our best interests: sometimes honoring God, caring for this or that neighbor, and honoring parts of Creation in some respect, while at least as often ignoring or defying God, snubbing or exploiting our neighbors, and neglecting or oppressing the world in our charge.

In God's goodness, God seeks to arrest this situation. God seeks to provide us a fresh start, untrammelled by the past. And God seeks to guide us in a course of recovery and rehabilitation such that we reach our full potential. In order to accomplish these three goals, God has providentially arranged the world such that it assists him remarkably well in this venture of global reclamation.

First, the world teaches us about sin and evil. It alerts us to our negative situation, sometimes with shocking force and overwhelming detail. It shows us something of the magnitude of our deviation from God's good will and the extent of the deadly consequences of our sin. It demonstrates both our limitations and our defects, and thus something of our great need of both forgiveness and rehabilitation. It proves that the problem is not confined to "lower" races or classes or to a single sex. And the world depicts the awful truth about us in the face of our proud denial that anything is really, permanently wrong that education, or technology, or mysticism, or revolution cannot soon solve.

Cornelius Plantinga warns us that sin makes us "religiously... unmusical.... Moral beauty begins to bore us. The idea that the human race needs a Savior sounds quaint."[22] But the world we inhabit provides us information in every day, and experiences in every life, that puncture our carefully and expensively constructed airbags and confront us with grim realities head-on. We hate it. It hurts—badly. But an inescapable reality check is what anyone needs first in order to begin a transition from deadly lifestyle to eternal life.

Our world also tells us, secondly, that we are not merely loathsome creatures deserving extermination. The world astonishingly assures us instead that we are creatures whom God still loves, who are capable of being restored, and who could

---

22. Cornelius Plantinga, *Not the Way It's Supposed to Be: A Breviary of Sin* (Grand Rapids, MI/Leicester, UK: Eerdmans/Apollos, 1995), xiii.

again be beautiful and strong and noble. It gives us hope that rescue is possible and, indeed, available—that there is a Savior who meets our need of forgiveness of our past and healing of our illnesses, moral and otherwise. The Bible tells us that God has provided a wide range of revelation to assure us of God's existence, of God's goodness, of God's goodwill toward us, and of God's provisions for our salvation. And, as I will detail presently, it is God's people who are charged with broadcasting this good news with clarity and persuasiveness to everyone else on the globe.

Thirdly, our world provides us opportunities for personal growth that take us beyond the eradication of our faults and the reorientation of our loves to enroll us in a regimen of maturation. Our world provides many opportunities to learn about and to do good. Indeed, we now are engaged in the task known as *tikkun olam*, the "repair of the world," as well as maximizing its good potential. Others are in need, whether because of their own choices, or those of others, or because of natural evil. Their need beckons to us, and we respond—somehow. For whether we turn away, or vacillate, or defer a decision, each is a significant ethical response that marks us and moves us along to one final condition or another. We live in a world in which suffering, whether our own or others', challenges us to go beyond our current state of personal development to greater moral virtue. Indeed, engaging our world in this way helps us, as Plantinga puts it, to "cultivate a taste for this project [of shalom], to become more and more the sort of person for whom eternal life with God would be sheer heaven."[23]

Our world is, in effect, a kind of boot camp, a university, a twelve-step group, an extended family, a war zone, and a pilgrimage all at once. It challenges us every day, from every angle, to grow up—and does so without allowing us to be so crushed by evil, whether our own or others', that we could not possibly complete the regimen. As in the case of suffering Job, God restrains evil (whether Satan or some other instigator) so as not to defeat God's ultimate purposes, not to press us beyond our capacities. Martin Luther avers:

> the power of the devil is not as great as it appears to be outwardly; for if he had full power to rage as he pleased, you would not live for one hour or retain safe and intact a single sheep, a crop in the field, corn in the barn, and, in short, any of those things which pertain to this life.... To be sure, he causes disturbance, and yet he is not able to carry out what he most desires, to overthrow all things....[24]

The world, to be sure, sometimes seems to say that virtue is foolish and vice is shrewd. In a world whose systems are so infected by sin, we ought to expect that sometimes evil will succeed. Yet even then, a deeper order often prevails and justice

---

23. C. Plantinga, *Not the Way It's Supposed to Be*, 37.

24. LW 6:90f; quoted in Hans Schwarz, *Evil: A Historical and Theological Perspective*, trans. Mark W. Worthing (Minneapolis, MN: Fortress, 1995), 146.

is done. We glimpse the temporariness and artificiality of systems that reward evil, and we sense the permanence and basicality of true justice, however intermittent, even elusive, it seems to be.

Even if, however, we grant this benign and salubrious understanding of the world (and I immediately recognize that it can be difficult to do so!), we might wonder epistemologically why God both allows the world to be ambiguous in some key respects (sometimes the wicked prosper and the righteous perish; sometimes the rain—and the lava—falls on the just and the unjust alike) and allows our own interpreting of the world to be both limited and distorted. If the world is supposed to function in the salutary ways I suggest, why does it function so poorly relative to the outcomes for which the world is thus designed—and why do our cognitive abilities function so poorly relative to those outcomes also? Moreover, how can we human beings possibly fulfill the Creation mandate to cultivate the earth if our cognitive processes are too limited to comprehend the various challenges we encounter, let alone actually malfunctioning because of sin?

Again, the answer comes that the world is in fact the sort of place that prompts questions like those and it is also the sort of place in which God kindly replies to them—at least (and this is the crucial point) to the extent necessary for us to know what we need to know in order to do what we need to do and become what we need to become. Since the world is so decidedly ambiguous and since our abilities to understand it are both so constrained and so compromised, God has provided extra resources to compensate for this difficult situation. In particular, God has provided revelation—of what we could not possibly know on our own, even if we were in our right minds and the world was as it should be, and also of what we would know if all, including us, were well.

Chief among God's media of revelation, furthermore, have been God's personal communications via the Holy Spirit, mostly obviously through prophecy and the Bible and pre-eminently via the career of Jesus Christ. To all of these revelations, and to the ongoing guidance of God's Spirit, testifies the Christian church. To the vocation of the church, then, we now turn to continue our exploration of the implications of vocation for epistemology. For it is in the calling and experience of the church that we see all of the resources for Christian thinking—which, we shall also see, is just human thinking supplemented by emergency measures—come together in a practical pattern nicely suited to the needs of our time.

When Christ took his leave of the disciples, he issued them one particular command: to disperse throughout the world and make people his followers:

> And Jesus came and said to them, "All authority in heaven and on earth has been given to me. Go therefore and make disciples of all nations, baptizing them in the name of the Father and of the Son and of the Holy Spirit, and teaching them to obey everything that I have commanded you. And remember, I am with you always, to the end of the age."
> (Matt. 28:18-20)

This is the distinctive Christian mission. We must immediately be clear that this calling does not replace the call of God upon all human beings, the Creation commandments. Christians do not stop being human beings by dint of becoming Christians. Indeed, most of what Christians do each day is generically human, not distinctively Christian. (One pauses to consider the Christian rising from his Christian chair to leave his Christian house in order to retrieve his Christian lawn mower from the Christian garage and begin mowing, Christianly, his Christian yard.) But Christ did call his church to a distinctive activity, namely, drawing men and women to himself and forming them into disciples.

This is a kind of re-creational task: go out into all the world and make shalom (shades of Genesis 1), except this time God's servants are to focus on redeeming human beings who are not just *wild*, but *wrong*. The Christian calling was made necessary by the Fall, as Jesus' own life and work was so necessitated. Sin has broken our natural human inclination to love God, love our neighbor, and love the rest of creation. It has deranged us, in fact, so that we tend strongly not to love God, or our neighbor, or the world. We therefore tend strongly to act destructively, rather than constructively, wrecking rather than creating shalom, alternately torturing and idolizing our fellow creatures, and generally convincing ourselves that we are right when we are patently wrong.

We therefore need to be arrested in our confusion and rebellion, sobered up, calmed down, repaired, revitalized, and rehabilitated. In short, we need to follow Jesus out of the pit we have dug for ourselves—and for everything else—and up into the light of shalom and the cosmos God intended us to enjoy and participate in. God meets us in the persons of our fellow human beings who themselves have gotten off the wrong path and, by God's gifts, onto the right one.

This work of declaring the Alternative Message of a way out and up, of living a pattern of life inspired by that good news, and of shaping other people into disciples who can speak and walk accordingly—this transformative work is the distinctive work of Christians, empowered, of course, by God. It is assigned to us, not on the basis of any conspicuous virtue we possess, but in the nature of the case. Christians are the only people in the world whose religion is named for Christ. We are the only people in the world who put Jesus in the center, where he belongs. We are the only people in the world who proclaim, "Jesus is Lord." Therefore we are the only people in the world who *can* and *want* to bear witness to Jesus, who can invite others to repent and believe this good news, and who can teach people how to become disciples of Jesus.

Everything else we are and do particularly *as Christians* connects with this mission. That is not to say that this mission is the sole *activity* of the church—*contra* much of the evangelical tradition and some elements of the "missional church" movement of our day.[25] To think this way is to substitute what Christians *distinctly* are to do for *all* that Christians are to do. Again, the Creation Commandments have

---

25. Darrell L. Guder, ed, *Missional Church: A Vision for the Sending of the Church in North America* (Grand Rapids, MI: Eerdmans, 1998).

priority. They are what human beings normally, and normatively, do. Thus the church engages in worship of God because that is the correct and healthful human response to God, to love God with all one's heart, soul, mind, and strength—not merely because engaging in worship somehow helps the church perform its mission better, although it *does*. The church also cares for its own in fellowship because that is what people do when they are rightly related in shalom and love each other as themselves—not merely because fellowship strengthens the Body of Christ for service to others, although it *does*. In particular, it just isn't true, despite its frequent repetition in some circles, that "the church is the one society that exists for the benefit of its non-members." That's cute, but not correct. The same is true for Kierkegaard's popular image of the church as performers in worship with God as the audience. Worship is a *dialogue* between God and ourselves, and God blesses us far more than we bless God, even as God gives us gifts with which to bless each other as well. The church exists in what I call the "Win—Win—Win" dynamic of the Kingdom of God: we bless God, we bless the neighbor (including, here, the rest of creation), and we bless ourselves simultaneously in a reinforcing circle of love. For if I love you, I am blessed when you are blessed, and it is a blessing to me to have the privilege of blessing you. And so on, all 'round the circle.

Yet the church is indeed "missional" in its distinctive task of witnessing to Jesus Christ and making disciples. It pursues that task in at least three respects: testifying as witnesses, yes, but in two other modes as well.

As *witnesses*, the church experiences something and relates that experience to others. The central experience of the Christian church is Christ—not "religious feeling" or "spirituality" in general, not "God" or "the divine" in general, not "faith" or "religion" in general, but Jesus Christ. Inasmuch as the church witnesses to its experience of Jesus Christ—its reception of his revelation, its baptism in his Holy Spirit, its enjoyment of his church, its work with him in the world—then the church performs its distinctive task and adds immeasurably to shalom. (Inasmuch as the church speaks more generally and less particularly about Christ, it might still add to shalom. But now it does so as just one among many agencies of social reform, charity, moral uplift, spiritual experience, and the like—and often not the most effective or inspiring of such agencies.)

Again, let us be clear that worship and fellowship are not solely *for* mission. But genuine worship of Christ, corporately and individually, and genuine fellowship with other Christians provide regular occasions for encounter with Christ, thus giving the church something to witness and so to bear witness to others.

This honor of bearing witness to Christ would be glory enough, but Christ calls the church, secondly, to serve as *example*. Christians are to live in the light of the Kingdom of God, however imperfectly we perceive it and however inconstantly we practice its principles. We are called not merely to testify to something *over there* and *long ago*, although what has happened is indeed crucial to our testimony: "God was in Christ reconciling the world to himself" (II Cor. 5:19). Nor are we only to testify to something that is happening *here and now* and *among us*. But what has happened and what is happening can be witnessed by others who observe us. Albeit with the grace of the Holy Spirit, without whose ministry no truly spiritual thing can be apprehended (I Cor. 2:13–15), the new life of the Spirit can be seen and interpreted for what it is, as we act out at least an approximation of the Kingdom of God in our individual lives, yes, but especially in our churches, families, and other Christian organizations. For the "eternal life" we are promised in the gospel (e.g., John 3) as our present experience as well as our future hope is ζωη αιωνιος, literally, "the life of the age to come."[26]

So we care for the poor—the financially poor, yes, as we defy the power of Mammon by giving away our money with liberality and faith that God will always provide what we truly need. We also care for the poor in spirit, the depressed, the lonely, the unloved, the misfits and "losers" that society scorns and hurries past. We also care for the poor in spirit among the towers and mansions of the wealthy and influential, as God graciously confronts them with the vanity of all worldly things and their need for something, and Someone, more.

Beyond these acts of mission, however, we rejoice with each other in sincere fellow-feeling, rather than offering grudging congratulations through teeth grinding in envy, since we know that in God's economy of abundance there will be plenty of success and honor to go around. We put ourselves at each other's service, making the most of our talents, skills, and resources to the maximal benefit of all. We celebrate the arts, play sports and games, cook good food, and otherwise declare that the world is yet a gift from God and that he is a generous Lord who enjoys our enjoyment.[27] We pray for the day when suffering, sin, and absurdity are gone and all is light, goodness, and flourishing. And so we work: to do whatever little bit we can to honor God, bless others, and fulfill ourselves.[28] In lives well lived, we thus exemplify, as well as bear witness to, the abundant life offered the world in the Gospel.

---

26. Robert L. Wilken cites Michael Buckley, *At the Origins of Modern Atheism*, to remark that "to defend the existence of God, Christian thinkers in early modern times excluded all appeals to Christian behavior or practices, the very things that give Christianity its power and have been its most compelling testimony to the reality of God" (*Remembering the Christian Past* [Grand Rapids, MI: Eerdmans, 1995], 52). For further reflection on the ways in which Christians can exemplify the faith, please see my *Humble Apologetics: Defending the Faith Today* (New York: Oxford University Press, 2002), chap. 11.

27. John Calvin, no one's idea of an aesthete or epicure, remarks at length on the creative generosity of God, who endows food with pleasant taste as well as nutrients, trees and animals with beauty beyond natural necessity, precious stones and metals strictly for ornament and art, and concludes: "Away, then, with that inhuman philosophy which, while conceding only a necessary use of creatures, not only malignantly deprives us of the lawful fruit of God's beneficence but cannot be practiced unless it robs a man of all his senses and degrades him to a block" (*Institutes of the Christian Religion*, ed. John T. McNeill and trans. Ford Lewis Battles [Philadelphia: Westminster, 1960], I:726–27 (III, x, 2–3). I am grateful to Nicholas Wolterstorff for quoting this at the conclusion of a longer quoted passage in *Until Justice and Peace Embrace* (Grand Rapids, MI: Eerdmans, 1983), 131–32.

28. And while we rejoice in this great privilege, we can marvel at the humility of God, as a desperately hungry protagonist does in one of Lawrence Dorr's superb short stories, as he receives food from a nun: "Christ had died for him, died in real agony a real death. He was cramming the bread into his mouth, crying and chewing at the same time, overcome by a

Thirdly, Christ calls us beyond witness and example to be actual *agents* of his mission. Among the most extraordinary commands of the Bible is, in fact, the Great Commission: "go…and make disciples." Strictly speaking, of course, this command requires the impossible. We cannot even make *ourselves* into proper disciples, no matter how we instruct ourselves, remonstrate with ourselves, and pray for ourselves. Asceticism, mysticism, *lectio divina,* and other spiritual disciplines take us only so far, and not nearly far enough. We must be born again by the Spirit. Christ must form himself in us. So how can Christ thus plausibly command us to make disciples of others?

This last, great command of Jesus' earthly ministry comes with the promise of the Holy Spirit (Acts 1:8). We are called to do what is truly divine work, the hardest work in the world: changing people's *loves.* And there is no way we could begin to do this work unless the heart-transforming power of the Holy Spirit were coursing within us. But he *is* within us, and therefore "greater works than these" are commanded of us. We are to play an actual part in the drawing of men, women, and children to the Savior and help them respond to him more and more faithfully as Lord.

Having surveyed these three great modes of our distinctive calling as Christians, then, we note the synergy of obeying the Creation Commandments together with the Salvation (or as they are sometimes called) Redemption Commandments.

On the one hand, the Salvation Commandments exist, so to speak, for the larger purposes of the Creation Commandments. The Salvation Commandments are temporary, and direct us only in this particular phase of the great story of the Bible. For in the world to come, there will be no one to evangelize, for all who survive the Last Judgment will be, ipso facto, following Christ. Yes, we will all need to keep growing up, but our commitment to Christ will be established. The Creation Commandments, by contrast, are God's abiding will for humanity and the creation under our care—apposite in Eden, apposite after the Fall, apposite in our day, and apposite in the world to come. The Salvation Commandments were given, therefore, not to replace the Creation Commandments, but to serve them.

For to obey the Creation Commandments is, indeed, to live in the Kingdom of God. Thus Jesus' proclamation of the Kingdom is the proclamation that God is setting things right, with himself properly in the center and everyone and everything else accordingly being put in its proper place. To live in the light of the Kingdom is to live in shalom, and to seek the Kingdom is to seek a world in which the Creation Commandments are once again honored by everyone, every moment, in everything.

(It is this relationship of the Salvation Commandments to the Creation Commandments that I think best explains why the New Testament is preoccupied with

---

terrible sadness, pity for God, who chose him and relied on him to be a bearer and announcer of the divine revelation" (Lawrence Dorr, *A Bearer of Divine Revelation* [Grand Rapids, MI: Eerdmans, 2003], 97).

the latter. It is because the New Testament does indeed presume the Old, and therefore the Creation Commandments are never revoked, but rather assumed to be still in full sway. Thus the New Testament focuses upon the distinctive calling of the church and the project of redemption. The Old Testament—and, indeed, the apocalyptic passages in the New—remains as testimony to God's original, abiding, and final concern that all human beings garden the earth and thus promote and enjoy shalom.[29])

On the other hand, faithfulness to the Creation Commandments forms a vital part of our faithfulness to the Salvation Commandments. We will be better witnesses to God's work in Christ and the Kingdom he brings as we experience that Kingdom life. We will be better examples of Kingdom life as we practice it in its fullness. And we will be more effective agents of the Kingdom as our neighbors see the Kingdom life we live and are drawn, with the help of the Holy Spirit, to its impressive goodness.

Put negatively, it is a dark irony that Christian individuals and groups who narrow their understanding and practice of mission to evangelism end up less effective in that evangelism precisely because they are witnessing to, exemplifying, and acting on the basis of a truncated Gospel, an important but thin slice of Kingdom life. Indeed, evangelism can seem like a bizarre pyramid scheme in which no one gets rich: I recruit you so that you can recruit others so that they can recruit still others with the goal that everyone will be on our side—but for what? At best, it is a concern to rescue people from hell—no small matter, but how sad that the rescued now have nothing to do but rescue others, world without end. God rescues us in order to give us the amazing positive outcome of abundant life, not merely the double negative of "not hell." And Christians who believe *that*, and live accordingly, have much more to offer, and therefore will be more winsome, in their evangelism. The paradox is that we will be better evangelists precisely as we do not restrict ourselves to evangelism.

Vocation, therefore, deeply grounds and shapes our understanding of epistemology. It is time to harvest some basic principles from these considerations.

THE EPISTEMOLOGICAL IMPLICATIONS OF VOCATION

1. God has called us as humanity to make shalom—indeed, to *maximize* shalom—in the context of love for God, love for our neighbor, and love for all

---

29. David Martin notes this kind of restriction in the New Testament: "The New Testament gives us a language in which to understand and speak of redemptive sacrificial love but it has no language for just war, let alone mere warfare, unless we grossly misuse its metaphors of the sword of the spirit and the helmet of salvation. What then are we to do?" (*Christian Language in the Secular City*, 80). What we are to do is to access the whole Bible, see the Salvation Commandments in the light of the Creation Commandments, and trace out the implications for Christians who are called to obey them all—a project that I trust Martin himself would affirm (118).

creation. God therefore can be trusted to provide what we need in order to fulfill this vocation. Moreover, we can expect our fellow human beings to know what they need to know in order to continue the human work of making shalom, however compromised by sin that work has become. Thus we live in the tension of believing that human beings, and not just Christians, can practice effective medicine, or carpentry, or poetry, or politics even as we expect to see each of these pursuits marked, and to some extent warped, by evil. John Calvin, not known for his sunny view of fallen human nature, nonetheless affirms that

> the sons of Cain, though deprived of the Spirit of regeneration, were yet endued with gifts of no despicable kind; just as the experience of all ages teaches us how widely the rays of divine light have shone on unbelieving nations, for the benefit of the present life; and we see, at the present time, that the excellent gifts of the Spirit are diffused through the whole human race. Moreover, the liberal arts and sciences have descended to us from the heathen. We are, indeed, compelled to acknowledge that we have received astronomy, and the other parts of philosophy, medicines and the order of civil government, from them.[30]

2. Christ has called us as the church to make disciples throughout the world. Christ therefore can be trusted to provide what we need in order to fulfill this vocation. Moreover, we can expect our fellow Christians, even those with whom we have serious disagreements, to know what they need to know in order to continue the Christian work of making disciples. We live in the tension of believing that Christians can practice effective evangelism, or preaching, or education, or counseling even as we expect to see each of these pursuits marked, and to some extent warped, by evil.

3. Since evangelism and conversion are not only possible, but divinely mandated, we can have confidence that translation is possible, that interpersonal and cross-cultural communication can happen, and that people can actually have their minds changed for the better through serious conversation with those of even quite different views.

4. God calls particular groups of people and particular individuals to particular ways of making shalom and making disciples. Modern societies feature such diverse elements as various levels and agencies of the state, different forms of family, businesses, schools, health care facilities, churches, missionary agencies, mass entertainment and news media, and so on. These various instances of shalom-making and disciple-making have particular ways of knowing that are best suited to the fulfillment of their mission. These ways of knowing are not mutually exclusive, to be sure, but they also cannot be assumed to be the same. Rather, their ways of knowing might be expected to be at least somewhat different per their different functions.

---

30. John Calvin, *Commentaries on the First Book of Moses Called Genesis*, trans. John King (Edinburgh: Banner of Truth, 1975), 148–49.

Again, then, God can be trusted to provide these institutions and individuals distinctively what they need, including epistemically, to fulfill their callings. Moreover, these various institutions or communities can sometimes profit from appropriating alternative ways of knowing from others, as businesses can be helped to be more humane by critically considering how charities treat people, and churches can manage resources better by critically considering best business practices.

5. New occasions sometimes make new demands or provide new opportunities. Knowledge can become outdated. Ways of thinking can become outmoded. God is not surprised by anything new and can be counted on to help us respond adequately to whatever novel challenge we face. We therefore must hold both our knowledge and our ways of thinking appropriately, recognizing that as times change, we may have to change—yet we can be confident in God's provision for tomorrow epistemically every bit as much as we can pray in faith for our daily bread.

6. Some phenomena are currently, and perhaps forever, beyond our comprehension because of our inherent limitations. God can teach us some things, even reveal what we would otherwise not be capable of learning, but God cannot teach us what is beyond our (current or inherent) cognitive capacity. Like any good parent, instructor, or coach, God might well have to hold back on rendering for us the comprehensive truth of a matter in order to accommodate his teaching to our limitations.[31] As Emily Dickinson wrote:

> Tell all the Truth but tell it slant—
> Success in Circuit lies
> Too bright for our infirm Delight
> The Truth's superb surprise
>
> As Lightning to the Children eased
> With explanation kind
> The Truth must dazzle gradually
> Or every man be blind—

7. The world, and especially we, are affected by sin. Indeed, we can assume that because of the Fall, our original cognitive equipment is impaired. We believe that

---

31. Nicholas Wolterstorff grasps the nettle and writes, "It may even be that the belief-content of my authentic Christian commitment contains certain falsehood. Frequently in teaching children one tells them what is, strictly speaking, false. So also it may be that some of what God says to us is, strictly speaking, false, accommodated to our frailty. Yet it may be that we are obliged to believe it" (*Reason within the Bounds of Religion*, 2nd ed. [Grand Rapids, MI: Eerdmans, 1984 (1976)], 156). As we shall see below, John Chrysostom, Gregory of Nyssa, Thomas Aquinas, and John Calvin all agree that God accommodates revelation to our capacity such that what we are to believe is not in strict terms absolutely true, but it is what is the most helpful approximation of the truth for us to believe. John T. McNeill points out, as a key example, that Calvin eschews teaching predestination in his catechism for children (*The History and Character of Calvinism* [Oxford: Oxford University Press, 1954, 211).

God is at work to rescue us from it. Now, we might immediately infer that God will give us whatever we need to compensate for our deficiencies and so grant us infallibility, albeit via some sort of emergency provisions (such as immediate revelation from the Holy Spirit, or the clear message of Bible, or the trustworthy teaching of a human authority). But I think we would be wrong in that inference.

We must recall that God's intention toward us is to rescue us in order to transform us into all we can be. God's mission is not merely to make sure we have accurate knowledge of things. Indeed, reflection on the problem of evil has shown us that God has provided an odd kind of world that is suited to help us in our extremely mixed-up state. In such a world, straightforward analysis and straight-line inference might work well in some situations, but sometimes they might not, and might instead have to yield to intuition, paradox, or even outright mystery. For God is teaching us other things besides facts about the universe. Fundamentally, in fact, God is teaching us about himself and us, and particularly how our relationship has become so badly damaged, the peril we are in, and what must be done to remedy the situation. Furthermore, God is not merely teaching us in terms of conveying information, but in terms of training our character. And long-term training in new habits of living, especially new habits that are in some respects at cross-purposes with what was previously familiar and comforting and self-aggrandizing, might require all sorts of counter-intuitive experiences, including unexpected epistemic phenomena.

God therefore can be trusted to provide what we need in order to escape sin and embark upon new life. Such provision includes extraordinary, compensatory epistemological aid, such as revelation, the personal presence of the Holy Spirit, and the company of the Christian church. But such provision does not include resources that guarantee our infallibility.

8. Paradoxically, then, God's provision in this era of redemption might well include extended periods of ignorance of even important truths as part of an overarching scheme of global salvation. God might well allow individuals or groups even to think wrong thoughts in order to accomplish goods that can be achieved no better way. For example, I have argued elsewhere that the universal practice of patriarchy by the church—universal, that is, until modern times and with some suggestive exceptions along the way—has been condoned by God for strategic reasons. It was better for the church to conform to this outlook, even as it was softened and its effects ameliorated by Gospel principles, so that the highest concern, the spread of the Gospel, would not be held up by the social disruption that Christian feminism would have undoubtedly caused.[32]

---

32. See John G. Stackhouse, Jr., *Finally Feminist: A Pragmatic Christian Understanding of Gender* (Grand Rapids, MI: Baker Academic, 2005).

Similarly, I have become convinced that God allows individuals to think wrong thoughts in order to position them for maximum positive influence. I think of eminent scholarly colleagues whose approaches to matters of Biblical criticism or elements of doctrinal theology are, to my view, quite clearly mistaken but who would not have been awarded their positions of indubitably positive influence were they to hold to the views I think are more correct. I think of friends who accomplish enormous good as conscientious journalists among Jewish and Muslim communities who, were they to become Christian, would that moment forfeit their ability to serve in that way. I therefore wonder if God purposely delays their conversion in order to maximize shalom through them. God works wisely with what he has to work with and he understands "the way of the world" better than anyone. So I understand God to be pragmatically doing what needs to be done for the achievement of his own great purposes. For that person to be appointed to that chair at that university, he *cannot* hold to orthodox views of this or that. For this other person to be God's representative in that government agency, or military office, or executive suite, or artistic community, or activist headquarters, she has to be the sort of person *who can be welcomed into that situation*, and therefore might have to be allowed, by our shrewd, practical God, to hold views that are welcomed by those institutions but are ultimately wrong.

I recognize that this idea will startle and even offend some readers. But I ask such readers to consider the Bible heroes Joseph and Daniel. Joseph and Daniel are held up by Scripture, and in considerable biographical detail, as models of godly service and divinely appointed influence—even as types of Christ. They also, however, are depicted as using their God-given talents day by day in the smooth running of oppressive empires, respectively, the Egyptian and Babylonian. Church history is also full of ambiguous examples, whether popes using their office for good purposes that can be affirmed even by those who do not affirm papal supremacy; monks and monastic orders blessing individuals and whole regions in ways commendable even by those who question monasticism; or missionaries making concessions to the cultural norms and power structures of peoples they encounter in respects that might cause us to recoil but without which they might never have gotten a hearing. In the light of these examples, as well as the theo-logic of a properly pragmatic understanding of how God works providentially, I continue to believe that there is something important to this way of seeing things. God is concerned to advance his whole program of redemption and blessing, not merely to correct everyone's errors. And he evidently is willing to use shortcomings, blind spots, even errors for his purposes. Joseph himself consoles his brothers by reference to the pragmatics of Providence: "Even though you intended to do harm to me, God intended it for good" (Gen. 50:20).[33]

---

33. I am indebted particularly to Dietrich Bonhoeffer for this view of things. Consider, for example, this passage from his *Ethics*: "To what extent a human action serves the divine goal of history and thus actualizes good in history is something we cannot know with ultimate

9. Less scandalously, we can quite easily imagine how it serves God's good purposes to allow us, and even to prompt us, to believe things that are not strictly true. I am facing a terrifying diagnosis from my physician, and adopting an optimistic attitude (that is to say, one not truly proportionate to the information I have been provided) might well make the difference in my responding successfully to my medical challenge. You are hiking on a glacier and a crevasse opens up that must be jumped. Only a strongly positive attitude will let you summon up and concentrate your powers to make the best possible attempt at a life-saving leap—a leap that, objectively speaking, you have a very small chance of making. We in our missionary organization face a daunting financial challenge, and so we pray fervently for a solid day, thus drawing together as never before—even as God knows a check is already in the mail that will solve all our money woes.

10. We cannot, therefore, presume that practicing even the most responsible Christian epistemology guarantees epistemic success, if such success is understood in the normal sense of arriving at warranted truth. We can presume instead, however, that practicing responsible Christian thinking fulfills the will of God and thus corresponds to and cooperates with his overarching good plan for each of us and for the world. Like any other practice of the Christian life, therefore, Christian thinking is undertaken in faith that "God causes all things to work together for good to those who love God, to those who are called according to his purpose" (Rom. 8:28; NASB).[34]

---

certainty. That is left to the hidden counsel of God. . . . Those who act responsibly 'in accord with reality,' and deliver their action into God's hands, have to console themselves with faith in the forgiving and healing grace of God. They cannot prove that they are right, because living reality does not provide them with an unambiguous standard. What is more, they are faced with an even deeper and more mysterious abyss. God uses both good and evil to achieve the divine purpose, and, as far as human eyes can see, often does it in such a way that the 'good' causes harm and the 'evil' brings benefits. . . . Does this mean negating the distinction between good and evil? No, but it means that . . . the power of the divine guidance of history leaves human beings dependent on God's grace" (Dietrich Bonhoeffer, *Ethics*, ed. Clifford J. Green, trans. Reinhard Krauss, Charles C. West, and Douglas W. Stott [Minneapolis, MN: Fortress, 2005 (1949)], 378–79). I discuss Bonhoeffer's paradoxical views about God's providence at length in *Making the Best of It: Following Christ in the Real World* (New York: Oxford University Press, 2008), 115–59.

34. We thus must be careful not to overinterpret the data of our lives into a readily intelligible plotline of divine guidance. It is correct, healthy, and joyful to see our lives in terms of God's Great Story of creation, redemption, and final glory and to be expectant of God's providence over each moment of our lives as part of that Story. What we must beware, however, is the human penchant to see patterns, to make sense of things, even when we lack sufficient data, or look at the wrong data, or interpret things in a way highly advantageous to our personal agenda, and so on. Knowing the Great Story is salubrious; fitting every event of our lives into what we think is the disposition of Providence is parlous indeed.

3

Elements of the Basic Scheme

PROCEDURE

It will be obvious by now that the epistemology I will shortly present is a species of "critical realism."[1] By "realism," I mean the outlook that believes we have reliable access to reality. There is a world beyond myself, and a world beyond ourselves and our communal description of it, and that world is accessible to us.[2] It must be accessible to us, a Christian would affirm, or else we would not be able to fulfill our primary vocations. If we are to love God, we must have reliable apprehension of God.[3] If we are to love our neighbors, we must truly know them such that we can care for them aright. And if we are to cultivate the rest of our planet, we must have extensive and reliable knowledge of it. Realism is entailed by the most fundamental tenets of our religion.

---

1. By this term I do not mean the particular, and to my mind unenlightening, philosophy of Roy Bhaskar, who seems to have sought to appropriate this generic term for his own, odd epistemology.

2. I trust that experts will allow me thus to blur "realism" and "objectivism" in this way. The definition of "realism" is a vexed issue in the history of philosophy, of course, but I am trying to use it in a common and unambiguous way in this discussion.

3. In a stroke, I am parting with those who (over-)emphasize the transcendence of God, those who invoke Kierkegaard's "infinite qualitative difference" between us and God, and what we might call Barth's anti-description of God as *totaliter aliter*. On the basis of God's abundant revelation to us, we can say quite a bit about God with quite a bit of assurance. God "infinitely overflows my thin description" of him, as Kelly Clark avers, but so does a rock. Yet as I believe with some confidence that I have accurate and reliable impressions and concepts about the latter, so I do about the former as well. I daresay the *via negativa* is a useful exercise in both theology and geology, but there remain the positive findings of both disciplines, however qualified (and, to be sure, I will qualify them at length presently). Again, a *vocational* grounding for epistemology helps us avoid a popular, but nonsensical, commonplace in Christian thought. See Kelly James Clark, "Knowing the Unknowable God," *Books & Culture* 3 (September 1997): 29–30; the quotation is from p. 29.

Realists, then, have something vital to offer our bewildered neighbors. Faced with a world of competing options offered by apparently credible, even admirable, advocates, it is tempting to throw up one's hands and despair of finding out what is actually the case. Indeed, if one is thoroughly immersed in a postmodern outlook, to simply say, "I want to know the truth" triggers immediate self-doubt, even self-reproach.

Realism rebukes those who, as Pascal already warned, seek refuge in pluralism from the obligation to find the right way and live in it: "Those who do not love truth excuse themselves on the grounds that it is disputed and that very many people deny it" (*Pensée* 176). But this epistemological project obviously is not aimed at those who are trying to dodge reality so they can live as they like, but at those who are seeking to know it so they can live as they ought. Christianity offers grounds to believe that that quest is both worthy and rewarding.

Among the other tenets of the Christian religion, however, are grounds for *critical* qualification of that realism. Because we human beings are finite, we must beware of over-estimating the reliability of what we think we know. In the first place, we likely do not possess all of the pertinent data on a complex problem and we cannot know when we do possess all of the pertinent data. Tomorrow we might well find out something that changes much or all of what we think we know about a subject. Indeed, in the age of the Internet, our problem increasingly is the paradoxical whirlwind of too many data swarming across our screens and not enough data that we can trust as reliably sound. How can we know that we know what we need to know?

Secondly, we cannot be certain that our reasoning about, or our intuition regarding, the pertinent data is absolutely correct (again, in non-trivial, complex situations). Aristotle's way of thinking about physics was right in some respects, but then Newton provided better ways that corrected Aristotle. Einstein, Heisenberg, Bohr, and Planck in their turn improved upon aspects of Newton's thought. And, at least at the time of this writing, we still lack theory that brings together all of what even those four thinkers thought was true, let alone what other physicists have thought since then. Furthermore, since new discoveries and conceptualizations continue to arise in cognate fields—whether mathematics, other sciences, epistemology, or metaphysics—we cannot ever settle on a particular construal of physics as The One True Theory of Everything, despite breathless press releases from this or that scientist or laboratory. And if this finitude is true of physics, which since the Enlightenment has been the gold standard of knowledge, it is *a fortiori* true of other disciplines as well.[4]

---

4. George Steiner is trenchant on this situation in literature, and worth quoting at length:

"The arts of understanding (hermeneutics) are as manifold as their objects. Signs are unbounded: both in combinatorial modes and in potentialities of significance. There is nothing more unnerving in the human condition than the fact that we can mean and/or say *anything*.... The words which we use to elucidate or paraphrase or interpret ('translate') those of the message, of the text before us, share with that message or text a radical undecidability....

Our realism must be qualified, moreover, by appreciation of our *bias* and *interest*. We are not impersonal machines scanning the world for data and processing them according to disinterested algorithms. We tend to see things in particular ways and our minds tend to run in particular directions along particular lines of thought because of who we are and what we value. The cognitive is intrinsically connected with the affective and the moral. "I can't believe it!" is something we can exclaim not only because the proposition fails to square with our current understanding but also perhaps because it *hurts* us to acknowledge that it might be true, it at least *threatens* us in some way beyond the merely cognitive, and since we thus badly wish it weren't true, we literally have trouble believing it. As we will see again later, our senses prioritize what interests us most and our memories code experiences according to the feelings they arouse, since feelings are our most basic way of registering what matters and what doesn't, and feelings arise not only out of rational judgments but out of aesthetic, relational, and moral judgments as well.

There is nothing inherently sinister about this trait of ours to apprehend and comprehend the world in a way that furthers our interests. We, like other living things, want to survive and thrive, and our biological and cultural inheritances guide us in particular ways toward what we variously understand to be optimal living. Indeed, our various biases and interests can be positively helpful in our thinking: they prompt us to do that thinking in the first place; they incline us to pay attention to some things rather than others, things that a "neutral" or otherwise-inclined person might not examine as closely, or at all; and in some instances they equip us to interpret sympathetically a subject that someone with different prejudices would find much more difficult to understand. So long as we are willing to be "subject to the subject-matter," as David Martin puts it, so long as we are truly willing to practice *disciplined* thought such that our biases do not run roughshod over evidence and argument, we can be glad for the impetus and inclination with which our presuppositions and prejudices equip us for the task of thought.[5]

"On the other hand, the sign is encrusted, beyond lexical-grammatical definition, with phonetic, historical, social, idiomatic overtones and undertones.... Except in mathematical and logically formal notations, the semantic unit is never totally neutral or totally 'in play' (Wittgenstein's 'language games')." George Steiner, *Errata: An Examined Life* (New Haven, CT, and London: Yale University Press, 1997), 19–20; emphasis in original.

5. David Martin, *Reflections on Sociology and Theology* (Oxford: Clarendon, 1997), 90. Thomas Haskell writes of his own profession of history, in response to Peter Novick's influential book *That Noble Dream*: "Most historians, certainly the abler and more influential ones, recognize full well that fine history can be and routinely is written by politically committed scholars. Most historians just do not assign to 'neutrality' and 'disinterestedness' the inflated value that Novick suggests. Most, I think, would be aghast at the thought that historians must 'purge themselves of external loyalties' in order to do their job well. Seeing an analogy between the role of the judge and that of the historian does not imply any overestimation of the value of neutrality: judges, like historians, are expected to be open to rational persuasion, not to be indifferent about the great issues of their day or—bizarre thought—to abstain from judgment.... The demand is for detachment and fairness, not disengagement from life" ("Objectivity Is Not Neutrality: Rhetoric versus Practice in Peter Novick's *That Noble Dream*," chap. in *Objectivity Is*

Thus the specification of our finitude includes not only generic human limitations but also the particular boundaries and motivations evident in some people and not in others. Some of us find geology fascinating while others stare blankly at a bunch of rocks; some of us find psychology empowering while others recoil at the touchy-feely stuff; and some of us find theology illuminating while others scoff at what sounds like mumbo-jumbo. Some of us, moreover, want to advance the cause of a particular group of people, or protect a particular part of the natural world, or emphasize a particular aspect of the spiritual life. All of these pre-understandings and motives both limit us and equip us to engage in knowledge-making of a particular sort. "It's a good thing he cares so much about that detail of the Civil War, or butterfly anatomy, or justice for native peoples, or customer relations else we would never have learned...."

Beyond these various aspects of finitude, then, is the dimension of *fallenness*. We are not just interested, but wickedly interested, in some things more than others. We seek the welfare of those we like at the expense of those we don't, and we relish both the triumphs of our kind and the miseries of the "others." We have a taste for, even a compulsion toward, what even we ourselves recognize as evil. Epistemically this fact of our fallenness means, as we shall detail below, that we are inclined in certain respects both to perceive things wrongly and to process what we perceive wrongly as well.

Because of our finitude and fallenness, furthermore, we are necessarily dependent upon God, and in at least three ways relevant to epistemology. First, we rely on God for the "stuff" we apprehend and comprehend. This category of course includes the physical world and the world of human consciousness, but also special revelation God has added to supplement what we learn from the created order itself: visions, prophecies, miracles, inspired scriptures, and pre-eminently the person and career of Jesus Christ. What God chooses not to reveal, we do not know.[6]

Not Neutrality: Explanatory Schemes in History [Baltimore: Johns Hopkins University Press, 1998], 155).

6. Theologians might note that I have just skimmed over two massive categories: general and special revelation. In this epistemology, I am, as it were, widening the category of revelation to include *everything* we know, since without God showing it to us in his providential ordering of the world and of us, no knowing would be going on.

I am also widening the typical limits of special revelation. Typically, systematic theology has pointed especially to the Bible and to Jesus as the key events of special revelation. These are revelations not generally available, but specially available in just this document and just this person. I follow that tradition in privileging the Scripture and, even more, Jesus himself.

Special revelation, however, if it is defined simply as "revelation that is not generally available but made available on this occasion to this audience," takes in much more. Prophecy, whether in the Old Testament, New Testament, or Christian church to the present, counts as special revelation. God speaks directly and specifically to a particular audience in such communication. The Roman Catholic Church (albeit with various interpretations within it) has viewed Tradition as also a deposit of the Holy Spirit's special revelation. If Protestants disagree with that lofty estimation, what do we make instead of the history of doctrine, of liturgy, of Christian thought and life in general? Did God offer special revelation through the Nicene Creed, or the *solas* of the magisterial Reformation, or the piety of eighteenth century revivals, or the rise of

Second, we rely on God for our epistemic functioning, finite and fallen as we are. God supplements the epistemic abilities with which we were created by providing us with ongoing guidance, whether we are Christian or not, to help us understand and live properly in the world God created and of which he put us in charge. For all analytical insight, all creativity, and all wisdom comes from one Source, whether or not we happen to acknowledge that fountain of all goodness.

Third, we rely on God's provisioning us to fulfill our literally globe-spanning work with a world-encompassing view of things. In an age, that is, of almost inconceivable specialization of sciences and diversities of outlooks, we nonetheless can trust that God will help us find ways for human beings to cooperate with each other, including, of course, communication across disciplinary and cultural boundaries. We need not expect any final, comprehensive, and coherent worldview with a place for everything and everything in its place. But we do need to expect enough coherence across the board that we can cooperate in our work of making shalom. A vocational approach to epistemology, then, helps us ground one of the leading aspirations of our era of amazing and frightening pluralism: to overcome the results of Babel at least enough to build a life together, to seek the common good in global flourishing.[7]

In what follows, we will survey yet more ways in which we are dependent upon God epistemically. For now, at least, I trust it is clear how serious our qualifications must be of our claims to epistemic realism, even as we are clear that being "critical" does not mean being "skeptical." We do still believe—even as we acknowledge problems with our beliefs, our way of believing, the consistency of our believing,

---

Pentecostalism? It is hard to know where to draw the line here if we believe God truly led these divines to at least some important approximation of theological truth.

We might consider also the Holy Spirit's work of personal conviction of sin and offer of salvation through Christ. Is this special revelation? It certainly amounts to such for the individual involved. Some theologians might demur, pointing out that there is no new content being delivered here that hasn't been delivered already through the Bible. But does this response overemphasize propositional revelation, rather than focusing on the *actual operation*? What alternative category shall we use for what seems to be indeed a new work of revelation by which God shows an individual spiritual truth she did not apprehend before?

The ongoing personal guidance of Christians similarly belongs in this discussion. Evangelicals particularly are inclined to celebrate God's direction in their lives, and to testify to many occasions in which God moved them this way or that—whether as individuals or as groups. Does this count as special revelation? If it does, then perhaps we now recognize a quite broad category of special revelation by which the Holy Spirit reveals quite a lot of things to quite a lot of people, rather than restricting his activity to illuminating the Bible about the gospel of Jesus Christ—as some evangelical construals would have it.

My approach in this epistemology so rests *everything* we think we know on the providence of God that I find the categories of general and special revelation of limited use in this discourse. So that is why they do not appear. But, I assure the reader, I do not intend to blur any distinction or reduce any dignity accorded to the Bible as the Word of God written or, supremely, to our Lord Jesus as the Word of God incarnate.

7. Two very different sorts of aspiration in this direction emerged in the same year from authors of global significance: Hans Küng, *A Global Ethic for Global Politics and Economics* (Oxford: Oxford University Press, 1998); and Edward O. Wilson, *Consilience: The Unity of Knowledge* (New York: Knopf, 1998).

our behavior relative to our beliefs, and so on. We are not holding *everything* at arm's length, refusing to commit to any belief, much less a Big Story, out of skeptical fear of being bamboozled or, much worse, being co-opted into someone else's oppressive regime. No, we can be *convinced* and *committed* in our believing even as we remain *critical*—by which I simply mean intellectually both honest and humble.[8]

Since we do therefore acknowledge such qualifications, we must test this epistemological model as we test all intellectual proposals. Do the various elements of it combine into an orderly whole? Do its constituent claims find adequate grounding in the world as we know it? Does it equip us to negotiate reality effectively? And does it cover everything that needs to be covered without unnecessary complications? In sum, we will judge the model by the standard criteria of coherence, correspondence, pragmatic value, comprehensiveness, and parsimony. We will do so, moreover, with some appreciation for whatever intuitive appeal it may make to us, and particularly to whatever elegance it may present.

We will also be wary, however, of each of these values. Coherence can be won at the cost of excluding inconvenient truths, anomalies, outliers. We tend to see patterns where none exist, causal relationships that are merely correlations, narratives that are no more than coincidences. We can hardly do without considering correspondence, but correspondence to which data, gathered how, excluding what, according to which method and methodology, interpreted within what theory, furthering whose agenda/interests/concerns? The criterion of pragmatic value immediately raises suspicions as to how this knowledge helps whom to do what to what or whom, and thus whether this knowledge is "valuable" for all concerned or instead oppressive for some and cynically legitimizing for others. The criteria of comprehensiveness and parsimony can themselves be value-laden, as the question of "enough" is often a matter of "enough for whom in order to think or do what?" Intuitive appeal is obviously subjective in the most basic sense, depending entirely on the values and abilities of the person doing the intuiting. What might seem intuitively obvious to a philanthropist might not seem so to a loan shark, and what might impress a mechanical engineer might leave a dancer or a chef entirely unmoved. Finally, even the criterion of elegance, touted so often in modern physics especially as a clue to truth, must be kept at arm's length.[9] For physics itself was retarded

---

8. I am grateful to an essay by Brian Leftow that prompted me to make this distinction clear between "critical" and "skeptical": "From Jerusalem to Athens," in *God and the Philosophers: The Reconciliation of Faith and Reason*, ed. Thomas V. Morris (New York: Oxford University Press, 1994), 197. And for a suggestive and perceptive wrestling by a Christian critical realist with two more postmodernly skeptical Christian counterparts, see Peter Payne, "A Review Essay of J. Richard Middleton and Brian J. Walsh's "Truth Is Stranger than It Used to Be," *Religious and Theological Students Fellowship Bulletin* 13 (November 1996): 16–25.

9. In what is often cited as a classic modern statement of the epistemological value of beauty, Paul Dirac concludes his survey of twentieth-century physics thus: "There is a moral to this story, namely, that it is more important to have beauty in one's equations than to have them fit experiment. . . . It seems that if one is working from the point of view of getting beauty in one's equations, and if one has really a sound insight, one is on a sure line of progress" (P. A. M. Dirac, "The Evolution of the Physicist's Picture of Nature," *Scientific American* (May 1963): 47. To be sure,

for centuries by just such a value, as the orbits of the planets were presumed to be perfectly (= elegantly) circular (Galileo was notoriously stubborn on this point), as pleasing musical intervals were presumed to be simple fractions (Galileo's father, Vincenzo, as it happens, wrote an iconoclastic work on lute-tuning), and so on.[10] Elegance too often amounts to saying, "This is the way the world *ought* to be" rather than "This is the way the world actually seems to be."[11] As David Berlinski says, "If it is beauty that governs the mathematician's soul, it is truth and certainty that remind him of his duty."[12]

With these caveats in mind, we will deploy these criteria as the best we have, acknowledged across cultures and centuries as reasonably reliable indications of where the truth lies. We turn, then, to the scheme itself.

A SKETCH OF THE MODEL

Human beings have five resources upon which to draw in our thinking. Experience is obviously the first one that comes to mind: our sense experiences, of course; the

---

Dirac means a very particular kind of beauty here: the beauty of the well-formed mathematical equation, and *not* the beauty of the vivid and coherent mental image of the phenomena in question. For later in this article Dirac scoffs at "the philosopher" for "wanting to have a satisfying description of nature" by way of "a consistent picture" versus "the physicist" who has "all he needs" if he "knows how to calculate results and compare them with experiment" (48). It seems, then, that Dirac is confident that the world is such a beautifully ordered place that elegant theories will, if founded on genuine insight (= grasp of reality), coincide with experimental results. The Christian, who believes in such a universe, can reply, "*Bien sûr*, Monsieur Dirac!" But to simplify Dirac's views, as so many do, to a championing of beautiful theory *over* rigorous experiment is to simplify much too much. For a more recent championing of elegance along similar lines (so to speak), see Brian Greene, *The Elegant Universe: Superstrings, Hidden Dimensions, and the Quest for the Ultimate Theory* 2nd ed. (New York: W. W. Norton, 2003 [1999]).

10. T. F. Torrance, among others, observes that the sacramental view of the world so characteristic of the medieval mind retarded the emergence of scientific thinking in its expectation that the natural world would reflect aesthetic and spiritual norms derived from theology and philosophy. See T. F. Torrance, *Theological Science* (Edinburgh: T. & T. Clark, 1996); and Carolly Erickson, *The Medieval Vision: Essays in History and Perception* (New York: Oxford University Press, 1976). Mark Noll warns modern American evangelicals that they are anti-intellectual in a curiously similar way: they, too, tend to discuss the world merely by expositing sacred texts—in their case, the Bible—and pronouncing about the way the world *must* be rather than looking *directly at the world*. See Mark A. Noll, *The Scandal of the Evangelical Mind* (Grand Rapids, MI: Eerdmans, 1994).

11. Michael Polanyi rehabilitates this kind of language, at least in part, by recognizing its special meaning in terms of corresponding to the underlying logic or structure of the cosmos. Such words as "simplicity," "symmetry," and "economy," Polanyi writes (and, I am adding, "elegance"), "are contributing elements in the excellence of a theory, but can account for its merit only if the meanings of these terms are stretched far beyond their usual scope, so as to include the much deeper qualities ... [,] those peculiar intellectual harmonies which reveal, more profoundly and permanently than any sense-experience, the presence of objective truth" (Michael Polanyi, *Personal Knowledge: Towards a Post-Critical Philosophy* [Chicago: University of Chicago Press, 1958], 16). Polanyi famously extends this aesthetic dimension of knowledge in his advocacy of the term "connoisseurship" in scientific work (*Personal Knowledge*, 54–55).

12. David Berlinski, "Iterations of Immortality," *Harper's* 300 (January 2000): 15–16.

experience of our own interior life (*cogito*); experiences of other persons or entities and perhaps extra dimensions of our cosmos or other realms entirely; and the experiences of others—or, more precisely, accounts of those experiences. Indeed, particular versions of others' experiences and reflections come to us in three additional resources: (1) tradition—what a community judges to be worth passing on to newcomers (what happens to survive might be *mistaken* for tradition, but all would agree that it ought not to be so); (2) the findings of the various intellectual disciplines, sciences, *Wissenschaften*: from physics to philology, from chemistry to cosmology, and from fractal geometry to French literary theory; and (3) art, whether novels, sculptures, costumes, dances, architectural blueprints, or string quartets. To these generic human resources the Christian adds the category of Scripture, the Bible understood as a literary compendium in which God communicates to us authoritatively in a way God does not through any other medium.

Each of these resources deserves description in some detail. That description will be more intelligible, however, if it is undertaken within a sketch of the rest of the model.

We typically draw on these five resources—or whichever of them we believe will be pertinent to a given subject—by way of three modes of apprehension and consideration: reason, intuition, and imagination. We will devote considerable attention not only to defining these three modes but also to defining their interaction—imagination, for example, providing reason with a number of possible alternative explanations among which it can select as the most likely. We then will consider some of the implications of the fact that we only ever have our own particular *apprehensions* and *interpretations* of these resources to work with in these three modes, a consideration that reminds us of how intensely subjective our thinking must be.

That subjectivity, moreover, is determined to a considerable extent by the social contexts in which we have lived and now do live. Each of us has been marked and shaped and motivated by the various groups we have inhabited since birth. We will see how social contexts both limit us and also offer a measure of liberation from our limitations.

Alas, our limitations include moral twistedness with epistemic ramifications. So we must get clear just how we tend to see what we want to see and believe what we want to believe—and how what we want has been affected by sin such that we are cognitively impaired, not just limited. We then will examine Christian remedies to this spiritual debility and its epistemological implications.

Finally, we shall consider the work of Christian thinking once more within the overarching context of our twofold vocation of cooperating with God's mission of redeeming the world while continuing to ply our generic human trade, so to speak, of cultivating shalom. We will see that each of us is called to practice responsible Christian thinking with vigor and rigor, but that the shape of that practice will vary according to our particular vocations—thus laying no unrealistic expectations on anyone, but calling everyone to the full and proper use of his or her God-given resources according to the challenges of his or her mission in life.

FIVE RESOURCES

Experience

We need not linger over the obvious categories of experience—sense experiences, memories, awareness of one's own consciousness, and so on—except to make a couple of basic observations.

First, as common sense tells us, our apprehension of the world via these resources seems generally reliable, but occasionally not—and the unreliability seems to increase as our experience varies from the quotidian. Ordinarily, that is, our senses, memory, self-consciousness, and so on provide us with information by which to steer our lives happily enough. But, as Ebenezer Scrooge noted, even "a little thing can make them cheat." The cause of confusion might indeed be an upset stomach that brings on bad dreams. But it can be something much milder and yet also equally delusional.

I scan a crowd of arriving airplane passengers in search of my beloved and make a series of false, momentary identifications as wish-fulfillment dominates my brain's face-recognition. Finally, however, we are reunited, and I am sure I parked the car on the second level as I always do, only to find it eventually on the third—oh, yes, I remember now: the second level was uncharacteristically full and I was thinking only of your imminent arrival so I didn't pay full attention to where I parked. Anyway, now that we're finally together every single thing you say is witty and delightful and I also seem to be much more amusing than usual....

It's one illusion—or, at least, one partly illusory experience—after another. Thomas Kuhn points to an even more radical qualification of sense experience:

> Much neural processing takes place between the receipt of a stimulus and the awareness of a sensation. Among the few things that we know about it with assurance are: that the same stimulus can produce very different sensations; and, finally, that the route from stimulus to sensation is in part conditioned by education. Individuals raised in different societies behave on some occasion as though they saw different things... [and thus] *in some sense* live in different worlds.[13]

We can all think of examples in which our experience becomes less reliably intelligible: extreme weather, painful illness, severe frustration, imminent danger, the prospect of great success, and so on. We will return in the last chapter to this crucial question of the qualification of our interpretation of experience. For now, we can observe simply that as a matter of course we both trust our interpretations of experience and yet at times also mistrust them, depending on either evidence that we are misunderstanding this particular sensation or awareness that we are in an

---

13. Thomas S. Kuhn, *The Structure of Scientific Revolutions*, 2nd ed. (Chicago: University of Chicago Press, 1970 [1962]), 192–93; emphasis in original.

extraordinary situation and should therefore interpret some or all sensations more carefully than usual.

Second, it is curious to note that contemporary philosophers are agreed that none of these experiential resources can be validated noncircularly. One cannot verify sense experience without in some key way assuming the validity of sense experience. The same is true of memory beliefs, belief in other minds, and so on. One goes back through cultural history from popular movies ("Inception," "The Matrix," "Total Recall") to contemporary analytical philosophy's "mad scientist" trope of a "brain in a vat," to René Descartes's postulation of an "evil demon" prompting us to illusory impressions of the world, to Zhuang-zi's wondering whether he was a man dreaming he is a butterfly or a butterfly dreaming he is a man.

It is crucial to recognize that we are not dealing with a simple matter of acknowledging the obvious. As Stephen Davis says, when we encounter our friend Smith "we simply do not bother to worry about the logical possibility that last night Smith died and that God decided to create, simultaneously and through the same causal processes, two equal Smith duplicates, one of which, say, is here before me . . . and the other of which is in hiding in Paraguay."[14] We are dealing with epistemic doubt up and down the register. There is no way for us to escape ourselves, so to speak, to validate even these most fundamental of connections to the world beyond our consciousness. Again, we find that we are in the position of having to trust them without being able to establish with some sort of objective certainty that they are in fact reliable.[15]

On the vocational basis of this model, however, we have grounds to trust our experience as generally reliable. For we could not successfully care for each

---

14. Stephen T. Davis, *Risen Indeed: Making Sense of the Resurrection* (Grand Rapids, MI: Eerdmans, 1993), 146.

15. Alvin Plantinga is much bolder than I on this point, averring that even *God* cannot transcend himself to analyze the reliability of his belief-forming mechanisms. Let us heed particularly, however, the robust good sense (one is tempted, in the light of Plantinga's affinity for Thomas Reid, to say "common sense") in his concluding sentence:

> "Not even God himself, necessarily omniscient as he is, can give a noncircular argument for the reliability of his ways of forming beliefs. God himself is trapped inside the circle of his own ideas. About all we can say about God's ways of forming beliefs is that it is necessary, in the broadly logical sense, that a proposition *p* is true if and only if God believes *p*. Of course God knows that and knows, therefore, that all of his beliefs are true. However (naturally enough), he knows this only by virtue of relying on his ways of forming beliefs. If, *per impossibile*, he became a bit apprehensive about the reliability of those ways of forming beliefs, he would be in the same boat as we are about that question. He couldn't give an epistemically noncircular argument for the reliability of his ways of forming beliefs; for the beliefs constituting the premises of any such argument would themselves have been formed in those ways. But any epistemic debility that afflicts a necessarily omniscient being is hardly worth worrying about" (Alvin Plantinga, *Warranted Christian Belief* [New York: Oxford University Press, 2000], 125).

For support from a quite different quarter, see Thomas Nagel, *The Last Word* (New York: Oxford University Press, 1997).

other and the world without a generally reliable apprehension of, yes, each other and the world. The main argument posed by many realists against radical skeptics is the multifold validity of science and technology. Our ability to describe nature such that we can predict what will happen (from solar eclipses to subatomic events) and our related ability to devise ways to interact with nature such that we get the results we predict and prefer (from skyscrapers to nanobots) are best explained by a realist epistemology: we are perceiving what's there. *Mutatis mutandis*, we interact with each other, on scales small and large, and the success of those interactions (we do seem to understand each other's messages; we do seem to cooperate productively on matters of common interest) is best explained, again, by a realist epistemology.

Basic components of a Theory of Everything in cosmic physics, however, are still conceptually up for grabs, from dark energy and dark matter to strings and superstrings. Even if we are not familiar with current cosmology, furthermore, no one needs to tell us that our technologies don't always work and that sometimes they do "work" but in weird and unpredictably unhelpful ways.

More troubling, to be sure, is the research that shows how routinely we misinterpret the world. Most troubling of all is the recent finding that vast amounts of medical research—not the gold, but the platinum, standard of research, since it deals with the most obviously significant of scientific research fields—is not only unverified, but demonstrably wrong. We will detail this research in the last chapter, but for now, the immediate lesson is clear: If our top scientific minds can make huge mistakes in interpreting experience, then so can I.

Our sense of vocation therefore justifies trusting our interpretation of experience, for without reasonably reliable interpretations we can't get out of bed, let alone be and do what God intends for us to be and do. The doctrine of vocation also reminds us, however, that we can trust God to provide for us *only* the knowledge we need to fulfill our particular callings, and that this knowledge thus must be understood in a highly qualified way, subject always to amplification, correction, or even replacement. Therefore we must hold this knowledge humbly, open-handedly, before each other and especially before God.

We also must hold all sorts of experiences gratefully. Beverly Wildung Harrison reminds us, and particularly readers of academic books, that

all our knowledge, including our moral knowledge, is body-mediated knowledge. All knowledge is rooted in our sensuality. We know and value the world, *if* we know and value it, through our ability to touch, to hear, to see. *Perception* is foundational to *conception*. Ideas are dependent on our sensuality.... When we cannot feel, literally, we lose our connectedness to the world.... If feeling is damaged or cut off, our power to image the world and act into it is destroyed and our rationality is impaired. But it is not merely the power to conceive the world that is lost. Our power to value the world gives way as well. If we are not perceptive in discerning our feelings, or if we do not know what we feel, we cannot be effective moral agents.... In the absence of feeling there is no rational ability to evaluate what is happening.... Many people live so much in their heads that they no longer feel their connectedness to other living things.[16]

The Nazi bureaucrat in his office consigning masses to their deaths via his typewriter and pen is on a continuum with politicians behind closed doors and church or academic committees in small rooms sensorily cut off from those most affected by their decisions. Such sense-deprivation chambers serve to render them as unempathetic as any sociopath, as any late-night Internet flamer staring at his screen as his fingers fly to punish a real human being who is present to his consciousness as only an acrid wisp of infuriating text. A brief walk in the park to smell the flowers won't in itself cure what's wrong with us, of course. Some of the Nazi leaders were notoriously fond of music, painting, and scenery. But reduced contact with, and interest in, the sensual experiences of life cannot help but reduce our field of perception, and therefore cannot help but reduce the accuracy, power, and faithfulness of our thinking in at least some crucial respects.

Indeed, science itself was held back by the Greek preference for deductive reasoning. Yes, they realized, inductive reasoning was, at its best, probabilistic. For real knowledge of the way things indubitably are, inference from axioms is the way to go. Alas, they thus enthroned science in an armchair rather than sending it out into the field. Only when the world failed to act quite the way Aristotle ruled it must act did science shed its quest for logical certainty in the hope of at least not being wildly wrong (as Aristotle was too often) and gaining at least an approximate grasp of reality.[17]

Christians, and people of certain other outlooks, report other kinds of experiences: mystical experiences. Such experiences vary in specificity from a fleeting feeling that the world of the five senses and self-awareness (if we bundle together under that heading self-consciousness, memory, beliefs, and so on) is not all there

---

16. Beverly Wildung Harrison, "The Power of Anger in the Work of Love: Christian Ethics for Women and Other Strangers," chap. in *Feminist Theology: A Reader*, ed. Ann Loades (London: SPCK and Louisville, KY: Westminster/John Knox, 1990), 205.

17. Students of intellectual history will see at once that I am radically reducing an extremely complex and contested story into a single paragraph. Still, I think that's basically what happened, and so do lots of people more informed and insightful than I. For a pithy and sprightly introduction to these questions, see Loren Wilkinson, "Cheeses, Chartreuse, Owls, and a Synchrotron: Some Thoughts from France on Science and Taste," *Crux* 42 (Spring 2006): 9–16. I am indebted to more extended introductions to these questions, of course, and they appear throughout the notes to this book. In addition to those, see the following: Herbert Butterfield, *The Origins of Modern Science, 1300–1800* (Toronto and Vancouver: Clarke, Irwin, 1977); Toby E. Huff, *The Rise of Early Modern Science: Islam, China and the West*, 2nd ed. (Cambridge: Cambridge University Press, 2003 [1993]); Huff, *Early Modern Science, Intellectual Curiosity and the Scientific Revolution: A Global Perspective* (Cambridge: Cambridge University Press, 2010); Eugene M. Klaaren, *Religious Origins of Modern Science: Belief in Creation in Seventeenth-Century Thought* (Grand Rapids, MI: Eerdmans, 1977); David C. Lindberg and Ronald L. Numbers, eds., *God and Nature: Historical Essays on the Encounter between Christianity and Science* (Berkeley: University of California Press, 1986); and Alfred North Whitehead, *Science and the Modern World* (New York: Free Press, 1925).

is to the cosmos, that there is Something More, to an unforgettable encounter with a particular deity, replete with parallels to experiences of one or more of the five senses and a verbal communication of some sort.

More particularly, Christians believe that we need the Holy Spirit of God to both show us and convince us that the Bible is not just a collection of ancient religious writings but also the very Word of God; that Jesus is not just a more-or-less respectable rabbi but the very Incarnation of God; that the Gospel message is not just one of the world's many religious teachings but the very truth of God's plan of salvation; and so on. Experiences of God's Spirit, that is, are required to cross what is otherwise an unbridgeable gap between the extant evidence and our current reasoning abilities, on one side, and the great truths of the Christian faith on the other.[18] You can't get there from here: There are no arguments available to bring someone to the conclusions necessary to embrace the Christian religion—about the Bible, about Jesus, about salvation, and the rest. Leaving aside for the moment the vexed question of the noetic effects of sin, these tenets are simply too wonder-full, too strange, and too beyond our normal experiences to be inferred in the normal modes of reasoning from the available evidence. No, they must be *shown* or, as theologians prefer to say, *revealed*. As Jesus once said to Peter, who came to the shocking conclusion that his Master was the Messiah rather than simply an extraordinary prophet, "Blessed are you, Simon son of Jonah! For flesh and blood has not revealed this to you, but my Father in heaven" (Matt. 16:16).[19]

Philosophers, social scientists, and medical researchers join the rest of us in wondering about the epistemic value of such experiences. Are reports of such experiences reports merely about states of mind—that is, reports about the psychological condition of the person or group having them—or are they reports (also) about the cosmos, the way Columbus's reports about discovering new lands were, despite his evident confusion about just what he experienced (the Indies? the Americas?) referring to something actual outside his own head?[20]

---

18. Calvin's classic statement on this matter reads, in part, as follows: "Those whom the Holy Spirit has inwardly taught truly rest upon Scripture, and that Scripture indeed is self-authenticated; hence, it is not right to subject it to proof and reasoning. And the certainty it deserves with us, it attains by the testimony of the Spirit.... Therefore, illumined by his power, we believe neither by our own nor by anyone else's judgment that Scripture is from God; but above human judgment we affirm with utter certainty (*just as if we were gazing upon the majesty of God himself*) that it has flowed to us from the very mouth of God by the ministry of men....

"Such, then, is.... a feeling that can be born only of heavenly revelation. I speak of nothing other than what each believer experiences within himself—though my words fall far beneath a just explanation of the matter" (*Institutes* I.vii.5; emphasis added).

19. For contemporary epistemological reflections on the work of the Holy Spirit, see Alvin Plantinga, *Warranted Christian Belief*, 244–52, 258–66, 284–89.

20. For a concise statement of philosophical incredulity of the epistemic value of religious experience with an attempt to validate it as nonetheless inspiring to virtue—a condescending approach to religion that evokes Voltaire's cynical erection of a chapel so that his estate workers would remain docile—see John D. Caputo, "On Being Clear about Faith," *Books & Culture*

Extra-sensory perception, premonition, and telepathy are modern categories of such experiences while visions, dreams, inclinations, "words of knowledge," "burnings in the bosom," and the like are phrases from religious traditions—but they all raise the question of whether in fact some human beings, at some time or times, have had experiences beyond what we secularized moderns would call the mundane, the cosmos of the physical senses plus self-awareness. Scientists have announced that they can stimulate the brain so as to produce experiences typically categorized as religious, from a general sense of the transcendent looming over the world to visions of general phenomena such as lights, tunnels, and so on. To date, so far as I know, none of these researchers have prompted someone to envision Krishna or Jesus or some other quite particular and recognizable deity. The experiences remain only suggestive in their abstraction. And the claims of such scientists, while interesting, do not in fact speak to our question. For artificially inducing the taste of almonds or licorice by applying electricity to the correct region of the brain says nothing about whether there are in fact almonds or licorice whips in existence and whether some human beings are reliably reporting experiences of them.

Perhaps no one has done more to rehabilitate the epistemic status of mystical religious experience than the late William Alston. In a range of published work, culminating particularly in his groundbreaking study *Perceiving God*, Alston argued that mystical perception is indeed entitled to the status of being considered a genuine avenue to truth (he calls it a "full-fledged perceptual doxastic practice").[21] Mystical perception, Alston avers, is remarkably parallel to sense experience and ought to be conceived of in a similar scheme: the appropriate epistemic faculty considers appropriate data using the appropriate practice and thereby comes to appropriate conclusions. Like sense experience, reports of mystical experience are properly subject to reasonable doubt and must submit to appropriate lines of rational questioning. If it can repel these possible "defeaters" and, indeed, produce some significant self-support, it ought to be taken seriously.

Also like sense experience, however, there is no non-circular way to argue for the reliability of mystical experience. Moreover, if one approaches reports of mystical experience from a worldview closed to the very idea that there is anything "there" of which to have experiences, or to the idea that human beings could possibly have any such faculty to perceive phenomena beyond the five physical senses and self-awareness, then there is no categorical argument to be offered in return—as there never is to closed-minded skepticism. One *might* be hallucinating; one *might* be troubled by an evil demon; one *might* be trapped in "The Matrix"; one *might* be a butterfly dreaming he is a man. But to those who are at least theoretically open to the existence of phenomena in the cosmos other than those perceived by the five senses

(November 2006): 40–42. A more extended treatment is his *The Weakness of God: A Theology of the Event* (Bloomington: Indiana University Press, 2006).

21. William P. Alston, *Perceiving God: The Epistemology of Religious Experience* (Ithaca, NY: Cornell University Press, 1991), 7.

and self-awareness, then appropriate tests can be run—and are indeed run by sensible believers—to distinguish between genuine apprehensions of divine phenomena versus the products of wishful thinking, delusion, psychosis, brain injury, deception by a third party, "groupthink," and so on.

Such tests would include the tests one would apply to judge the veracity of any other experience, including sense experience: analysis of the situation in which one had the experience to estimate the extent to which it would conduce toward clarity versus confusion; analysis of oneself—one's mental and physical health, one's expectations and fears, one's training in interpreting that particular genus of experience—in sum, one's ability to interpret the kind of experience one had; corroboration by others who are equipped and positioned to hold a pertinent opinion; coherence with other things one holds to be true; the existence of corroborating physical evidence (a security camera happens to record something relevant; a piece of cloth in the vicinity undergoes a change consistent with the experience); and so on.[22]

The irony of Alston's meticulous work is that it, in effect, de-mystifies mystical experience as it renders such experience both plausible and, to a considerable extent, criticizable. It re-locates mystical experience from some borderland where it is defended by zealots as infallible while being generally ignored by the majority to a central position alongside other, more generally accepted forms of knowledge that are (also) well attested across the globe and capable of subjection to rational interrogation.

This discussion of how one's own experience might be tested at least in part by reference to others' experiences reminds us of an avenue to knowledge leading in the other direction. We have our own experiences to consider, yes, but also those of other people. To be sure, one never has access to someone else's experience per se, but only to an account of that experience. Yet while other people's interpretations of their experiences can be illuminating, especially if such people are unusually wise or possess unusual gifts of vivid rendition, we can go beyond their interpretations to consider the experiences themselves. For experiences are not always and completely imprisoned in the interpretations by which they are related to others. It is a common experience, in fact, that someone can have an experience and relate it to someone else who may then interpret it quite differently. Indeed, it even happens that the first person comes around to agreeing with the second person's interpretation: "Oh, I see now. Yes, you're right: that is probably what happened, not what I was thinking."

The corrigibility of interpretations of experience, and particularly of mystical experience, is thus crucial to a healthy, responsible, humble, and confident mode of Christian thinking. Christians cannot be Christians without being open to mystical

---

22. The classic work of discerning valid spiritual experience from mere "enthusiasm" is Jonathan Edwards, *Religious Affections*, ed. John E. Smith (New Haven, CT: Yale University Press, 1959 [1746]).

experience. What Christian would want to be closed to it? But the radical cognitive style of mysticism I discussed earlier is hereby disqualified as indeed radical, cutting back to the root of experience and laying waste in the process other good resources God provides to both test the provenance of an experience and our interpretation of it. We can gratefully receive all sorts of experiences from the hand of the God who calls us and leads us in fulfilling our callings while we must use our God-given resources to ascertain just what experiences we are having, their validity, and their genuine implications.

Tradition

We recall that the word "tradition" comes from the Latin word *traditio*, which is the process of "handing over." We can identify negative, neutral, and positive senses to this term for our purposes. The dark side of the word connects with the word "traitor," one who hands over treasures or secrets or simply his allegiance to an enemy. The (neutral) core of the word describes just whatever is "handed over" from one generation to the next, from insiders to newcomers, from superiors to inferiors, as in "this is (just) a tradition of the team/company/neighborhood." And the bright side of the word has to do with the best, most prized and significant elements of an organization or community being shared with and entrusted to those who will carry on its life.

The modern Christian thinker typically is the recipient therefore of a wide range of traditions, because she inhabits a wide range of groups each of which has a tradition that she is expected to willingly receive and in which she is expected to fully participate.

One thus ends up with a lot of laundry to do. How so? If we consider how clothing is dictated by the tradition of an institution, and if we consider how different some institutions are from others in our lives, then we go literally through a lot of clothes: suits for this, jeans for that, sportswear here, loungewear there. And just as we change our clothes to fit the tradition of our next appointment, we adjust our cognitive style and our values as well, as we have previously noted. We become different versions of ourselves in order to fit best into this or that culture.

The worrisome challenge here, of course, is that we will take on traditions in which we do not truly believe and to which we ought not to subscribe. Yet the overarching, interlocking, and mutually confirming traditions of a place can so constrain and reassure us that we can unthinkingly be implicated in quite anti-Christian thought and action. It all seems so plausible when I'm at work that the single most important thing in life is the stability and prosperity of the company. It just seems right when I'm at the gym to assess people by the beauty and performance of their bodies. Of course, mere worldly things mean nothing to me when I'm gazing up at the Cross during hymn-singing in church on Sunday morning.

So tradition must be scrutinized as must any other aspect of life in order to determine what is truly conducive to shalom-making and what is off-kilter but still useful, what is seriously compromised but still the least-bad option, and what must be avoided as simply evil no matter how attractive it appears. Moreover, what is true of traditions throughout the various sectors of contemporary life is true also of tradition in the church. "We've always done it this way" is easy enough to scorn as an insufficient justification for a practice one doesn't like, but one would be foolish to underestimate the power many traditions carry because they do, in fact, manifest the basic culture of an institution or community even as they carry the inertia of customary use. Much of what is done according to tradition is done not out of slavish, mindless conformity to the past which a mere word of clarity will dispel, but out of a genuine satisfaction, for better or for worse, with the way things are, to which any question, let alone challenge, is to be repelled as a threat. Indeed, those who are currently in positions of authority, power, comfort, and esteem are *ipso facto* those who have benefitted most from the system as it is, and particularly from everyone observing tradition, so they are unlikely to countenance anything that might alter the system that has rewarded them. Not only the leaders, however, but everyone who is invested in the community will naturally look askance at whatever threatens to disturb its smooth continuance.

The thinking person nonetheless must recognize tensions among the various traditions and cultures she encounters—she can't give them all the money and time and attention and devotion they prefer her to give. She must critique this or that aspect of tradition in this or that situation as unhealthy, even counterproductive to the express purposes of that culture, as well as to her own. She must rank traditions in a hierarchy of importance and domain, so that each is kept in its proper place in her life and doesn't disrupt the proper functioning of other modes. She must square all of the various traditions of her life with her understanding of the core of her identity as a human being and as a Christian. And to do this she must find a good way to bring tradition into critical and constructive conversation with the other avenues to knowledge she enjoys.

With all of these caveats about tradition, however, ought to come celebration as well. One of the benefits of formal education, but also of much folklore, is the access it gives to the deliverances of great minds, ideas, and stories of the past. These can be greatly *evil* or otherwise repellent, to be sure, but even then often instructive. Tradition thus offers us a dizzying array of new conversation partners in our thought. True, we can consult our current friends, relations, pastors, teachers, and contemporary experts, but we also may converse with Kong-zi (Confucius), Thucydides, Marcus Aurelius, Shankara, Moses Maimonides, Abu Hamid al-Ghazali, René Descartes, or James Madison—each of whom influenced a major tradition. As Christians, furthermore, we will want to listen to Augustine, Maximus the Confessor, Thomas Aquinas, Martin Luther, Teresa of Ávila, and Charles Wesley if once we have been introduced to them and then know where to find them!

Tradition is more than reading "Greats," furthermore, more than conferring with the fine minds of the past. As the reference to Charles Wesley (rather than John) indicates, Christian tradition includes practices and artifacts: liturgy, devotional disciplines, poetry, hymnody, hierarchy, architecture, and other ways in which Christians have expressed and lived their faith. And the parallels with other traditions I trust are obvious: national anthems, folk songs, proverbs, medicines, rites of passage, holidays, uniforms, greetings, honors—we live amid a welter of significant, even sacred, times and places and words and actions and objects. These are the consolidations and epitomes of the convictions of our forebears. Behavior is dialectically related to thought, and by doing what they did, we can more readily think and feel as they did—with, one hopes, similar benefits for our thought and life. Our failure to undertake and to exegete such traditions, to mine them of their value and values, and instead to dismiss them as merely passé (as if to be "past" is just to be "worse"!) demonstrates our stupidity, not that of our "funny old ancestors."[23]

Tradition for some people, including some Christians, is a familiar and comfortable harness they put on to guide their every move. Tradition for others is a straitjacket that straps them into uncomfortable and unhelpful positions against their better judgment. Instead, however, tradition should be a closet of outfits—and by outfits I have in mind "outfitters" who provide us not only with clothing but also with other useful tools for the journey. We cannot simply put on a previous era's way of thinking and doing, let alone pile on costumes from multiple times and places. As it is, we have to put on and take off various ensembles every day in modern life. But we can try out the patterns of the past, study them, and design what we need for today with an informed and appreciative knowledge of the past. Where they fit perennial needs, traditions can be appropriated with little strain. Where they respond to specific circumstances quite unlike our own, they can be examined for particular relevancies and then set aside.

To use a different metaphor, a more Biblical one, tradition is the great cloud of witnesses that urge us on and can help us if we will consult them and their legacies with respect and realism. We should neither follow them slavishly (as some enthusiasts do) nor reject them reflexively (as some ecclesiastical entrepreneurs and iconoclasts do). Instead, as G. K. Chesterton wisely put it, respecting tradition means giving your ancestors a vote: not all the votes, but some votes, in our deliberations. [24]

Paradoxically, such an attitude toward tradition both frees us from servitude to the past (we take it seriously, but not too seriously), and also from servitude to the

---

23. A fascinating provocation in this regard is provided by philosophers Vrinda Dalmiya and Linda Alcoff, "Are 'Old Wives' Tales' Justified?" in *Feminist Epistemologies*, ed. Linda Alcoff and Elizabeth Potter (New York: Routledge, 1993), 217–44.

24. G. K. Chesterton, *Orthodoxy* (Garden City, NY: Image, 1959 [1908]), 48. A similar balance is struck by Jaroslav Pelikan, who defends the perennial value of tradition as a resource while warning against its stultifying effects as a rule: see Jaroslav Pelikan, *The Vindication of Tradition* (New Haven, CT, and London: Yale University Press, 1984), esp. 65–82.

present, "the small and arrogant oligarchy of those who merely happen to be walking about," as Chesterton puts it.[25] And thus we return to my sartorial imagery: serious consultation of tradition beckons us to escape the current fads masquerading as "tradition" as we find that we have *not* always done it this way and in fact may have done it better at some other time and place.

What, then, about capital-T Tradition as theological readers have been patiently expecting me to describe it, namely, the accumulated legacy of reflection on doctrine, piety, and practice throughout the history of the church?

I actually have little more to say specifically about ecclesiastical tradition. It is not foundational and supremely normative, as the Bible is. (We will discuss the Bible much more thoroughly in a moment.) Each element of church tradition instead must be interpreted and weighed for its relevance and value.[26] Not everything Irenaeus or Luther said is equally true or important—for us or for ever. Not every argument can be settled merely by invoking Augustine or Aquinas—or C. S. Lewis, for that matter. Even the Apostles' Creed has at least one pocket of deep obscurity ("he descended into hell") while the Nicene Creed, seems rather wordy, even redundant, in its parallel phrases ("God of God, Light of Light, Very God of Very God").[27] Many Christians would not join in the rigorous and extensive doctrinal demands of the last clause of the Athanasian Creed ("This is the catholic faith; which except a man believe truly and firmly, he cannot be saved"), nor of those of more recent and particular confessional vintage. (I have in mind the cursing or "detesting" of the Anabaptists and their doctrine in the Anglican 42 Articles of 1553 and the Belgic Confession of 1561.)

Tradition instead, as Richard Bauckham puts it, is "essentially a hermeneutical process, in which the message of Scripture is interpreted and developed. As such it takes place in a tension between the guidance of the Spirit, who preserves the church from irreparable apostasy, and the fallibility of the church as a human society."[28] John Webster writes similarly, "'Tradition' is best conceived of as a [human] *hearing* of the Word rather than a fresh act of [divine] *speaking*."[29]

---

25. Chesterton, *Orthodoxy.*

26. Edification is, after all, the whole point of tradition: Ellen T. Charry, *By the Renewing of Your Minds: The Pastoral Function of Christian Doctrine* (Oxford: Oxford University Press, 1997).

27. My professor of Reformation thought, B.A. Gerrish, first brought to my attention Calvin's misgivings about both the authenticity and wording of both the Athanasian and Nicene Creeds: see *The Old Protestantism and the New: Essays on the Reformation Heritage* (Chicago: University of Chicago Press, 1982), 382n56. Gerrish draws especially on W. Nijenhuis, "Calvin's Attitude toward the Symbols of the Early Church during the Conflict with Caroli," *Ecclesia Reformata: Studies on the Reformation*, Kerkhistorische Bijdragen, no. 3 (Leiden: E.J. Brill, 1972), 73–96. Dawn DeVries refers also to this question in Calvin: "'Inspired Heterodoxy'? The Freedom of Theological Inquiry and the Well-Being of the Church," in *Theology as Conversation*, ed. Bruce L. McCormack and Kimlyn J. Bender (Grand Rapids, MI: Eerdmans, 2009), 125–27.

28. Richard Bauckham, *God and the Crisis of Freedom: Biblical and Contemporary Perspectives* (Louisville, KY, and London: Westminster John Knox, 2002), 99. This quotation appears in a particularly brilliant discussion of "Authority and Tradition," 91–115.

29. John Webster, *Holy Scripture: A Dogmatic Sketch* (Cambridge: Cambridge University Press, 2003), 51.

We are thus stupid if we are not grateful for the work of our forebears and foolish if we fail to offer proper deference to our spiritual and intellectual betters, past or present. There is no brief here for anti-clericalism nor for a disregard of the work of theological scholarship painstakingly wrought over the centuries. (We shall deal with the question of discerning and deferring to authorities below, including ecclesiastical ones. I am not sure, however, that I shall satisfy even post–Vatican II Catholics in this regard, alas.) Indeed, tremendous confusion has been wrought at just this point between defenders of *sola scriptura* and even quite moderate defenders of the "rule of faith," the great creeds, and Christian tradition in general. As most orthodox Christians would agree, *of course* Scripture trumps any theological summary of its teaching. The whole purpose of such statements is, after all, to render Scripture faithfully and they thus are always corrigible in the light of further knowledge of Scripture.

Yet the awesome authority of Scripture does not transfer to the act of interpreting Scripture, nor to the results of that action. There is wisdom in the early Christian adoption of rules of faith precisely over against just any interpretation of Scripture that challenged the community's tradition. Rules of faith were developed, in fact, mainly against heretics who were confident that their interpretations of doctrine were better grounded in the Bible than were orthodox tenets. Because the Bible is both so complex and so important, rendering its messages correctly is a task properly fenced about by prudent guidance found in the consensus of the church's teachers.

So the hermeneutical circle once again comes into play, with creeds and the like functioning as "interpretations of the whole" that are ever open to improvement by successive readings of "the parts" of Scripture, but those interpretations that have stood the test of wide and long adherence by the church are properly deferred to against just any reading of the Bible that challenges them, not because tradition matters more than Scripture, but because *tried and true interpretations of Scripture that have thus become tradition are to be preferred* prima facie *against novel alternatives as a simple matter of rationality*. This point is thus a simple one hermeneutically, but it too often gets clouded by passionate and needless defenses of Scripture versus the church, the Word of God versus the word of humans, and so on.

Having said all that on behalf of tradition, we nonetheless are irresponsible if we shirk the task of listening to what the Spirit of the Lord is saying today in and to the church and to test everything we hear from tradition by everything else we think we know in the light of the deliverances of the other intellectual resources God gives us. As Brian Hebblethwaite says,

> The authority of the tradition lies fairly and squarely in its content, in the way it commends itself to historical judgment, to rational comprehension and to experiential authentication. In particular, ... its authority lies in the moral and religious value to be found in it.[30]

---

30. Brian Hebblethwaite, *The Incarnation: Collected Essays in Christology* (Cambridge: Cambridge University Press, 1987), 43.

Furthermore, we cannot possibly take in every bit of tradition accumulated in the ecclesiastical storehouses of the world, and must instead depend on the Spirit to draw our attention to whatever particular elements of the tradition will equip us well for the demands of our vocation in this moment.[31]

What else, then, beyond our experiences and the traditions of the past, will help us be faithful in those vocations? To the disciplines of discovery we now turn.

Scholarship

By "scholarship" I mean simply the deliverances of the academic disciplines, the orderly investigation of and reflection upon the world. Symptomatic of what Mark Noll has discussed as "the scandal of the evangelical mind" is that fact that many of his fellow evangelicals need to be persuaded that scholarly learning is a gift of God to be gratefully received and diligently pursued. The anti-intellectualism within evangelicalism is well known, alas, and it is evident in many other communities of Christians as well. There are plenty of historical explanations why so many

---

31. Theologians will recognize that I have compacted a great many theses into just a couple of paragraphs here. The current dialogue—at its worst, a controversy, at its best, a collaboration—regarding the theological interpretation of Scripture is one I hope to engage in more fully and directly elsewhere. For now, I simply declare that *of course* the historical-critical study of Scripture is *part* of what it means to understand Scripture well, just as it is a part of understanding, say, Homer or any other text (as Frank Turner demonstrates, the historical-critical method flowers particularly around the study of these two classical texts: *The Greek Heritage in Victorian Britain* [New Haven, CT: Yale University Press, 1984]). Likewise, however, *of course* the modern study of the Bible should benefit all it can from the wisdom of previous Biblical interpreters, both because they interpreted the Bible as human beings exploring generic and perennial human issues (so we can connect with their interpretations) but also because they also were particular human beings investigating the Bible in circumstances and ways not our own (so we can learn new things from their interpretations). Furthermore, the fact that a previous author or council or tradition, no matter how eminent, interpreted a text in this or that way does not outlaw an alternative interpretation, since even the Roman Catholic Church sees only popes as infallible, and only on rare occasions. Augustine, Aquinas, Luther, Wesley, Schleiermacher, Barth—none of these forebears are Jesus, so we receive from them as we ought, both gratefully and critically.

I recognize that there is at least one other major issue in this discussion, namely, the problematic nature of allegorical interpretation. I confess to being not greatly exercised on this question, following Augustine and Aquinas, not to mention Luther, Calvin, and other Protestants, in averring the basic and pre-eminent status of the literal level of interpretation. If a text can then be read at other levels in an edifying way (which cannot, *ipso facto*, be a way that contradicts, or is even rendered even slightly implausible by, the literal meaning of the text), I welcome that reading. My welcome, however, will be ever cautious, as the history of interpretation is replete with examples of ingenious extravagances replacing sober rendering of the plain meaning of the text. The Song of Songs is *not*, that is, primarily a book about Christ and the Church, and devoting too much attention to the allegorical mode celebrating the latter motif risks missing the revelation originally given at the literal level. Likewise, however, to dismiss out of hand centuries of pious meditation on this text as an elaboration of the splendid affirmation that Christ and the Church will love each other as intensely as any human lovers would be a sad price to pay indeed for a conservative literalism.

Christians are so suspicious of the sector comprising universities, intellectuals, journals of ideas, and the like, but we will not indulge ourselves in exploring that fascinating question here.[32] For our purposes it will suffice to show that Christians ought not to resist intellectual engagement, but instead ought to be in the forefront of each field—as, indeed, many are, despite the misgivings or even opposition of our religious communities.

The fundamental reason Christians ought to be learning from the scholarly disciplines is that Christians are simply trying to become fully functioning human beings, by way of the redemptive work God is doing within and among us. And fully functioning human beings need the deliverances of scholarship in order to be and do what we are supposed to be and do.

Clearly, if we are to "be" at all, we need to know how to procure the essentials of bodily life. The sciences help us find, procure, and prepare properly for consumption the water and food we need each day. The sciences help us understand the world well enough, furthermore, to exercise our calling of caring for each other and for the rest of Creation. We need a generally reliable understanding of what helps our fellow creatures flourish or compels them to decline. And the more we explore and discover, the better we can fulfill our vocations.

Since what it means for human beings, as well as other creatures, to flourish is a very wide concept, we need to engage in disciplines sufficiently expansive so as to neglect no part of our lives before God. Thus we validate not only the aspects of intellectual work that pertain to water and food production, safety, shelter, and the like, but also those that pertain to artistic production and appreciation, moral clarity and sophistication, recreational exercise and enjoyment, and spiritual purification and maturation. Beyond improving our lives and those in our care in these ways, furthermore, we human beings flourish in the sheer delight of investigating the marvelous world God has made to share with us, investigation that provides the corollary benefit of expanded and enriched appreciation for God.

With a properly global view of shalom and of our calling to engage in a world of shalom-making, Christians ought to be among the enthusiasts of every discipline, no matter how arcane or plain, sophisticated or simple. There is no actual conflict between *any* science and Christianity, nor is there any opposition between what is authentically good in any culture and the Christian gospel that comes not only to correct and supplement it, but also to validate and celebrate it.

Yet, one might ask, isn't this view of scholarship naïve? Don't we all engage in every intellectual pursuit, as we engage in any other activity, from a particular place as particular people with a particular agenda? Isn't all thinking inescapably *tribal*?

---

32. I have explored it elsewhere: see "Why Johnny Can't Produce Christian Scholarship: A Reflection on Real-Life Impediments," in *Evangelical Landscapes: Facing Critical Issues of the Day* (Grand Rapids, MI: Baker Academic, 2002), 141–60.

I will have much more to say on this issue in the remainder of this book, but for now I will simply defend the scholarly disciplines as genuine *disciplines*: genuine regimens the observance of which has a good record of producing knowledge. I may be a Christian historian or a Marxist historian or what I imagine to be a completely "objective" historian, but my work must conform to the generally agreed canons of the discipline of history—standards accepted by my profession as to what counts as evidence, what counts as enough evidence of the right sort, what counts as proper argumentation, and so on—or it will be disregarded. If it does meet those standards, however, then those who disagree with me must argue according to the same canons or be disqualified. People of very different outlooks, therefore, nonetheless can learn from each other as they all practice the same discipline.

To be sure, there may come a time in the investigation of a problem when differences of prior commitments cause historians (or other "scientists") to irremediably part company. Christians are open in a way Marxists generally are not to both religion and the supernatural playing irreducibly key parts in history. So in some instances (although, it must be clear, not all, since Marxists and Christians do hold a number of beliefs in common), the Marxist and the Christian will stare at the same facts and draw different conclusions. Since miracles simply don't happen, according to the Marxist worldview, reports of wonders among a Nigerian tribe converting to Christianity from animism must be reports of something else: a mass delusion, a misinterpretation of psychosomatic healing, or the like. The Christian is, or ought to be, wide open to the possibility of mass delusion, misinterpretation, and similar plausible interpretations, but is also open to the possibility that genuinely supernatural events are taking place. The difference of historical interpretation is a difference occurring much farther back up the road: at the metaphysical level, at the place where one decides what actors there are and aren't in historical events, and at the epistemological level, as to whether the actions of each are in some way discernible by historical investigation.

In most instances, however, scholars (whether of history or of chemistry, of linguistics or of music theory) are not faced with data that expose the zones in which their worldviews radically diverge, but instead usually spend their time in the places of intersection deriving results that all can validate and celebrate.

Have genuine conflicts arisen, however, between the current thinking in a particular discipline and the current thinking in a particular Christian community? Of course. Have genuine conflicts arisen between aspects of a particular culture and the pronouncements of Christian missionaries or converts regarding those aspects? Of course. How, then, Christian experience, tradition, and the Bible are best related to each other and to the disciplines is a question we have yet to discuss. But before we do, we need to examine both what we mean by the fourth resource, another aspect of cultural life we call "art," and then the particular text that Christians revere as different than all the other resources we have at hand, the Bible.

As the Christian person draws together the materials for her deliberation on a subject—and, as we have already intimated and will later discuss in detail, this picture is almost amusingly oversimplified, as if the person in question has an utterly blank mind, devoid of previous information or opinion, and yet somehow collects just the right information upon which to reflect—she will properly consider including works of art. For art-making is a means of both exploring and expressing what is, what is not, and what might be. And it is good for the responsible thinker to consider what is with reference to the information, opinion, and provocation rendered by art, even as it is good for her also to ponder what is not, by contrast, and what might be, by warning or encouragement.

An important confusion, alas, often arises in discussions of works of art as windows onto the world. Literature, for instance, is often commended to students as a way of experiencing other places and times, and to interact with a wide range of other people in circumstances quite like or quite unlike one's own. So far, so good— so long as we recall that literature provides us with *a particular author's rendering* of his or her subject, not of the subject—or manifold constituent subjects—thus rendered.

One does not, then, encounter a young, frustrated physician's wife in *Madame Bovary*, but a thirty-five-year-old male writer's depiction of such a person. I put it this way indeed to evoke doubt about taking at face value *any* thirty-five-year-old man's extended account of a young woman's romantic history. *Madame Bovary* was, of course, denounced as pornographic, and among the crimes of pornography is that it doesn't tell the truth about the way women and men actually are. We then need good reasons to believe that *Madame Bovary* tells us anything about the world other than the state of Gustave Flaubert's mind at the time—if even *that* is portrayed for us in any reliable way in the novel, a contention over which much hermeneutical ink has been spilled.

Likewise, Charles Dickens does not simply show us what industrial London was like, but, like any artist, creates a fictional world that more or less conveys his vision and message to the reader. Because it is fiction, it is not *necessarily* any more accurate a rendering of an actual place and society than is J. R. R. Tolkien's *Lord of the Rings*.

What good, then, is art to the thinking person—as opposed to the one seeking escape, or amusement, or thrills, and so on?

Every account of the world we have is, indeed, an account. It is a rendering, a depiction, a combination of information and interpretation. All interpretation is, in a basic sense, a work of art, or artifice, of "making," because it is not the thing itself, the referent, but a constructed thing, a reference. When we are conferring over something that confuses us, we ask each other for an interpretation and say, "What do you *make* of that?" So immediately we see that "art" is not in some utterly separate category from the work of thinking (!), but that inescapably terms and concepts in epistemology overlap with or even are simply borrowed from the world of art.

For art forms are languages, literally media of expression. Some are more clear and direct while others have a superior capacity for subtlety, profundity, or ambiguity. Rock music, for example, expresses certain ranges of experience, emotion, and concern much more powerfully than would, say, chamber music (and vice versa), while a symphony orchestra can take us places that a bluegrass band, however gifted, could not (and vice versa). Acrylic paint, oils, watercolors, pastels, pen- and ink—each is a language (or perhaps a dialect) via which one can do, say, transmit, evoke some things better and other things not so well. What is made via these media, then, deserves our consideration (at least sometimes) as particular, peculiar expressions of human interest.

Moreover, as C. S. Lewis averred, everything is real. The question is, a real what?[33] So when we encounter a work of art, we don't properly pose the question, "Is this real or not?" but "In what respects is this real? In what aspects is it real? In what prospects is it real?" In what modes and to what extent does the world that this art projects (in Nicholas Wolterstorff's locution) correspond with the actual world?[34] What parts or "sides" of it do that corresponding? And what does it tell us about what *might* be real—in some alternative place or time, under other circumstances, in the future, or whatever?

To be clear, the value of a work of art of course does not reside *entirely* in its depiction of reality. Indeed, art serves many valid purposes and representing reality is not even its primary purpose.[35] What I am arguing for in this discussion is its genuine value, sometimes controverted but usually ignored, as an aid to reflective thought. (One has to page through a lot of discussions of epistemology to find art even mentioned as a relevant resource.) Art *suggests*, and suggestions are helpful in a way that sheer facts, or widely agreed interpretations, or tightly constructed arguments are not. The way forward in thinking often relies heavily on "what if" and "maybe," along with what is self-evident or incontrovertible. Indeed, many intellectual breakthroughs have occurred in the realm of the symbolic, the narratival, the "thought-experimental," even the visionary—and then hard evidence and disciplined reasoning comes along later to construct, test, and validate such insights. (August Kekulé's daydream that prompted his conceptualization of the benzene molecule comes immediately to mind.)

33. C. S. Lewis, *Letters to Malcolm, Chiefly on Prayer* (London: Harcourt, Brace, and World, 1963), p. 80.

34. Nicholas Wolterstorff, "The Action of World-Projection," chap. in *Art in Action* (Grand Rapids, MI: Eerdmans, 1980), 122–55.

35. Dorothy Sayers remarks that "the true work of art...is something new; it is not primarily the copy or representation of anything." A truly Christian aesthetic, she avers, rests foundationally on the idea that human beings, in the image of God, are to create (what is new), not merely manufacture (what is already present). See "Toward a Christian Esthetic" [*sic*], in Dorothy L. Sayers, *The Whimsical Christian* (New York: Collier Books, 1987 [1969]), 73–91; the quotation is on p. 83. See also Arthur C. Danto, *The Transfiguration of the Commonplace: A Philosophy of Art* (Cambridge, MA: Harvard University Press, 1981).

Art, moreover, enriches our thinking in a range of ways. It adds (back) all our senses to our consideration and thus gives us more to work with metaphorically and thus conceptually: smells, textures, shapes, tastes, weights, colors, and more. Metaphors therefore arise to expand our list of options, clarify our comprehension of problems, and open our imaginations to innovations. Art combines into new units and conversations what had been distinct, even distant, in our minds heretofore. One cannot, and therefore does not, imagine that a solution could lie in that direction, in that combination of elements; then an artist shows one a chimera, a juxtaposition, a marriage, an amalgam. "This *could* be like that; these *could* be combined with those after all."

Art at once exaggerates and reduces as it frames, focuses, fabricates, and fixes into form. It positions us in unusual angles of vision, heightens our awareness, removes what Coleridge called "the film of familiarity" from our perception, opens up new landscapes, spotlights relations, poses alternatives, introduces possibilities.[36] From Aesop's fables to Jesus' parables, from *Blade Runner*'s dystopian Los Angeles to Frank Lloyd Wright's fabulous mile-high Illinois Tower, from the dreamscapes of Hieronymus Bosch to those of Salvador Dalí, from Noh masks to Picasso portraits, art nudges us, gestures to us, even dashes ice water across our faces so that we exclaim, "Wow, I never *saw* that before. It's not all there is to the matter, of course, but still, there is something here I simply must consider...." Art reminds and it surprises, it cajoles and it berates, it seduces and it shocks, it disturbs and it assures, it unites and it divides—all so that we apprehend and interpret the world differently and better. And *that* is a set of tasks obviously helpful to the project of responsible thinking.

How one ought to integrate what one learns from art with what one learns from the other resources is a matter to which we will turn shortly. But before we do, we need to take note of the uniquely Christian resource in this group, the Bible.

Scripture

One good way to introduce the role of the Bible in Christian thought is to get clear what sort of thing the Bible is and what it is for. Bear with me as I make what will seem to the knowledgeable reader a series of elementary observations, for I hope to make some theological hay out of them in due course.

The Bible on my shelf is an English-language translation rendered by an international committee of Anglophone scholars in various branches of theology and history—and perhaps an expert stylist or two. Whatever translation it is, it emerges from a particular network of scholars and churches: not all scholars in all relevant fields throughout the world were involved in this translation, of course, and it represents only certain denominations and traditions whose interests the publisher

---

36. S. T. Coleridge, *Biographia Literaria*, ch. xiv.

hopes to serve. It therefore reflects particular kinds and levels of education in translators and readers, as well as particular cultural norms, commonplaces, background knowledge, and expectations.

In the translators' *modus operandi*, previous translations might be consulted. Certainly previous translations will be resonant in each translator's head as he cannot help but recall, however dimly or even implicitly, previous renderings of Bibles he has encountered. Focus, however, will normally be upon the Hebrew and Greek texts in the standard editions, with perhaps reference also to works discussing the variants, text-histories, and so on of those Hebrew and Greek texts. For the "Bible behind the Bible" that we have is in a fragmented state: thousands of fragments, in fact, held in collections all over the scholarly world. Scholars pore over these fragments, arrange them in what they think are helpful order (e.g., text "families" of what appear to be related renditions), and do their best to construct what they believe is the Hebrew or Greek of—well, of what?

At this point, one might expect the phrase, "the original." But the textual history of the Bible is complicated, as is the history of its emergence into the form recognized by the believing community as the correct, final form—the canon of Scripture. At least some of the books in the Bible appear to be stitched together from previous documents. (In the computer age, we would say "cut-and-pasted.") The evidence in a particular book of the Bible might indicate that an author borrowed from a previous text—perhaps an Old Testament historian relying on a previous royal chronicle or a Gospel writer drawing on a collection of Jesus' sayings. Or it might appear that long passages are taken from a previous text, perhaps even whole, and grafted into a new work—so the supposition that the Book of Isaiah may be a compilation of two or even three books, and that some of Paul's epistles are literary patchworks of two or more letters.

What this information means, then, is that we have fragments/portions before the Bible becomes *the Bible*, so to speak, and we have fragments/portions of it afterward. What we do not have, however, is a single, intact, authoritative Hebrew Bible dating from Old Testament times, nor a single, intact, authoritative Greek New Testament dating from apostolic times.

True, we have the Septuagint, which was, it seems, the *functioning* Scripture of Jews at the time of Jesus. But it is a Greek translation of a lost Hebrew original. And we have many, many manuscripts of the Greek New Testament, some of them quite early—dating back to within decades of the composition of the originals. Experts therefore believe that the Hebrew and Greek texts we have been able to reconstruct are remarkably close to—again, what?

Not, to be sure, to "the autographs," those wonderful, mysterious "documents" thought to have emerged from the pens of the divinely inspired Biblical writers and defended as "inerrant" by Protestant Christians since at least the later nineteenth century.[37] For what, we might ask, would count as an "autograph" of a Biblical book—

---

37. The classic work here is A. A. Hodge and B. B. Warfield, "Inspiration," in *The Princeton Theology 1812–1921*, ed. Mark A. Noll (Grand Rapids, MI: Baker, 1983), 218–32.

like Isaiah or like any of the books of the Pentateuch—that seem to most scholars, even quite conservative ones, not to have come from the pen of a single author? No, what is on offer in the authoritative Hebrew and Greek texts we have today is what scholarship believes is a very close rendering of what was the authoritative Hebrew text of late Old Testament Israel, out of which the Septuagint was translated, and what was the Greek New Testament as it circulated in its various individual elements (and *not*, in fact, as "the New Testament" until the third or fourth century) in the apostolic church. These texts are what we *guess* are the words of the *canon*, the version of the Bible *recognized by the people of God* as *Scripture*. We mean by "the people of God" either intertestamental Israel with its Tanakh or the New Testament church with both the Old Testament and the emerging New one—as the church followed the lead of its Lord in accepting the Old Testament as the Word of God and then gratefully received new Words of God to interpret the new covenant they entered through the career of Jesus.

Inspiration, then, is best understood as divine superintendence of the entire process: the right authors write the right words and the right editorial process gathers those words together into books and then collections of books that the people of God recognize as truly Scripture that they receive gratefully from God as though God himself had authored them.[38] Maximally, so to speak, Christians believe with B. B. Warfield that God selected particular authors and editors and so guided their work that what emerged in the canonical process was exactly, word for word, what God intended to be written and thus can be received as a text authored by God, as well as by his human co-authors.[39] Minimally, it seems to me, Christians must affirm an understanding of inspiration along the lines set out by Nicholas Wolterstorff: God "appropriated" the various literary elements of the Bible and guided their compilation into just this canon, thus putting his imprimatur on it and commending it

---

38. John Webster puts thus the process of inspiration (he idiosyncratically uses the term "sanctification" so as to include the Spirit's illumination of Scripture to believers): "Sanctification can thus properly be extended to the processes of the production of the text—not simply authorship (as, so often, in older theories of inspiration) but also the complex histories of pre-literary and literary tradition, redaction and compilation. It will, likewise, be extended to the post-history of the text, most particularly to canonisation (understood as the church's Spirit-produced acknowledgment of the testimony of Scripture) and to interpretation (understood as Spirit-illumined repentant and faithful attention to the presence of God)" (*Holy Scripture*, 30). This understanding avoids the dichotomy that vexes so many moderns as they believe the Church is calling on them, intolerably, to affirm the Bible as "God's immutable self-revelation for all time [that escapes] the relativities of historical and cultural conditioning" (Hebblethwaite, *The Incarnation*, 105). Some Christians do issue such a call, but it is certainly not the only orthodox way to view inspiration. One need not feel, as even theologians seem to feel, forced to choose between belief in divine revelation via Scripture and a Bible that is evidently marked by human limitations.

39. A selection of relevant essays by Warfield can be found in Mark A. Noll, ed., *The Princeton Theology 1812–1921* (Grand Rapids, MI: Baker Academic, 1983).

as his Word to us.[40] In either version, and of every one in between, the Bible thus comes to us as the Word of God, a text God expects us to read and heed as God's own message.[41]

Yet what, still, does all this mean? What kind of a book is the Bible and therefore *how* are we to "read and heed" it? To make a few points more clear, we might say this: The Bible is not the Qur'an. The Qur'an is understood traditionally to be the "recitation" of the very words of God, mediated by the angel Gabriel to Muhammad or received directly by intuition in Muhammad's mind. Since every word of the Qur'an was received by dictation, the Qur'an is revered as authored by God alone (no human authorship is involved) and is thus aesthetically, as well as morally and factually, perfect. Arabic, therefore, must be learned by every pious Muslim so as to enjoy the beauty, as well as the goodness and truth, of the very speech of God.

To be sure, many Christians have believed and claimed and done the same sorts of things in regard to the Bible. Divine dictation of the Bible is a commonly assumed oversimplification Christian teachers everywhere must root out of their students' minds—for no educated reader of the Bible would defend, say, its grammar at every point as being perfect Hebrew or Greek. Quite the contrary: the reader of the original Biblical languages immediately recognizes various authorial voices in the various books, and no one would confuse fisherman Peter with rabbi Paul.

Yet if Christians ought not to defend the Bible as perfect in every respect, as educated Christians have always realized we shouldn't, then to what extent ought we to tolerate imperfections in Scripture? To what extent can we tolerate them before the Bible no longer can be received as divinely authored and mandated?

---

40. "All that is necessary for the whole to be God's book is that all the human discourse it contains have been appropriated by God, as one single book, for God's discourse. If it is the Christian Bible we are speaking of, the event which *counts as* God's appropriating this totality as the medium of God's own discourse is presumably that rather drawn out event consisting of the Church's settling on the totality as its canon" (Nicholas Wolterstorff, *Divine Discourse: Philosophical Reflections on the Claim that God Speaks* [Cambridge: Cambridge University Press, 1995], 54). John Webster objects that such a view can amount to "a curious textual equivalent of adoptionism," but Webster himself warns against pressing analogies too far between the inspiration of Scripture and the Incarnation of the Son of God (*Holy Scripture: A Dogmatic Sketch* [Cambridge: Cambridge University Press, 2003], 24; cf. 22–23). Wolterstorff's point is that if God has signed (off on) the Bible, so to speak, He has authorized it, and thereby officially authored it. And that is minimally what matters to the orthodox Christian.

41. Orthodox Christianity thus reveres the Bible as God's Word written, even as it also affirms that revelation comes to a reader only by the illumination of the Holy Spirit. The Bible, that is, truly is an artifact of God's revelation: it simply *is* revelation whether or not any human reader recognizes it as such. But we do not receive revelation from it unless God commends it to us. Thus John Webster puts the emphasis in the right place: "Inspiration is not primarily a textual property but a divine movement and therefore a divine moving" (*Holy Scripture*, 36). God's revelation is not simply an action in the past: "There! I've taken great trouble to produce the Bible. Now read it." God's revelation continues as God's Spirit opens up the Bible to the reader who attends to it in expectancy, in faith.

It is striking, actually, how much imperfection in the Bible Christians have tolerated throughout Christian history, even—and sometimes especially—among those who most vociferously champion the Bible's plenary verbal inerrancy. The earliest Christians, of course, were Jews working mostly with the Septuagint, not the Hebrew Bible. Furthermore, the Septuagint they were actually working with much of the time, including when some of them were authoring parts of the New Testament from prison cells, was the "Septuagint" they had memorized, rather than a definitive text ready to hand. Thus we see New Testament quotations of Old Testament texts that are not, in fact, quotations of the Hebrew Bible but quotations of the Septuagint—and even some of those are only fairly-remembered-but-not-exact renditions of the Septuagint. Mark that these imperfect quotations are now themselves enshrined in, and as, Holy Scripture.

The earliest Christians, moreover, were edifying each other with Scripture both Old and New, yes, but also with fine books of Christian instruction such as the *Shepherd* of Hermas and the *Didache*. Nothing wrong with that, of course, and what is interesting for our purposes is that a few of such books were considered seriously *as Scripture* for at least a century or two before the consensus of the faithful adjudged them definitively as simply good Christian teaching. Stranger still, perhaps, is the career of certain books that would eventually be recognized as Scripture moving in and out of the shadows of churchly use and regard, whether the latter two letters of John, II Peter, Jude, the anonymous letter to the Hebrews, the Apocalypse, and more. If a basic hermeneutical principle is to "read Scripture with Scripture" and a basic theological priority, which I shall return to presently, is to interpret "the whole counsel of God," it is remarkable that the early Christians, for a couple of centuries it seems, were without an agreed canon of just the right books "in" and all the other books, however edifying, "out." At the same time, we must recognize that the vast majority of the pages of the New Testament, including all four Gospels, Acts, and the major letters of Paul, were almost undisputedly and universally accepted as Scripture from very early on.

Until very recently, furthermore, this situation was *normal* for Christians *everywhere*: translations (of greater or lesser value) of a canon that might be too large (especially in the eyes of Protestants, who do not regard the Apocrypha as canonical) but was also frequently small—as churches could not obtain copies of the whole of Scripture, nor could many clergy, let alone laity, read the more difficult passages in the vernacular or Latin, let alone Hebrew or Greek, thus rendering *the actual Bible in use* much smaller than the full canon. Indeed, it is only in our own day, and only in the highly educated global North-West, that one finds excellent translations and original language texts of the whole Bible published in affordable editions to a literate church. *Everywhere* else, Christians work with a Bible that is something other than ideal—and often something very much other than ideal.

Evangelical Protestants, furthermore, who have been in the vanguard of those defending the plenary verbal inerrancy of the Bible, are also those whose evangelistic zeal has compelled them to translate the Bible into most of the world's languages. Note that this zeal has not compelled evangelicals to insist that newly evangelized peoples all learn Hebrew and Greek in order to read the Bible "properly" in the original tongues—as Muslim teachers do with the Qur'an and Arabic. Instead, evangelical missionaries work hard to render the Scripture in the plainest language possible, sacrificing delicate nuance for broad intelligibility and speedy completion so as to achieve the widest and quickest dissemination of the Word of Life. While evangelicals particularly in America engage in the luxury of periodic furious and expensive arguments over this or that new translation as if the fate of the church hangs in the balance, evangelicals elsewhere live happily with the roughest of translations so long as they serve the purpose of promoting authentic Christian faith.[42] Indeed, the very willingness of Christians to translate the Bible demonstrates the basic Christian conviction that God's Word can be expressed fruitfully in any language (= culture) and also an acceptance of the fact that shades of meaning open up in a new language even as that new language also constrains what can be said—as any technology both provides and withholds.[43]

The fundamental posture of the Christian is to "trust and obey," and the Bible provides the ground and content for faith as well as the life practice incumbent upon those who believe the gospel. It tells us what is true about God, the world, and everything and how we therefore are to live in the light of that truth. Christians recognize that the basic contours of the Gospel story and the fundamental patterns of Christian worship, fellowship, and mission are evident to faithful readers of the Bible—for the centuries have shown individual after individual, and culture after culture, reading the same Book and coming to the same basic conclusions, albeit with sometimes spectacularly different responses. Despite, indeed, those manifestly different responses—as different as a Quaker prayer meeting differs from a Latin American street parade for the Virgin Mary, or as a theological seminar at Edinburgh differs from a healing service in Nigeria—textbooks on world religions routinely define Christianity by way of the same fundamental beliefs and practices, and rarely differ much in their respective accounts. It is the same religion all over the world, shaped by reading the same Book in whatever language it is rendered and however *well* it has been rendered.

---

42. See Mark A. Noll, *Between Faith and Criticism: Evangelicals, Scholarship, and the Bible in America*, 2nd ed. (Vancouver: Regent College, 2004 [1991]); and Peter J. Thuesen, *In Discordance with the Scriptures: American Protestant Battles Over Translating the Bible* (New York and Oxford: Oxford University Press, 1999). Elsewhere, Noll quotes Myles Smith, the author of the translators' "note to the reader" in the 1611 version of the King James Bible, darling of fundamentalists: "the very meanest translation of the Bible in *English* ... containeth the word of God, yea, is the word of God" (Mark A. Noll, "Long Live the King," *Books & Culture* [November 2011]: 12; emphasis in original).

43. See Lamin Sanneh, *Translating the Message: The Missionary Impact on Culture*, 2nd ed. (Maryknoll, NY: Orbis, 2009 [1989]), on a range of issues involved in the translation of the Bible, with particular reference to Africa and the differences with Islam.

We observe, then, that God has used the Bible to good effect over the centuries in what for some will be a startling variety of forms, none of which look exactly like the Bible on the reader's shelf. Fights to the death about Bible translations or dogmatic statements of the Bible's flawlessness seem wildly out of keeping with the actual career of the Bible.

Steering happily into the other ditch, however, is hardly the right response to these observations. Flawed renditions of Scripture interpreted by hermeneutically deficient teachers to vulnerably ignorant communities explains a lot of what is wrong in the global church. Ongoing efforts to refine Biblical translations, produce better tools for theological study, and improve Scriptural interpretation thereby for the good of the church are entirely laudable. The need for the best possible Bibles and the best possible hermeneutics in every community is keen.

Among the most important of those good interpretative practices, however, is an implication of our discussion of the Bible's protean shape through the centuries and across cultures. We must avoid constructing theology out of particular words or phrases in the Bible—or, as sometimes has happened, defend particular doctrines by reference to one or a few arcane phrases of Scripture—and instead derive our theology from "the whole counsel of God" (Acts 20:27) according to the whole Book of God. Yes, the Trinitarian decision at Nicaea did hinge on a single letter, and the smallest letter, of the Greek alphabet. A mere pen-stroke of an *iota* separated those who believed the Son was of the "same substance" as the Father (*homoousios*) from those who believed the Son was of "similar substance" as the Father (*homoiousios*). But these terms were not themselves Scriptural terms, and the complex and crucial matter of the ontology of the Trinity was not resolved by referring to single bits of Bible words. These terms came from Greek metaphysics and were used to summarize, as banners, careful readings of the whole Bible in concert with the best philosophy and most fervent piety of the time.

We therefore should be on our guard against the twin mistakes of arguing from our favorite snippets of Scripture and of arguing from our favorite themes of Scripture. Both modes truncate the Bible and we must constantly submit our summaries—whether rendered in proof-texts or epitomes—to critique: *Is that all* the Bible usefully says about this question?

Furthermore, the "whole counsel of God" must be understood (in a key argument of this book) in the light of the "*whole* whole counsel of God": in the context of everything that God has revealed, has *shown*, to us via human traditions, scholarship, art, and experiences—not only in terms of what has been revealed in the text of the Bible. In reference to the "*whole* whole counsel of God" is how the church, at its best, has always resolved doctrinal and ethical challenges, and it is how we must continue to engage them today.

Given this sketch of the nature of the Bible and its inspiration, what, then, is it for?

Posing this question immediately helps us recognize the narrowness of much modern argument that focuses upon the *truth* of the Bible. The evangelical championing of "inerrancy" is an understandable response to several preceding centuries of critics charging that the Bible was, indeed, widely and deeply erroneous. The Bible got its historical facts wrong (in both testaments), its scientific facts wrong (from its first chapter onwards), its moral facts wrong (with a bloodthirsty God wiping out whole populations in Genesis through Revelation)—even its own internal calendar wrong (from how many years the Israelites were in Egypt to how many days Christ was dead before his resurrection). Wrong, wrong, wrong.

These were serious charges, of course. The logic of the Christian religion, following the logic of its Jewish predecessor, is that God can be trusted and loved and obeyed on the basis of truths we know about God: truths about how God made the world and why; truths about God acting benevolently toward his people throughout history; truths about God's moral goodness despite appearances to the contrary; and truths pre-eminently about the life, work, and teachings of Jesus Christ. The Christian faith is about trusting a God who has acted in history such that we have reliable information about him and can live accordingly. It is not, by contrast, simply one group's retelling of some perennial philosophy, a universal mysticism or moralism that is clothed in various expressions around the world and amounts to the same glorious thing however impressive or crude its particular cultural trappings. No, this religion poses the "scandal of particularity" quite acutely: "God was in Christ reconciling the world to himself" (2 Cor. 5:19), and this God is the God of Abraham, Isaac, and Jacob; the God who brought Israel out of the land of Egypt to the Promised Land; the God who raised this Jesus from the dead and made him both Lord and Christ. So if at least this array of crucial facts is wrong, it's all wrong. No wonder, then, that faithful Christians in the modern era have fortified the ramparts regarding the truth of the Bible.

Nonetheless, to aver *only* that the Bible is true is to misconstrue its nature and purpose. The Apostle Paul, himself both an impressive student of Scripture and by God's grace an author of much of it, sets out the one Biblical epitome of Scripture's divine origin and object:

> The sacred writings . . . are able to instruct you for salvation through faith in Christ Jesus. All scripture is inspired by God and is useful for teaching, for reproof, for correction, and for training in righteousness, so that everyone who belongs to God may be proficient, equipped for every good work.
>
> (2 Tim. 3:15–17)

The Bible's fundamental purpose is to tell people what we need to know in order to put our faith in Jesus and thus receive God's salvation. More explicitly, the Scriptures teach us, yes, but they also reprove us (calling us to account when we are misbehaving), correct us (factually, yes, but also morally, spiritually, and every other way germane to our walk with God), and train us in the patterns of right living—shalom-making—so that each Christian will be fully equipped to do excellent work in the world.[44]

---

44. John Webster, echoing Calvin, puts the functions of Scripture concisely: "announcing the gospel, reproving idolatry and fostering true piety" (*Holy Scripture*, 74). This focus on what

This compact package, then, opens up to show us that the Bible is not only true in its facts and moral teachings, but it is *effective* as a training tool in its multifarious modes: promises, threats, warnings, comforts, commands, prohibitions, histories, prophecies, laws, proverbs, songs, musings, parables, doctrines, poems, and more. To say that this remarkable array of genres is "true" (or, to use the defensive double negative, "not errant") is thus to say not enough and of the right sort. "Infallible" is better, in that it gets at the Bible as a *functioning* thing, a book intended to achieve a purpose at which it does not fail. But another double negative will not do to express the positive virtues of the Holy Scriptures.

Better, then, to affirm that the Bible is the Word of God and does what God inspired it to do—which is what Paul affirms in 2 Timothy. *The Bible is what it is in order to do what it is intended to do.* If a passage of the Bible has to be historically reliable to achieve its purposes—as I understand the Bible's several accounts of Jesus' resurrection have to be—then the Christian can take it to be historically reliable.[45] If a passage of the Bible depicts historical developments in stylized literary terms, which is what I understand most of the first eleven chapters of Genesis to do, that part of the Bible is that kind of literature in order to accomplish what that part of the Bible is supposed to accomplish—namely, to provide a trans-culturally intelligible introduction to God, the world, the human race, the human predicament, and therefore the context in which the whole remainder of the Bible's story of redemption will be understood best.[46]

So is the Bible true? Yes, in the sense that it is never false, never deceptive, never misleading. But, again, double negatives do not suffice. The Bible tells us what we need to know, and in the way we need to know it. More generally, however—since the purpose of the Bible is not just to help us know things, as if the purpose of salvation was to be informed of certain truths—the Bible does what it is supposed to do.

---

the Bible *effects* rather than on theories as to what it *is* characterizes leaders of modern evangelicalism such as James Orr: see James Orr, *Revelation and Inspiration* (New York: Scribner's, 1910); Glen G. Scorgie, *A Call for Continuity: The Theological Contribution of James Orr* (Macon, GA: Mercer University Press, 1988).

45. We want to remember, of course, Aristotle's advice not to seek more precision than the subject itself admits of (*Nicomachean Ethics*, I.3).

46. As Calvin attests, "the Holy Spirit would rather speak childishly than unintelligibly to the humble and unlearned" (*Commentary on the Book of Psalms*, trans. James Anderson, 5 vols. (Edinburgh: Calvin Translation Society, 1845), 5: 168. Rodney Stark quotes John Chrysostom, Gregory of Nyssa, and Thomas Aquinas (along with John Calvin elsewhere in his corpus) making the same point: *Cities of God: The Real Story of How Christianity Became an Urban Movement and Conquered Rome* (San Francisco: HarperSanFrancisco, 2006), 106–7. Presumably, later generations of Christians, aided by increases in human knowledge, by changes in perspective, and by continued Scripture study and theological reflection, all guided by the Spirit's ongoing tutelage, can spot at least some of these "accommodations" in Scripture so as to evidence this general principle. As an example of what I trust is all of these factors at work, I offer my own small book, *Finally Feminist: A Pragmatic Christian Understanding of Gender* (Grand Rapids, MI: Baker Academic, 2005).

It is *effective*. In every passage, it is everything it needs to be in order to accomplish what God wants to accomplish: our salvation, our training in righteousness, and our usefulness to others in their salvation and training as well—all so that we human beings can resume our proper functioning in love for God, love for each other, and love for the rest of our fellow creatures "in every good work." As the Psalmist says, God's Word is "a lamp to my feet and a light for my path" (Ps. 119:105). It illuminates the world so that I can get where I am going as effectively as possible.

In the light of these considerations, then, we must appreciate that interpreting the Bible is as much like a musical performance as it is like a reading report. The Bible, as is suggested by a wide range of modern authors (from David Bosch to Ellen Charry to George Steiner to Kevin Vanhoozer), is meant to be performed as a mission, a liturgy, a score or a script. As each performance of a musical piece *is* an interpretation of that composition, so each action of the Christian as directed by God per the Bible is an interpretation of God's Word of blessing, or command, or warning, or reassurance. "This," we declare by our actions as well as our words, "is what we believe God means in the Bible by loving your neighbor, or doing justice, or glorifying God, or making shalom."[47]

Nowadays, it must be asserted to one or another group of Bible readers that there is no shortcut to understanding the Bible. In particular, commitment to neither extreme of "rigorous historical study" nor of "inerrancy" sorts things out easily. We need something that includes what is right about these commitments and yet goes beyond them.

In some ways these terms stand for "inductive" versus "deductive" approaches to the Bible. In the former case, the scholar examines the text with the instruments of historical, literary, anthropological, and other kinds of academic study and tries thereby to ascertain just what can be fairly said, according to the standards of these disciplines, of the Bible's truth. In the latter case, the scholar assumes that the Bible is true and then proceeds to research with this in mind, framing historical or exegetical or theological study around this prior conviction.

Surely, though, both of these approaches have some merit even as both also fall short. The believer is entitled—nay, wise and correct—to begin Scriptural study with the prior conviction that the Bible is divinely inspired. This is the historic position of all mainstream Christian thinking, and it is difficult to see why a Christian ought to depart from it. At a minimum, then, the Christian ought to proceed from the assumption that the Bible is not mistaken in its teaching, but can in fact be relied upon as divinely given precisely to render that teaching effectively. Moreover, since the Bible is God's Book, its various elements, however diverse, can be expected

---

47. I have in mind such works as David Bosch, *Transforming Mission: Paradigm Shifts in Theology of Mission* (Maryknoll, NY: Orbis, 2006); Ellen T. Charry, *By the Renewing of Your Minds: The Pastoral Function of Christian Doctrine* (New York and Oxford: Oxford University Press, 1997); George Steiner, *Real Presences* (Chicago: University of Chicago Press, 1989); and Kevin J. Vanhoozer, *The Drama of Doctrine: A Canonical Linguistic Approach to Christian Doctrine* (Louisville, KY: Westminster John Knox, 2005).

to co-operate with each other, so to speak, in furthering God's mission. One thus expects complementarity, reinforcement, elaboration, extension, qualification, and, ultimately, harmony among the voices of Scripture, since the one voice of God speaks through them all to one sovereign purpose: the redemption of the world.

One does not, to put it the other way, entertain the possibility that the Bible might in fact be simply wrong about its message. It may well be, naturally, that in the course of exegesis one will feel compelled to revise one's *interpretation* of what the Bible says in this or that passage. It may even be that one comes to see a particular passage as a divinely inspired (and therefore reliable) record of a decidedly human and even ungodly sentiment or conviction, as some believing scholars have seen part or all of the Book of Ecclesiastes, for instance. But the Christian scholar none-theless proceeds to Scriptural study with a belief that the Bible is God's Word in whatever sense pertains to the genre of the work under investigation. She thus pro-ceeds, in an expression almost lost today but common in nineteenth-century dis-cussions of higher criticism, *reverently*. She uses all the appropriate academic tools available to her, but deploys them as a child of God respectfully and expectantly listening for God to speak.[48]

Conversely, simply declaring the Bible "inerrant" *solves* little, as scholarly iner-rantists themselves recognize.[49] However lofty one's presuppositions about the inspiration and character of Scripture, one must humbly attend to the phenomena of Scripture with sophisticated care. There is therefore a hermeneutical circle here, too, as prior commitments about the Bible as the Word of God are refined by inves-tigation to see just *what* Word and *what kind of* Word God has provided for us, even as rigorous exegetical study is guided by the conviction that the Bible *is* the Word of God and therefore various interpretative possibilities are likely and various others—however excitingly revolutionary—simply are not worth the trouble to consider.[50]

---

48. Veteran Biblical scholar Bruce Waltke wryly quotes Puritan John Owen in this regard and adds his own contemporary reference: "John Owen noted that apart from the Spirit people are 'inclined to all things that are vain, curious, superstitious, carnal suited unto the interests of pride, lust, and all manner of corrupt affections.' An honest reader of the learned journals in biblical studies must acknowledge this fact" (Bruce K. Waltke, "Exegesis and the Spiritual Life: Theology as Spiritual Formation," *Crux* 30 [September 1994]: 33; the quotation is cited from John Owen, *The Works of John Owen* [London: T. & T. Clark, 1862], 4: n.p.).

49. See Norman L. Geisler, ed., *Inerrancy* (Grand Rapids, MI: Zondervan, 1980).

50. It is this fundamental, and appropriate, faith in God's revelation in Scripture that has prompted so many Christians to insist that every single detail in the Bible is straightforwardly and utterly true as that reader understands the requirements of truth for each such detail. It therefore comes as a shock, particularly to contemporary defenders of inerrancy, who are per-haps most conspicuous today among Anglophone members of the Reformed tradition, to find that John Calvin and Charles Hodge are among those orthodox Bible readers who thought that the Bible does, indeed, contain what to these readers were minor and literally insignificant mis-takes. On Calvin, see B. A. Gerrish, *The Old Protestantism and the New: Essays on the Reformation Heritage* (Chicago: University of Chicago Press, 1982), 63 (and see the literature there cited). On Charles Hodge, see his *Systematic Theology* (New York: Scribner's, 1871), 1:170.

An example from the last generation of Biblical scholarship illustrates something of this creative tension.[51] American Robert Gundry was voted out of the Evangelical Theological Society (ETS) in the mid-1980s because his commentary on the Gospel according to Matthew was judged to be contrary to the ETS's endorsement of biblical inerrancy.[52] Among Gundry's controversial conclusions was that the story of the Magi visiting the infant Jesus was a form of Jewish midrash, an illustrative story intended to make important theological points but not expected by the author to be understood as literal history, as an account of actual wise men traversing "field and fountain, moor and mountain" to worship Israel's new king.

Clearly this view of Matthew's gospel would upset the majority of Christians, who have traditionally believed that this story depicts actual events. It upsets me, since I agree that it does. But Gundry himself affirmed his belief in inerrancy. The Bible itself was not wrong, he contended, let alone misleading—except to those who were interpreting it badly. The author of the first Gospel is telling an edifying, if unhistorical, story that he expected his Jewish Christian audience to understand *as such*. It is we moderns who have misunderstood its intent and thus the nature of its truth. What it was intended to convey, Gundry concluded, is true.

This version of inerrancy did not please the majority of the ETS members who attended the stormy meeting at which Gundry's membership was terminated. But in the pages of the ETS's own journal, a well-known defender of inerrancy, D. A. Carson, granted Gundry's point entirely and stated that argument with Gundry's work had to proceed at a quite different level, the level of actual exegesis (as in "what *did* Matthew intend here?"). By his own lights, Carson agreed, Gundry was an inerrantist.

From that affirmation, then, the rest of the work of Biblical interpretation proceeds. The Bible is true, yes, but it is much more than *merely* true. It is efficacious: it gets done what God wants it to do—namely, to assist in the project of God's Spirit to reform human beings into the image of Christ. And to assist with all *that* seems to have required the Bible to be a very strange book indeed. For the Bible has needed to be astonishingly versatile: capable of converting people in two millennia (and counting) in every ethnic group, class, and situation and guiding them into mature, shalom-producing discipleship to Jesus. To be able to speak to such various audiences in such various contexts has apparently required a book of books, a congeries of poetry, prophecy, history, wisdom, epistles, and even an invented genre, gospels. The Bible is like an enormous repertoire of themes (David Martin) from which, when all goes well, the Holy Spirit helps the church in its each instance select

---

51. For a pithy survey of American evangelicals' complex relationship with Scripture and "inerrancy" in particular, see Gary Dorrien, *The Remaking of Evangelical Theology* (Louisville, KY: Westminster John Knox, 1998), 13–47.

52. I recount and reflect upon this story here: "Who Follows in His Train? E. J. Carnell as a Model for Evangelical Theology," *Crux* 21 (June 1985): 19–27. All citations for what follows appear in this article.

what will help them do what needs to be done.[53] It is a library: coherent, yes, but also so unfathomably rich as to challenge any summary, including even the great creeds—which, understood aright, are themselves merely tools, statements crafted by particular people in particular contexts to accomplish particular objectives. Furthermore, any such summaries—whether rendered via metaphysical schemata, grand narratives, poetic evocations, or otherwise—are not finally reducible to each other, as the contents of the Bible's revelation address us in a variety of ways per the variety of needs we have. We need parables to be explained, yes—the disciples themselves did, and Jesus commends them for asking rather than settling for mere amusement as did the crowds who heard and departed—but then we need to freshly encounter them *as parables*, explosive images and tales meant to shake us up. It is simply stupid to decry propositions as if careful thought about Christian matters can proceed happily without them. Propositions are keenly important in getting clear both basic and detailed understandings of crucial Biblical truths. But propositions are not the only way to render the Word of God and they are not sufficient to do all God wants done through his verbal revelation. Lorraine Code says in a broader context that

> images, metaphors, imaginings, and a governing imaginary are more and other than mere rhetorical devices, superimposed upon or embellishing an otherwise flat-footedly literal language capable, without their help, of mapping the "outside world" congruently and with no leftovers.[54]

The Bible presents us with an array of speech-acts (J. L. Austin) meant to *get things done*, to accomplish God's mission. Commands, promises, threats, assurances, blessings, curses, reminiscences, forecasts, warnings, proverbs, illustrations, suggestions, examples, exhortations, instructions—the Bible ranges widely in its semantic forms in order to accomplish a wide range of tasks in each Christian and each Christian community.

Currently among evangelical theological scholars there is a movement away from the stringent, even astringent, methodology of historical-critical Biblical interpretation toward so-called spiritual or theological interpretation of Scripture.[55] The immediate danger here is that historical and systematic theologians will elbow

---

53. John Webster is quite vehement on this point, and rightly so: "Worship, proclamation and ruling do not *make use* of the canon, as if it were a catalogue of resources through which the church could browse and from which it could select what it considered fitting or tasteful for some particular occasion; rather, they are acts which are at all points shaped by the canon and what it sets before the church" (*Holy Scripture*, 65).

54. Lorraine Code, *Ecological Thinking: The Politics of Epistemic Location* (Oxford and New York: Oxford University Press, 2006), 213.

55. J. Todd Billings, *The Word of God for the People of God: An Entryway to the Theological Interpretation of Scripture* (Grand Rapids, MI: Eerdmans, 2010); Daniel J. Treier, *Introducing Theological Interpretation of Scripture: Recovering a Christian Practice* (Grand Rapids, MI: Baker Academic, 2008).

aside Biblical scholars rather than cooperate with them. Thus there would be two distinct discourses, the former informed by the history of interpretation and the latter informed by the historical context of the Biblical texts themselves—as if responsible interpretation could ever be done without consulting all of these resources. Who would responsibly attempt to exposit Plato without understanding the cultural context of his day *and* conversing with the history of philosophy since then?

What has happened, to be sure, is that a particular hegemony has dominated the professional study of the Bible since at least the middle of the nineteenth century, a hegemony that has tended to reduce the sphere of plausible interpretation of the text to what any credentialed historian could accept—including Jewish or even atheistic historians.[56] This reductionist historical approach narrowed Bible study still further in that no subsequent interpreters in the history of the Church would be consulted in the process of exegesis due to the conviction that pre-modern writers *ipso facto* were unaware of both the pertinent historical knowledge and the pertinent historicist methodology necessary to study the Bible properly—quite apart from those interpreters' unfortunately obvious and controlling theological biases, such as presuming the Bible would not contradict itself since it was authored ultimately by God. The bibliographies of such run-of-the-mill scholarship therefore feature only two kinds of literature: the ancient Near Eastern literature contemporary to the Biblical materials in view plus notable commentaries and other publications of modern historical-critical scholars. The intervening two-thousand-year gap yawns conspicuously.

It is commonplace among critics of the historical-critical method to point out its failure to arrive at anything like a "scientific" consensus on most matters to which it has been devoted. Some progress, however, has been made such that there is, for example, a general consensus that some of the books of the Old Testament are composites of previous writings, rather than single books produced by a single author, and a consensus that the books of the New Testament were written by apostles or those in the apostolic circle less than a century after Jesus' death. On more particular matters, there is a consensus that the "long ending" of Mark is not part of the original gospel, nor the beloved story of Jesus and the woman caught in adultery. It is too easy to say that the story of the historical-critical method is simply one of ironic sterility.

---

56. For examples of, and mordant reflections upon, these developments, see John J. Collins, "Historical Criticism and the State of Biblical Theology," *The Christian Century* (July 28, 1993): 743–47; Van A. Harvey, *The Historian and the Believer: The Morality of Historical Knowledge and Christian Belief* (Philadelphia: Westminster Press, 1966); Eta Linnemann, *Historical Criticism of the Bible: Methodology or Ideology? Reflections of a Bultmannian Turned Evangelical*, trans. Robert W. Yarbrough (Grand Rapids, MI: Baker Academic, 1990); Plantinga, ch.12; Christopher R. Seitz, "The Changing Face of Old Testament Studies," *The Christian Century* (October 21, 1992): 932–35; and Peter Van Inwagen, "Skeptical of the Skeptics," *Books & Culture* 3 (May 1997): 29–30.

Nonetheless, from a Christian point of view, it also makes no sense for the Christian student of Scripture to pretend methodologically not to believe things she does in fact believe. Since she believes that the religious logic of the Old Testament depends on the historicity of God's saving acts (*since* God did that back then and there, *then* we can trust him here and now), she believes that the historical accounts in the Old Testament have to be generally true. Since she believes, for a more particular example, that God does not, in fact, hate women and that God did, in fact, inspire the Scripture for the good of all people, including women, she will look askance at the so-called "texts of terror" and will find that they do not, in fact, merely endorse patriarchy, let alone misogyny. [57] She will find, to the contrary, that the men committing violence in these stories are shown to be fools and thus are implicitly condemned by the ethical standards of the canon in which the narratives are found. When she turns to the New Testament, believing as she does, she will expect a close—not a distant, let alone a contradictory—relationship between the so-called Jesus of history and the Christ of faith.[58]

To be sure, she cannot simply play her "orthodox doctrine" card and sidestep the scholarly demands of her discipline. She has all the usual obligations of linguistic facility, historical knowledge, logical rigor, and so on. But her beliefs prompt her to look at the evidence differently than would someone of a secularist or minimalist outlook. And she might well include certain data in her argument—such as the belief that God exists and participated in the lives of God's people in evident ways, as attested in the Bible. So long as she is not arguing improperly, she is entitled to bring forward concepts and data she believes are true and germane. The mere fact that someone else doesn't hold to those concepts or data says nothing *prima facie* about their legitimacy. And in a postmodern context in which we recognize the irreducible reality of presuppositions guiding everyone's work, she may have to rest content with convincing only some of her colleagues—a situation, we might observe, that is not unlike the general state of the art as it is.

It would also make no sense for a Bible scholar to ignore two thousand years of Christian reflection on these texts, since the primary reason to study the Bible is to gain acquaintance of God, to grow in wisdom, and to perform one's vocation properly—all activities in which our forebears truly go before us and about which some of them can be expected to be expert in various respects. Technical scientific knowledge, yes, is not likely to be found in ancient texts, but wisdom routinely is. It is also true that cultures can forget what they once knew, particularly when it comes to matters of morality and prudence. So to grasp what God is saying today in this or that Biblical text, it would be well both to study the original context(s) thoroughly

---

57. Phyllis Trible, *Texts of Terror: Literary-Feminist Readings of Biblical Narratives* (Philadelphia: Fortress Press, 1984).

58. See Iain Provan, V. Philips Long, and Tremper Longman III, *A Biblical History of Israel* (Louisville, KY: Westminster/John Knox, 2003); C. Stephen Evans, *The Historical Christ and the Jesus of Faith: The Incarnational Narrative as History* (Oxford: Clarendon Press, 1996).

and to learn from subsequent Christian reflection, in its wide range of contexts, upon those texts.

So far, then, so good: All we are asserting here is that in the study of the Bible, as in any other study, the Christian bring to bear everything she knows that promises to be pertinent to that study. Secondary questions immediately arise, of course, such as the continuing relevance of once-popular interpretative methods, whether fourfold allegorizing and typologizing, privileging of Christological themes even in the Old Testament, and so on. But these and other questions must be resolved according to the express nature and purpose of Scripture. To the extent that these methods aid in truly expositing Scripture—truly *exposing* its message—in order to facilitate our faithful reception of it, we can welcome them. To the extent that something else is going on, whether mere ingenuity or the smuggling in of external agendas, let alone the subversion of the text to say something other than it says, then the danger must be denounced as such.

To understand and then to apply the apposite Biblical message to a particular community in a particular context requires gifted and trained individuals—what the New Testament calls, variously, pastors, teachers, evangelists, prophets, apostles, elders, and the like. The doctrine of the "perspicuity of Scripture" was formulated in Protestant polemics against the Roman Catholic warning that only the clergy could, and therefore should, interpret Scripture, and that they should do so only in concert with the tradition and teaching office of the Church. Protestants, disillusioned with the deliverances of the clergy of their day in the late medieval and early modern period of European history—a time replete with extravagant sins among the Renaissance popes and their curiae, exploitative selling of indulgences, impoverishing and life-threatening pilgrimages undertaken to reduce the threat of thousands of years of painful purgatory, and the like—retorted that the gospel of a carpenter relayed by fishermen was intelligible to anyone.

The Protestants said such things, of course, right up until a new front of theological controversy opened up on their left, so to speak, and the radical reformers took the ball and ran with it, some quite far into heresy, others certainly into new forms of theology and practice that quite undercut the previously unquestioned assumptions of (magisterial) Reformers and Catholics alike, whether church–state cooperation, Christ's presence in the Eucharist, the baptism of infants, and so on. Thus the mainstream Protestant Reformation fairly quickly rejoined the rest of the church against the radicals to insist that the Bible was yet complex enough to require the services of a class of trained interpreters to assist the rest of the church in its reading of Scripture.

What was radical in the sixteenth and seventeenth centuries, to be sure, has become common in the (radically) democratic cultures of contemporary modernity with its emphasis on the sovereign self interpreting and deciding for itself about the whole world, not just the Bible. In the populism so typical of American culture since the nineteenth century and now common so broadly elsewhere, authoritative teachers can spring up at any time, in any place, validated only by their appeal to a populace of followers. No credentialing by any seminary, university, denomination, or government is any longer required. Our Teacher says what I agree should be said, and that's why I follow his teachings. Thus in the wide-open religious markets particularly of Africa, South America, Korea, and China, but also of the former Soviet Union, among immigrants in the great cities of Europe, and parts of the ever-fertile religious soil of the American Midwest, South, and southern California, all sorts of teachers are, in fact, doing a good business. Churches of all sorts recognize that the Bible is, in fact, a pretty complicated collection of literatures. What distinguishes Christians from each other in this regard is, then, the basis on which teachers are recognized and the extent to which they wield interpretative authority. For our purposes, however, we can simply note the perennial need for teaching, and later we will discuss how authorities—for Scripture teaching and for everything else—can most reliably be discerned.

John Webster warns us of a perennial danger in all such talk of the Bible, no matter how lofty the predications of it, no matter how reverent the attitude toward it. Indeed, our very regard for Holy Scripture can incline us to a serious misunderstanding of its nature and use: "Accounts of scriptural inspiration are not infrequently curiously deistic, in so far as the biblical text can itself become a revelatory agent by virtue of an act of divine inspiration in the past."[59] Christians are neither deists nor Muslims: We do not properly understand the *scriptures* to be our primary authority for faith and practice (or anything else), but *God*. The fundamental dynamic of our religion is not the exegesis and application of a holy book. It is attending to Jesus' voice—through the humble and careful interpretation of the Bible, of course, but also of every other resource God has provided us, from physics to philosophy, from quotidian experiences to spectacular miracles, and from ancient proverbs to the latest Internet meme.

How, then, in cooperation with the Spirit of Jesus, is the Christian responsibly to conduct her consultation of the five resources we have set out for her? How is she then to connect them? And if Christians affirm, as they generally do, that the Bible is our supreme authority in faith and practice, how does she rightly relate her Bible study to her other studies—particularly if what she has concluded is true or right or beautiful somewhere else seems to conflict with what she finds in Scripture? To those elements of the model we now proceed.

THREE MODES OF APPREHENSION AND CONSIDERATION

Intuition

We use intuition in what appear to be several different ways.[60] In the first use, we refer to intuition as a kind of unusual, even extra-sensory perception. People "just

---

59. *Holy Scripture*, 36.

60. I formulated most of these ideas, such as they are, without knowing much about Michael Polanyi's work, which I have read only belatedly, if also gratefully. He makes much of intuition and related modes of knowing. For an introduction to these themes in his work, see Mark T.

know" that the missing object can be found in that unlikely place or that harm will come to that person soon. Perhaps they see a vision or hear a voice, but normally there is merely an inkling, a conviction or a sense (n.b.) that X *is* the case, despite not being able to supply a chain of data and inference to that conclusion. Intuition here is an apprehension of what is not commonly available experience.

"Women's intuition" is an interesting bridge to the second usage, for by this cliché we might mean that a woman perceives data that others don't, but we might also mean that a woman puts generally available data together immediately so as to perceive *better* what others do perceive and yet ignore. Either way, we note that a woman *just knows* that this man is dangerous, or that that woman is lying, or that the scheme we're discussing just doesn't make sense.

The second usage, then, is the case of an experienced expert instantly discerning a situation to which an ordinary person would be oblivious. The data are all there, but the non-expert doesn't process them the way the expert does. Think of the mechanic who *just knows* what's wrong with the engine, the chef who *just knows* what's missing in the sauce, or the musician who *just knows* that in the sixty-fifth measure the piece modulated up a minor third—or can even predict that it will.[61] It would be silly to discount these apprehensions merely because the experts involved cannot immediately specify just what data and what modes of reasoning lie behind them. Indeed, we trust our well-being to the intuition of pilots, surgeons, nurses, police officers, and others who have trained their intuition to produce reliable results quickly in the heat of trying moments.

Furthermore, intuition of a sort has a distinguished intellectual heritage, particularly emerging in modern European hermeneutics as Friedrich Schleiermacher, Leopold von Ranke, and others responded to the challenges of Kant's bifurcation of knowledge into noumena and phenomena. Intuition in this scholarly form of Romanticism is informed by rigorous analysis of texts and contexts, and does not so much go beyond them as integrate them with an imaginative connection to other people, places, and times. The intuitive interpreter then can say, in Ranke's famous formulation, *wie es eigentlich gewesen*, what "actually" or (more powerfully) what "essentially" happened, what was truly meant.[62]

Mitchell, "The Tacit Dimension: A New Paradigm for Knowing" chap. in *Michael Polanyi* [Wilmington, DE: ISI Books, 2006], 59–103).

61. Daniel Kahneman concludes about this kind of intuition, "Valid intuitions develop when experts have learned to recognize familiar elements in a new situation and to act in a manner that is appropriate to it" (*Thinking, Fast and Slow* [New York: Farrar, Straus and Giroux, 2011]), 12.

62. A highly accessible introduction to Schleiermacher can be found in B. A. Gerrish, *A Prince of the Church: Schleiermacher and the Beginnings of Modern Theology* (London: SCM Press, 1984). For Ranke, see Georg G. Iggers and Konrad von Moltke, "Introduction" to Leopold von Ranke, *The Theory and Practice of History*, ed. Georg G. Iggers and Konrad von Moltke, trans. Wilma A. Iggers and Konrad von Moltke (New York: Irvington, 1983), esp. xix, xlvii–liv.

In the so-called Reformed epistemology that has been so helpful to me, Alvin Plantinga describes two mental functions that seem intuitive along some of the lines we have just encountered. Plantinga has coined the term *basic beliefs* for beliefs we form instantly upon apprehending a certain situation. "There is a tree" is not a conviction we form via a chain of inferences from a bunch of data we carefully interpret into the conclusion that standing there is, in fact, a tree. No, upon seeing the tree we immediately, automatically, and I would say intuitively believe that "there is a tree."

In his masterwork, *Warrant and Christian Belief,* Plantinga then makes considerable use of this concept as he asserts, in the company of Aquinas and Calvin, that human beings have a *sensus divinitatis,* an apprehension of the divine, that is as basic as beholding a tree. Plantinga goes on at great length then to specify what qualifications must obtain for human beings so to perceive God—much as his epistemological compatriot William Alston did in justifying what he calls Christian Mystical Experience.[63] In both philosophers' epistemologies, then, an important place is reserved for the direct apprehension of God and of other spiritual realities. [64] And this conviction reflects their regard for a Bible teaching often neglected in epistemological discourse: "O *taste* and *see* that the Lord is good" (Ps. 34:8; emphasis

---

63. Plantinga is not entirely clear as to whether he thinks the *sensus divinitatis* is an innate sense of the existence of God or is, at least, the capacity for sensing, in the right circumstances, the existence of God. Following Romans 1, he believes that the *sensus divinitatis* has been deeply compromised in the human race, but can yet be, and is being, enjoyed by many. See *Warranted Christian Belief* (New York and Oxford: Oxford University Press, 2000), esp. chaps. 6 and 8. Alston, *Perceiving God.*

64. Plantinga seems to think that *faith* is a kind of "belief-producing *process* or activity, like perception or memory" (*Warranted Christian Belief,* 256), but I confess I cannot make sense of his claim. Convictions about God seem to be formed in us in a variety of ways—whether direct apprehension of God in mystical experience, inferring truths about God from other kinds of observation, accepting the teaching of the Scriptures, bowing to the authority of our spiritual betters, and more. But I don't see *faith* as some special kind of belief-producing *operation,* but rather an *attitude* of trust based on what I think I know about some source of knowledge (e.g., from what I know of it, or him, I can rely on this book, or this teacher) that opens me up to receiving more truth from that source. Indeed, Plantinga quotes Aquinas in his argument, but I think Aquinas is actually on *my* side in this friendly quarrel: "Faith is a habit of the mind whereby eternal life is begun in us, making the intellect assent to what is non-apparent" (*Summa Theologiae* II-II, q.4, a.i, *respondeo;* quoted in *Warranted Christian Belief,* 266).

Perhaps Plantinga (and Calvin, whom he follows particularly on this question) uses the term "faith" for what is, in the terminology I am using, spiritual *intuition.* Brother Lawrence, via his interviewer Joseph de Beaufort, speaks similarly of this question thus: "[Brother Lawrence] told me several times that everything he said, read, and even wrote himself seemed insipid in comparison with what faith revealed to him concerning the grandeurs of God and Jesus Christ. 'He alone,' he said, 'is capable of making himself known as he really is. We seek in reasoning and in the sciences—as in a poor copy—what we fail to see in an excellent original. God paints himself in the depths of our souls" (Joseph de Beaufort, "The Ways of Brother Lawrence," in *The Practice of the Presence of God by Brother Lawrence,* ed. Conrad de Meester, trans. Salvadore Sciurba [Washington, DC: Institute of Carmelite Studies, 1994 (1694)], 114).

added)—a teaching echoed in Pascal's oft-quoted, if not always well understood, claim that "the heart has its reasons of which reason knows nothing" (*Pensée* 277).

These various types of intuition thus share a basic quality: the sense of directly apprehending something, whether a physical object, or an aesthetic pattern, or a moral condition, or a spiritual presence. Intuition is what we mean by *just seeing* or *just knowing* something.[65] Indeed, there is a wide range of occupations that train people's intuitions, literally training their emotions, so that they will respond properly to stimuli even if they cannot articulate why they form the judgments they do.[66] Again, if we consider mechanics, pilots, surgeons, counselors, mediators, artists, talent scouts, sommeliers, and more, we can observe how valuable a well-tuned intuitive ability can be.[67]

Intuition is hardly infallible, of course. Indeed, a great deal of epistemology and psychology has been devoted to showing how our intuitions, certain as they *feel*, can lead us astray.[68] Let's consider two examples, from opposite ideological viewpoints, on the idea of God—a subject of obvious importance about which everyone has some intuitions.

Atheists typically argue that the problem of evil poses insuperable difficulties for orthodox believers. From David Hume to Richard Dawkins, it is just intuitively obvious to such critics that a Supreme Being would never design a world that is so obviously makeshift, dangerous, and painful. On the other end of the ideological spectrum, orthodox theologians from the patristic period to the present affirm the immutability, even the impassibility, of God because of their strong intuition that a Supreme Being *ipso facto* can neither change nor suffer. In both cases, the reply can come that it would be well to look hard(er) at the information and interpretative options available, rather than close off possibilities simply because one currently

---

65. Elaine Scarry suggests that encountering beauty "provides by its compelling 'clear discernibility' an introduction (perhaps even our first introduction) to the state of certainty." One has trouble even considering that one might be wrong about one's intuition that *that* is *beautiful* (Elaine Scarry, *On Beauty and Being Just* [Princeton, NJ: Princeton University Press, 1999], 31).

66. One thinks of Polanyi's commendation of *connoisseurship* and of Steiner's assertion that "the humanities are susceptible neither to crucial experiments nor to verification (except on a material, documentary level). Our responses to them are narratives of intuition....The only propositions are those of personal choice, of taste, of echoing affinity or deafness" (*Errata: An Examined Life* [New Haven, CT and London: Yale University Press, 1997], 5–6).

67. Students have occasionally asked me where *emotions* fit into my scheme, if they do at all. It seems to me they fit here, as signals that one's perceptions or conceptions are getting "hotter" or "colder," better or worse. Many is the time I have pored over a manuscript and just felt that something was wrong. It might have taken several revisitings to get clear what exactly was wrong in the writing, let alone to fix it. But the initial emotion (in my case, a sort of dread bordering on nausea, alas), was reliable, triggered as it is by years of experience in reading and writing. Those years, moreover, have taught me to pay attention to that emotion rather than shy away from it, unpleasant as it is. (Readers of this book, of course, will wonder why that emotion wasn't triggered much more often, and I can only nod in sad acquiescence.)

68. Malcolm Gladwell rather famously extols the virtues of intuition even as he then provides, somewhat contradictorily, ample grounds to doubt it in *Blink: The Power of Thinking without Thinking* (New York and Boston: Little, Brown, 2005).

cannot imagine how *A* or *B* can be the case. One is reminded of God telling Moses in the burning bush that God's name would be "I AM WHO I AM," (Ex. 3:14) rather than whatever conception of deity would come to the mind of a contemporary Egyptian or Israelite. The world, as G. K. Chesterton enjoyed reminding us, is much stranger than we expect, and actually examining what it is provides better knowledge than serenely supposing what it must be.[69]

Intuition is also not to be despised, however, as some modern forms of epistemology have done. As Thomas Morris says, "To ask why anyone should ever rely on intuition is like asking why anyone should ever believe what seems to him to be true."[70] We do in fact intuit a great deal of the world around us, and we have to be able to do so in order to negotiate the complex sensorium we inhabit. Who could possibly walk from the bedroom to the kitchen, let alone drive a car, if all knowledge had to be worked up by gathering and then sifting through the wide range of available sense impressions, holding them up carefully against all possible interpretative options, with data and interpretations then sorted out in a rigorous dialectic to the best possible conclusion?

We find we are thus repeating ourselves, for we came to these conclusions already when we discussed experience as a resource. Intuition is the mode by which we receive experiences and immediately form beliefs, whether those experiences are ordinary sense impressions, or gleanings from introspection, or patterns of sense impressions only expertise can discern, or spiritual realities only some are equipped and positioned to encounter.

Moving to situations that cannot be adequately comprehended by intuition requires use of other faculties: imagination and reason. To them we now turn.

Imagination

Imagination functions for us intellectually in at least four ways. First, imagination provides ways of connecting our intuitions—our initial apprehensions of sense experiences, yes, but also our readings or our recollections of tradition, the sciences, art, and Scripture. Intuition is our "reading" of the world in the sense of a

---

69. G. K. Chesterton, *Orthodoxy*, and especially "The Paradoxes of Christianity"; and *The Everlasting Man* (New York: Doubleday, 1955 [1925]), especially II, 3: "The Strangest Story in the World," 202–17.

70. Thomas V. Morris, *Our Idea of God: An Introduction to Philosophical Theology* (Downers Grove, IL: InterVarsity, 1991), 39. Ironically, Morris's own use of "perfect being theology" as a method in this volume is vulnerable to the charge of excessive reliance on intuition and not enough reliance on Scripture, particularly in his preference for "two-minds" Christology instead of kenotic Christology. For discussions of the latter, which do specifically claim to put the Biblical evidence ahead of philosophical intuition, see C. Stephen Evans, *Exploring Kenotic Christology: The Self-Emptying of God* (New York and Oxford: Oxford University Press, 2006); and John G. Stackhouse, Jr., "Jesus Christ," in *The Oxford Handbook of Evangelical Theology*, ed. Gerald D. McDermott (New York and Oxford: Oxford University Press, 2010), 146–58.

meter "reading" hydraulic flow or a tuner "reading" electrical signals such that a television screen lights up in a certain pattern. Imagination arranges these readings into patterns for us to consider.

In the previous discussion, we noted that our minds sometimes jump directly to a conclusion when we have certain experiences. We announce, "I see a tree," without sorting through various alternative interpretations of our experience. But of course sometimes we hesitate, even in the presence of what looks like it might be a tree. Imagination, then, helps us apprehend what we are experiencing by furnishing us with interpretative possibilities. "That looks like it *might* be a tree, but I don't feel right about stopping there. For it also looks like it *could* be a blossom of cauliflower, and also a lot like a kind of coral—and now you're telling me that it is some kind of *brain*?" Imagination concatenates the various elements of an experience into possible interpretative units for our evaluation. It provides us options for identifying what it is we are experiencing.

As interpretation proceeds, secondly, imagination can assist by offering us thought experiments. As Einstein considered theories of relativity, he famously thought about trains and light beams. He could do mathematics at a very high level, of course, but the math part of the theory had to wait until he imagined people dealing with flashes of light on moving trains and then thought through the implications of this imaginary situation. The experimental/observational part of the theory of relativity would have to wait still longer.[71] (I would scarcely be the first to connect Einstein's notorious resistance to quantum theory with the fact that most of what it asserts cannot be imagined but only asserted on the ground that it makes some of the math work out and renders at least somewhat coherent the results of a variety of experiments.[72])

C. S. Lewis, in a generally overlooked essay, speaks of the crucial importance of metaphors in our thinking, metaphors furnished by our imaginations. "When we pass beyond pointing to individual sensible objects," he writes, "when we being to think of causes, relations, of mental states or acts, we become incurably metaphorical."[73] We

---

71. In an oft-quoted interview, Einstein testifies as follows: "I believe in intuitions and inspirations. I sometimes feel that I am right. I do not know that I am. When two expeditions of scientists, financed by the Royal Academy, went forth to test my theory of relativity, I was convinced that their conclusions would tally with my hypothesis. I was not surprised when the eclipse of May 29, 1919, confirmed my intuitions. I would have been surprised if I had been wrong."

[Interviewer:] "Then you trust more to your imagination than to your knowledge?"

"I am enough of the artist to draw freely upon my imagination. Imagination is more important than knowledge. Knowledge is limited. Imagination encircles the world" ("What Life Means to Einstein: An Interview by George Sylvester Viereck," *The Saturday Evening Post* [26 October 1929]: 117).

72. I was not a little comforted to read John Polkinghorne conclude his *Quantum Theory: A Very Short Introduction* with the confession that neither he nor his colleagues held coherent pictures in their heads of what they were talking about (New York and Oxford: Oxford University Press, 2002).

73. C. S. Lewis, "Bluspels and Flalanspheres: A Semantic Nightmare," in *Selected Literary Essays*, ed. Walter Hooper (Cambridge: Cambridge University Press, 1969), 263.

connect the elements of our apprehension by way of things we think we already understand, and thus in the presence of this new thing begin to run through the similar possibilities by way of metaphor: "This seems to be *like* a...." As George Lakoff and Mark Johnson suggest, metaphor "unites reason and imagination...[as] metaphor is one of our most important tools for trying to comprehend partially what cannot [yet] be comprehended totally."[74]

Imagination enriches our interpretation, thirdly, by helping us to enter into the interpretative situations, and thus to grasp better the interpretations, of those significantly different from ourselves. To be sure, we must avoid the arrogant naïveté that supposes we can drop nicely into just any alternative interpretative paradigm and fully comprehend it, only then to pop out again to return to our own schema with whatever we found fruitful to consider in the other. Truly understanding a truly different interpretation requires considerable learning, but also moral virtues such as humility, discipline, sympathy, and flexibility in the service of a versatile imagination. With such imagination, however, one can come at least to a beneficial approximation: "Well, I think I can see how someone in that situation *could* think that—and this is what I've learned...."[75]

Beyond thought experiments to help us think through what is the case and beyond enabling us to consider others' interpretations of what is the case, imagination, fourthly, can test interpretative options by extending them into what is *not* the case—not yet, or not in our experience. Here is the imaginative realm of extrapolations, ramifications, and reductios. "What would things be like if *X* really were the case?" Psychological, sociological, religious, ethical, historical and technological ideas have been tested for years this way in science fiction, fantasy, and other forms of wildly imaginative—but also often quite rigorously logical—fiction. Moreover, we can extend this consideration of the value of imagination in the testing of theories into the realm of action. If we conclude *X*, what then follows for moral practice? What is the best thing to do, not just think? Logic plays a non-negotiable part in such thinking, of course, but so does imagination.[76]

It is crucial, then, to note that a limited imagination poses a significant limit to all forms of thought above the most mechanical/algorithmic. We cannot consider

---

74. George Lakoff and Mark Johnson, *Metaphors We Live by* (Chicago: University of Chicago Press, 1980), 193.

75. I trust it is clear, therefore, that I am not advocating the strong (actually, quite mystical) goal of *Verstehen*, an actual entering-into of the outlook of someone of a different time and place, that animates Leopold von Ranke and his historicist successors. I am thinking in the more circumspect, but still ambitious, terms of Clifford Geertz's advocacy of "thick description" of a situation such that it, and its main subjects, become truly intelligible to the informed and sympathetic observer: Leopold von Ranke, *The Theory and Practice of History*, reprint ed. (New York: Irvington, 1983); Clifford Geertz, *The Interpretation of Cultures: Selected Essays* (New York: Basic Books, 1973).

76. I thus promiscuously combine Coleridge's secondary form of "imagination" (which he valorizes) with what he calls "fancy" (which he does not). See his *Biographia Literaria* (London, 1817), ch. 13.

as a possibility what doesn't occur to us to imagine in the first place. The cultivation of a bold imagination that is both free and equipped to wander widely while also remaining in productive contact with the matter at hand is a crucial desideratum of serious thought. And the cultivation of a bold imagination, one might observe, has not everywhere and always been highly prized among Christians.

Indeed, if we go beyond the situation of coming to an initial interpretation of a matter to that of changing our minds from one conclusion to another, it is clear that only a vividly imagined alternative will have any chance of affecting our outlook and behavior. We will stick with what we know unless given an adequately powerful motive to give it up, and imagination's power to depict the alternative and its ramifications plays a crucial part in that process. We will return to this question of how we change our minds, not just make them up in the first place, again and again in what follows. For now, however, we can turn to the last stage in our scheme of apprehension and consideration.

Reason

Thomas Morris provides a highly intelligible and sensible definition of reason which, although it needs supplementation by the explicit inclusion of imagination per the previous discussion (I expect Morris would include imagination under reason in this definition), will serve us well:

> Human reason is just the power we have to organize and interpret our sense experience (what we see, hear, touch, taste, smell, or sense in any other way) [Morris would be including all of what I mean by "intuition" here] as well as the power to draw conclusions that move beyond the confines of immediate experience. We sometimes talk of reason as if it were a separate organ for discovering truth. It is better thought of as a cluster of skills and abilities, abilities to work with and process what we're given as we make contact with the outside world and reflect on ourselves.[77]

If intuition is about immediacy, and imagination about possibility, reason is about comprehension, evaluation, and decision. Reason makes sure that elements of our thought relate properly with each other (coherence) and with the part of the world they describe (correspondence).

At least since the Romantic critique of the Enlightenment, and actually much further back in the dismissal of theology by mystics, reason has been accused of arrogant objectification, of cold-eyed appraisal of "the other," of enjoying an artificial and ultimately unjustified perch on the judgment seat of the world. Yet it remains hard to imagine how some key aspects of life would be better without reason's discipline, its appeal to reality rather than to prejudice, preference, passion, or

---

77. Thomas V. Morris, *Making Sense of It All: Pascal and the Meaning of Life* (Grand Rapids, MI: Eerdmans, 1992), 66–67.

power. The university itself operates under the aegis of reason, whatever else also goes on therein. Are the critics of reason truly prepared to do without the fruits of science and technology? The correct response to the undeniable overreach of reason and its devotees in so much of the modern world cannot be to abandon it.

The Christian view of human reason strikes a balance between expecting too much and expecting too little from human rationality. The Bible's repeated affirmation that the world, let alone God, is too complex for our final comprehension cautions us against epistemological hubris. We can note that this caution extends not only to non-Christian thinking but to Christian thinking as well. Even God's favorites—indeed, *especially* God's favorites—and in both Testaments proclaim the surpassing greatness of the mind of God and God's design of the world. From the whirling declarations of God to Job to the almost indescribable visions vouchsafed to John in the Apocalypse, the message is clear that even our own planet, even our very selves, remain mysterious to us in important respects.

Thus the Christian thinker is not troubled by modern critiques of knowledge (or ancient ones, for that matter) that put us humans in our place, *sub specie aeternitatis*. When Thomas Kuhn's brilliant discussion of *The Structure of Scientific Revolutions* startles us with its radical historicizing and politicizing of the archetype of all modern rationality, physics itself, we are yet not dismayed and can appreciate Kuhn's implicit warning against epistemological presumption. When Nicholas Wolterstorff mounts his unanswerable attack on what he calls "classical foundationalism" in his *Reason within the Bounds of Religion*, showing that the modern insistence that only what is indisputably and immediately available to the senses or self-evident to reason can be trusted as the basis for the rest of human thought, the Christian rejoices in the freedom to draw on a much wider range of resources.[78] And when Lorraine Code's masterpiece of feminist epistemology, *Ecological Thinking*, locates our rationality within one or another social location such that we are always thinking as the particular people we are and not as "humanity-in-general," the Christian who sees in the Bible human beings as necessarily male or female, old or young, married or single, of one or another community in one or another occupation within one or another nation, carries on as best she can in her particular situation and vocation.[79]

To these seminal thinkers about thinking, as well as a few more, we will return presently. But for now, we can affirm also that a Christian view of things resists any wholesale disparagement of reason.

Disparagement of reason, as we have seen, can come in various forms. Mystics claim direct intuition of divinely revealed truths, while conservatives need only to recite their divinely given traditions. Both types of Christian thinking fear and reject

---

78. Nicholas Wolterstorff, *Reason within the Bounds of Religion*, 2nd ed. (Grand Rapids, MI: Eerdmans, 1984 [1976]).

79. Lorraine Code, *Ecological Thinking: The Politics of Epistemic Location* (Oxford and New York: Oxford University Press, 2006).

reason as "worldly," as somehow a devilish replacement for a proper Christian attitude of mere receptivity to God's directly given gifts. Even in Christian academic circles, logical reflection is disparaged in some quarters as sterile, objectifying, "logocentric," "phallocentric," ethereal, and the like, while *narrative* is championed as vital, organic, embodied, grounded, and so on. (Traditionally this argument has been put as contrasting an alien "Hellenistic/Greek" mentality with an authentic, "Hebraic/Jewish" outlook, an antinomy with more than a few resemblances to the still older "Apollonian" versus "Dionysian" conflicts among intellectuals of quite different stripes.)

As Christians, of course, these antagonists of reason will sometimes resort to Scripture to make their case, with reference invariably to this *locus classicus*:

> For Christ did not send me to baptize but to proclaim the gospel, and not with eloquent wisdom, so that the cross of Christ might not be emptied of its power. For the message about the cross is foolishness to those who are perishing, but to us who are being saved it is the power of God. For it is written, "I will destroy the wisdom of the wise, and the discernment of the discerning I will thwart." Where is the one who is wise? Where is the scribe? Where is the debater of this age? Has not God made foolish the wisdom of the world? For since, in the wisdom of God, the world did not know God through wisdom, God decided, through the foolishness of our proclamation, to save those who believe. For Jews demand signs and Greeks desire wisdom, but we proclaim Christ crucified, a stumbling block to Jews and foolishness to Gentiles, but to those who are the called, both Jews and Greeks, Christ the power of God and the wisdom of God. For God's foolishness is wiser than human wisdom, and God's weakness is stronger than human strength. Consider your own call, brothers and sisters: not many of you were wise by human standards, not many were powerful, not many were of noble birth. But God chose what is foolish in the world to shame the wise; God chose what is weak in the world to shame the strong; God chose what is low and despised in the world, things that are not, to reduce to nothing things that are, so that no one might boast in the presence of God. He is the source of your life in Christ Jesus, who became for us wisdom from God, and righteousness and sanctification and redemption, in order that, as it is written, "Let the one who boasts, boast in the Lord."
>
> When I came to you, brothers and sisters, I did not come proclaiming the mystery of God to you in lofty words or wisdom. For I decided to know nothing among you except Jesus Christ, and him crucified. And I came to you in weakness and in fear and in much trembling. My speech and my proclamation were not with plausible words of wisdom, but with a demonstration of the Spirit and of power, so that your faith might rest not on human wisdom but on the power of God.
>
> (1 Cor. 1:17–2:5).

Any reader of this book who has gotten this far likely doesn't need a long defense of the use of reason, but it is worth pausing a moment to understand at least elementarily what is and isn't being said by the Apostle in this oft-cited text.

Paul preaches to the Corinthians a transcendent message, one that comes from God as revelation rather than from human traditions or ratiocination. These Gentile

Christians apparently suffered from considerably inflated self-esteem, and Paul puts them in their place, as he places the best of human insight—Jewish or Gentile—in its place. The crucified and resurrected Lord of glory is precisely what *no one expected* as the definitive revelation of God and as the decisive mode of human salvation. No one, then, can claim epistemological mastery over the great things of God: they come from above, to our surprise and even our shock such that our greatest human intellectual traditions either stumble in confusion or recoil in scorn from such an apparently incongruous message: God was on a Cross reconciling the world to himself. This message, Paul avers, is not one you can be talked into, nor is it one you can discover on your own terms. God must uncover, must reveal it, and you must come to terms with it. The very message and mode of the Gospel drive us to the posture of submission to the surpassing, surprising greatness of God—or drive us away.

Having made that fundamental point clear, however, Paul then goes immediately on to connect it with the wisdom he has temporarily set aside:

> Yet among the mature we do speak wisdom, though it is not a wisdom of this age or of the rulers of this age, who are doomed to perish. But we speak God's wisdom, secret and hidden, which God decreed before the ages for our glory. None of the rulers of this age understood this; for if they had, they would not have crucified the Lord of glory. But, as it is written, "What no eye has seen, nor ear heard, nor the human heart conceived, what God has prepared for those who love him"—these things God has revealed to us through the Spirit; for the Spirit searches everything, even the depths of God. For what human being knows what is truly human except the human spirit that is within? So also no one comprehends what is truly God's except the Spirit of God. Now we have received not the spirit of the world, but the Spirit that is from God, so that we may understand the gifts bestowed on us by God. And we speak of these things in words not taught by human wisdom but taught by the Spirit, interpreting spiritual things to those who are spiritual. Those who are unspiritual do not receive the gifts of God's Spirit, for they are foolishness to them, and they are unable to understand them because they are spiritually discerned.
>
> (I Cor. 2:6–14)

Of course, Paul is saying, we value wisdom, including straightforward propositions about the way the world is, from proverbs to doctrines. Our Scripture is full of such teaching; whole books are devoted to it. And I myself, he says, am a highly trained rabbi, taught not only by Gamaliel but by Jesus himself. So of course we make use of human reason. But it is reason that has been informed and transformed by the gospel. More than that, in fact, it is reason that has been enlivened and enlightened by the very Spirit of God such that we now can recognize as true what otherwise we also would have rejected as utterly implausible, as simply irreconcilable with what we "know" is true.

We will later say much more about the role of the Holy Spirit in Christian thought. For now, we will be glad just to recognize that this text does not, in fact, disparage human reason but instead puts it in its place: under the Gospel, under the Spirit, under the supreme revelation of God in Christ. Rightly functioning reason is reason that gets the basic things right and puts first things first. And it does so only as a responsible recipient of God's gifting, not as a boastful hero of intellectual prowess.

We recall, in this light, that without reason we can hardly perform God's basic calling upon our lives as human beings to cultivate the world. We certainly cannot worship God with our minds, as Jesus taught us to do as he reiterated the Great Commandment and laid stress (by adding a term for it) on the mind. (Matt. 22:37) We can hardly love each other properly if we cannot think intelligently about what that would mean in any given case. And we cannot perform God's calling of Christians to make disciples without rationality, either, as God gave us much complex reading material and skilled teachers to help us understand what it means to follow Jesus aright.

There is no brief offered here, therefore, for *rationalism*, for any glorification of reason above its proper station. Reason remains a humble worker going about its normal business of noticing, sorting, and arranging as best it can, according to the disciplines it has learned along the way and drawing on the right mode or modes of reasoning appropriate to the occasion, the materials presented to it moment by moment in the providence of God. We do not bow before the power of reason, but instead give thanks to God who gave us this power, who calls us to use it in worthy enterprises, and who promises to assist us in its most effective and honorable use.[80]

How, then, do we reason? More broadly, how do we draw on these various resources according to the different modes of apprehension and consideration at our disposal? To the collecting and coordination of the fruits of these gifts we now turn.

---

80. Some readers may wonder if I am nodding to the ghosts of Max Weber and Jacques Ellul in this implicit caution about reason—and technology—as idols. I am.

4

The Basic Scheme

INTERPRETATION AND THE PENTALECTIC

All five resources we encountered in the last chapter—experience, tradition, sciences, art, and Scripture—stand ready to assist Christians in responsible thought. Yet in at least four key respects we have less at our disposal than it may appear we have. First, we have only as much of those resources as we have acquired. We can consider only the experiences we ourselves have had plus those of other people to which we have some kind of access. Clearly, the sum total of human experiences (let alone the experiences of other beings) is not on our mental table, so to speak, as we think about this or that issue. We can get up from the table and seek out more, to be sure, but whatever we harvest, that is what we have to work with. The same is true, obviously, of the other four resources as well. If we have not listened to the teachers of tradition, if we have not learned geology or economics or music, if we have not yet encountered this or that work of art, and if have not studied parts of the Bible, then they are absent from our consideration.

Second, we have only as much of those resources as we have in our minds while we are thinking. Obviously, I cannot deploy information I have forgotten. If I know where to look, I can retrieve it, but I do have to remember that I have forgotten something important even to initiate that search, I have to recall where it may now be found, and I have to reinsert it into my mind along with whatever else I currently recall so as to actually use it. Even allowing, as we must, for the workings of intuition, which can draw upon things we have learned even if we cannot immediately bring them to consciousness, the point remains that we cannot work with what we have truly and completely forgotten.

Third, I can work with only as much of those resources as I choose—consciously or not—to reflect upon. If it doesn't somehow occur to me to connect Michelangelo's statue of David with my present study of the Bible's accounts of David, then even though I have seen the statue and could recall it easily at will, it is effectively absent to me in this case. Indeed, we should acknowledge again in this regard the influence our emotions have on our thinking. We might not connect the current situation with one in our childhood, say, or in the experience of a friend, or an enemy, precisely because at some level we do not *want* to connect them. Our cognitive function is affected, perhaps improved but also perhaps impaired, by motives and obstacles originating in our affections, rather than merely in our reason.

Fourth, our situation is more circumscribed still. Whatever of the five resources I have learned and recall and choose to consider, I can work with only in the form of my *interpretation* of each. While, say, Einstein's papers on relativity lie on the desk in front of me, what I actually have to work with in my consideration of contemporary physics is what I actually *comprehend* of Einstein's work. I might be staring directly at Picasso's *Guernica*, but only what actually impresses me can go into my reflection—and what will impress me will depend upon a wide range of factors, such as my own experiences of war, my knowledge of the Spanish Civil War and Picasso's connections with it, my understanding of Picasso's formal agenda at this stage of his career, and so on. And to the extent I lack the requisite scientific or aesthetic ability to fully comprehend these works of genius (I use the word "genius" to underline the surplus of meaning I surely will miss in each case), I will lack what those resources offer. I am working, always, only with my interpretations of those resources, not the resources themselves.

Recalling Jacques Derrida's *On Grammatology* as well as semiotic reflections by Umberto Eco prompts me to note that words (and, as we have referred to Picasso, we ought to extrapolate this observation to refer to all signs), always come with their previous uses aboard, so to speak—or, at least, those uses recognized at some level, even if only unconsciously, by authors and audiences. The task of interpretation is thus often multilayered and multidimensionally dynamic as connotations and denotations interact in our minds, and as we succeed or fail in discerning whatever similar interaction in the author's mind affects his communication to us.[1]

What must seem a simple point I trust will nonetheless go deeply into our epistemological awareness—as it evidently does not, even among (and sometimes especially among) some brilliant and highly educated people. In any situation of even moderate complexity, we are only ever working with a truncated and distorted apprehension of its elements. (So much, then, for talk of mastery, command, and control.)[2]

It perhaps is worthwhile, then, to consider briefly what we mean by the vexed word-set of "reality, interpretation, and truth." *Reality* is whatever is. Reality is what,

---

1. Jacques Derrida, *Of Grammatology*, trans. Gayatri Chakravorty Spivak (Baltimore: Johns Hopkins University Press, 1976); Umberto Eco, *A Theory of Semiotics* (Bloomington, IN: Indiana University Press, 1978). See also George Steiner, *Errata: An Examined Life* (New Haven, CT and London: Yale University Press, 1997).

2. Michael Polanyi drily complicates things even more: "For just as, owing to the ultimately tacit character of all our knowledge, we remain ever unable to say all that we know, so also, in view of the tacit character of meaning, we can never quite know what is implied in what we say" (Michael Polanyi, *Personal Knowledge: Towards a Post-Critical Philosophy* [Chicago: University of Chicago Press, 1958], 95). But I trust the situation is complicated enough by now for the general point to stand.

and the way, things are. Perhaps there is just One Thing, whether that be the universe, or Brahman, or God. Maybe there are two things or lots of things. But whatever is actually real, that is what we should mean by "reality."

We perceive things, and we interpret them.[3] We name them, or paint them, or represent them in some other way. These *interpretations* of ours, then, are our attempts to "re-present" reality in some approximate form. So a map re-presents the streets of Chicago, say, by showing them in relation to each other, to Lake Michigan, and to the points of the compass.

Now our interpretations are not exactly like the reality they represent—at least, not any complex reality. If we want to re-present reality in an exact one-to-one way, we would simply have to duplicate it.[4] To produce such a totally exact "map" of downtown Chicago, we would have to construct a parallel Loop—Sears Tower and Chicago River, and all—down to the subatomic level. (Indeed, in order to make the representation exact, to push this thought experiment right off the edge into absurdity, we would have to have it occupy the same position in space-time as the original.) So our interpretations (again, of complex realities) always sacrifice certain aspects or dimensions of the reality they represent in order to get a particular job done. A typical street map helps us drive around the city. An unusual street map for city engineers shows the structure of the subterranean conduits for water, gas, electricity, sewage, and so on. A map you'll never see shows all of the people who happened to be on those streets on a particular moment on a particular afternoon. No map of anything complex (nor any portrait, or biography, or poem, or chemical analysis) describes everything of the reality it depicts.

Now, to what extent can we call a map true? *Truth* is a quality or a property, not a thing. There is no such *thing* as truth, if by that we mean a substance or an entity anywhere in the cosmos that one could conceivably visit and witness—as Plato apparently thought one could in the realm of the perfect Forms. Truth is a quality of an interpretation as follows: *To the extent that the interpretation corresponds to the*

---

3. This distinction so concerned Paul Tillich that he preferred to speak of "encounter" for the "pretheoretical" moment of perception and "experience" for "a theoretically interpreted encounter." Rather than introducing a new term, however, I trust that I can make this distinction clear in what follows as it needs to be. See Paul Tillich, "The Problem of Theological Method," *Journal of Religion* 27 (January 1947): 17.

4. George Steiner comments: "No repetition of measurement, however closely calibrated, in whatever controlled vacuum it was carried out, could ever be perfectly the same. It would deviate by some trillionth of an inch, by a nanosecond, by the breadth of a hair—itself a teeming immensity—from any preceding measurement....There [can] be no perfect facsimile of anything,...the identical word spoken twice, even in lightning-quick reiteration, [is] not and [cannot] be the same" (*Errata*, 3). For a detailed depiction of the staggering complexities of recording speech accurately, see Jane A. Edwards, "The Transcription of Discourse," in *The Handbook of Discourse Analysis*, ed. Deborah Schiffrin, Deborah Tannen and Heidi E. Hamilton (Oxford: Blackwell, 2003); Blackwell Reference Online 13 December 2007 <http://www.blackwellreference.com/subscriber/tocnode?id=g9780631205968_chunk_g978063120596818>.

reality it represents, it is *true*. William Alston, among the most vigorous defenders of such conceptions in our time, puts it more technically:

> A statement...is true if and only if what the statement is about is as the statement says it is. Alternatively in terms of propositions, the conception is such that the schema "It is true that p if and only if p" yields a (necessarily, conceptually, analytically) true statement for any substitution instance.[5]

So if my hand-drawn map of downtown Chicago does in fact position the Art Institute correctly relative to the John Hancock tower (such an artful map would consist of a single line running more or less vertically with the scribbled label "Michigan Avenue" on it and the word "North" scrawled at the top), then it would be a true map—in the binary sense that (a) it is not false and (b) the message it is intending to convey, it does in fact convey.

Now a map can be true *more or less*, and in two respects. In an *absolute* sense, as we have seen, no map is completely true as no map can possibly represent every detail of the reality it describes. My map does not include the famous sculpted lions on the steps of the Art Institute, nor does it depict the trademark gridwork on the face of the Hancock. To the extent that our interpretations of anything fall short of complete correspondence with the reality they represent, they are less than fully true.

Let's be slightly more provocative on this point, by way of geographer Mark Monmonier's admissions:

> A good map tells a multitude of little white lies; it suppresses truth to help the user see what needs to be seen. Reality is three-dimensional, rich in detail, and far too factual to allow a complete yet uncluttered two-dimensional graphic scale model. Indeed, a map that did not generalize would be useless. But the value of a map depends on how well its generalized geometry and generalized content reflect the chosen aspect of reality.[6]

The fact that a map doesn't tell the whole, entire truth thus doesn't usually bother us because we usually apply a *relative* standard—technically, a *pragmatic* standard—to interpretations instead. We expect interpretations to perform certain limited tasks,

---

5. William P. Alston, *A Realist Conception of Truth* (Ithaca, NY: Cornell University Press: 1996), 1. Alston harks back to Aristotle's rather droll description of telling the truth: "To say of what is that it is and of what is not that it is not, is true" (*Metaphysics* IV, 6, 1001b, 28; quoted in Alston, *Realist Conception*, 6).

6. Mark Monmonier, *How to Lie with Maps*, 2nd ed. (Chicago and London: University of Chicago Press, 1996 [1991]), 25. Monmonier's fascinating volume is, in fact, an extended essay on this point. For extended consideration of the dialectic of maps and consciousness in western culture, see Toby Lester, *The Fourth Part of the World: The Race to the Ends of the Earth, and the Epic Story of the Map That Gave America Its Name* (New York: Free Press, 2009).

and they are true to the extent that they perform those tasks.[7] If my map really does guide you from one Chicago landmark to another, then it is true ("as far as it goes," we might say). If Newton's laws of motion helped NASA put Apollo 11 on the moon, they were true ("true enough," we might say)—even though we know that Einstein, Planck, Heisenberg & Company had complicated Sir Isaac's laws half a century before the space program began. So *truth* is a quality of *interpretations* or *representations* by which we denote the *extent* to which they resemble *reality*—both in an absolute sense (technically, according to their *correspondence*) and in a relative sense of their usefulness in that task (technically, according to their *pragmatic value*).[8] It is obvious that a map is more or less true in these ways.[9]

We use "true" also to describe things that don't seem immediately interpretive or representational. We speak of a true friend, by which we mean that, on the whole, she acts the way a friend ought to act. Her behavior is a "re-presentation" of "friend-hood." Christians affirm the claim of our Lord Jesus that he is the Truth (John 14:6) in that he properly represents God. It doesn't make sense, that is, to say that *God* is the Truth, because God isn't a representation of some other reality. God is the Reality *about which* Jesus is the "exact representation" (Heb. 1:3; NIV).[10]

---

7. This point is critically true in regard to the vexed question of the existence and nature of God: "It is only when people find themselves actually receiving God's grace and interacting with God that their minds and hearts achieve the full assurance of conviction in the truth of Christianity. It takes not only thinking but also action to achieve conviction" (Diogenes Allen, *Christian Belief in a Postmodern World: The Full Wealth of Conviction* [Louisville, KY: Westminster/John Knox, 1989], 9).

8. The Hebrew word *'emeth* in fact contains these various definitions of correspondence, faithfulness, reliability, soundness, and the like. John Polkinghorne concisely makes the point, as scientists usually do, that the best reason to believe that a proposition is pragmatically useful is that it does, indeed, correspond to the reality it describes (*Quantum Theory: A Very Short Introduction* [Oxford: Oxford University Press, 2002], 82–86).

9. Mark Mitchell points to Michael Polanyi's distinction between *verification* of scientific claims and the *validation* of religious or artistic ones, drawing on C. S. Lewis's distinction between "looking at" and "looking along." But I'm not confident this distinction can in fact be mapped onto "science versus religion" (or art, for that matter). Both discourses make testable claims about the way things are and both provide frames of reference within which one goes on to live in certain ways and not others with results that can be assessed as positive or negative. Thus both science and religion can properly be held to account in terms of correspondence and pragmatism (with coherence as a third epistemological desideratum). See *Michael Polanyi* (Wilmington, DE: ISI Books, 2006), 125–26.

10. Some Christians say in this regard that "truth is personal." If by that they mean to aver that ultimate reality is, in the Christian view of things, God, and that God is personal, and so truth is personal, then of course there's no argument. But not much is gained, either, and instead we simply have a fuzzy equation of "reality" and "truth" that the present discussion is aimed at clarifying. If, instead, they mean that truth is best apprehended by the whole person, rather than by sheer sensation and intellection—perhaps along the lines offered by Polanyi in *Personal Knowledge*—then of course my scheme agrees, even as "truth is personal" is an odd way to put the matter. ("Reception and recognition of truth is personal" might be more accurate.) Indeed, I cannot think of a way in which the phrase "truth is personal" actually does clarify anything, so I do not use it, despite its popularity in some circles with which I otherwise have affinity.

Some people say, "There is no absolute truth," but let's step lightly past the apparent self-contradiction: "There is no absolute truth, including this categorical assertion that 'there is no absolute truth.'" There is another problem. Yes, there is no "truth" in the sense of an entity called "Truth" floating somewhere in the heavens. But there is indeed absolute truth in the sense that a numeral (say, "5") can exactly represent the reality of the number of digits on my hand: five. The difficulties for us come when we are attempting to know *complex* realities and to determine how well we know them.

To say, as some do, that "you have your reality, and I have mine" is usually to mean, "You have your *interpretation* of reality, and I have my *interpretation* of reality, and those may not agree." Still, it could yet be entirely literal to say, "That's your reality, and it's not mine." Suppose I say, "Chicago is a great city. It's sophisticated, energetic, welcoming, and entertaining." That is the way I have experienced it. Suppose someone else, however, says, "Chicago is a nightmare. Illegal drugs, violence, poverty, and racism—that's Chicago." If that person did not experience the *parts* of Chicago that I did when I lived there (as a middle-class white student living in Hyde Park while attending the University of Chicago), but experienced instead a childhood in the horrors of the Cabrini Green or Robert Taylor Homes projects, then we are literally talking about two different realities. Our mistake is not in using the term "realities," for we really did experience very different things, and our interpretations are each true as far as each goes. Our mistake instead is to generalize from our limited experience of only a select part of that city to the city as a whole.

A further complication arises as we recall that both our neural physiology and our cultural conditioning—which are, to be sure, complexly intertwined—cause us to interpret stimuli not only with different intuitions but even as different sensations. How one literally sees what is happening on a street in Chicago will vary with the individual to at least some extent, and perhaps to a drastic extent—as we consider how, variously, a needy drug addict, a detective, a gang leader, a socialite, and a French tourist would take in all the stimuli offered by a block of the Magnificent Mile retail district or of the ravaged slums of the South Side.[11]

We should say more carefully something like this: "My experience of parts of the huge and variegated city of Chicago was as follows...." So my interpretation of Chicago is limited, and therefore to some extent wrong (because some parts of Chicago do not correspond to it), but also to some extent right (because some parts

---

11. Thomas Kuhn discusses how a change in paradigm prompts scientists both to see differently what they had seen in another way before and also to pay attention to, even to seek out, what they had heretofore not experienced. In these respects, he writes, it is as if they lived in a different world—or, in the terms of my illustration, a different Chicago. Consider a pampered North Sider and a street-savvy woman from the South Side who fall in love. In each other's company, each discovers an "alternative" Chicago, both dispositionally and geographically. Thus a change of "worldview" is experienced in more than one key respect as a change of world. See chapter 10 of *The Structure of Scientific Revolutions*, 2nd ed. (Chicago: University of Chicago Press, 1970 [1962]), 111–35.

do). This discussion points up the mistake committed by so many people today, including Christians, who claim that when there are two competing claims about something, at least one of them must be wrong. It could be instead that both of them are partly wrong and partly right, or each right about the part that it actually represents but wrong about other parts that are properly included in the subject under discussion.[12]

Such a consideration then brings us to a key observation. Knowledge, like truth, can be understood in binary terms: you either know it or you don't. It's either true or false. But there is more, much more, to knowing than that.

Knowledge and truth exist also on a continuum. Just as some maps are truer than others—more detail, more consistent scaling, and so on—so some forms of knowledge are greater than others. If you ask me, "Do you know Jim?" I can answer in binary terms, either yes or no. But it also makes sense to ask me, "How well do you know Jim?" and then I answer on some sort of axis: "Well, I know him better than I know Alex, but of course I know my close friends better still." My knowledge of Jim, the truth I have about him, is now better expressed on a scale.

Knowledge of someone or something, moreover, can be considered on multiple axes. "Well, I know Jim pretty well professionally, but I hardly know him personally at all." "I know that car is pretty fast, but I have no idea of its reliability or its comfort." "I've taken that road in daylight, but never at night." "I can recommend her as a cooperative person when things are going smoothly, but I frankly have no idea what she's like under stress." With complex realities, our knowledge increases with various interactions in various circumstances, whether we are learning about a poem, a gun, a garden, an institution, or a person.

Finally, we seem able to possess knowledge in one part of ourselves without it residing in other parts. How common it is for someone to say, "I always knew that X, but I didn't really believe it until now." Head and heart seem sometimes to be disconnected: "I knew that, but I didn't really feel its reality until—." And wisdom is applying what we know ("cognitively," or "in our heads," we might say) to actual practice. So to say that we "know" something is often not a simple matter.

A similar range of uses appears in the Bible. The Bible speaks of knowing God or not knowing God, knowing the truth or not knowing it. But it also speaks of *growing* in the knowledge of God. The Apostle Paul paradoxically says at one point that the whole quest of his life is this: "I want to know him" (Phil. 3:10)—when the reader is assumed to be confident that Paul already does know Jesus, in a binary

---

12. Andrew Walls makes a similar in regard to diversity of interpretations of Christianity itself: "We therefore have a paradox: the very universality of the Gospel, the fact that it is for *everyone*, leads to a variety of perceptions and applications of it. Responsive hearers of the Gospel respond in terms of their own lives. They must make sense of the Jesus Act within the play as they have seen it, and on the part of the stage within their field of vision. By the same token, the very universality of the Scriptures ensures a variety of specific interpretations and applications" (*The Missionary Movement in Christian History: Studies in the Transmission of Faith* [Maryknoll, NY: Orbis, 1996], 46).

sense. But Paul is talking about a fullness of knowledge compared with which his current state of acquaintance seems to him only elementary. Similarly, Paul writes elsewhere, "Now I know only in part; then I will know fully" (1 Cor. 13:12). And, of course, the Bible is constantly exhorting the people of God to *truly* hear what is being said *even as they are, right then, hearing what is being said.*

Well-meaning Christians constantly get confused on this question, as if the Bible's references to "knowing" or "truth" always mean "knowing exactly, completely, and certainly."[13] Nowhere in the Bible, in fact, does it say that we will know the truth about any *complex* subject *exactly, completely,* and *certainly,* as if we are utterly right and could not possibly be wrong. The Bible does not claim that we have that kind of intellectual prowess and position: Only God does.

Instead, the Bible teaches, we walk by faith, not by sight (2 Cor. 5:7). This crucial phrase means that we walk in situations of uncertainty according to what we have learned about God. We must trust what we think we know, just as we must trust what we think we know about our ski instructor to follow him down a difficult hill. If we knew *certainly,* then we would not have to trust: we would simply "know" in an absolute sense and go off skiing by ourselves. But we do *not* know most things certainly.

Of course, we know some things with a high degree of "persuadedness"—I'm quite sure that I'm typing on my laptop just now and not merely dreaming that I'm doing so. In this sense, as I have already allowed, I can say that I am certain—that is, as a description of my state of mind. As C. S. Lewis puts it, the situation is one of "psychological exclusion of doubt, though not a logical exclusion of dispute."[14] For since I am not God and do not have access to all of reality perfectly interpreted,

---

13. E. D. Hirsch, Jr., not widely understood to be a radical skeptic, says, "It is a logical mistake to confuse the impossibility of certainty in understanding with the impossibility of understanding. It is a similar, though more subtle, mistake to identify knowledge with certainty. A good many disciplines do not pretend to certainty, and the more sophisticated the methodology of the discipline, the less likely that its goal will be defined as certainty of knowledge" (*Validity in Interpretation* [New Haven, CT: Yale University Press, 1967], 17).

14. C. S. Lewis, "On Obstinacy in Belief," in *The World's Last Night and Other Essays* (New York: Harcourt Brace Jovanovich, 1960), 16. I am, it must be allowed, putting Lewis's words to my own purposes, since in this quotation he actually refers to "belief" and in this essay he distinguishes between "belief" and "knowledge" in a way I don't—or, at least, not quite in this way. Lewis suggests that knowledge is beyond both psychological doubt and logical questioning, while belief, even the strongest belief, is held with the acknowledgment that logical questioning is not excluded. I am saying instead that what he defines as very strong belief here is in fact the situation for all of our claims to knowledge. Faith, by apparent contrast, is the venturing into the unknown, the act of truly putting oneself at some kind of risk, on the basis of what one thinks one knows. Yet what one thinks one knows, I am arguing, is itself a decidedly uncertain foundation for faith. Indeed, the central thrust of this book is that our epistemic situation is, in a crucial sense, that of faith "all the way down."

Strictly speaking, I suppose one could therefore call my scheme a species of *fideism.* But fideism normally is understood as being in some basic opposition to reason, and obviously my scheme has nothing to do with such an antinomy. So I am burying this question of fideism deep in the footnotes, where it belongs.

I cannot say beyond a shadow of doubt that I am *not* dreaming right now. How could I know a thing like that with certainty? I can't. And if I can't know something as basic as that in a truly certain way, then I can't know anything beyond my own immediate experiences in a certain way.[15]

With this severe caveat in mind, Christian thinkers thus consult all five resources. This consultation is not a simple matter, however, of stopping off to attend to each in turn. What has become obvious to many in the postmodern situation (and was obvious to many of our predecessors, despite this generation's self-congratulation that we are the first to notice this fact) is that each of the five resources shape—and *ought* to shape—our interpretation of the others. We now routinely ask these sorts of questions: Will a Christian neuropsychologist consider certain possible theories regarding the mind/brain relationship that someone who disbelieves in the spiritual life of a person, the "soul," will not? Do paleontological ideas properly pertain to Scriptural interpretation of the Creation and Flood stories in Genesis? What does our experience of women and men in various homes, churches, and societies have to say to help us understand the Bible and tradition regarding gender? What insights and examples—both positive and negative, surely—does the history of the church offer us as we consider the right use of money, or involvement in secular politics?

This sort of question often must be handled delicately. We must refrain from rushing in with an explanation that appears ready to hand—whether a "God of the gaps" or any other *deus ex machina*—when more patient and circumspect investigation and consideration might turn up something more subtle and unexpected. Disciplinary boundaries ought to be respected also as ways of fending off reductionism ("This chemistry problem is nothing but physics" or "This religious phenomenon is nothing but sociology"). We ought to observe disciplinary chastity, so to speak, until we become convinced that we simply must seek explanation at some other level or in some other field. Then the disciplinary boundaries are properly crossed as we bring all of what we know to bear on the problems in this or that particular area of inquiry.[16]

---

15. Among the other sources cited in this discussion, see Susan E. Schreiner, *Are You Alone Wise? The Search for Certainty in the Early Modern Era* (New York and Oxford: Oxford University Press, 2010).

16. This is the sense in which "methodological atheism" makes sense for Christians—or, better, a methodological *secularity* that confines itself to natural phenomena and explanation in the investigation of the world God made *to be largely intelligible as such*. The term "atheism" goes too far, I think, as the very grounds for believing in an intelligible world, taking it seriously, and so on are grounded, for the Christian, in his or her theological commitments. But the term "secularity" works to circumscribe methodologically any investigation in any discipline in order to promote optimal activity in that discipline: "Let's see what we can figure out without recourse to divine intervention. We might eventually conclude that, indeed, the phenomenon can be explained well, or at all, only by invoking God's direct action—as in, say, the creation of the cosmos or the resurrection of Jesus, for which explanations we also, to be sure, have express Scriptural warrants. But for everything for which we do *not* have inspired explanations, let's attribute it to God's unmediated

I therefore coin a word, *pentalectic,* that resembles a more familiar word, *dialectic,* which means "conversation between." A pentalectic thus is a five-way conversation among our interpretations of experience, tradition, scholarship, art, and Scripture. Epistemologists speak of different varieties of hermeneutical circles. One has one's general sense of the matter, one encounters new information from one or more of these resources, and this new information confirms or modifies one's general sense. This is the familiar dialectic between "the whole" and "the parts." In reference to the pentalectic, the idea would be that with each pass through the five resources, the understanding of each of the other four and of the overall issue in question can become more clear and full. Thus the hermeneutical circle becomes a spiral, heading (one trusts) toward greater apprehension of reality.

Even the image of a circle is too neat, moreover, since the vectors go every which way, the interpretation of each element at least potentially affecting the interpretation of the others and of the whole. Each relationship is dialectical, conversational—which means at least potentially *both* "back and forth" *and* "ongoing." We interpretively pause from time to time, of course, whether because we are content with a conclusion, or because we have insufficient grounds to decide among interpretative options, or because we have insufficient input to even formulate possible interpretations. But the web of relationships is only ever temporarily, provisionally, at rest. Some new element—a new datum (or the loss of an old one), or a new way of interpreting the data on board—sets the web buzzing again and the conversation resumes. We are ever only where and what we are, but interacting with what is beyond and other than us, so that our thinking takes place in the tension of both centripetal and centrifugal forces.

THE AUTHORITY OF THE BIBLE

In undertaking such a pentalectic, our interpretation of the Bible must be *primum inter pares.* I say *"inter pares"* because in the case of each of the five resources we have only our interpretations to work with, and thus we must face the sobering reality that our interpretation of the Bible is not necessarily more accurate than our interpretation of God's world apprehended by us in other ways. The fact that the Bible is God's Word written does not miraculously make up for our own interpretative deficiencies. Indeed, some of us might be *terrible* Bible interpreters, on the one hand, and capable scientists, historians, or architects, on the other, in which case our

---

activity only as a last resort, since as soon as we decide that 'It's a miracle,' investigation stops." On this multifaceted question arising in American scholarship, see George M. Marsden, *The Soul of the American University: From Protestant Establishment to Established Nonbelief* (New York and Oxford: Oxford University Press, 1994), esp. 150–66.

knowledge of one of the latter resources will be more reliable, all things considered, than our Bible reading.[17]

The Bible yet must hold first place among these resources as God's unique self-expression: a text understood and gratefully accepted by the Christian church as guaranteed by God to be what God wants us to have as God's written revelation to us.[18] Moreover, God has promised God's people the tutelary ministry of the Holy Spirit to open the meaning of the Bible to us in our particular circumstances and needs. So whatever we may acknowledge about our limitations as Bible interpreters, Christians properly take as a basic principle of responsible thinking that we shall always seek the Bible's teaching relevant to our concern and receive it as the divinely authoritative gift it is. As Bonhoeffer urges us, in words of startling relevance to our own context,

> We must become acquainted with the Scriptures first and foremost for the sake of our salvation. But, besides this,... how are we ever to gain certainty and confidence in our personal deeds and church activity if we do not stand on solid biblical ground? It is not our heart that determines our course, but God's Word. But who in this day has any proper awareness of the need for evidence from Scripture? How often do we hear innumerable arguments "from life" and "from experience" to justify the most crucial decisions? Yet the evidence of Scripture is excluded even though it would perhaps point in exactly the opposite direction. It is not surprising, of course, that those who attempt to discredit the evidence of Scripture are the people who themselves do not seriously read, know, or make a thorough study of the Scriptures. But those who are not willing to learn how to deal with the Scriptures for themselves are not Protestant Christians [*evangelischer Christ*].[19]

---

17. That is, just any interpretation of just any Scripture does not trump a carefully wrought analysis of science—or the intuition of a mystical experience. A theory in paleontology or psychology might well offer a much clearer view of the subject under discussion than a bad interpretation of a few Bible verses. And a strongly felt impression that God is directing in a particular direction might well be a truer revelation than the reflexive deployment of favorite Bible passages by those feeling threatened by something new.

18. It is refreshing to have philosophical theologians and theologically interested philosophers caution us against giving pride of place to even the most carefully wrought conceptual schemes regarding divine things over against the teaching of the Bible. Ronald Feenstra points to Anselm as a classic example of what we might call "perfect being" theology, by which one attributes "great-making properties" to God to a maximal degree, and warns, "If Christians use Anselmian methods to articulate their concept of God, they must use these methods only insofar as they reflect what Scripture says about God. And if there is any conflict between the deliverances of Scripture and the deliverances of the Anselmian method, Christian theologians should favour what Scripture says" (Ronald J. Feenstra, "A Kenotic Christology of the Divine Attributes," in *Exploring Kenotic Christology: The Self-Emptying of God*, ed. C. Stephen Evans [Oxford: Oxford University Press, 2006], 162).

19. Dietrich Bonhoeffer, *Life Together*, ed. Geoffrey B. Kelly, trans. Daniel W. Bloesch and James H. Burtness (Minneapolis: Fortress, 2005 [1939]), 63.

Furthermore, as a complementary principle, we shall *not* decide a matter *against* what we interpret the Bible to say. Yes, we freely admit that our interpretation of the Bible is finite (and fallen) and that tomorrow or next year we might well change our minds about that interpretation. But to go deliberately *against* what we believe God's Word is saying would be, in the words of Luther at the Diet of Worms, to go against the Christian conscience, a conscience that is "bound to the Word of God," and to do so would be "neither right nor safe." To decide and to act against our interpretation of the Bible is to set aside what light we perceive of the map God provided to orient us.[20] To shift frames of reference to that of the scholarly disciplines, "no aspect of a theology...is acceptable if it can be biblically patently falsified."[21]

It would be flatly foolish, that is, to turn away from the very manual with which has God equipped the church and that God has promised to use to make Christians "proficient" in our callings (2 Tim. 3:17). Yes, we should strive, using everything we know, to improve our interpretation of the world, and in the course of that endeavor we might well alter for the better our navigational conclusions or our methods of running the ship. We must not, however, disparage what light and wisdom we do think we have from God's Word written, particularly as we have on board a Guide who has promised to help us make good use of it.[22]

The Christian therefore, as a matter of good method, never decides a matter against what she thinks the Scripture says, even as she remains open to improving her interpretation of Scripture, of the other resources involved, and of the matter at hand.[23] In the meanwhile, furthermore, she might well decide to defer making up her mind on a matter in which her interpretation of two or more sources seems to

---

20. In this advice I merely echo what Augustine says more authoritatively and eloquently in *De doctrina christiana* (*On Christian Teaching*). A terse and eloquent contemporary statement of this principle is provided by Merold Westphal, who says, "The Bible is the only ultimate standard for the community of faith, the one card that cannot be trumped. We cannot simply disregard our best judgments about what it teaches, however fallible those judgments may be" ("Saving *Sola Scriptura* from Rhem and the Rationalists," *Perspectives* [February 1993]: 11).

21. Miroslav Volf, *Work in the Spirit: Toward a Theology of Work* (Eugene, OR: Wipf and Stock, 2001 [1991]), 79.

22. Alvin Plantinga puts the matter succinctly: "Scripture itself is taken to be a wholly authoritative and trustworthy guide to faith and morals; it is authoritative and trustworthy because it is a revelation from God, a matter of God's speaking to us. Once it is clear, therefore, what the teaching of a given bit of Scripture is, the question of the truth and acceptability of that teaching is settled.... Once convinced that God *is* proposing XYZ for our belief, we do not go on to ask whether it is true, or whether God has made a good case for it. God is not required to make a case" (*Warranted Christian Belief*, 383–84). Thus, as Richard Bauckham concurs, "reason [is] not deployed as a critical principle, only as an expository one" (*God and the Crisis of Freedom: Biblical and Contemporary Perspectives* [Louisville, KY, and London: Westminster/John Knox, 2002], 51).

23. James Brownson puts it carefully: "Of course, a selective and distorted reading of Scripture itself can...lead one to idolatrous conceptions of God. An emphasis on Scripture as norm does not automatically guarantee the integrity of the theology that is purportedly normed by Scripture. Yet it must be recognized that the neglect of the normative function of Scripture precludes even the *possibility* of any such corrective element in the process of engaging in

conflict. To decide to *not* decide is often to make the best decision possible in the circumstances, and the Christian scores no points for dogmatically insisting on deciding based on her interpretation of Scripture when it seems to be contradicted by other things she knows, or ought to know, from other epistemic gifts of God.[24]

Let me be clear that I am not now contradicting what I just took pains to say in the previous paragraphs. If one's interpretation of Scripture seems to lead to beliefs or actions that do not square with what else one thinks one knows (from one's surveying of experience, tradition, scholarship, and art), one rightly pauses and prays for more light, rather than bullheadedly asserting *one's interpretation of Scripture* in a blaze of zeal without knowledge. The authority of Scripture itself is not in question here. One is trying to understand God via the *many* media through which God communicates with us. Contradiction among those media simply gives the responsible person serious pause. In such instances, therefore, it would be better for the Christian first to recognize the contradiction in her gleanings from the various resources; then perhaps go around the various pertinent resources again to see if more knowledge can be gained or new interpretations formulated to resolve the contradiction; and, if that doesn't resolve the issue, wait (upon God) for the situation somehow to change so she may come eventually to a satisfactory conclusion.[25]

What if, however, she finds herself in a situation such that she cannot defer some sort of conclusion until all of her beliefs come nicely into harmony on a particular issue? What if she really has to decide now, or soon, with no prospect of a total consensus of all she believes? The Christian will then pray (!) and particularly pray that God will direct her to whatever option will best advance God's purposes in the world. Note that she will not pray primarily to come to a right conclusion. She may well pray for that—of course she should. But her primary prayer will be *vocational* and *missional*, truly pragmatic. For she knows that God's purposes normally are indeed advanced best by Christians believing true things, but not always. And so she will steer by the preponderance of evidence and argument she has—what else can she do?—while also asking God to intervene in her mind or in the circumstances of

---

theological discourse" (James V. Brownson, "Thoughts on God-Language," *Perspectives* [March 1993], 14).

24. Galileo Galilei, having averred the supremacy of theology as "queen of the sciences" in that theology deals with the most important matters of life, also warns us against simplistically dictating to the other sciences what they must conclude on the basis of our interpretation of theology: "To require astronomers to endeavor to protect themselves against their own observations and demonstrations, namely to show that these are nothing but fallacies and sophisms, is to demand they do the impossible; for that would be to require that they not only should not see what they see and not understand what they understand, but also that in their research they should find the contrary of what they find" ("Letter to the Grand Duchess Christina [1615]," in *The Galileo Affair: A Documentary History*, ed. Maurice Finocchiaro [Berkeley: University of California Press, 1989], 101).

25. I testify to my own experience of such a process in "How to Produce an Egalitarian Man," chap. in *How I Changed My Mind about Women in Leadership: Compelling Stories from Prominent Evangelicals*, ed. Alan F. Johnson (Grand Rapids, MI: Zondervan, 2010), 235–43.

her life such that God's will be done whether she concludes something truthful, or erroneous, or something in between.

Perhaps instead of a simple hermeneutical spiral, however, the image of a web or network will serve us better in considering the pentalectic, as our attending to this or that resource is always conducted with at least implicit reference to our apprehension of the others.

HYPOTHETICAL THINKING: WEBS AND ECOLOGIES

When we think about things, we usually are quite particular. We ask particular questions and expect particular sorts of answers.

Q: Why is the sky blue?
A: Because of the way light reflects off it, and refracts through it, to our eyes and because of the way our eyes and brains then interpret that light.
Q: Why do people offer incense to Buddhas and Bodhisattvas at the local Buddhist temple?
A: Because those beings enjoy receiving such devotion and generously respond with supernatural favors.
Q: Why am I constantly short of cash?
A: Because I am not paid what I'm worth in this philistine society that refuses to recognize true genius.

These answers satisfy the questioner, of course, only if he shares with the answerer a considerable number of assumptions about the world. Each of these answers (and, indeed, each of the questions) assumes a particular understanding of the universe: of physics and biology in the first case; of religion in the second case; and of both society and my abilities in the third case.

Not sharing this understanding will lead to very different answers, and even a breakdown in communication:

Q: Why is the sky blue?
A: Because the occupying alien forces are cloaking their massive armada of spaceships that are currently in orbit around the earth with this opaque blue screen.
Q: Why do people offer incense to Buddhas and Bodhisattvas at the local Buddhist temple?
A: Because Satan has blinded their eyes to the existence of the true God, and they erroneously believe they can earn the favor of nonexistent spiritual beings.
Q: Why am I constantly short of cash?
A: Because society infallibly rewards only industriousness and talent with financial success.

An answer "works" only within a set of assumptions about the subject in question, each of which assumptions could well be examined for its own warrants. When we answer a question, we are in fact advancing what scientists sometimes call a hypothesis, an intelligent guess as to what is the case in any particular instance based on what we already think we know about the world. We then try out such guesses on this or that new situation and see how they fit.[26] That is, we do not simply open our eyes in a situation with no idea of what it is and then just start inferring conclusions from the impressions we receive. Our interpretations are always conversations, negotiations, among our assumptions and expectations and what we are now experiencing. We are not obliged to work up our beliefs from some kind of zero position, as if we could actually start thinking from scratch without already believing a considerable number of propositions about the world and as if the evidence in the matter we are investigating will simply, directly, inexorably lead us to a single satisfactory explanation. Instead, we are obliged only to do what we actually do: experience something, hypothesize about it, and then submit our guesses to any appropriate rigorous testing.

We are wise to recognize that all human thought is conducted in this way.[27] We encounter a situation; we encounter that situation both with some assumptions as to what things are and how they work in such a situation, and with some expectations as to how they will, or at least might, behave in this new situation; as we experience it, we compose our best guess as to how to understand that experience; and, if necessary, we adjust our assumptions and explanations accordingly. Thus the hermeneutical spiral continues to turn.[28]

Let us also be clear that by "hypotheses" we truly mean what scientists mean: "hypotheses" is a term that includes *narratives* as well as propositions, equations,

---

26. I have found that John Hick speaks in a somewhat similar way about our thought: *An Interpretation of Religion: Human Responses to the Transcendent* (New Haven, CT: Yale University Press, 1989), 138–39. Professor Hick and I do not, however, agree on everything.

27. Ah, how the stock of various disciplines has risen and fallen. Natural science, of course, is now the bluest of blue chips. But a century or so ago, natural science was seen by some, at least, to be not true, since it was merely hypothetical, and thus not a fit subject for a Cambridge B.A. See Noel Annan, *The Dons: Mentors, Eccentrics, and Geniuses* (Chicago: University of Chicago Press, 1999), 119. Peter F. Drucker uses the language of testing hypotheses in the quite different domain of management: see "Effective Decisions," chap. in *The Essential Drucker* (New York: HarperCollins, 1991 [1966]), 241–60.

28. One might wonder if I am leaving out deduction. But deductions themselves depend on beliefs we have drawn from experience. To enjoy the reassuring solidity of a syllogism, one must draw major and minor premises from the stock of what all right-thinking people know is true. (Yes, I do intend the irony.) But "all men are mortal" is not itself deductively derivable from other premises that are either self-evident or necessarily true, but is instead an inductive argument from "our" experience of "men"—namely, that we know of no men who are immortal, and all that we know about men indicates that they are not capable of immortality. But those beliefs are inductively drawn from observing men and making generalized statements about them. Such statements are generalizations *just so far as we know*. Hypothetical thinking, in the way I am using the term, is therefore true of all the thinking we do.

and the like. For cosmology, paleontology and geology are what we can call *histor-ical* sciences, sciences that investigate what happened long ago and perhaps also far away. They rely, to be sure, on knowledge that can be proved in laboratory experi-ments as to what things are and how thing normally behave, but these sciences reach far beyond the purview of the lab to events that occurred once, or at least to matters and events that cannot be replicated in any laboratory.

Again, all science must *ipso facto* proceed from fundamental convictions about the world (e.g., the reliability of sense perception and memory beliefs, the regu-larity of natural processes, that the cosmos at far removes in time or at very large or very small scales behaves the way it does now at the "medium" levels we believe we perceive and understand well, that divine beings haven't tried to fool us by strewing the world with bad data, and so on) that are not themselves obviously testable by experiment. These convictions, I am suggesting, constitute overarching narratives within which particular experiments on what we *can* examine take place, experi-ments that provide correspondence-type validation that then can lend credibility to beliefs—these overarching narratives—that are thus justified by coherence with such validated findings.[29]

To reiterate: we include in the terminology of hypotheses those conceptions at the scale of grand theory and worldview, the "paradigms" and *les grands récits*, the models and "metanarratives" or "master narratives" that ground, direct, and curtail our thinking in both the broadest and most fundamental respects. Indeed, to use Keith Yandell's suggestive phrase, they are "total interpretations."[30]

---

29. Physicist Ernest Zebrowski remarks, "To a great extent, and more than most of the pub-lic may realize, all science rests on historical foundations. No science student is expected to re-peat Pasteur's experiments in developing a vaccine for rabies or Fizeau's experiments in measuring the speed of light in moving fluids. Scientists acknowledge these results on the weight of their historical documentation—accepting the fact that the experiments were actu-ally performed in the past, that they yielded the reported results, and that the methodologies have already been critically reviewed and analyzed....What science students learn is largely history." Furthermore, many sciences, such as his own field of natural disasters, offer the chal-lenge of "irreproducibility....A phenomenon like a volcanic eruption gives you only one shot. You can't recreate the volcano in the laboratory, much less test it repeatedly." Science of the present as well as of the distant past rests importantly and in several respects on major assump-tions and narrative structures about the way the world is. See Ernest Zebrowski, Jr., *Perils of a Restless Planet: Scientific Perspectives on Natural Disasters* (Cambridge: Cambridge University Press, 1997), 20–21.

30. In a magisterial essay remarkable at once for both its sweep and concision, sociologist of religion David Martin scores his colleagues for repeatedly letting unthinking subscription to master narratives obscure what is "sociologically obvious" in the major problematics of secular-ization theory, modernization and religion, and more: "Science and Secularization," chap. in *The Future of Christianity: Reflections on Violence and Democracy, Religion and Secularization* (Farnham, UK: Ashgate, 2011), 119–31. The resurgence of the category of narrative in the-ology per se began with Hans W. Frei, *The Eclipse of Biblical Narrative: A Study in Eighteenth and Nineteenth Century Hermeneutics* (New Haven, CT: Yale University Press, 1974); see also Stanley Hauerwas and L. Gregory Jones, eds., *Why Narrative? Readings in Narrative Theology* (Grand Rapids, MI: Eerdmans, 1989). For "total interpretations," see Keith E. Yandell, *Basic Issues in the Philosophy of Religion* (Boston: Allyn and Bacon, 1971), 218.

We also recognize that our understanding of the world is both framed by and articulated in metaphors. George Lakoff and Mark Johnson have gone to considerable trouble, in their now-classic work *Metaphors We Live by*, to show that we cannot think without metaphors. An argument is like a battle, rather than like a dance—this is one of their favorite examples of how metaphors at once both illuminate and conceal realities and possibilities in a situation. Thus, metaphors are both false and true: "*A is B*" is false in any sense of strict identity (my love is not, in fact, a vivid flower; Jesus is, not in fact, a door or a shepherd), while it is also true in that something about *A* is like something about *B*, and a good metaphor puts that point with illuminating power (my love is indeed like a red, red rose; Jesus is indeed like a door and a shepherd; and these similarities matter even as it is important to bear in mind the dissimilarities as well). Rather like technologies generally, metaphors both give and withhold, they open up and they contain, they prompt certain actions ("Well, if an argument is a war, then I shall...") and they bracket out others ("Why should I treat him courteously, let alone consider agreeing with him on that point, when we're at war?"). The metaphors we live by are codings of some of the hypotheses we live by: the world is like this, even if it is not *exactly* this, and also (by silent implication) it is *not* like that. Once again, we encounter the tension between our grasping something of reality without being able to claim that we grasp it all.[31]

Anthony Thiselton commends the work of Ian T. Ramsey in this respect, referring to metaphors along with other conceptual schemata as "models":

> Ramsey was one among many Christian philosophers of religion who recognized that controlling models offer organizing power and integrating vision but also potentially constructive seduction in religion. Pictures and metaphors can monopolize attention and thereby distort rational judgment. Thus pictures of God as judge can, for example, damaged the guilt-obsessed, while pictures of God as lover can inflate the over-confi dent. Hence Ramsay stressed that *isolated* or *single* controlling models could seduce, distort, or deceive. He refused, however, to reject models as necessarily deceptive.

---

31. George Lakoff and Mark Johnson, *Metaphors We Live by* (Chicago: University of Chicago Press, 1980). See also C. S. Lewis, "'Horrid Red Things,'" chap. in *Miracles* (San Francisco: HarperCollins, 2001 [1947]), 107–27. A general book on epistemology is not the place to discuss issues within particular disciplines, but may I simply signal my worry that some of my theological colleagues, in their laudable concern for appropriate humility in theological matters, overstate the case by suggesting that we have *only* metaphors at our disposal. To say (correctly) that we cannot possibly claim comprehensive knowledge of God, the world, or the great truths of the Gospel does not mean that we then have *only* metaphors by which to describe them. The fact that I do not know everything about Chicago does not mean that I do not know some things about it and can state them plainly. Christians in fact do aver propositions ("God is one," "God was in Christ") and narratives ("Jesus was born of the Virgin Mary," "God resurrected Jesus from the dead") that are not metaphorical, but are, in the Christian understanding, simply, literally true. And it matters a great deal that these statements are not metaphorical, but literally true. Once again, we must not avoid one epistemological extreme by veering determinedly into the other.

He proposed two key safeguards. First, models, symbols, or pictures should be used in *plurality*, in *multi-form* clusters. Second, models should be qualified by other language which serves to cancel off unwanted or manipulative resonances. Such models retain the power to disclose truth and (as Tillich also claims) "to open up new levels of reality." But they need not elude disciplined, self-critical thought.

A variety of models which operate together provides what Ramsay calls "checks and balances."[32]

The theologian will quickly recall the usefulness and appropriateness of keeping in mind multiple "theories" or "motifs" regarding the Atonement, none of which captures all that the Bible has to say about the mysterious work of God in Christ, and all of which together balance any tendency to oversimplify and even misrepresent the character of God in this central event of salvation history.[33] Scholars of organizational behavior, to select a quite different field, will recognize that in some respects a company is like a family, but also like an army, like a neighborhood, like a tribe, and so on, and leadership of any such group requires a flexibility and versatility equal to the task of referring rapidly and nimbly to various models in response to a given challenge. The various metaphors are tried out on the situation to see to what extent they illuminate it and are validated in turn, and thus not just any model will do, not just any summary will suffice—even as their multiplicity cautions us of the limitations of any conceptualization of complex phenomena.

Returning, then, to the discourse of general epistemology, we can observe that our conceptualizations of things in one or another domain will sometimes take the form of general propositions ("One ought not to spend more than one earns"), equations ("My salary – my deductions – my taxes – my discretionary spending = increasing debt"), narratives ("Last year I spent more than I earned, and every year before that for the last decade or more. I find that I therefore have become resentful and bitter"), or metaphors ("I'm being crushed by a mountain of debt"). In sum, by "hypotheses" in this conversation I mean *any* representation we might construct of our perception of reality, including not only narratives but other, non- or at least not-so-discursive genres, such as poetry, painting, and the like.[34]

The web of our various beliefs therefore forms the context in which we encounter something new to interpret, and this act of interpretation provides an occasion not

---

32. Anthony C. Thiselton, *Interpreting God and the Postmodern Self: On Meaning, Manipulation, and Promise* (Edinburgh: T. & T. Clark and Grand Rapids, MI: Eerdmans, 1995), 29; emphasis in original. Thiselton refers particularly to Ian T. Ramsey, *Religious Language: An Empirical Placing of Theological Phrases* (London: SCM, 1957).

33. See Janet Martin Soskice, *Metaphor and Religious Language* (New York and Oxford: Oxford University Press, 1987).

34. Thus George Lindbeck declares that "a religion may be pictured as a single gigantic proposition," albeit one composed of innumerable smaller propositions (George A. Lindbeck, *The Nature of Doctrine: Religion and Theology in a Postliberal Age* [Philadelphia: Westminster Press, 1984], 51).

only for the acquisition of new knowledge, but also at least potentially for a revision of what we previously believed as the new knowledge must be accommodated in the pentalectical network.

Let's suppose we have encountered a flock of sheep, which creatures we have previously encountered only in books, and we conclude that "all sheep are white." We later encounter a similar situation, apply our hypothesis, and see how it works then. If it works perfectly, we are pleased. "Here's another flock of sheep, and behold, they are all white." If it works pretty well but doesn't quite fit a new circumstance, we tinker with the hypothesis and improve it—or perhaps we just store away this oddity for future consideration. "Here, apparently, is a black sheep. It must be some sort of exception to the rule. But it's just one strange datum in a strange world, so it's no big deal." If our white-sheep hypothesis works badly on another occasion, however, we consider whether the new situation really is similar to the previous one. "Hmm. Here are quite a lot of what look very much like grey and black sheep. To be sure, maybe these aren't sheep at all, but some other species. Or perhaps someone has deliberately dyed the sheep's natural white wool." Maybe the hypothesis is still just fine and we need instead another hypothesis to suit a different challenge. "This flock over here are indeed sheep and they are white. Those mottled ones over there turn out to be goats. Sheep *are* white." But perhaps we conclude that this new situation really is like the previous one and yet the hypothesis doesn't work satisfactorily. So we consider a radical change in our hypothesis, or abandon it for a new one. "I now believe that sheep naturally occur in a variety of colors."

Therefore, when we are thinking about things, we are always assessing particular elements within systems of explanation, rather than mere brute facts or discrete notions.[35] Indeed, our assumptions about how the world is shape our actual perception such that, in certain cases, we literally cannot see (or otherwise sense) what is before us because we lack an interpretative scheme in which to process it. Neuroscientists detail rare syndromes in which certain patients take in the same sensory stimuli as a normal person but experience importantly different perceptions and form drastically abnormal conclusions. Oliver Sacks's popular book, for example, describes *The Man Who Mistook His Wife for a Hat*.[36] Much more commonly,

---

35. Larry Laudan sets out a scheme, reminiscent of both Thomas Kuhn and Nicholas Wolterstorff's schemata, connecting the world "outside" with the world "inside" (that is, inside our heads, our conceptual world) via a nested set of experimental data, theories about that data, research traditions that govern theorizing, and worldviews that comprise our most basic convictions. Each of these elements, furthermore, are in a dialectical relationship with each other. A diagram of Laudan's model appears in Paul G. Hiebert, *Transforming Worldviews: An Anthropological Understanding of How People Change* (Grand Rapids, MI: Baker Academic, 2008), 80; Hiebert cites Larry Laudan, *Progress and Its Problems: Towards a Theory of Scientific Growth* (Berkeley: University of California Press, 1977), n.p.

36. Oliver Sacks, *The Man Who Mistook His Wife for a Hat* (New York: HarperPerennial, 1990). Consider also the horrifying phenomenon of Capgras syndrome, in which sufferers believe their loved ones have been taken over by body doubles: Thomas Grüter and Ulrich Kraft, "Alien Friends," *Scientific American Mind* (March 24, 2005): 58 62. Sense experiences

a concertgoer dragged along by his sophisticated friend hears the same sounds, but perceives only noise in the Hindemith symphony or the Coltrane saxophone solo while his friend nods and smiles at all she "hears." Another hapless date finds himself at a gallery of art from a very different culture. He sees all the colors and shapes and textures that everyone else does, but because he lacks anthropological and aesthetic categories, his immediate and lasting impression is that it is just junk: bizarre and ugly, leaving only a faint and unpleasant impression.

What has seemed to many to be an absurd claim that there is no such thing as a fact now perhaps makes sense. If we mean by "fact" an actual *event*, then of course there are facts. Things happen, and as they actually happen, they are facts. If it is the case that Columbus sailed the ocean blue in fourteen hundred and ninety-two, then it is a fact that he did, regardless of anyone's interpretative scheme. But if by "fact" we mean "a *statement* that provides an *account* of an event," then we now must take this language of hypotheses into account. For facts in this sense are truly connected with, and in some sense (although, of course, not completely) constituted by, our assumptions.

If I assert, for example, that "this computer screen is grey," I am simultaneously asserting other ideas as well, only some of which I can give for examples here: that the screen appears grey to me via the interpretation of sense experience by my mind, which is trained to label such data as "computer," "screen," "grey," and so on; I can normally trust such experiences and interpretations; I expect that other people see things in similar ways so that my claim that "this computer screen is grey" will make sense to them and correspond to their own experience were they to sit here now and look in this direction at the object before me; and so on.

Thus the simple and rather uninteresting assertion that "the computer screen is grey" implicitly asserts an entire model of human perception and interpretation. (And here is where things get more interesting for the epistemologist.) Arguments with my proposal that "this computer screen is grey" could take place *within* the model, as in "Well, *I* believe the screen is actually *green* and that you therefore must have a visual disorder—let's call some other people over to take a look." The general model of "perceiving computer screens" is accepted by both of us in this argument, and the disagreement remains within the model.

Someone else, however, could challenge my contention regarding a grey computer screen from *outside* the more general model of perception and interpretation I hold: "You believe that you see a grey computer screen. Such a belief, however, is just another illusion in the common human confusion of believing in a world of particular objects. Ultimate reality instead consists in the cosmic Oneness of all being. It would be better for you somehow to get past this preoccupation with particulars and concentrate upon experiencing the unity of all." Thus we see how epistemology depends upon metaphysics. Our "image of knowledge"—what we take to

---

and intuitions ("This looks like my brother but I don't feel it is he") clearly are out of sync with each other, thus producing this terrible form of cognitive dissonance.

be the valid sources, purposes, and principles of verification in any consideration of the world—depends on our image of the world: what it is, and what it is for.[37]

Clearly, then, our beliefs at one level are formed within the influence—even a kind of "force field"—of more basic, more important beliefs. Indeed, if the dominant convictions between the sender of a message and the receiver of it differ too much, the message itself becomes distorted to fit the receiver's outlook. What is meant as a peace offering is interpreted as a provocation. Christian missionaries might be gratified to see their converts happily naming worship spaces, festivals, and amulets after Christian saints, but if the underlying convictions have not been truly altered, there is no real conversion but only a superficial syncretism, a relabeling of an otherwise unchanged spiritual alternative.[38] A plastic statuette of the Virgin Mary in a Spanish Catholic home does not mean the same thing as its twin that shows up in an Indian Hindu shrine.

When we are making affirmations about true and false—or, for that matter, about right and wrong, or beautiful and ugly—it therefore would be more accurate for us to speak in terms of *hypotheses* by which we seek to explain our experiences and judgments. "This assertion," we should say, "is the best we have formulated so far to explain what we understand to be the pertinent data." In cases of disagreement, we ought properly to abandon simplistic assertions of mere facts to more accurate and appropriate comparisons of the relative strengths of this hypothesis versus that one, while also recognizing that the power of this hypothesis to convince will depend importantly on the holding of *other* hypotheses of a certain sort. Those who make their living as negotiators realize that often the parties in conflict don't agree even on what stand as the main issues, or on how to proceed in dialogue, or on what will count as a good argument. These differences must be articulated and resolved if the parties have any hope of agreeing on the particular point in question.

This reference to negotiation underscores a pluralist, postmodern recognition that the Christian will accept as "evidence" or "good reason" some things that others will not. Sense experience, intuition, Scriptural teaching, church tradition, mystical experience, and rigorous logic, among other resources to which a Christian might refer, have each been rejected by one or another alternative ideology or religion. A helpful semantic move, then, can be made away from loaded terms such as "evidence" and "reason" to the more generic terms of "grounds" or "warrants" or "justification." This lets us put the question, in any given dispute, as follows: What *grounds* do you have to believe what you believe?[39]

---

37. The concept of "images of knowledge" was introduced to me by Paul Mendes-Flohr, "Images of Knowledge in Modern Jewish Thought," *Criterion* (Spring 1997): 4–5.

38. This is the burden of Hiebert, *Transforming Worldviews*. It is also a theme throughout David Martin's sociological *oeuvre*, such as in *On Secularization: Towards a Revised General Theory* (Aldershot, UK: Ashgate, 2005).

39. Let me signal that Alvin Plantinga's distinctive use of the word "warrant" is not the same as mine. His is specially suited to his epistemological agenda of showing what it is that, when added to a true belief, makes it *knowledge* (rather than, say, a lucky guess). He says that "warrant"

Someone might well then be able to appreciate that *within* a given system of thought, her neighbor indeed has sufficient grounds for him to give it assent. A sympathetic and imaginative Christian can see how a Buddhist could decide to aim at achieving nirvana, since nirvana, in a Buddhist frame of reference, is the highest good available. Likewise, the Buddhist could see why his Christian friend looks forward instead to enjoying residence in the New Jerusalem. The Christian will still disagree, however, with important elements of her neighbor's overarching system of belief (that is, with Buddhism), and thus will find the grounds for desiring nirvana to be less than convincing (that is, measured according to her own *Christian* system). The Buddhist would return the favor, understanding why the New Jerusalem seems attractive but simply not accepting the wide range of beliefs necessary to accept the arguments supporting hope in the eventual advent of such a splendid destiny. To put it more starkly, if "God is dead," as Nietzsche believed, then a Nietzschean approach to life makes sense—at least, it does if you're one of the *Übermenschen* with the talent and wealth to realize your aspirations. Christianity necessarily looks like a gigantic social conspiracy of the weak and ignoble against the great and high-minded. But within a Christian frame of reference, Nietzscheanism looks preposterously short-sighted, trading an eternity of blissful shalom for a few decades of self-indulgence.

Critical thinking in a postmodern context, therefore, appreciates that disagreements are not always over particular propositions A or B, but over entire complexes of ideas, whole models of explanation that in turn reside within worldviews—however coherent or incoherent one's worldview might be. In such cases, disagreement is not so much a matter of whether A or B is the case—or, as Lorraine Code points out, knowledge is not simply a matter of "S-knows-that-p," the classic formulation in analytical philosophy—as of whether one model is more effective in explaining all of the relevant data than another.[40] If there is too much variance in their larger models of explanation, two observers cannot come to agreement on A or B because, among

---

is that added something. (Of course, he is much more specific and interesting than that: see his *Warranted Christian Belief* [New York and Oxford: Oxford University Press, 2000]).

My use is more commonplace. I mean by "warrant" simply whatever it is that gives us the basis to believe this or that. It might be a sense impression, or the word of a trusted friend, or a cogent argument, or something else. My answer to the question, "Why do you believe p?" is my warrant or my grounds or my justification. (I recognize also that the term "justification" is also something of a weasel-word in technical epistemology. I expect that readers of this volume will understand it well enough in context as a generic term.)

40. "Such empirical claims [as 'S-knows-that-p'] are uncontested only within that same narrow purview from which so many of these examples are drawn. Their epistemic pertinence diminishes in situations whose complexity differs in both kind and degree from anything potentially derivable from accumulations of such stripped-down claims; and their capacity to address the specificities of knowers, situations, and events disruptive of the settled frame in which such knowings pass as paradigmatic is equally hard to discern. In short, 'S-knows-that-p' claims are representative, exemplary across a far narrower range than orthodox empiricist epistemologists tend to allow....They are communal for/to only a certain select community of knowers who...come across as solitary individuals...sealed up within their own imaginings. Openings for deliberation or negotiation are not easy to discern" (Lorraine Code, *Ecological Thinking: The Politics of Epistemic Location* [Oxford and New York: Oxford University Press, 2006], 216).

other things, their criteria for evaluating the validity or value of A and B are too different. To be sure, they might well agree on lots of other things, as their worldviews, like Venn circles, overlap. But where they don't overlap, whole reaches of facts and hypotheses may be affected and they may literally talk past each other. When we are deciding upon a matter, therefore, an important part of the decision is to decide at what *level* we are to make our choice. Are we differing most importantly at the level of facts, or of explanations of this set of facts, or of theories about how this sort of thing occurs, or of whole worldviews about the way the world is constituted?

We also, it must be reiterated, decide about A or B at least partly, and perhaps entirely, on how we feel about A or B aesthetically or morally. Will believing A mean I now must accept something I find to be ugly or merely insipid? By believing B am I now granting legitimacy to behavior I previously have found repellent or just inane? Worldviews, as anthropologists remind us, are properly understood as constellations of cognitive, affective, and moral convictions, systems of beliefs (in this broad sense) that connect with each other and sometimes pose critical implications for each other. Disagreeing with someone on one level sometimes means a conflict also on another: "That Francis Bacon painting is terrible art because it not only is disturbing, it also conflicts with my belief that the purpose of art is always to promote beauty" or "If I adopt this new understanding of Middle Eastern history, I am now going to have to change how I feel about Jews/Israelis/Arabs/Palestinians/terrorists/soldiers...."

Many Christians still do not recognize this principle. They focus their disputes instead upon only "A or B." For example, they believe it is sufficient to ask, "Did Jesus rise from the dead or not?" They fail to recognize that some people don't care about historical evidence and argument; others freely believe in all sorts of supernatural events from which the Christian would want to distinguish the resurrection of Christ; and still others are so secularist in their views that *any* alternative explanation is preferable to the implausible assertion that a deity resurrected an ancient Jewish teacher in order to make him Lord of the universe.[41] Christians also frequently fail to appreciate fully—as many of their non-Christian friends actually do appreciate— that for an interlocutor to grant the truth of the claim for the historicity of Jesus' resurrection really might point toward religious conversion, which would throw into disarray their whole moral and relational situation, challenging much of what and

41. Michael Polanyi points to hostile responses to the highly controversial experiments of Duke University psychologist J. B. Rhine on ESP and in doing so illustrates what are in fact the popular and the actual versions of Ockham's Razor: "Extra-sensory perception is of course the simplest explanation for them, if you are prepared to believe in extra-sensory perception. Yet most scientists today would prefer some other explanation, however, complicated, if only it lay within the scope of hither-to known physical interactions. To them it appears more 'economical' not to introduce a new principle if we can possibly manage with those already accepted; and they are even prepared to disregard Rhine's observations until such time as these can be fitted into the existing framework of natural laws" (*Personal Knowledge*, 166). We will say more about this scientific resistance to possibly revolutionary knowledge presently (although I won't say any more about Rhine, whose work has been widely debunked), particularly in regard to the work of Thomas Kuhn and Lorraine Code.

whom they love every bit as much as it challenges their rational understanding of an event purported to occur outside Jerusalem two thousand years ago. Failure to see just how differently our neighbors can think and believe will doom conversations to frustration, whether between a Christian and a Hindu, say, or between an Enlightenment-style thinker and a postmodernist.[42]

Ideally, we ought to appreciate that each hypothesis is, by definition, only a provisional, "working" model, rather than a statement of absolute truth, right here, right now.[43] As provisional explanations, furthermore, we should be open not only to comparing our hypotheses with others in order to judge their relative merits, but also to improving or even replacing our hypotheses, since they are only humanly devised instruments to help us make sense of something. We thus should distinguish between our understandable loyalties to particular thought-systems that have helped us in the past, and critical openness to new hypotheses that might help us better in the future.[44]

PLAUSIBILITY VERSUS CREDIBILITY

E. E. Evans-Pritchard conducted famous anthropological studies among the Azande of Sudan in the 1920s. He found that the Azande, like most tribal peoples the world over, understood sickness and health primarily in terms of magic and witchcraft. When someone fell ill, it was because he had offended a spirit, or a shaman, or someone

---

42. I deal with these implications of religious conversion in *Can God Be Trusted? Faith and the Challenge of Evil*, 2nd ed. (Downers Grove, IL: IVP, 2009 [1998]).

43. George Lindbeck offers important reflections on the implications of this way of construing even whole worldviews, religions, philosophies: "In this perspective, the reasonableness of a religion is largely a function of its assimilative powers, of its ability to provide an intelligible interpretation in its own terms of the varied situations and realities adherents encounter. The religions we call primitive regularly fail this test when confronted with major changes, while the world religions have developed greater resources for coping with vicissitude. Thus, although a religion is not susceptible to decisive disproof, it is subject ... to rational testing procedures not wholly unlike those which apply to general scientific theories or paradigms. ... Confirmation or disconfirmation occurs through an accumulation of successes or failures in making practically and cognitively coherent sense of relevant data, and the process does not conclude, in the case of religions, until the disappearance of the last communities of believers or, if the faith survives, until the end of history" (George A. Lindbeck, *The Nature of Doctrine: Religion and Theology in a Postliberal Age* [Philadelphia: Westminster, 1984], 131).

44. "Now, the truth is that knowledge consists of conjectured explanations—guesses about what really is (or really should be, or might be) out there in all those worlds. Even in the hard sciences, these guesses have no foundations and don't need justification. Why? Because genuine knowledge, though by definition it does *contain* truth, almost always contains error as well. So it is not 'true' in the sense studied in mathematics and logic. Thinking consists of *criticizing* and correcting partially true guesses with the intention of locating and eliminating the errors and misconceptions in them, *not* generating or justifying extrapolations from sense data" (David Deutsch, "Creative Blocks," *Aeon* (3 October 2012): http://www.aeonmagazine.com/being-human/david-deutsch-artificial-intelligence/; accessed 7 October 2012.

else who had enlisted a shaman's aid in retribution. Within this web of belief, the sensible—yes, logical—thing to do when faced with sickness was to consult the shaman and make things right with the offended party. Ritual, sacrifice, restitution, and so on all would be entailed, and then one could expect to recover one's health.

Well, we know better, don't we? So, blessed with our superior knowledge, we fly over to Africa in our huge silver bird. We alight from the plane wearing our priestly garments (lab coats) and greet the assembled Azande.

"O Azande!" we say. "We hear that you understand sickness and health in terms of witchcraft."

The Azande, a noble and patient people, respond, "That is true."

"O Azande!" we say again. "Have you not heard of microbiology, of Louis Pasteur, of bacteria, and of antibiotics?"

The Azande, a noble and patient people, respond, "No, we have not."

"O Azande!" we repeat, thoroughly caught up now in our role as beneficent saviors, "let us explain to you how wrong you are about illness and how our way of understanding is correct."

The Azande, a people whose nobility and patience is now being tried, continue to listen.

"You see," we say animatedly, "there are these teeny weeny *bugs* all over the place. You can't see them; you can't smell them; you can't hear them or feel them—*but they're there!* We have special machines that help us to see them."

One of the Azande, who has visited a city, pipes up helpfully. "You mean, movie projectors?"

"No, no!" we reply, aghast. "We mean machines that show us what is really there, not what is not there that others want us to pretend is there."

The Azande begin to shift nervously, unclear now about the sanity of our civilization. So we press on with even more enthusiasm.

"Now these bugs that you can't see or hear or feel crawl over your skin and into your body through your nose and ears and eyes and mouth and cuts in your skin. Yes, you don't sense them doing it, but they do it all the time. And once inside, they breed and breed and breed until there are thousands of them, then *millions* of them, then BILLIONS of them all over the inside of your body.

"And that mass of bugs inside you," we conclude with a flourish, "is what makes you sick."

The Azande, a noble and patient people, look at each other for a long moment. Then the leader responds: "Thank-you very much for that fascinating presentation. But I think we'll just stick with the witchcraft paradigm. It's worked pretty well for us so far and your alternative seems, well...," he smiles at the man beside him, who broadly smiles back, "*implausible.*"[45]

---

45. The first account I read of this famous research, published as E. E. Evans-Prichard, *Witchcraft, Oracles, and Magic among the Azande* (Oxford: Oxford University Press, 1937), was in William C. Placher, *Unapologetic Theology: A Christian Voice in a Pluralistic Conversation*

One more example, this one literally closer to home, to illustrate how what first might seem implausible to us might be made plausible after all. Let's suppose that at breakfast this morning, I complained to my spouse that I was feeling a bit unwell. I described my symptoms, and as a health professional (which she is) she quickly offered a diagnosis.

"It's because you wear too much blue."

I am incredulous, of course. What she suggests is preposterous. "What are you talking about? How can my wearing too much blue make me feel like I have the 'flu?"

"Well," she calmly explains, "the most common blue dye used nowadays—Blue No. 3—is extracted from a plant whose juices are mildly toxic to human beings. If you wear blue once in a while, there's no problem. But wearing it as often as you do means that a little bit leaches into your skin each day, and when it accumulates you become sick."

"Oh," I say in a small, respectful voice, overcome by what seems to be irrefutable science. "Maybe I *do* wear too much blue...."

The amusement we might feel in reading such stories is, in fact, the point. The explanations offered are not simply unusual, or unlikely, or even quite difficult to believe without further evidence. They are *laughable*. They don't count as even *possible* alternatives; they are not worth a moment's consideration. They do not fall within the range of theories that, given one's worldview, one is disposed to entertain seriously.[46] To use Thomas Kuhn's language, when an explanation from one paradigm of knowledge encounters a community working with a quite different paradigm, the latter tend not to denounce the proffered explanation as merely inferior

(Louisville, KY: Westminster/John Knox Press, 1989), chap. 4, 55–73. Philosophers Peter Winch and Kai Nielsen touched off a lasting debate in the 1960s over issues arising from this research: Placher's notes include many of the relevant citations. Michael Polanyi astringently notes in this regard that "the rules of induction have lent their support throughout the ages to beliefs that are contrary to those of science. Astrology has been sustained for 3000 years by empirical evidence confirming the predictions of horoscopes. This represents the longest chain of historically known empirical generalizations.... Almost every major systematic error which has deluded men for thousands of years relied on practical experience. Horoscopes, incantations, oracles, magic, witchcraft, the cure of witch doctors and of medical practitioners before the advent of modern medicine, were all firmly established through the centuries in the eye of the public by their supposed practical successes" (*Personal Knowledge*, 168, 183). Indeed, Polanyi deals with this very study of the Azande himself: 288–94. For a clever exercise in viewing a modern society anthropologically, with the problem of plausibility in the foreground, see Umberto Eco, "Industry and Sexual Repression in a Po Valley Society," chap. in Umberto Eco, *Misreadings*, trans. William Weaver (London: Picador, 1994), 69–93.

46. On such "control beliefs," see Nicholas Wolterstorff, *Reason within the Bounds of Religion*, 2nd ed. (Grand Rapids, MI: Eerdmans, 1984); and his extension of these reflections in "Theology and Science: Listening to Each Other," in *Religion and Science: History, Method, Dialogue*, ed. W. Mark Richardson and Wesley J. Wildman (New York: Routledge, 1996), 95–104.

or even as bad science. The other community tends to treat the suggestion as *not science at all*. It is simply implausible, irrational, not worth taking seriously.[47]

Before one can get to the question upon which we usually focus when we're making up our minds, the question of *credibility*—of the available explanations for X, which is the best?—one has to address the question of *plausibility*—what determines which explanations will be made available and taken seriously as such? In which direction and at what ought one to look when investigating? What data are worth attending to? How ought they to be classified and related in analysis? What contending theories of their relationship and implication shall be applied and adjudicated? What criteria shall be used against which the rivals will be judged? In sum, *what counts as evidence and rationality* in this case? The question of credibility is, What ought I to believe? The prior question of plausibility asks, What *might* I believe? To combine these two categories, then: What is the range of plausible options among which I ought properly to look for the most credible answer to this question?[48]

We see again that we do not come as blank slates to reasoning—or to any other kind of judgment. (Kenneth Koch reminds us that poets similarly have their own standards for "what kind of inspiration the poet will get, or respond to, and will certainly influence all the maneuvers made in writing the poem." What doesn't meet the minimum standard, that is, will not even be rejected, since it will not ever be taken on board for consideration in the first place.[49]) We cannot engage in any

---

47. Polanyi writes, "Adherents of one persuasion may refuse to recognize any intellectual merit in those of a rival persuasion, calling them cranks, frauds or fools" (221). In this passage he refers to "clashes between different [philosophical], religious or artistic movements," but what he says could apply as easily to natural and social scientists as well. John Lennox quotes Nobel laureate Christian de Duve equating "rational explanation" with "naturalistic" or "atheistic" explanation. Polemicists like Richard Dawkins make this category mistake all the time, and willfully, but it is sobering to read someone make the same equation at the very point of advocating epistemic humility: "[Naturalism is] a working hypothesis that we should be prepared to abandon if faced with facts that defy every attempt at rational explanation" (*Life Evolving: Molecules, Mind, and Meaning* [New York and Oxford: Oxford University Press, 2002], 84; quoted in John C. Lennox, *God's Undertaker: Has Science Buried God?* [Oxford: Lion, 2009], 34).

48. Considerable effort has been expended on behalf of the Christian religion in terms of plausibility, and particularly the question of coherence: Does Christianity make assertions that actually make sense (before we ask about whether they are adequately grounded)? See, for example, William P. Alston's *oeuvre* on justification, beginning with *Epistemic Justification: Essays in the Theory of Knowledge* (Ithaca, NY and London: Cornell University Press, 1989); Alston, *Perceiving God: The Epistemology of Religious Experience* (Ithaca, NY: Cornell University Press, 1991); Alvin Plantinga's trilogy on warrant, which begins with *Warrant: The Current Debate* (New York and Oxford: Oxford University Press, 1993); Richard Swinburne's trilogy that begins with *The Coherence of Theism* (Oxford: Clarendon, 1977); Swinburne, *Epistemic Justification* (Oxford: Clarendon, 2001); and Nicholas Wolterstorff, *Divine Discourse: Philosophical Reflections on the Claim That God Speaks* (Cambridge: Cambridge University Press, 1995).

49. Kenneth Koch, *Making Your Own Days: The Pleasures of Reading and Writing Poetry* (New York: Simon & Schuster, 1998), 95.

reasoning without some prior grasp of logic; some prior confidence in sense experience, memory, and other modes of perception; some prior expectation that the world is usually orderly and so are our thought processes and so intelligible patterns can be discerned by us; and so on. Nor could we reason if we did not already have some idea of what things are worth examining, what questions are worth asking, what cause-and-effect relationships were plausible and which were not. We simply cannot be, and are not, open to everything: we need focus and that means limitation, usually quite drastic limitation, as to what we will admit even to the outer court of plausibility.

Bowing to the dominance of laboratory science as our current cultural paragon of epistemic virtue, let us undertake a bold experiment.[50] I have in my left hand a beaker containing some (I suppose a scientist would say exactly how much) red liquid (again, I'm confident a scientist would be more specific) and in my right hand a beaker containing pretty much the same amount of blue liquid. As my assistant, you are charged with observing and noting anything significant. As we approach the high drama of my pouring the red liquid into the beaker containing the blue liquid, however, I notice your eyes straying out the window. It is the first day of early summer, and a number of students are celebrating the warmth by wearing relatively few clothes. As a man of science, I am focused entirely on the joy of chemistry. You, however, keep watching various attractive people go by.

Despite my mild, but firm, remonstrations that you attend to the beakers, at the critical moment you glance outside again, only to witness a cyclist suddenly lose his balance and fall. You whirl back to me, as I now hold an empty beaker in one hand and beaker of, yes, purple liquid in the other, and exclaim, "That's amazing!"

"What is amazing?" I ask morosely, since according to my hypothesis the liquids were supposed to burst into a nice small sphere of green flame.

"The combination of those liquids forces a mild loss of equilibrium such that anyone nearby riding a bike will fall."

This story sounds like merely another illustration of implausibility, but we have two new points to record. The first is that the choice to look at the beakers rather than at something else is made within an encompassing set of beliefs, or hypotheses, as to how the world works such that I was confident that the results of the experiment would be confined to the immediate vicinity of the beakers. Thus I upbraided

---

50. I do pause briefly to note what Jeffrey Burton Russell notes about the medieval outlook: "The physical cosmos is the allegory of the truly real cosmos, which is God's utterance or song. Physics is an inferior truth pointing to the greater truth, which is theological, moral, and even divine. . . . Indeed, the modern material worldview is almost a total inversion of the moral worldview of the thirteenth and fourteenth centuries" (Jeffrey Burton Russell, *A History of Heaven: The Singing Silence* [Princeton, NJ: Princeton University Press, 1997], 126). I trust it is clear that I am not proposing in this book yet another revolution of the hierarchy of disciplines, but instead am suggesting that all our knowledge, whether of theology or of natural science, is subject to the same fundamental qualifications.

you for looking in an apparently irrelevant direction: There was, in my understanding of things, no good reason to look elsewhere than at the beakers.

"How closed-minded!" you might reply, and I would have to bow to the validity of the charge. We human beings cannot keep track of everything at once, so we make choices as to where to direct our attention based on our presuppositions as to how things are.

Michael Polanyi concurs:

> Life is too short to allow us to go on testing millions of false [hypotheses] in order to hit on a true one. It is of the essence of the scientific method to select for verification hypotheses having a *high* chance of being true. To select good questions for investigation is the mark of scientific talent.... The same holds for the process of verification. Things are not labeled "evidence" in nature, but are evidence only to the extent to which they are accepted as such by us as observers.... No scientist can forgo selecting his evidence in the light of heuristic expectations.[51]

The second, related point, however, is that science has progressed at times by someone noticing something outside the normal, expected range of observation and discovering an important new connection. Velcro, artificial sweeteners, Teflon, the microwave oven, and many other staples of modern life were discovered by scientific minds looking in an unusual, even apparently unwarranted, direction. What counts as relevant evidence is very much a moot point, but evidence that does not currently pass muster with the current paradigm as the right sort of evidence (= simply "evidence") must usually pass a very demanding test indeed to be taken seriously. For to accept it into the argument, everyone involved in the discussion must be willing to alter, even if only for the sake of argument, the paradigm itself, and in many cases, for many people, that is difficult—if not impossible—to do. "To even start considering that kind of thing is just ridiculous!" someone sputters, and we know we have another plausibility problem on our hands. Paradigms are technologies and share key traits of technologies: they enable us to do some things while preventing us from doing other, even closely related, things.

Lorraine Code and her fellow feminist epistemologists expose a dark side to this issue. What counts as evidence and what counts as a good argument are frequently based on assumptions that are morally and politically dubious, if not evil. The testimony of female patients that they are enduring significant pain is a case in point. Male physicians, working from a model of the body that takes the male body as normative, working from a view of science that takes laboratory research (and thus only evidence that can appear in that setting) as normative, and thus working from a set of tests and results designed for normal (= male) bodies have routinely failed to link such testimony with any clear physiological problem. The test results—the

---

51. Polanyi, *Personal Knowledge*, 30.

only evidence that matters—come back ambiguous or even negative, and therefore provide no grounds for the physician to proceed. Customarily, then, physicians have attributed such "undefined disorders"—that include the cardiac condition known as "syndrome X" and chronic fatigue syndrome—to (mere) psychological distress. "It's all in your head" is the answer offered in more or less soothing tones, and analgesics and sedatives are then prescribed.

Research into this phenomenon, however, has shown that (a) the pain or other unwelcome symptom in many cases is due to distinctive features of *female* anatomy and physiology; (b) the trouble in some other cases is due to environmental causes not replicable in a lab or hospital—the usual "control" environments for "normal" medical science; and (c) the suffering in still other cases is, indeed, psychologically prompted, for which the appropriate cure would be, indeed, psychological rather than chemical.[52]

Nicholas Wolterstorff has pressed this matter on behalf of a different group of epistemologically marginalized people, namely, Christians. In his little classic, *Reason within the Bounds of Religion*, he demolishes the claims of what he terms "foundationalism" or, more precisely, "classical foundationalism." This fundamental conviction of the governing elites of modern intellectual life insists that anything deserving the status of knowledge must be worked up from, or be itself, either something evident to the senses or something rationally self-evident. This foundation, Wolterstorff shows, is far too slender a basis upon which to rest the whole of the knowledge-seeking enterprise. Worse, it lacks the ability to justify even itself, since the requirement that all knowledge be derivative from or be itself what is evident to the senses or be rationally self-evident isn't *any* of those things.[53]

It is better, Wolterstorff argues—in a way remarkably congenial to a wide range of contemporary epistemologists, from Kuhn to Polanyi to Code—for each person or community to start with whatever beliefs they hold to be foundational, to begin within their own worldview, and to then construct knowledge on that basis. One doesn't have to start from scratch—as if anyone could! There is no "first position" to which all responsible thinkers must return and from which all responsible thinking then must proceed. Instead, we ought—and we are epistemologically justified—to make the best sense of things we can, according to whatever beliefs/presuppositions/paradigms we take for granted. Start with whatever you like, then see how you do.

---

52. Lorraine Code, *Ecological Thinking: The Politics of Epistemic Location* (Oxford and New York: Oxford University Press, 2006), 112–17, 185–90.

53. Wolterstorff knows his contemporary philosophy and so also treats of the more recent version of classical foundationalism that substitutes descriptions of one's own states of mind (as in "I report that I have the strong impression that I am seeing a tree") for "evident to the senses," which of course reduces the scope of knowledge even further. See Wolterstorff, *Reason within the Bounds of Religion*, chap. 6. And for a powerful extension of Wolterstorff's demolition of classical foundationalism, see Plantinga, *Warranted Christian Belief*, chap. 3.

One might well ask, however, what saves this approach to knowledge-making from sheer antirealistic relativism. What keeps this approach from validating the manifestly mistaken assertions of flat-earthers—or schizophrenics? Is it perfectly all right for anyone to start with just any old beliefs and come to just any old conclusions?

At least two types of vulnerability make this approach properly, rigorously responsible. The first is the common insistence among these thinkers that any claims to knowledge, including even one's fundamental beliefs (Wolterstorff calls them "control beliefs"), are vulnerable to prospective "qualifiers" or "defeaters": evidence and argument that call them into question.[54] The world is what it is, and ideas—from very particular hypotheses on up to entire worldviews—that can be shown to explain the world badly by their failure to deal adequately with qualifiers or defeaters must be improved, repaired, or replaced. Put positively, as David Wolfe puts it, to limited knowers such as ourselves who can never be entirely certain of anything much, "the only credentials ... a true scheme could provide would be its ability to withstand continued criticism. The best in human knowledge consists in interpretive schemes which have withstood strong criticism."[55] Start with whatever you like, then see how you do. The world is, as Mark Richardson and Wesley Wildman remind us, "the ultimate 'dialogue partner' that corrects and improves our ... beliefs about it."[56] This vulnerability keeps such epistemologies, and mine, *realistic*.

Until such time as such challengers arise, however, each person or community is rationally entitled to believe as they do and construct knowledge accordingly. They might be actually wrong about this or that—and who would claim to be completely and accurately right about everything?—but they are not intellectually irresponsible for continuing to believe ideas that have served them well enough thus far. Secularist rationality is not the only game in town, and it must not be allowed to set the terms for everyone else's quest for truth.

The second vulnerability is predictive ability—both in terms of what we can immediately infer from any idea we hold and in terms of what we cannot currently foresee as its predictive power. As Polanyi puts it with natural science particularly in view,

---

54. Wolterstorff, chaps. 11–13; Code: "Pressures, destabilizations, ruptures, breaks—from above, within, or below—repeated explanatory stress, may become so insistent that the imaginary [= governing model or hypothesis] can no longer accommodate it in its seamlessly enveloping story. Clearly, the center can no longer hold" (224). A fine explanation of defeaters is given in Plantinga, *Warranted Christian Belief*, chap. 11.

55. David L. Wolfe, *Epistemology: The Justification of Belief* (Downers Grove, IL: InterVarsity, 1982), 65.

56. W. Mark Richardson and Wesley J. Wildman, "General Introduction," to *Religion and Science: History, Method, Dialogue*, ed. W. Mark Richardson and Wesley J. Wildman (New York: Routledge, 1996), xiv.

a theory which we acclaim as rational...is thereby accredited with predictive powers. We accept it in the hope of making contact with reality; so that, being really true, our theory may yet show forth its truth through future centuries in ways undreamed of by its authors.[57]

Since we believe p to be true, we can expect to see q—and do we? Moreover, since we believe p to be true, we can expect to see other things in due course that p in some way anticipates: "You know, I never thought about it before, but what happened today is exactly what we might have expected to experience, given p."

We can start with whatever we like, and then see how we do. The world provides an abundance of occasions to test our hypotheses.[58] And on some occasions the world will provide intransigent and significant anomalies that provoke us to reconsider details of our paradigms, while on special occasions (we might say) the world crashes through our frameworks and compels us to convert to some radically alternative way of thinking. ("No, that is not going to fly. Ever." "Yes, she actually does love me, despite all appearances to the contrary.")

To be sure, it is not always immediately obvious just what needs to change in our scheme to explain any particular set of anomalies. Perhaps our natural science needs to change; perhaps our Bible interpretation; or perhaps our trust in the reliability of our research assistant! As we probe for just what is wrong, we cannot subject everything in our mental schemes to simultaneous assessment: "Maybe my senses are deceiving me! And maybe my memory...and my assumption that there are other minds out there...and...." Even our process of diagnosing what is malfunctioning in our theorizing, that is, is conducted according to what we believe is more or less likely to be the problem because of what we think is more or less likely to be true. (I have a lot of confidence in the deliverances of my senses, less in my interpretation of the Bible, and still less in my understanding of natural science. My research assistants, I am glad to report, have so far been infallible.) Still, we can methodically check our thinking in each respect in hope of finding a satisfactory way to incorporate the anomalies into a coherent framework.[59]

---

57. Polanyi, *Personal Knowledge*, 5.

58. William Alston says, "Using commonly accepted, workaday standards for knowledge, it is only an extreme skeptic who doubts that we know many things that go beyond our speech acts, beliefs, and their propositional contents. And that being the case, we are well supplied with facts that we can examine to determine whether any of them render this or that propositional attitude or assertion true. It doesn't matter how we came by this knowledge, or what credentials it exhibits, provided its credentials qualify it as genuine knowledge. We may have attained the knowledge by some relatively direct route, such as introspection or perception, or by some more indirect route, like induction, argument to the best explanation, or taking Y (a reliable sign of Z) to indicate that Z obtains. It doesn't matter. So long as we *know* that Z obtains, that is enough to give us a sufficient condition for the truth of Z, on a realist conception of truth. No doubt, we do not have as much knowledge of objective fact as we would like. But we are not as bereft of it as the [extreme skeptics] would have us believe" (*A Realist Conception of Truth* [Ithaca, NY: Cornell University Press, 1996], 101).

59. Polanyi comments, "When text and meaning fall apart we must choose whether to

We all resist alternatives initially, and if they are too different we laugh them off as implausible.[60] But sometimes individuals and even whole communities face what to them are incontrovertible and important realities that their hypotheses cannot absorb and manage. The former paradigm collapses, in whole or in part; a liminal state of confusion, investigation, new theorizing, and testing occurs; and, if all goes well, a new model of comprehension emerges. Conversion, we must note, does occur in the world. *People do change their minds.* It doesn't occur easily, but it does occur—in individuals, groups, and whole societies. And as a general principle it is, of course, good that conversion occurs: Who wants to be imprisoned forever in a defective, and yet incorrigible, understanding?

No one's worldview is impervious to the world. Responsible thinking actively seeks to be responsive to the world and gladly, if also cautiously, adapts to new apprehensions of reality. Sometimes that adaptation requires significant change of a trusted paradigm in the face of what were initially implausible, but then increasingly persuasive, evidences that reality is better understood another way. So be it. The epistemology offered here is thus a form of realism, a confidence that we do have at least *some* access to things as they are and that things as they are *can get through to us, whatever our prejudices and presuppositions.*[61]

---

(1) (a) Correct the meaning of the text.
    (b) Re-interpret the text.
(2) Re-interpret experience.
(3) Dismiss the text as meaningless" (*Personal Knowledge*, 109).

60. See Howard Gardner, *Changing Minds: The Art and Science of Changing Our Own and Other People's Minds* (New York: Harvard Business School Press, 2004), for reflections on why it is difficult to alter one's own, or someone else's, views. John Locke offers us a classic image of even—or, in this case, especially—scholarly resistance to new ideas, in a way eerily prescient of Thomas Kuhn's argument that old-timers basically cannot adapt to radically new paradigms and that new paradigms come to dominate only when defenders of the previous one lose power, most obviously by dying: "Would it not be an insufferable thing for a learned professor, and that which his scarlet would blush at, to have his authority of forty years' standing wrought out of hardrock Greek and Latin, with no small expense of time and candle, and confirmed by general tradition, and a reverend beard, in an instant overturned by an upstart novelist [by which Locke means "purveyor of something new"]? Can any one expect that he should be made to confess, that what he taught his scholars thirty years ago, was all error and mistake; and that he sold them hard words and ignorance at a very dear rate?" (*An Essay concerning Human Understanding*, ed. A. S. Pringle-Pattison [Oxford: Clarendon, 1928], IV, xx, 11, pp. 366–67).

61. Alongside the philosophical works cited here in this regard, I have been helped by historical and social scientific accounts of conversion. See, for example, Jerald C. Brauer, "Conversion: From Puritanism to Revivalism," *Journal of Religion* 58 (1978): 227–43; Lewis R. Rambo, *Understanding Religious Conversion* (New Haven and London: Yale University Press, 1993); Gardner, *Changing Minds*; and Paul Hiebert, *Transforming Worldviews: An Anthropological Understanding of How People Change* (Grand Rapids, MI: Baker Academic, 2008).

As this book will continue to detail, however, this realism is a heavily qualified, "critical" realism. We can hardly claim that every change of mind is a change for the better, prompted by a clearer or more comprehensive apprehension of reality. If all conversion were in one direction we might be tempted to think so, but it obviously is not. Sometimes the best explanation for a change of mind is that one has encountered elements of the world previously unknown, ignored, or misunderstood, or new, and realism is thus justified. But sometimes that isn't the best explanation for an altered opinion or even a wholesale conversion. We make up our minds under competing influences, and it is time to examine more of them now.

THE SOCIAL CONTEXT OF OUR THINKING

Anthropologists, sociologists, and psychologists broadly agree that human thinking is deeply affected by our social environment. Epistemologists, economists, and political scientists, let alone scientists and engineers, have been much slower to recognize that fact.[62] (Indeed, I have often reflected on the fact that several Nobel Prizes in economics have been won by thinkers at the University of Chicago for noticing that human beings are more than mere rational choice machines, an insight those of us in the Divinity School, a short walk across campus, rather took for granted.) In these latter disciplines, the "knower" is a very particular sort of person, as Lorraine Code tellingly depicts him:

> He has existed only in narrowly conceived theoretical places, abstracted and isolated from the exigencies and vagaries of human lives; and whenever he has figured in philosophical-political theory, he has been presumptively male, usually white, privileged, able-bodied, articulate, and educated. Of particular significance for my purposes is his principled isolation from the implications of corporeality, from the minutiae of individuality and situatedness, and from actively informed or motivated participation in concerns that surface insistently in everyday interactions marked by vulnerability and trust and/or in experiences of trauma and crisis, where the requirements of responsible knowing are particularly urgent.

In reaction to this model, some enthusiasts have gone so far as to say that our experience of reality is fundamentally "socially constructed." By this they mean more than the truism that our social situations affect how we think. They mean that we all think *primarily* or even *entirely* in terms set for us by individuals and communities that have figured prominently in our lives: parents, siblings, teachers, educational institutions, friends, enemies, heroes, authors, churches, cultural organizations,

---

62. Wry reflections on this oft-remarked phenomenon can be enjoyed here: Gordon Bigelow, "Let There Be Markets: The Evangelical Roots of Economics," *Harper's* 310 (May 2005): 33–38.

ethnic groups, classes, governments, entertainment and news media, and so on. Truly radical social constructivists would reduce our thoughts to mere artifacts of the multiple social contexts of our lives. This is a profoundly anti-humanist assertion with grave consequences, not least in terms of the worth of the human person and its implications for justice. (Amnesty International, more than twenty years ago, convened a conference at Oxford University asking speakers to consider whether the self "as construed by the liberal tradition still exist[s]" and, if it doesn't, "whose human rights are we [= we Amnesty activists] defending?"[63]

This extreme construal of the human person and thus of human knowledge also has the baleful entailment of being vulnerable to any *ad hominem* argument an opponent cares to lob: "Yes, well, that's just what a [person affected by this or that social context] *would* say." The modern drive toward the ideal of disembodied, generic human minds reflecting only on publicly accepted data according to the most prestigious intellectual conventions of the time arose largely from the desire to avoid the charge of interested, therefore biased, and therefore dubious "knowledge" and to arrive instead at what was actually, rather than preferably, the case. The abandonment of such an ideal as unavailable without surrendering knowledge to a mere contest of propagandas is the challenge of any postmodern epistemology.

Well short of any extreme social constructivism, however, we can begin our reflection on the social context of our thought by noticing that even strikingly original thinkers throughout history show themselves to be men and women "of their times," working within—even as they stretch and perhaps reshape—the categories and convictions of their day. No one except fellow artists in the same cultural context writes poetry like Homer, or composes music like Bach, or paints portraits like Picasso. Indeed, every one of us works within the most obvious cultural context of all: the language or languages we learn. Without subscribing to anything like the so-called Sapir-Whorf hypothesis, we nonetheless can easily agree that each language provides both possibilities and constraints, open doors and solid walls, vistas and cloud banks. As Polanyi says, "I cannot speak except from inside a language."[64]

When we move, moreover, from the level of German or Chinese (recognizing that there are significantly different creative alternatives in the variety of dialects within those rich traditions) to consider the languages of musical genres (e.g., the conventions of baroque counterpoint or early punk rock), painting styles (e.g., late Renaissance mannerism versus abstract expressionism), or computer programming (BASIC compared with UNIX), or even return to English to ponder the semantics of telegraphy versus texting, the reality of language's influence becomes obvious, even as its particulars remain fascinating.

By extension, we confront the social practices that both encourage and inhibit, that direct and restrain, our thought. It is difficult to reflect upon what one takes for

---

63. Barbara Johnson, "Introduction," in *Freedom and Interpretation: The Oxford Amnesty Lectures 1992* (New York: Basic, 1994), 2; quoted in Code, 201.

64. *Personal Knowledge*, 253.

granted, of course, but consider just two examples of how social practices shape our thinking.

A documentary film is shown at a local festival. The festival convenors want to aid the audience's reflection on the movie, so they invite the director to say a few words afterward and they also invite an academic specialist to critique the film. The cultural expectations of the largely white, largely Canadian, and largely urban audience clearly govern what happens in the exchange. Despite evidently deep and passionate differences of opinion, the panelists and the audience members speak in relatively moderate tones and civilly indicate their differences and concerns. An audience member who deviates from that norm in expressing herself less discreetly and more combatively meets with murmurs of disapproval. The announced expertise of the one panelist clearly cows some audience members (but not all), while the very presence of the director makes every criticism of the film now a matter of personal attack, a mode of encounter white Canadians tend to reserve rather strictly for political rallies and hockey games. The stilted "one question per person" expectation, with no give-and-take "as we want to give everyone a chance" (to what? perform? contribute? be validated?), obviously compromises the intellectual quality of the proceedings in some respects. But the social pressure to speak moderately, briefly, and in turn allows for intelligent encounter that might otherwise quickly descend into battle or mutual excommunication.[65]

A controversial motion is tabled in the latter part of the annual business meeting of a Christian congregation. It comes from the board of elders with the blessing of the pastoral staff. The chairman of the board takes time to frame the issue and to set out the terms of the discussion from the position of power: the lectern at the front of the room, amplified (in both respects) by a public address system. Before debate is allowed, he indicates that the hour is late and "we all want to get home." The social practices observed in such a meeting virtually guarantee that the motion will receive only superficial scrutiny. Indeed, anyone who mounts a serious challenge from the floor is not generally regarded as making a positive intellectual contribution to the mutual consideration of this important issue, but as a dangerous deviant disrupting the harmony of the congregation. It being a religious meeting, every action is charged with religious significance: difference, and especially dissent, now carries ominous spiritual implications. If one attended this meeting with the assumption that the only value at work here was to make the best decision possible in terms of the intrinsic merits of the proposal, one would be quickly corrected by the social practices of the collective.

Social practices thus can affect quite profoundly the possibilities and impossibilities for serious thought in a given situation. What is habitually done when a

---

65. I don't mean this last word only figuratively, of course. It might well change the nature of certain Christian arguments if the participants had to, say, take communion together, or pray for each other, or wash each other's feet at the beginning, end, or perhaps especially in the middle of the debate.

group needs to consider a matter, what is allowable, what is disallowed, what is even thinkable to do or say—all of these expectations are encoded in rituals and responses, in modes and mores, in permissions and denials both expressed and tacit. How do we think? Whom do we consult, and how? What do we bring to the table, and how do we deal with what is presented? How do we express ourselves and how do we entertain each other's thoughts? Who is invited, who is ignored, and who is opposed as a matter of course?[66]

Coming to terms with social realities and growing in this dimension of self-consciousness helps us understand both what and how we think. We might well ask ourselves, and others, "*Where* did you read the Bible, or conduct that experiment, or observe those people—and *with whom*?" This awareness helps us determine what ideas we have received from these influences and to recognize why it is that we hold them. This further understanding thus positions us to accept or to alter what and how we think, to at least some extent. It also can humble us with the fact of our own limitations.[67]

For some time now, contemporary theology—not least among evangelical Christians—has decried individualism in theology in favor of a renewed emphasis upon thinking "in community." This emphasis upon theology as the activity of the Christian community per se, rather than of just isolated Christian individuals, echoes the convictions of great theologians of the past who also viewed theology always in the context of the church, whether Thomas Aquinas, John Calvin, F. D. E. Schleiermacher or Karl Barth. In the recently renewed emphasis upon the creeds, "the undivided church," and "the Fathers"; in the fresh regard for the intuitions, convictions, and practices of laypeople; and in the new recognition that the Christian church is both global and local—and thus Christian thinking ought to benefit from the wisdom of quite different believers while properly speaking with an indigenous voice—the theologian hears the call to conduct her work in a broad context with due deference to the *consensus fidelium* and due recognition of one's own embeddedness in a particular context.[68] What is true for the theologian, then, is true, *mutatis mutandis*, for all Christian thinkers.

---

66. Kathryn Tanner relates theological thinking and social practices suggestively in *Theories of Culture: A New Agenda for Theology* (Minneapolis, MN: Fortress, 1997).

67. Along with the sources cited here, see "Conviviality," chap. in Michael Polanyi, *Personal Knowledge*, 203–45.

68. For examples among a host of others, see Robert E. Webber, *Ancient-Future Faith: Rethinking Evangelicalism for a Postmodern World* (Grand Rapids, MI: Baker, 1999); Kenneth Tanner and Christopher Hall, eds., *Ancient & Postmodern Christianity: Paleo-Orthodoxy in the 21st Century—Essays in Honor of Thomas C. Oden* (Downers Grove, IL: IVP Academic, 2008); George A. Lindbeck, *The Nature of Doctrine: Religion and Theology in a Postliberal Age* (Philadelphia: Westminster Press, 1984); Daniel J. Treier, *Introducing Theological Interpretation of Scripture: Recovering a Christian Practice* (Grand Rapids, MI: Baker Academic, 2008); Richard J. Mouw, *Consulting the Faithful: What Christian Intellectuals Can Learn from Popular Religion* (Grand Rapids, MI: Eerdmans, 1994); Robert Schreiter, *Constructing Local Theologies*

Some of this rhetoric about community and church and ecumenicity and so on sounds, to be sure, romantically unrealistic. "If only we would think together as a nice, big family we would come up with much better theology." Communities connect us with a world in some respects bigger than ourselves, but no bigger than the community itself. Thus thinkers are constrained by the facts, interpretations, frames of reference, and possibilities acknowledged as plausible that are available to them in that cultural context. They generally share their community's values, including its sinful or stupid ones, its blind spots and rationalizations of evil, its complacency about unjust advantages it enjoys and its resistance to anything that challenges what it understands to be its wellbeing. Reinhold Niebuhr worked tirelessly to warn his fellow American liberals of the error of their utopian views of social transformation. He wrote of *Moral Man and Immoral Society*, arguing at length that groups often believe and act *worse* than individuals—and, indeed, worse than the individuals who constitute the group would act on their own.[69] Furthermore, groups can, like individuals can, drive a hermeneutical spiral *away* from reality, *away* from the true, the good, and the beautiful. Racist attitudes and policies in both the American South and Apartheid South Africa started small-scale and inchoate, only later to be fully thematized in elaborate apologetics as each society felt pressure to justify its oppressive values and structures. The thinking about race relations, about anthropology, about justice, about the Bible, and about God in fact became worse and worse.[70] Societies, like individuals, are both finite and fallen.

Thomas Kuhn's classic study of *The Structure of Scientific Revolutions* helps us here.[71] Kuhn famously (or "notoriously," depending on your viewpoint) historicized and politicized the so-called hard sciences, notably physics and chemistry. Kuhn showed that the great advances of science—including such fundamental features as heliocentrism and the discovery of oxygen—are understood best not as a series of simple intellectual insights (great minds enjoying a string of "Eureka!" moments),

(Maryknoll, NY: Orbis, 1985); Craig Ott and Harold Netland, eds., *Globalizing Theology: Belief and Practice in an Era of World Christianity* (Grand Rapids, MI: Baker Academic, 2006).

69. Reinhold Niebuhr, *Moral Man and Immoral Society: A Study in Ethics and Politics* (New York: Charles Scribner's Sons, 1960 [1932]).

70. See Mark A. Noll, "The Bible and Slavery," chap. in *America's God: From Jonathan Edwards to Abraham Lincoln* (New York: Oxford University Press, 2002), 386–401; Irving Hexham, *The Irony of Apartheid: The Struggle for National Independence of Afrikaner Calvinism against British Imperialism* (New York: Edwin Mellen, 1981). See also Christine Rosen, *Preaching Eugenics: Religious Leaders and the American Eugenics Movement* (New York: Oxford University Press, 2004). Lorraine Code comments: "Ecological thinking will yield no 'poet's utopia,' such as Richard Rorty's free-play of the ironic liberal imagination promises. Ecosystems—both metaphorical and literal—are as cruel as they are kind, as unpredictable and overwhelming as they are orderly and nurturant, as unsentimentally destructive of their less viable members as they are cooperative and mutually sustaining; and ecological thinking is as available for feeding self-serving romantic fantasies as for inspiring socially responsible transformations" (6).

71. Kuhn, *The Structure of Scientific Revolutions*.

but within a historical narrative that is fraught with alliances, ideologies, agendas, and power.

Strikingly new ways of seeing things—if they have the potential to change science significantly, they are new *paradigms*, in Kuhn's wildly influential terminology—emerge in particular sets of historical circumstances. These are usually a concatenation of nagging problems, whether with the theory or the data, afflicting the current paradigm; younger scholars, or perhaps older ones who do not enjoy positions of central prestige and influence, who are not fully invested in the accepted model, paying careful attention to these problems and willing to think outside the model; new equipment becoming available, whether coincidentally or by design, that can analyze data pertinent to comparing the current paradigm with an alternative; and so on. Eventually, a group—really, a kind of alliance—of scholars forms around a particular novel option and campaigns for its acceptance. Some other scholars convert to the cause, while yet others resist.

If the differences run too deep—if the question is not that of refining the existing model but of replacing it—then, Kuhn contends, there is no way to arbitrate the discussion in a neutral way by reference to generally accepted beliefs, since some of those beliefs themselves are on the table. Each must decide for himself or herself in comparing the theories with each other and with the whatever data seem pertinent; the struggle for supremacy—in the various relevant arenas, whether universities, presses, meetings, and so on—proceeds apace; and eventually either proponents of the old model beat back the challengers or the new model triumphs in what is—note the political connotation—a scientific *revolution*.[72]

---

72. Nancey Murphy points to W.v.O. Quine's borrowing of an image from Otto Neurath (!): "We are like people on a ship; we can repair and change the ship bit by bit, plank by plank. The ship stays afloat only because at each alteration we keep the bulk of it intact" (W.v.O. Quine, *Word and Object* [Cambridge, MA: MIT Press, 1960], 3–4; cited in Nancey Murphy, *Reasoning and Rhetoric in Religion* [Valley Forge, PA: Trinity, 1994], 205). Kuhn's "paradigm shift" in this imagery would be to abandon a ship judged to be no longer seaworthy for another that one believes will perform better.

I might briefly pause to acknowledge that Kuhn has a more radical idea still in his idea of paradigm shifts—namely, that one model is abandoned for another not simply because the latter solves the problems recognized in the former but inadequately solved by it, but also, or even primarily, because the latter opens up new questions entirely and leaves the problems of the past behind. I think that that way of seeing scientific revolutions in particular and intellectual paradigm shifts in general is a trifle extreme, however. It is likely true in some cases (no scientist seriously pursues astrology or alchemy anymore), but the general questions of science and of human inquiry in general remain: What is the world? Where did it come from? Where is it going? What's wrong with it, and what can we do about that? While I recognize that paradigms can obscure as well as reveal, I am dubious about the idea that truly valid questions may be abandoned in the limitations of the new model. Any questions "left over" from the previous paradigm would make sense and therefore have enduring validity in the new one if they did in fact point to phenomena to be explained. Perhaps they are temporarily ignored in the enthusiasm for the main features of the new model. But if they point to realities, they will not go away. Indeed, if we did actually start to see evidence that, say, the gravitational force of the moon or the radiation from distant stars did affect human behavior, or that the subatomic particles of base metals could be rearranged to form more valuable metals, we would take up the old questions with alacrity. (I will drop the

Many of those who have a reverence for science have been dismayed by Kuhn's depiction of how science advances in times of significant theoretical crisis.[73] Kuhn is adamant, however, that while the scientific method works fine in day-to-day "normal" science—that is, scientific work conducted within an agreed-upon paradigm—it is not the route by which scientists in fact develop alternative ways of seeing something nor how one alternative becomes accepted over others.[74] There is always more than science involved in major developments in science.[75]

Does Kuhn's work therefore undercut the reliability of the hard sciences, and therefore (as we moderns would reflexively think) of all knowledge? Are the established facts merely the orthodoxy that has been advanced by the strongest party?[76]

---

matter here, however, since even if I am wrong about this issue, nothing much is affected in the present discussion.)

73. My own students in the history of theology have been likewise appalled at the machinations surrounding the emergence of the great ecumenical creeds of the Church, as the standard patristic histories detail. For example, see Henry Chadwick, *The Early Church* (London: Penguin, 1967); W. H. C. Frend, *The Rise of Christianity* (Philadelphia: Fortress, 1984); and the like. Kuhn himself refers to theology explicitly at a number of key junctures, but usually only with tantalizing brevity. For his part, Polanyi straightforwardly speaks of "conversion" in quasi-religious terms as the agenda in scientific controversy: *Personal Knowledge*, 150–51.

74. A more recent history, this time focusing on chemistry, confirms this basic sense of how science proceeds: Patrick Coffey, *Cathedrals of Science: The Personalities and Rivalries that Made Modern Chemistry* (New York and Oxford: Oxford University Press UP, 2008). See also István Hargittai's account of the Nobel Prize, *The Road to Stockholm: Nobel Prizes, Science, and Scientists* (New York and Oxford: Oxford University Press, 2002).

75. Barry Commoner, himself a scientist, writes about the sacred status of the "myth" that DNA explains all there is to explain about our make-up: "To some degree the theory has been protected from criticism by a device more common to religion than to science: dissent, or merely the discovery of a discordant fact, is a punishable offense, a heresy that might easily lead to professional ostracism. Much of this bias can be attributed to institutional inertia, a failure of rigor, but there are other, more insidious reasons why molecular geneticists might be satisfied with the status quo; the central dogma has given them such a satisfying, seductively simplistic explanation of heredity that it seemed sacrilegious to entertain doubts. The central dogma was simply too good not to be true." Commoner observes that this resistance to basic scientific integrity had an economic dimension as well: simplistic understanding of genes undergirded massive projects in commercial genetic engineering of foods that would become utterly dubious the moment the complexity of the situation became apparent. See Barry Commoner, "Unraveling the DNA Myth: The Spurious Foundation of Genetic Engineering," *Harper's* (February 2002): 39–47. The quotation is from p. 47.

76. One thinks of Matthew Prior's devastating proto-Kuhnian critique:

"Man does with dangerous curiosity
        Those unfathomed wonders try:
With fancied rules and arbitrary laws
Matter and motion he restrains;
And studied lines and fictious circles draws:
        Then with imagined sovereignty
        Lord of his new *Hypothesis* he reigns.
        He reigns: How long? 'till some usurper rise;
        And he too, mighty thoughtful, mighty wise,

Some understand Kuhn that way. Alternatively, I see Kuhn's scheme to rest on the idea that paradigms are called into question only when they fail to work to everyone's satisfaction, particularly in the face of factual anomalies. A new generation of scientists, disgruntled because they haven't been able to rise to positions of eminence, cannot simply launch a revolution out of envy alone. One cannot plausibly, let alone admirably, think just whatever one prefers to think.[77] There has to be something *there* sufficient to justify a quite new model, even as those with power will tend (as Lord Acton warned in a different register) to exaggerate, underplay, or otherwise construe the situation in accord with their interests.

Andrew Walls points to similar phenomena in terms of tribal religious conversions:

> The impact on Africa of alien influences from the Western world produced an array of reasons within the traditional framework of thinking to seek for radical religious adjustment and change. The religious effects of a river dam, of a concrete building constructed over the abode of the water spirit, of an exodus of young men to work for cash, of a virus caught from incomers for which the local society has no immunity—these things are potentially more shattering religiously [and, I am saying, epistemologically] than years of preaching to a stable and satisfied society. In stable primal societies the tradition of the elders—a body of knowledge, wisdom, and interpretation built up over centuries— provides the means of coping with every conceivable situation. But when situations arise for which the tradition has no answers, the society may be in danger of disintegration unless it can find either a means of containing the invading elements or a new rule of life to act as an alternative or supplementary tradition.[78]

Lorraine Code seems to combine the realms of Kuhn and Walls as she calls us to recognize the fundamentally *ecological* nature of our thinking: that we conduct our investigation of the world as particular sorts of people in particular parts of the

---

Studies new lines, and other circles feigns.
From this last toil again what knowledge flows?
Just as much, perhaps, as shows
That all his predecessor's rules
Were empty cant, all *Jargon* of the schools;
That he on t'other's ruin rears his throne;
And shows his friend's mistake, and thence confirms his own."

("On Exodus 3:14 'I am that I am': An Ode," in *Poems on Several Occasions*, 2nd ed. [London: Jacob Tonson, 1709 (1688)], 4; emphasis in original; I have modernized spellings.)

77. Indeed, sociologist Steven Goldberg cites a fundamental principle of any reputable inquiry: "If you are happy with the conclusions reached by your research, double-check and triple-check those conclusions" ("The Erosion of the Social Sciences" in *Dumbing Down: Essays on the Strip-Mining of American Culture*, ed. Katharine Washburn and John F. Thornton [New York: W. W. Norton, 1996], 97).

78. Andrew Walls, *The Missionary Movement in Christian History: Studies in the Transmission of Faith* (Maryknoll, NY: Orbis, 1996), 90–91.

world, deeply affected by the particularity of ourselves and our environment. Code in fact prompts us to move beyond the customary postmodern recognition of the *social* context of our thinking—the standard, and important, categories of race, class, sexuality, age, and the like—to consider the complete range of dimensions of our existence... and thus of our thought. We therefore ought to add the geographical and corporeal nature of our being into account, intertwined as these factors are with the political, sexual, religious, and other dimensions of culture.

Life is different, and so thinking is different, in a hot place versus a cold one versus a temperate one. Life is different, and so thinking is different, if you are in danger from natural disaster, famine, or bellicose neighbors.[79] Virginia Woolf famously considered the counterfactual idea of Shakespeare's sister needing a range of concrete circumstances in which to do work that would give her a literary voice, including "A Room of One's Own."[80] Those who have a room, furthermore, conduct their thinking (and communicating) in a very particular room. Thinking isn't necessarily going to be the same beneath the Gothic fan ceilings of an Oxbridge college and under the thatch of an African mission school, or in a Hong Kong high-rise versus a sprawling, windswept prairie campus. Thinking almost certainly isn't going to be the same if you and your community are running the show in a prosperous and stable situation versus being on the run in a desperate one.

To this broadly spatial consideration, furthermore, we might here add the dimension of time and the effects of particular circumstances upon *this moment* of thinking. A little reflection tells any of us that we have thought differently at different times both because under different circumstances and because we ourselves were in some key respects different people then. "Depend upon it, sir, when a man knows he is to be hanged in a fortnight, it concentrates his mind wonderfully," Samuel Johnson is reported to have said. At the other end of the scale, as we combine now both the temporal and the spatial, weeks of leisure by a

---

79. Here—partly prompted by the *Annales* historians' (over-)emphasis on physical geography and partly prompted by liberation theology's focus upon extreme and dangerous social, economic, and political situations—I extend Code's categories. Her discussion of the "geographical," for instance, is restricted to different kinds of buildings: offices, laboratories, homes, and so on. Climate, availability of food, war or the threat of war, and so on, don't figure in her account—but easily could, so I trust my extensions are legitimate. And particularly since the Christian tradition rests in large part on epistles written in prison or exile to audiences threatened by or even experiencing persecution, Christians particularly want to be alert to the ways in which knowledge can be found and shared in extreme situations and not only in normal ones—toward the latter of which attitudes modern knowledge-seeking tends (that is, knowledge is what is found in safe, orderly environments, whether archives, laboratories, or private rooms.) Indeed, a challenge for Christian thinking today is the recognition and critical reception of knowledge claims being made by those in volatile situations, whether by Christians reporting extraordinary ways to understand God's healing power in charismatic movements in Africa; political options arising in Latin America, Singapore, or Korea; or the anarchist, communitarian, monastic, and other radical ecclesiastical and public policy proposals being advocated by many Christians working among the most troubled in European, North American, and Australasian cities.

80. Virginia Woolf, *A Room of One's Own* (London: Hogarth, 1929).

mountain lake offer the mind freedom to wander over terrains normally ignored in the press of everyday life that forces one to take tried-and-true paths.[81] Holding the gun—or the flowers, or the court order, or the keys—prompts one to see things differently than if one is facing the gun or the flowers or the court order or the keys.[82]

Different situations, then, prompt different kinds of thought. Not all of them will be as valuable as each other: it is reliably reported that one's ruminations when intoxicated usually turn out, upon sober reconsideration, to be less impressive than they had originally appeared. But it is well for us to recognize that things occur to people in some circumstances that don't otherwise occur to anyone, and that some circumstances thus put people in epistemically *privileged* situations, whether permanently or temporarily. "Ah, *now* I see! It looks very different when I'm in *this* situation" is hardly a rare experience, and responsible thinkers therefore ought to seek out either the situations or the people in those situations who can provide special, even superior, angles of vision on the subject. As Susan Babbitt puts it, "Rather than requiring information in order to make the right choices, individuals sometimes have to make certain choices and take actions *first* in order to bring about the conditions under which information, if it is available can be properly approached.[83]

We must locate ourselves properly, furthermore, not just to improve our thinking, to move from "good" to "better," but also to guard our thinking against the misunderstandings, delusions, and even propaganda fostered by some environments. As late as the 1980s in West Texas, where I worked for a couple of summers, everyone I met (and they were all middle-class white Texans) shared a common attitude toward both blacks and Mexicans, a common "understanding" that these minorities were, as entire groups, lazy, barely competent, and dangerous. Memoirs and histories of those growing up in Nazi Germany, Apartheid South Africa, Maoist China, and other cultures vastly deranged by evil ideology show that the part of the (social) world we are experiencing might, in fact, lie to us, distort the true nature of things, and both enforce and reinforce errors in our thinking. After all, many communities and institutions are not centrally concerned with discerning truth, and thus participation in such groups inclines each constituent individual away from the truths that are inconvenient for the group's central purposes (whether wealth, status, security, fame, vengeance, pleasure, and so on). Many groups, in fact, thrive only on the basis of systemic misrepresentations of the truth—that is, on deep and abiding lies: slaves, or employees, or women are like children who warrant both

---

81. This is a recurring theme in Mihaly Csikszentmihalyi, *Creativity: Flow and the Psychology of Discovery and Invention* (New York: Harper, 1996).

82. The first speech I ever gave was a reflection on John Howard Griffin, *Black Like Me* (New York: Houghton Mifflin, 1961). For a schoolchild in northern Ontario, as I was at the time, the experience of reading and reflecting on this book was epistemologically disturbing at a fundamental level—a disturbance for which I remain grateful.

83. Susan E. Babbitt, "Feminism and Objective Interests," in *Feminist Epistemologies*, ed. Linda Alcoff and Elizabeth Potter (New York: Routledge, 1993), 260.

control and condescension; one race is superior to all others and therefore deserves whatever privileges it can garner; riches, power, and honour come inexorably to those who succeed by dint of individual effort and talent; this system is a pure meritocracy such that those higher up in the pecking order entirely deserve their positions.

Such situations notoriously foster false consciousness—in everyone involved. Those with power think themselves to be entirely entitled to it; those without it think themselves also to occupy their appropriate station in life. Whether in the feudal hierarchy in which everyone believes in the divine right of kings, and therefore by implication in the unquestionable authority of a local lord, or in a patriarchy in which everyone believes in the husband's priority in all family matters, even at the cost of the well-bring of wife and children (and, to be sure, of the husband himself), false consciousness is a pervasive epistemic state that only radically different experiences—anomalies great enough to rock these settled paradigms—can even begin to challenge.[84]

What is true in such situations that seem obviously harmful to knowledge-seeking is true also in situations closer to home: even a relatively modest amount of wealth and education insulates us against the realities of, say, the lives of those we hire for domestic duties or menial jobs at work, the lives of prisoners and their families, the lives of street people, the lives of the mentally ill. We—and the politicians our money pays to represent us—routinely make policy decisions that shape the worlds of such people without any of us spending even a single hour in the horrifying realities of their daily lives. *How can we really know what we're talking about?* Epistemology turns out, once again, to be inescapably political and economic, as well as intellectual.[85]

Dietrich Bonhoeffer, like me a well-educated son of a successful physician living a comfortable bourgeois life in a western society, was forced to see things from a

---

84. Susan Babbitt writes, "It is often painfully futile and startlingly insensitive to try to help someone out of a difficult situation by simply giving her more information. Telling someone that she is living her life wrongly is not usually helpful and often quite damaging. However, by changing someone's situation we are sometimes in fact supplying that person with relevant information" ("Feminism and Objective Interests," 257). On the Uncle Tom, Self-Deprecator, and the Deferential Wife, see Thomas Hill, Jr., "Servility and Self-Respect," *The Monist* 57 (1973): 87–104.

85. The vector of influence can point the other way, of course. Not only do political realities qualify our epistemology, but, as Locke intended, our epistemology ought to qualify our politics. Bold certainty might well lead to inflexible and extreme political stands and strategies; a strong sense of the fallibility of all human thinking might well lead to more modest, conservative, incrementalist approaches to social change. I cannot embark on that question here, of course, but I have offered an ethics and an apologetics grounded in this epistemology here: *Making the Best of It: Following Christ in the Real World* (New York and Oxford: Oxford University Press, 2008); *Humble Apologetics: Defending the Faith Today* (New York and Oxford: Oxford University Press, 2003).

radically different perspective when he was cast into prison by the Nazis. Unlike me, Bonhoeffer learned to appreciate the value of "the view from below":

> There remains an experience of incomparable value. We have for once learnt to see the great events of world history from below, from the perspective of the outcast, the suspects, the maltreated, the powerless, the oppressed, the reviled—in short, from the perspective of those who suffer. The important thing is that neither bitterness nor envy should have gnawed at the heart during this time, but we should have come to look with new eyes at matters great and small, sorrow and joy, strength and weakness; that our perception of generosity, humanity, justice and mercy should have become clearer, freer, less corruptible. We have to learn that personal suffering is a more effective key, a more rewarding principle for exploring the world in thought and action, than personal good fortune.[86]

As Gustavo Gutiérrez and the liberationist tradition he fathered have reminded their fellow Christians, we read the Bible differently, and better, when we heed the testimony of those on the receiving end of power—as the apostles were. So, too, do we read much else differently, and better.[87]

Lest we imagine, moreover, that Kuhn's reflections do not apply to us because we are not engaged in scientific world-shaking, or that Code's warnings do not apply to us at least when we are engaged in disciplined scholarly pursuits, or that Bonhoeffer's and Gutiérrez's experiences seem the stuff of nightmarish movies, sociologist Michèle Lamont informs us that at the highest reaches of academic decision-making, history and politics reign as well.

Herself a member of the academic elite (she holds a multi-pronged professorship at Harvard), Lamont examined the way academicians recognize excellence. Among the ways available to professors to do so (such as, indeed, granting positions at top-flight schools, but also publication by élite book presses and journals, awarding professional society prizes, and so on) are the decisions to grant funds for research via the top agencies. "Peer review" is the gold standard of academic life,

---

86. Dietrich Bonhoeffer, *Letters and Papers from Prison*, ed. Eberhard Bethge, trans. Frank Clarke, Reginald Fuller, and John Bowden, enlarged ed. (New York: Macmillan, 1971 [1953]), 17.

87. Gustavo Gutiérrez, *A Theology of Liberation: History, Politics, and Salvation*, trans. Sister Caridad Inda and John Eagleson, rev. ed. (Maryknoll, NY: Orbis Books, 1988 [1973]). This discussion of how we can, and should, seek alternative viewpoints and contexts is, in part, a response to the challenge laid down by George Mavrodes more than twenty years ago as he asked Merold Westphal, "How can I tell which part of my own philosophy has been badly warped by sin?...What I need are examples of Christian philosophers who make serious use of the idea that sin has a damaging effect on *their own* intellectual lives and who then illustrate the ways in which they detect those effects, how they avoid equally damaging effects of sin when they endeavor to correct the original damage, and so on" ("A Futile Search for Sin," *Perspectives* [January 1993], 9).

and it doesn't get more gilded than the fellowships, field research grants, and oper-ating grants offered by the handful of élite agencies she studied.

She found that "excellence" was indeed the sole stated standard by which the various committees made their judgments. But as she watched them work, inter-viewed the panelists, and then saw the results, she concluded that there was much more going on in the decision-making process than the disinterested quest for su-perb scholarship. "Peer review is an interactional and an emotional undertaking," she concludes, with the conversational and larger political dynamics of the commit-tee itself playing a large role in the deliberations, including bargaining (Lamont literally calls it "horse trading"), gossip (her word), intimidation, alliances, even fatigue and ill-timed humor during the proceedings. "Pleasure, saving face, and maintaining one's self-concept" among the panelists were obvious and important motives for their decisions—*about other people's research careers*. And "homophilic judgments are pervasive across the social sciences and the humanities"—that is, awards are made to researchers whose work both resembles and reinforces the work of the panelists themselves. Far from the ideal of committees resolutely wrestling with decisions until the most worthy candidates eventually emerge to their just des-erts, Lamont saw a lot of "satisficing" going on, what she describes as "making good enough," rather than optimal, decisions.[88]

We must not be sentimental, therefore, about "community" in our thinking. Sentimental championing of communal thinking takes insufficiently into account the continuing need for prophetic (reminding) and creative (discovering) thought proffered by individuals or small fellowships of intellectual innovators. Furthermore, communities of *Christians* do not escape the dynamics of group behavior that may impede the Spirit's voice. Consider Francis, Luther, Kierkegaard, and others who spoke a shockingly alternative word to the dominant theology of their churches, let alone the apostles themselves who testified against their Jewish compatriots. In fact, Paul provides for us an example of innovative dissent even within the early Christian community as he challenges the Jewish church with the legitimacy and success of the Gentile mission. I note in this regard that the theologians who are usually cited,

---

88. Michèle Lamont, *How Professors Think: Inside the Curious World of Academic Judgment* (Cambridge, MA, and London: Harvard University Press, 2009), 20–21. As a career academi-cian myself, I found much to contemplate in this work, not least as Lamont discovered that "program officers do not force panelists to respect [the] guidelines.... Panelists are given full sovereignty over decision making" (29). The book offers fascinating glimpses into American academic disciplinary cultures as well, with philosophers stubbornly insisting on arcaneness to the point of unintelligibility outside their field, anthropologists sanctimoniously citing no one but other anthropologists, and English literature specialists destroying their field by decades of poststructuralist doubt to the point that no one else thinks they have standards for excellence any more, either. This dispiriting situation is so widely recognized in academia, in fact, that tes-timonies and *cris de coeur* regularly appear in the professional press, such as these: Stephen H. Balch, "The Antidote to Academic Orthodoxy," *The Chronicle of Higher Education* (23 April 2004): B7–9; and Lawrence H. Keeley, Preface to *War before Civilization* (New York and Oxford: Oxford University Press, 1996), vii–ix.

as I cited them, as paragons of "churchly" theology—Aquinas, Calvin, Schleiermacher, Barth—were each strikingly innovative, characteristically calling the churches of their day to something other and better than what they were typically teaching and practicing. And let us remember that we are never dealing with "the church" per se, but with only particular churches, congregations, clergy, documents, traditions, seminaries, and so on. To insist, therefore, that "the church" ought to have something like "epistemological priority" is merely to sloganeer. Any Christian epistemology must be wary of any method that eulogizes the ecclesial context of Christian thought without serious qualifications.

David Wells points to two kinds of individualism arising in early modernity, not one, and sees the truly Christian version, which he traces to the Protestant Reformation, as in fact robustly resisting the other:

> Each source, the Reformation and the Enlightenment, has produced its own kind of individualism. As a rough generalization, we might say that Reformation individualism produces people whose life choices and values have a seriousness and intensity about them that reflect their recognition of an ultimate divine accountability. It is this sense of a moral universe presided over by God that drives this individualism to eschew all competing authorities, including those of the state, the Church, and, most importantly, the self.[89]

(By contrast, the alternative form of individualism manifests the congeries of bad traits typically denounced in such discourse: hubris, autonomy, arrogance, will-to-power, and the like.)

Individuality thus properly construed is a crucial value of the Christian religion, and individuality of thought needs to be prized and protected alongside due regard for communities and traditions. We must consider whether a given family, church, denomination, school, or agency does in fact validate, even welcome, innovative thinking that, in the nature of the case, calls into question one or more elements of that institution's beliefs and practices. Improvement isn't possible without such a

---

89. David F. Wells, *No Place for Truth, or, Whatever Happened to Evangelical Theology?* (Grand Rapids, MI: Eerdmans, 1993), 141. Glenn Tinder offers a powerful set of reflections on this theme: "Hope for the kingdom of heaven relativizes all institutions, and among these it relativizes the Church. It compels Christians to look on the churches critically and to support them only conditionally. Private judgment in religious matters is not merely a right which some, such as Martin Luther, have been bold enough to claim. It is a burdensome obligation, forced upon every Christian by the imperfection of the churches. Like every human being, a Christian is set apart from all others by a separate mind and a separate will. In contemporary social thought, as we have noted, 'individualism' has become a pejorative term. It might be argued, however, that individualism originates in God. Not only did God refrain from giving us a common mind and will; he did not elect to save us in groups. Salvation depends always on a personal commitment, and this commitment can cause one to be not only isolated and scorned but even killed. Each one alone must decide what is true and false, and right and wrong. Granted, the surrounding social order helps one do this; but the social order offers nothing that can take the place of personal resolution and effort" (*The Fabric of Hope: An Essay* [Atlanta, GA: Scholars Press, 1999], 106).

culture of hospitality to creativity, even as organizations naturally protect themselves against just any novelty or mutation that might in fact be a waste or a threat. Intentional and rigorous regimes of appropriately scaled experimentation and evaluation make the most sense of the tensions involved in valuing both individuality and community in responsible Christian thought.

There is more to say, in fact, about how we Christians can improve our thinking in the light of the social realities we inhabit. The positive side of our social relatedness is that no one has to go it alone. Each of us has to think *for* himself or herself, but we need not, and should not, and actually cannot think *by* ourselves. Indeed, as Richard Niebuhr warned, "without companions, collaborators, teachers, corroborating witnesses, I am at the mercy of my imaginations."[90] We have the resources of our various communities at our disposal. Families provide us with memories, lore, habits, interests, identities, and lifelong acquaintances linked by fundamental bonds. (Of course, families can be and in at least some ways usually are restricting and even destructive, but most still provide us with some positive help as well. Fundamentally, they give us a place to start out, with some initial directions and tools.) Schools, friendships, neighborhoods, churches, clubs, teams—all of these shape our values, increase our knowledge, and clarify our goals. One learns much through these various social experiences, including (and sometimes especially) the demanding and even painful ones. We can be pressed by these social forces to consider ideas we would never have entertained on our own. We can be kept from error by the current of the opinions of others close to us. And we can learn a great deal if we attend carefully to what others know and do.

It perhaps would be well to state bluntly the elementary point that these various social forces *do vary*. In certain situations of cultural homogeneity, they might well overlap and reinforce each other. But for many people today, and particularly those of us experiencing a postmodern situation, life is negotiated among a variety of social contexts with differing, even competing, narratives. We therefore must be as aware as we can be of the plurality, even the competition, of the social influences upon us. Some cancel each other out; some pull us this way and then that; some show up at certain times and others at others. We are not simply the sum of our experiences in some easy sense, but rather we move through a complex field of forces that does not yield readily to analysis.

To improve our thinking, nonetheless, we can deliberately alter our social situation. Not all of us will be able to perform the same alterations, but each of us can do some things to improve our situation for better Christian thinking. We tend increasingly to resemble those with whom we consort—even unwillingly. In particular, we take on the intellectual contours and currents of the minds of our friends and of anyone else with whom we spend a great deal of time, just as our choices in clothing and entertainment reflect these social influences. Thus we have the creative possibility

---

90. H. Richard Niebuhr, *Christ and Culture* (New York: Harper & Row, 1951), 245.

of being more deliberate about the sorts of people with whom we choose to consort, however much other relationships in our lives (in families or workplaces, for example) cannot be altered. We can decide, that is, whom we want to think like by adjusting our company. Most communities offer social alternatives, whether book clubs through libraries, part-time courses at universities, small groups in churches, student fellowships in universities, and so on. We can select which books, magazines, television programs, movies, websites, and social media in which to immerse ourselves. Each such choice connects us with another individual and usually a larger social world that shapes us every minute we inhabit it. As I tell college students, if you want to get smarter, get smarter friends. If one wants to pray or meditate better, one joins a monastery. If one wants not only to learn more, but to become a certain kind of thinker because one is a certain kind of person, one enrolls in a certain kind of school, immersion in which will re-form one into that kind of person. If one wants truly to see things from a different point of view—and recall that how we see things depends greatly on what we value and how we feel, not just on what we rationally process—then one ought to enter a different community: a different church, a different economic class, a different neighborhood, a different leisure scene, a different language group. In those social settings, what seemed strange, even absurd, or perhaps even repellent might now seem at least plausible: these apparently decent people hold to those beliefs and seem nonetheless innocuous, if not actually attractive. These social situations—what I call *plausibility places*—can help us immensely to encounter authentically what is not already ingredient in our own mental cosmos.

To be sure, one of the main reasons Christians should regularly participate in a local church and particularly in a strongly supportive fellowship of like-minded believers is to reinforce for themselves the persuasiveness of their religion in a culture that poses so many and such constant pressures to invalidate, even to render implausible, Christian belief and practice. Even a small, dedicated band can resist powerful cultural influences, as Christian renewal movements have shown throughout church history, if they will intentionally and frequently engage in communal practices of reiteration of their distinctive values.[91]

Howard Gardner's principle of "multiple intelligences" is by now a matter of common acceptance, thematizing as it does the rather commonsensical observation that there are different kinds of "smart."[92] The ivory-tower academician can parse ancient languages but needs a janitor to fix the squeak in his office chair. The mechanically practical janitor, however, himself needs a differently trained mechanic to repair his car, or service his laptop computer, or even replace the engine in

---

91. A particularly suggestive study of early modern Protestant renewal movements' varied ways of applying this principle is Howard A. Snyder, *Signs of the Spirit: How God Reshapes the Church* (Grand Rapids, MI: Zondervan, 1989).

92. Howard Gardner, *Frames of Mind: The Theory of Multiple Intelligences*, 3rd ed. (New York: Basic, 2011 [1983]).

the vacuum cleaner he uses every day. Similarly, the professor of ancient languages must call on his colleagues in cognate languages, ancient history, historical geography, and other disciplines to truly master his own subject. And consider the almost overwhelming network of varying outlooks and expertises that support and feed into the consultation of the average patient with the average family physician. In the complex interdependence of modern society, we have come to depend upon, if not fully appreciate, a wide range of expertise.

Even within the same subject or discipline, moreover, perceptions and interpretations can vary, with more than one of them deserving of respect. (I include this last clause since someone might easily acknowledge the existence of various viewpoints while claiming that his alone is correct.) So in considering any complex problem, we do well to seek out those whose knowledge, analytical approach, and wisdom varies significantly from our own. It should be obvious to everyone by now that people interpret the world differently, even people trained similarly with similar aptitudes. What is not obvious, alas, is that different interpretative stances can produce different, and differently helpful, conclusions. Collaboration is widely practiced, of course, but I daresay yet not widely enough. It is, after all, so much more comfortable to work with people of a similar outlook. But such comfort can be enjoyed, it is plain to see, at the risk of missing vital aspects of, even keys to, the problems we want to solve. The serious investigator will always seek out even contrary viewpoints in order to get maximum exposure to her subject and the widest possible range of plausible interpretations. Even one's (intellectual) enemies cannot be wrong about everything, and they might this time be right about something important.[93]

The same principle holds for communities of thinkers. If we want both to maximize the scope of our knowledge and to minimize the limiting and even crippling effects on our thought of the defects of our particular culture, we ought to consult thinkers in significantly different communities—and especially communities strategically selected so as to give us the most helpfully different perspectives possible.[94] So groups of men will consider consulting groups of women, and vice versa. Parents' conversations will be enriched by approaching children seriously for their views on matters of common concern. Rich and poor, powerful and weak, North and South, and then beyond these familiar—but still significant—pairings to the likes of Christians consulting with Muslims, Buddhists, Marxists, and Nietzcheans;

---

93. Mark Monmonier asks, "Should not the viewer be given several maps?" rather than just one, given how each interpretation (= map) necessarily represses some data and emphasizes others, including the relationships among the data points. See Mark Monmonier, *How to Lie with Maps*, 2nd ed. (Chicago and London: University of Chicago Press, 1996 [1991]), 162. His book is replete with startling examples of the usefulness of multiple overlapping representations of the "same" reality.

94. Paul Griffiths argues in this vein for vigorous apologetical exchanges among proponents of various religions: Paul J. Griffiths, *An Apology for Apologetics: A Study in the Logic of Interreligious Dialogue* (Maryknoll, NY: Orbis, 1991).

Americans consulting with Canadians, New Zealanders, Chinese, Argentinians, and Kenyans; social democrats consulting with monarchists, libertarians, anarchists, and communists; senior executives consulting with middle managers, front-line workers, union representatives, suppliers, customers, ex-customers, even competitors; and so on. In a society in which we can opt to consume most of public life—and notably now the daily news itself—through media conforming (to) our preferred interpretative filters, we must determine to avoid an increasingly narrow and continually reinforced outlook—unless we really do consider our outlook exactly correct. Until we do think that, however, we must then compensate for our weaknesses and, if all goes well, for what we do not even recognize as weaknesses by seeking contact with societies that what will best help us in that worthy work.

One more fundamental principle here is a basic psychological one. We will benefit from consulting other people simply because they are not involved in the same decision-provoking situation in which we find ourselves. Precisely because they are not experiencing the pressure of making this decision and then living with the consequences, they are freer to consider a wider range of data and interpretations than we likely are, and freer to evaluate conceptual and practical options that someone actually in the situation would naturally prefer to ignore. In particular, if we are stressed we will be strongly inclined toward averting risk, and therefore thinking conventionally, rather than toward maximizing benefit and thinking creatively. This basic principle explains why talking things out with someone else often increases the net wisdom in the deliberation, even if the other person is very similar to oneself. Precisely because she is not in the situation prompting the conversation, she will have energy to spend on thinking that I have to devote to managing anxiety, anticipating outcomes, and the like.

Finally, there is the category of love. If, as Paul says, it is the greatest of all spiritual gifts, it ought to be operative in our thinking. A "hermeneutics of love" is the counterbalance to the "hermeneutics of suspicion," both of which are justified by Christian doctrine. Love prompts us to communicate and collaborate. Love prompts us to respect and to pay attention to the other. Love prompts us to give the benefit of the doubt rather than impose an unbearable burden of proof. Love prompts us to empathetic awareness, to realizing how someone *could* actually think that, after all. Love prompts us to consider even changing our mind. It is good to have faith in the epistemological project, to hope for a rewarding outcome to our thinking. Best of all, it is good to exercise love in the process with love—benefiting others according to our calling—also as the outcome.[95]

In sum, to ascertain the truth as well as one can, one ought to take one's circumstances into account and complement them with the perspectives of others—or even of oneself at other times. In this key respect, a postmodern outlook can be positive

---

95. Alan Jacobs, *A Theology of Reading: The Hermeneutics of Love* (Boulder, CO: Westview, 2001). Augustine introduces love of neighbor as ingredient in the interpretative task in Book I of *De doctrina christiana*.

(I can enrich and correct my own, limited view with others') rather than negative (I am stuck with only my little fragment of the truth), constructive rather then (merely) deconstructive.

An obvious caveat must be added, however, to all this positive talk about seeking knowledge and wisdom from others, including very different others. The warning is simply that with increasing difference come increasing difficulties of understanding each other. Translation—not just in the narrow linguistic sense but in the full sense of getting as much of the other's meaning as possible—is a deeply vexed issue, even to people who speak the same language, are of the same class, and are working in the same context, as all of us ruefully recognize as soon as we pause to recall communication snafus at home, school, church, or work. I *thought* what I was saying (or writing or—worst of all, perhaps—e-mailing) was perfectly clear. Then, alas, I find out that I have puzzled one person, offended another, and angered a third.

Unlike most speakers, professors have the opportunity to literally examine their audiences to see how effective our communication has been. Market research companies spend vast resources trying to ascertain what voters and consumers think about this or that, but we professors have people pay us to ascertain the efficacy of our utterances. And the picture is not, as you would expect, an entirely pretty one. All professors have their favorite stories of miscommunication, but the worst for me have to do with students who not only get something wrong, and get something quite important wrong (such as, say, basic doctrines of the Christian faith in my theology courses), but then deferentially attribute their heresy *to me*. "As Professor Stackhouse said in class . . . " go the damning words, and I gasp in horror. How could you possibly have thought I meant to communicate *that*?

To move from one example of hermeneutical horror to another, consider troubled couples in marriage counseling. Over weeks, months, and even years, they painstakingly learn to ascertain much more clearly all that they are in fact communicating to each other and all that they are in fact failing to communicate. Session after session goes by in which spouses learn how bewilderingly and importantly vexed their communication actually is, even between people who know each other well, who inhabit the same literal space but also economic and social spaces as well, and who have loved each other and therefore cared very much what the other one is saying. What ought to be an ideal interpretative context is in fact a fascinatingly, distressingly complex one.

The danger, then, in seeking out others' opinions is that one will mistranslate them in any of a variety of common ways: one will reshape every communication into an affirmation of one's own views; one will filter out whatever content is novel and receive only what is familiar, whether welcome or not; one will go the other extreme and pay disproportionate attention to what is unusual and fail to appreciate the common affirmations; one will misunderstand how the unexpected elements connect properly to the expected ones (since the nexus is itself unexpected); one will misconstrue whatever is not straightforward and univocal, whether metaphor, humor, irony, sarcasm, allusion, cliché, euphemism, veiled threat, implicit promise, and so on. When we undertake the worthy effort to solicit different views, therefore, we must prepare ourselves properly to attend adequately to each message and messenger. Otherwise, we will simply colonize, co-opt, corrupt, contradict, or even combat what is being offered to us as gift.[96]

Indeed, our interests cannot be entirely laid aside in any such conversation—and in many cases they ought not to be, anyway, if they are legitimate. So we must enter into such conversations not only as collaborations but also as negotiations. Power, privilege, possibility—they are often at stake in our discussions of what and how things are. We are foolish to ignore factors that indeed shape and direct our thinking, so we ought to acknowledge our interests in this way also. Thus we can try to appreciate not only why our interlocutors have difficulty coming around to our point of view (for they might well have to give up certain advantages to do so) but also why we ourselves seem unable to grasp, let alone fully sympathize with, their outlook (for to do so might well cost us too much). Negotiation is entailed by a candid and humble recognition that it is enormously difficult, and perhaps in some cases impossible, to think entirely like someone in a very different situation with very different interests particularly if to do so would mean surrendering something important, whether self-respect, a tenet of our worldview, a superior political or economic position, or the like. Thus the best we can do, if we truly believe our perspective is not the only valid one and needs whatever correction and supplementation it can receive, is to engage in good-faith negotiating.[97] As Helen Longino acknowledges, "the point of dialogue from this point of view is not to produce a general and universal consensus but to make possible the refinement, correction, rejection, and sharing of models. Alliances, mergers, and revisions of standards as well as of models are all possible consequences of this dialogic interaction."[98]

Negotiation is also the only positive course of action—versus sheer domination that essentially negates the other as his or her viewpoint is summarily ruled out—in situations involving people of different social positions and degrees of power: parents and children, husbands and wives, bosses and employees, officers and enlisted personnel, teachers and students, lead investigators and research staff. We all will learn more if we are willing to truly negotiate, rather than co-opt, caricature, contain, or crush alternative interpretations.

---

96. Anthony Thiselton warns us similarly: "Only understanding texts and selfhood in *their otherness and alienness* can make it possible for them to address us in ways that avoid readings already domesticated and made bland by our construing them *as products of our own world* (*Interpreting God and the Postmodern Self: On Meaning, Manipulation, and Promise* [Edinburgh: T. & T. Clark and Grand Rapids, MI: Eerdmans, 1995], 56; emphasis in original).

97. Code's discussion—and her sources—are helpful on these points: see Code, ch. 6.

98. Helen E. Longino, "Subjects, Power, and Knowledge," in *Feminist Epistemologies* (New York: Routledge, 1993), 117. This, of course, is a major theme in Hans-Georg Gadamer, *Truth and Method*, trans. J. Weinsheimer and D. G. Marshall, 2nd rev. ed. (New York: Crossroad, 2004).

An obvious test of the fidelity of one's construal of others' views, furthermore, is to submit one's interpretation *of* them *to* them—or at least to other experts on their views. I trust it is clear that nothing, however, can guarantee faithful interpretation. One might fail to render one's interpretation in a way that will make sense to those from whom one learned—consider the difficulties facing a scientist who tries to check his understanding of a jungle people's recommendation of the medicinal effects of a particular plant with his original informants who do not understand modern pharmacology. And one's consulting experts might be caught up in a currently fashionable paradigm that is not, in fact, very close to the truth of the matter. So certainty is not on offer here, as it has not been on offer generally in this model! But one does what one can, and this is part of what one can do. As Michael Oakeshott puts it, in terms of society-wide encounters,

> Perhaps we may think of the components of culture as voices, each the expression of a
> distinct condition and understanding of the world and a distinct idiom of human
> self-understanding, and of the culture itself as these voices joined, as such voices could
> only be joined, in a conversation—an endless unrehearsed intellectual adventure in
> which, in imagination, we enter into a variety of modes of understanding the world and
> ourselves and are not disconcerted by the differences or dismayed by the inconclusive-
> ness of it all.[99]

This positive approach to epistemic difference, furthermore, puts conflict itself in a positive light. Some conflict, of course, arises from bad motives and can result only in, at best, mitigated evil and compromised good. But often conflict is simply the result of good people bringing good, but different, ideas to matters of common concern. Conflict can be understood then as the passionate registering of these differences.[100] Rick Kennedy exhorts us to "dinner-table obligations, wide-angle listening, and benefit-of-the-doubt hospitality" as minimal standards for paying proper attention to others, however strange or even hostile they may initially appear to be.[101] From there, negotiation can bring about an understanding and a situation better than any party originally enjoyed. Knowledge-making is always political and is obviously so in such situations, as people work together in common cause doing the best they can to cooperate—in both understanding and application—while recognizing their perduring differences. Lorraine Code offers a characteristically rich paragraph in this regard:

---

99. Michael Oakeshott, *The Voice of Liberal Learning* (New Haven, CT: Yale University Press, 1989), 38–39.

100. See John Feikens, "Conflict: Its Resolution and the Completion of Creation," chap. in *Seeking Understanding: The Stob Lectures, 1986–1998* (Grand Rapids, MI: Eerdmans, 2001), 343–72.

101. Rick Kennedy, "Educating Bees: Humility as a Craft in Classical and Christian Liberal Arts," *Christian Scholar's Review* 42 (Fall 2012): 40.

My discussion...throughout this book proposes that the stripped-down fiction of uniformly perceptive, autonomous knowers confronting self-announcing facts should yield to an imaginary of knowledge construction as a social-communal-political process, where items of would-be knowledge are embedded in discourses, informed by interests that are themselves open to critical scrutiny and by hierarchies of power and privilege, uneven credulity, and the pragmatics of conferring or withholding trust.[102]

In such a situation, Code says, voices previously subjugated can be heard with the promise of benefitting all who will heed them. Only with the recognition of such fundamental qualifications can we escape the trap of arrogant narrowness, the conceit that we know all we need to know—or, at least, that we know all we need to know about how to know. Instead, we can recognize our limited place in the complexity of the world and then communicate with fellow knowers toward mutual benefit.[103]

Code thus helpfully reinforces the postmodern affirmation that the classic model of the natural and applied sciences and of analytical philosophy—namely, the isolated, insular, universal subject S who "knows that p"—doesn't exist. Both theories of knowledge and knowledge claims must be appropriately qualified in terms of *which* "S" in *which* circumstances according to *which* interests conducted *which* sort of inquiry and now claims *which* conclusions. And because knowledge claims deeply affect, even as they are deeply affected by, power relations, it is well particularly for those not at the top of a social hierarchy to ponder carefully the true provenance of any assertions of truth. As Code trenchantly asks, "Whose knowledge are we talking about?"[104]

There seems a paradox at the heart of Code's scheme that secures her proposal within the general category of critical realism. Yes, one's knowledge claims and the knowledge claims of one's group must be qualified in terms of the situatedness of all (human) knowledge. But her model's advocacy of deliberate consultation with other people, critical self-awareness, and its very regard for the particulars of one's self and situation connects knowledge-seeking to a real world, however partially and distortedly apprehended:

---

102. Code, 192–93.

103. Along these lines see also Nancy Goldberger, Jill Tarule, Blythe Clinchy, and Mary Belenky, eds., *Knowledge, Differerence and Power: Essays Inspired by "Women's Ways of Knowing"* (New York: Basic, 1996). Elizabeth Fox-Genovese tellingly remarks that "the attentive reader will [notice that] much of what the feminist epistemologists value in women's ways of knowing bears a strong resemblance to Christianity" (*"Women's Ways of Knowing* Revisited: Feminism and the Epistemological Crisis of the West," *Books & Culture* [September 1997]: 18). I have indeed noticed that resemblance and am grateful for the work of many feminist epistemologists, despite the almost total lack of direct intersection between their work and that of orthodox Christian theological and philosophical inquirers such as I.

104. Code, 21.

The practice-dependent, communicative, deliberative processes of negotiation from which knowledge, on this model, is made and remade, its critical reflexivity, and its grounding in the "givenness" of the physical, historical, corporeal *Lebenswelt* guard against the subjectivism and/or relativism that have deterred philosophers from granting epistemic significance to place, particularity, imagination, and interpretation.[105]

I find Code's model to be remarkably congruent with that of some of my favourite Christian philosophers even as it adds crucial specific concerns that are generally underrepresented, if not simply absent, in Christian epistemology—feminist and ecological concerns in particular.[106] Her central theme of epistemological ecosystems in which each of us must live, even as we reach out to learn from and perhaps help others, connects with a strong Christian sense of both Providence and vocation. Christians confess that God made not only "heaven-and-earth-in-general" but each hill and vale, each river and harbor. God has placed each of us in particular situations in order to flourish in those situations as best we can and to work with God in God's overarching plan to rescue and renew the world. Vocational thinking, therefore, must be ecological thinking—and ecological thinking that takes account of the full *oikos*, including the Architect and Landlord of it all.[107]

---

105. Code, 6. Andrew Walls uses the theatre analogy to say, "Culture is simply a name for a location in the auditorium where the drama of life is in progress" (*The Missionary Movement in Christian History*, 44).

106. Here is another good place in which to discuss Alvin Plantinga's influential definition of *warrant*, that which adds to beliefs that happen to be true the status of being actual *knowledge* (rather than lucky truths we believe for no particularly good reason). Plantinga writes, "a belief has warrant just if it is produced by cognitive processes or faculties that are functioning properly, in a cognitive environment that is propitious for that exercise of cognitive powers, according to a design plan that is successfully aimed at the production of true belief" (*Warranted Christian Belief*, xi). That definition makes sense to me, and I deploy it here only because it includes an implicit warning that we will have trouble forming warranted true beliefs, we will have trouble gaining *knowledge*, in a cognitive environment that is *not* "propitious for that exercise of cognitive powers." Such environments, I am suggesting, are everywhere: environments so distorted by the interests of the dominant and the wicked that it is difficult to see straight, whether in a *barrio* or in a country club, in a gang meeting or in an academic conference. Racism, sexism, class advantage, family solidarity, nationalism, religious zeal, intellectual chauvinism—the world is full of powers that bend our view of things in a particular direction to a particular purpose. Canvassing the views of those who are outside our epistemological forcefields—allowing as thoroughly as possible that their thinking is shaped by others—gives us at least some opportunity to make allowances for the systemic distortions of our thought.

107. This approach seems to me to rescue postliberal theology from the tribal isolation that some of its proponents and opponents suggest it might entail. For candid and searching questions about postliberalism along this line, see William C. Placher, *Unapologetic Theology: A Christian Voice in a Pluralistic Conversation* (Louisville, KY: Westminster/John Knox, 1989); and Timothy R. Phillips and Dennis L. Okholm, eds., *The Nature of Confession: Evangelicals and Postliberals in Conversation* (Downers Grove, IL: InterVarsity, 1996).

CONSULTATION OF AUTHORITIES

A key aspect of our social situation is that most of what we know has been mediated to us by other people we have trusted to tell us what we cannot or would not learn directly. In a way, this epistemological interdependence reflects the economic and occupational interdependence of modern life, life in which we rely on other people for most of what we need done in our lives while we ourselves work at a particular job to help a lot of other people in that one particular respect. Specialization, and thus interdependence, is a fact of modern existence.

It was also a fact of premodern life. Tribal cultures featured the division of labor, even in families—the smallest social unit we have—between parents and children and usually between parents themselves as well. Tribal cultures also featured the transmission of knowledge from acknowledged experts to acknowledged learners: parents, older siblings, shamans or other spiritual leaders, wise women, senior hunters or soldiers, and, above all, the chief.

Michael Polanyi reminds us that the knowledge that is transmitted from expert to novice goes beyond facts and even skills to the realm of judgment, discernment, intuition, and what Polanyi calls *connoisseurship*. Because so much of what it means to *be* and to *perform as* a scientist (Polanyi's profession) or a physician, or lawyer, or firefighter, or pilot, or teacher, or scholar, or salesperson, and so on, depends upon what Polanyi calls "tacit knowledge," those who wish to learn must bind themselves to authorities—almost literally.[108] That is, such learners must become disciples, following a master in person, noticing what he says and does and trying to follow suit, conforming oneself to the ways of the master that are explicitly taught, of course, and are also implicitly "caught." No amount of technological cleverness will substitute for this "in-person" education.

(I might pause to note in this respect that "distance education" has its undeniable uses. This book, after all, is a technology of distance education. But distance education is powerless in the face of Polanyi's observation. So propagandists of distance education simply don't deal with it, and students who think they are getting an education just as good as one they would receive in a community of multiply reinforced values and subtle, intuitive signals are deeply mistaken—if not in fact misled.)

We might observe as a truism, therefore, that since one cannot become expert on everything in one's life and therefore capable of making an independent judgment on everything in one's life, then one properly trusts authorities in these areas

---

108. This perhaps is the place to note that what Polanyi calls "tacit knowledge" should better be called "tacit 'knowledge.'" By these scare quotes I mean to show that the "knowledge" in question is actually only whatever is assumed to be true by the master and, presumably, the guild of experts: what "all right-thinking people think." Whether such "knowledge" qualifies *as knowledge*, as something that is actually true, is moot. If this point isn't remembered, then the disciple is simply accepting whatever is offered by the master as truth, and I am confident Polanyi does not mean to recommend such an uncritical attitude.

in which one cannot become expert. Yet we ought to be able to see at this point in our discussion that *no one* is *that* kind of "expert" on *anything*. Only God apprehends perfectly and certainly, and all human thought, no matter how great, is both finite and fallen. Thus to ask, "Is it ever appropriate to believe something on the basis of someone else's authority?" is to ask what for human beings is an irrelevant question: we *have* to do so, and do so *almost always*. The issue instead is how we make use of authorities with both appropriate confidence and criticism, whatever our individual levels of expertise.[109]

C. S. Lewis, in the middle of the last century, detected a dangerous attitude emerging among modern people, an attitude that positions us between two sorts of wisdom and leaves us ignorantly and ignobly opining rather than wisely and humbly finding knowledge, whether on our own through genuine expertise or by submitting to the authority of others who have it:

> All over the world, until quite modern times, the direct insight of the mystics and the reasonings of the philosophers percolated to the mass of the people by authority and tradition; they could be received by those who were no great reasoners [or mystics] themselves in the concrete form of myth and ritual and the whole pattern of life. In the conditions produced by a century or so of [ideological] Naturalism, plain men are being forced to bear burdens which plain men were never expected to bear before. We must get the truth for ourselves or go without it....
>
> ...If we are content to go back and become humble plain men obeying a tradition, well. If we are ready to climb and struggle on till we become sages ourselves, better still. But the man who will neither obey wisdom in others nor adventure for her/himself is fatal. A society where the simple many obey the few seers can live: a society where all were seers could live even more fully. But a society where the mass is still simple and the seers are no longer attended to can achieve only superficiality, baseness, ugliness, and in the end extinction. On or back we must go; to stay here is death.[110]

We thus perhaps surprisingly encounter the ancient Christian motto of *fides quaerens intellectum*, "faith seeking understanding." For we cannot learn from a master if we do not trust him. And there is nothing spookily religious or supernatural about such faith, as Polanyi explains:

---

109. Dru Johnson provocatively draws on the temptation narrative in Genesis to assert that "the idea that knowledge begins with listening to the appropriate authority is exotic to many conceptions of epistemology....But the question God asks the man upon finding him in Genesis 3 is instructive. Notice that he does not ask the man, 'How did you deduce this knowledge of your nakedness?' Rather, he asks the man, 'Who told you?'" ("Scripture Is Not Our Dog," *Comment* [Fall 2012]: 45). Alvin Plantinga offers a cogent defense of testimony more generally in "Other Persons and Testimony," chap. in *Warrant and Proper Function* (New York: Oxford University Press, 1993), 65–88.

110. C. S. Lewis, *Miracles* (San Francisco: HarperCollins, 2001 [1947]), 66–67.

To learn by example is to submit to authority. You follow your master because you trust his manner of doing things even when you cannot analyze and account in detail for its effectiveness. By watching the master and emulating his efforts in the presence of his example, the apprentice unconsciously picks up the rules of the art, including those which are not explicitly known to the master himself. These hidden rules can be assimilated only by a person who surrenders himself to that extent uncritically to the imitation of another.[111]

This issue confronts us all, particularly as there is a manifest tendency in any subculture—including, and sometimes especially, intellectual and academic subcultures—to lionize certain heroes for a time and to hearken to them uncritically, while simultaneously despising others who are in fact worthy of serious attention and even emulation. So how can a serious person find authorities to believe?

Authorities ought to be respected by virtue of quality and relevance, rather than by mere virtue of office. In this I am striking a rather populist note. "Authority" has a political air to it, a sense of someone being granted and thus wielding power to which the rest of us ought to submit. Compare the word "expert" as an academic word, denoting someone who has acquired knowledge that others may access as a resource. In what follows, I am recommending that one submit to authorities not merely by dint of their office, however impressive, but by what can be established of their pertinent expertise. Thus I will henceforth use "expert" and "authority" interchangeably, unless the context clearly indicates otherwise. I am, yes, of the Canadian generation born on the hinge of the Baby Boomers and Generation X, and I therefore take as axiomatic that having authority in my thought is a power I myself grant to an individual (or institution), not something that I encounter as already a fixture on the landscape and to which I ought uncritically to yield. I recognize, to be sure, that many authorities have influenced me without my deliberate assent at the time, but over the years most of those, I expect, have been subjected to scrutiny, whether parents, teachers, coaches, conductors, churches, schools, national cultures, and the like. I try now, as I recommend others do, to draw only from authorities that qualify to me as deserving that status.

This principle that authority ought to be earned, so to speak, might seem obvious, but even communities that pride themselves on their supposed ability to regard persons and ideas critically and without prejudice—such as law courts, universities, and churches—demonstrate the common human trait of confusing status with worthiness. A critical understanding of institutions, however, tells us that the fact that someone occupies a position of prominence and power says nothing more than that the apposite system (whether educational, political, artistic, or whatever) has promoted him or her *in its own interests*. Those interests may or may not coincide with one's own; they may well not coincide with the disinterested pursuit of truth; and

---

111. Polanyi, *Personal Knowledge*, 53.

of course they may not coincide with the interests of the Kingdom of God. One therefore must resist deference to mere hierarchical eminence, and instead seek out authorities as one would seek out any other resource—by evidences of quality.

I trust it is clear that in this section I am carrying no brief for élitism, but instead am open quite widely to genuine expertise residing in all sorts of people regarding all sorts of matters.[112] Nicholas Wolterstorff warns us, in fact, that

> from Plato onwards, the standard imagery for what one does when entering the academy and engaging in *Wissenschaft* is that of *turning away* from the everyday. It would be possible to think of what transpires in the academy as the extension and intensification of what transpires in the everyday. In fact the dominant image has always been that of departure.[113]

Yet on many issues, only those on the point of the spear or on the receiving end of policies and practices have the information we need in order to understand what is going on. Only those with the expertise of being in *that* place in *that* role as *that* sort of person can advise us aright. So let us be careful not to restrict the idea of "possessing authoritative information and judgment" to the higher social classes—or to people of a certain age, or sex, and so on.

One therefore might well ask of prospective authorities—whether living or dead, whether individuals or institutions—something like the following list of qualifying questions. (Indeed, this list would serve, *mutatis mutandis*, as a useful checklist for ascertaining the reliability of testimony in general.) None of these questions, nor all of them together, can provide us with a guarantee that this resource will be correct, of course, but no list of questions in any complex matter will do that. So let us do what we can:

- What training did he receive, whether formal or informal? Who are his mentors—and what do we know about the mentors to help us determine the reliability of the mentee? Christians follow a rabbi uncredentialed by the authorities of his day, so we might be expected to remain unimpressed by "worldly" training. Yet Jesus was "credentialed" by God through signs and vouched for by the Holy Spirit, ultimately vindicated, as Peter preached in Acts 2, by God raising him from the dead. Paul and Luke, who were given the responsibility to write most of the New Testament, were among the best educated of all the early Christian leaders. So Christians need not be narrowly focused only on what might be valued as

---

112. In this regard, see the wise recommendations offered in Richard J. Mouw, *Consulting the Faithful: What Christian Intellectuals Can Learn from Popular Religion* (Grand Rapids, MI: Eerdmans, 1994).

113. Nicholas Wolterstorff, "Suffering, Power, and Privileged Cognitive Access," in *Christianity and Culture in the Crossfire*, ed. David A. Hoekema and Bobby Fong (Grand Rapids, MI: Eerdmans, 1997.

expert training in our culture (whether university degrees, experience in a successful business, and so on), but we will also use our God-given reason to determine whether the training in a given case is *relevant* and *adequate* to the role someone is to play. University degrees and business success thus might well be relevant and adequate from a Christian point of view.

- What abilities has he demonstrated and had affirmed by others? He might be well enough credentialed in a general sense, but has he yet shown that he has what it takes to be trusted on this matter? And what *pertinent* accomplishments can he demonstrate? Here we must beware the "halo effect" of bowing to someone's opinion about X when her genuine expertise is in area Y. Indeed, a related question is that of how he handles his own authority. Does he know his limits and either circumspectly remain within them or at least signal clearly when he goes beyond them?

- Who will vouch for him? What approval does he enjoy especially from authorities—individual or institutional—we already recognize? To be sure, in a given community or culture, there can be a "hall of mirrors" effect in which the various authorities reinforce each other's status while the entire group might be wrong-headed about the matter in question. (I have mentioned racist societies, and here I think of Christian denominations in which all the respected teachers vouch for each other, honor each other, trade podiums and pulpits, and the like—while the whole group is wrong about key matters.) If we suspect that such is the case we are facing, we have at least two options. We can consult other communities we respect to see what they think of our authorities or we can develop enough expertise in the matter ourselves as to check at least in part the expertise of the authorities in question. To take an example from a very different field, if I am trying to determine the reliability of the mechanics at my favorite garage, I can ask mechanics in other garages what they think of these mechanics, their competitors. A negative answer might not decide the issue, while a positive one likely would (unless, alas, there is a reason for collusion I must then discover). Alternatively, I could teach myself a particular aspect of automotive repair, set up a test, and see how well the mechanics do in that one small area of my personal expertise.

- What experiences have fostered in him an understanding of and sympathy for those he addresses? These are qualities essential to accurate and effective communication, without which pronouncements magisterially descend out of context and likely off the mark. The supermodel with genes for height and slimness and goaded by million-dollar incentives brightly encourages weight loss before an audience of ordinary people, glum with psychological and physiological problems unknown to her. The CEO who was heir to a family fortune and recipient of an élite education wonders at the poor sales of his book on how anyone can become financially successful. The western European diplomat shakes her head in perplexity at an African or Asian society's struggles with novel democratic polities and capitalist economies. Does the authority really know how his expertise can and cannot relate to those he seeks to inform?

- What moral character does he exhibit? For many people, significant moral failure simply disqualifies a person from any admiration, let alone deference. Others pay attention to moral failure as providing clues to the particular nature of a person's work. Still others are simply grateful for the good accomplished by another and place moral failings in a separate box.[114] The key question here is how germane is a person's particular kind of moral success or failure for the particular kind of authority he exercises. To be sure, the evident willingness to say or do the wrong thing *at all* raises the caution that one might be willing to do the wrong thing in a matter germane to one's sphere of authority. And since we Christians take for granted that *all* human beings are sinners, and thus are manifestly willing to do at least some things we shouldn't, vesting absolute trust in any human being is a bad idea. This basic principle seems truistic, except that even otherwise intelligent and prudent people epistemically fall in love, so to speak, with a particular author, or leader, or spiritual advisor, or school of thought, or institution and suspend their critical faculties regarding such an authority, accepting all that is said as infallible. Yet no one else is Jesus, no other book is the Bible, and we ought to remember that about *all* authorities and especially, of course, our favorites. More particular is the counsel to analyze clearly how moral failure in one zone can indeed relate to foolishness in another: recklessness here can imply recklessness there, cowardice in this instance can signal a general trait, and so on. Yet human beings are remarkable moral creatures such that some of us demonstrate a clear, even shocking, lack of integrity in some parts of our lives and flawless devotion to principle in others. Great care, then, must be taken neither to under- nor over-react to the presence of moral failure in an authority.
- Does he take his own advice? Strictly speaking, wisdom is wise even in the mouth of the fool, and a hypocrite can render helpful counsel. The so-called genetic fallacy is to judge the veracity of a proposition by one's estimation of its source. "Can any good thing come from Nazareth?" Yet one properly seeks integrity in authorities since the whole function of an authority is to tell one what one cannot discover or discern for oneself. Manifest incoherence in a person's life between preaching and practicing is cause for alarm, and likely one will therefore do better trusting someone who knows experientially as well as theoretically the truth of which he speaks. The authority doesn't have to be perfect, of course. Maybe he has received genuine insight he can offer to others even as he struggles with the same issues. But one rightly looks at least for genuine struggle and, preferably, a measure of success before one is willing to accept that insight authoritatively.

---

114. Authors such as Paul Johnson and Michael Jones are at least of the second order, but in some respects seem like the first, even though the subjects of their studies are manifestly talented and accomplished people: Paul Johnson, *Intellectuals* (London: Weidenfeld and Nicholson, 1988); E. Michael Jones, *Degenerate Moderns: Modernity as Rationalized Sexual Misbehavior* (San Francisco: Ignatius, 1993).

- In a similar vein, does he take anyone else's advice? How does he respond to evaluation, positive as well as negative, and what does that response tell you about him? Perhaps he responds badly: fawningly to praise and defensively, mean-spiritedly, even violently to criticism. Such a response does not invalidate his information or interpretation. Brilliant and creative people are not, after all, famous for their serene mental health. Furthermore, emotional instability does not necessarily mark a core resistance to valid critique, and many talented people do eventually respond constructively to substantial criticism. Those who do not, however, must be considered carefully as authorities since taking flattery at face value or stubbornly refusing to grant credence to criticism is to treat unwisely what are potential sources of knowledge, and that is hardly a commendable practice in someone you intend to trust to tell you things. The reverse situation, moreover, is also an occasion for caution. If the authority cedes too much credence to the advice of another, you now have to assess this other person or institution as an authority over your prospective authority. If you have come to admire, say, a Roman Catholic author who you then find is reflexively deferential to every papal pronouncement, you now have two authorities to assess: author and pope. If your favorite politician turns out to follow to the letter the social theories of a particular philosopher, you now have two evaluations to undertake. But not only do you have to assess both sources—perhaps you conclude that popes are in fact generally right about things—you have to assess, thirdly, what it means for your prospective authority to defer absolutely to the pope or the philosopher. Is that *attitude* all right with you in an authority, or do you seek someone who will critically assess *all* sources of knowledge he accesses?
- What is his worldview, including his values? To the extent that his worldview coincides with yours, intelligibility and applicability will be relatively straightforward. To the extent that it doesn't, slippages in translation and errors in utilization loom as constant dangers. It is simply natural to hear the familiar instead of the truly unusual, to neatly stretch or cut what we perceive to fit the Procrustean bed of our extant paradigm. So if we want to benefit from the offerings of an authority from a quite different outlook, we must take pains to interpret carefully and beware particularly of the "false cognates," the words that appear to mean the same thing in both his discourse and ours, and yet do not. The religious realm is full of examples of people misappropriating phrases, categories, and even whole works from one tradition to their own and thereby utterly recasting them into convenient caricatures. Jesus himself shows up all around the world not always in discernibly Christian form, whether as a fertility deity in Congo, a mild guru in India, or a model of macho masculinity in America.
- What have been the results for other people who have trusted him? This question is perhaps the most obvious and basic of all, and it is striking how often is not seriously posed (to dentists, mechanics, lawyers, and religious leaders, among

others whose careers one might think would be replete with obvious evidence as to competence).

- Finally, we can ask who is paying him. In whose interests does he work? *Why* is he saying what he is saying? We return, in fact, to the question of his social location versus yours. If he comes validated by a large, impressive organization, consider to what extent the outlook and interests of that organization comport with your own. He may well be speaking from a very different worldview and with an importantly different agenda from yours. You may still learn much from him as your worldviews and interests overlap sufficiently for there to be fruitful communication. But by all means get clear to whom you are listening, why he is speaking, and what you intend to gain from attending to him.

Only God is, after all, worthy of absolute trust, so one is foolish to trust even his ostensible servants too highly. Indeed, the religion of the Crucified One puts a question mark beside the pronouncements of all authorities, even—and perhaps especially—those who purport to speak the final truth above all possible dissent. But one is equally foolish to dispense with the genuine gifts of our fellow creatures. One must both learn and discern, both gratefully receive and critically examine, so as to profit best from the resources genuine authorities offer us all.

Furthermore, we do well to seek *more than one* authority on any given subject, not only for the greater enrichment she will provide alongside his, but also to mitigate the negative effects upon us of any individual authority's limitations and flaws. "In an abundance of counselors" there is both safety and victory (Prov. 11:14; 24:6).[115]

Our consideration of the social nature of thought returns us again to the maxim: One ought to think *for* oneself, but one cannot—and ought not to try to—think *by* oneself.[116] The responsible Christian thinker therefore tries to improve her social location accordingly.

---

115. At the conclusion of his book-long indictment of experts, David H. Freedman ruefully allows that we cannot do without them, and offers similar advice about how to select whom to believe: "Eleven Simple Never-Fail Rules for Not Being Misled by Experts," chap. in *Wrong: Why Experts Keep Failing Us—and How to Know When Not to Trust Them* (New York: Little, Brown, 2010), 203–30. For a fascinating consideration of authority from a multiplicity of angles and eras, see Bruce Lincoln, *Authority: Construction and Corrosion* (Chicago and London: University of Chicago Press, 1994). And for an amusing, and often bemusing, stroll through the errors of the expert, see Christopher Cerf and Victor Navasky, *The Experts Speak: The Definitive Compendium of Authoritative Misinformation*, expanded ed. (New York: Villard, 1998 [1984]).

116. I recognize that some in our culture, as in others, would not immediately receive this axiom as axiomatic. They have yielded their individual judgment to something greater than themselves, the accumulated wisdom and current judgment of a particular church, or tribe, or nation, or philosophy. "Why should I presume to know better than Mother Church/our ancestors/the experts/etc.?" I trust that I am making clear, however, that to so defer to this or that authority is itself a matter of individual agency, and not only just initially, but constantly as each life-challenge emerges and one in fact must decide anew whether to remain submissive to this or that authority.

This positive note nicely concludes this chapter on the basic scheme. In a perfect world, the conscientious and skillful practice of the scheme outlined here would yield knowledge, we would all be happy, and this book would be over. Alas, we do not live in that world, and so we must go on to consider how we ought to make up our minds in the world we actually inhabit. Psychologist Daniel Kahneman tells us a little bit about that world, and what he reveals isn't happy at all:

> Humans are incorrigibly inconsistent in making summary judgments of complex information [exactly the situation, of course, in which one seeks out an authority for help]. When asked to evaluate the same information twice, they frequently give different answers.... Experienced radiologists who evaluate chest X-rays as "normal" or "abnormal" contradict themselves 20% of the time when they see the same picture on separate occasions. A study of 101 independent auditors who were asked to evaluate the reliability of internal corporate audits revealed a similar degree of inconsistency. A review of 41 separate studies of the reliability of judgments made by auditors, pathologists, psychologists, organizational managers, and other professionals suggests that this level of inconsistency is typical, even when a case is reevaluated within a few minutes.[117]

Clearly, then, we have more work to do to devise an epistemology that will work in such an uncertain context.

---

117. Kahneman, 224–25.

5
Deciding in an Ambiguous World

O Lord, my maker and protector, who hast graciously sent me into this world to work out my salvation, enable me to drive from me all such unquiet and perplexing thoughts as may mislead or hinder me in the practice of those duties which thou hast required. When I behold the works of thy hands and consider the course of thy providence, give me grace always to remember that thy thoughts are not my thoughts, nor thy ways my ways. And while it shall please thee to continue me in this world where much is to be done and little to be known, teach me by thy Holy Spirit to withdraw my mind from unprofitable and dangerous enquiries, from difficulties vainly curious and doubts impossible to be solved. Let me rejoice in the light which thou hast imparted, let me serve thee with active zeal and humble confidence, and wait with patient expectation for the time in which the soul which thou receivest shall be satisfied with knowledge. Grant this, O Lord, for Jesus Christ's sake, amen.

Samuel Johnson

THE PRINCIPLE OF PROPORTIONATE ASSENT

After two centuries of religious and political upheaval in Britain, John Locke thought it was time to settle everyone down. The great political philosopher was also an epistemologist and epistemology came readily to the aid of his politics. Instead of prosecuting politics with a fanatical certainty that could tolerate no alternatives, he advised his reader, bethink yourself as to just how certain you can claim to be. You will find that you are not nearly so entitled to certainty as you thought you were. In fact, legitimate certainty is rare and restricted to only one choice zone: one's own mental states. (You cannot be less than certain, since you cannot possibly be wrong, about what you are experiencing at least in simple terms, whether, say, joy, or pain, or the sense that you are sitting on a chair. You might well not actually be sitting on a chair, but you certainly think you are, if you think you are.) The common epistemic situation instead is to be more or less convinced by more or less convincing evidences and inferences. The common *practice* to that point, to be sure, was to simply believe or not believe. Locke contended that his predecessors and

contemporaries had foolishly taken on board all sorts of dubious and even perni-
cious ideas without submitting them to the scrutiny of critical reason. Worse, they
then had elevated various versions of this mish-mash to the level of dogma, and
proceeded to fight religious wars over them. In short, people had not governed their
beliefs properly heretofore. The proper attitude, instead, Locke averred, is to proportion one's assent in any given case to the strength of the evidences as adjudicated
by reason. One thus is in an epistemological position to grant that other people's
views may have at least some grounding. One might even learn something from
particularly impressive alternatives. An attitude of tolerance for alternatives is thus
in order, fanaticism should disappear, and political, ideological, and even religious
pluralism can flourish.

Locke's wise warnings ring down the centuries. Bernard Lewis writes:

> Doubt is good and, indeed, is one of the mainsprings of Western civilization. It under-
> mines the certitudes that in other civilizations and in earlier stages of our own have fet-
> tered thought, weakened or ended tolerance, and prevented the emergence of that
> cooperation of opponents that we call democracy. It leads to questioning and thus to
> discoveries, and to new achievements and new knowledge, including the knowledge of
> other civilizations.[1]

The rational person ought, it seems to us, too, to proportion her belief to the warrants she has for it—and behave accordingly, with both due confidence and humility. We shall consider some heavy qualifications of this principle presently, but
for now let us proceed to consider how this principle might work out in practice.

It is at least theoretically possible that we are mistaken about even obvious and
important things. Yet there are many things about which we doubt very strongly that
we are mistaken. There are propositions and experiences about which we are, instead, virtually certain. "Two plus two equals four," I assert, with considerable assurance. "I am now reading a book," you might affirm with (almost as much? greater?)
vigor. Then there are propositions and experiences about which we have what we
might call "negative certainty": "$2 + 2 = 5$," for instance, seems certainly wrong, as
does the proposition "I am now looking at a book that is playing a piano nocturne."

In between these extremes, however, there is a range of propositions and experiences about which we have more or less confidence. "The square of the hypotenuse
of a right-angled triangle is equal to the sum of the squares of the other two sides"
seems to non-mathematicians to *sound* like the Pythagorean theorem. We were always *taught* that it is true. And we might even have measured a few triangles to test
it. But unless we have undertaken considerable and informed investigation into the
matter, we probably wouldn't affirm this theorem with the same intensity with

---

1. Lewis's words are attributed, without further information, to an unnamed article of his in
Commentary, December 1994, by Martin E. Marty in *Context* (1 March 1995): 2.

which we would affirm other items of our mathematical knowledge, such as "odd numbers are not divisible evenly by two." Furthermore, about still other propositions of mathematics—say, "The square root of 456,891 is 299"—we might have no immediate opinion at all.

What is true of propositions is also true of experiences. I am pretty sure I'm looking at a computer screen right now as I type these words. I am equally sure I am *not* looking at the brilliant new motion picture *The Computer Screen*. In between these two convictions, however, are others about this very same experience about which I am not so confident. I think I hear the murmur of the building's ventilation system, but it could also be the sound of construction on campus a distance away, or the muffled roar of a jet overhead. I'd have to listen for a few more moments to acquire more data in the hopes of settling this fascinating matter more firmly. And even if I did listen a while longer, I might still not be as sure about what I'm hearing as about what I'm seeing. (Indeed, maybe I'm just so excited about this whole question of background noise that the blood is rushing in my ears and I'm in an otherwise completely silent room.)

Every chemistry laboratory contains long glass tubes that stand upright on a desk and have little marks running up their heights with numbers at regular intervals. These devices are called "graduated cylinders," as you may recall fondly from your high school days. If one takes a cylinder marked for 100 ml and drops precisely 1 ml of water into it, is the cylinder now "wet" or "dry"?

The question, of course, is improperly posed. The whole point of a graduated cylinder is to make possible a "graduated" or proportionate answer, such as "the mostly dry tube yet contains a relatively small amount of water." (Scientists likely would be more precise.) So philosophers before and after John Locke have advocated a proportionate response from us in the case of each conviction we hold to be true. Rather than see everything in "binary" terms of black-or-white, true-or-false, all-or-nothing, they have suggested that we ought to proportion our assent to the quality of warrant we possess.

We, indeed, ought to proportion our assent to the ideas we encounter. We need, perhaps more self-consciously than we do, to measure out our agreement in strict proportion to the grounds we have for such agreement. Moreover, we ought to assent to things also in accordance with their importance in a given context. Clearly it would be foolish to cling fiercely to a trivial idea and equally foolish to be indifferent to issues of great moment.[2]

Thus we return for the moment to the metaphor of a "web" of belief. Our beliefs connect with each other and with the world—if not always very well, if the web is

---

2. Michael Polanyi and Mihaly Csikszentmihalyi both emphasize that truly creative, influential thinkers have a superior ability to discern which avenues of research are most likely to pay off in discoveries of importance and that, indeed, a reliable sense of what matters is crucial in channeling all scholarship such that it avoids spreading out into what Polanyi calls "a desert of trivialities" (Michael Polanyi, *Personal Knowledge: Towards a Post-Critical Philosophy* [Chicago: University of Chicago Press, 1958], 135; Mihaly Csikszentmihalyi, *Creativity: Flow and the Psychology of Discovery and Invention* [New York: Harper, 1996]).

ragged—with some beliefs being more crucial to the overall shape and strength of the web than others. Thus, again, a part of epistemological wisdom is to distinguish among our beliefs in terms of their importance as well as in terms of their warrant. Moreover, some strands of the web connect more or less solidly to the environment (think of them being warranted by correspondence), while others play a crucial role in the integrity of the web itself (think of them being warranted by coherence[3]), while still others form regions of the web that seem especially productive (think of them being warranted by pragmatism). Lastly, the web analogy reminds us that the web exists in time: that circumstances change and the web does, too, so that a belief that was once well warranted may have lost its grounding, while another has gained traction in the world; an overall shape that suited one (epistemic) environment needs to change in another; thus one or another quarter of the web needs repair or perhaps abandonment, while a once-productive area seems recently to have yielded little of value; and what used to be a key thread has been relegated to a dangling idea as the web's structure now depends on other convictions. The web metaphor thus combines a number of key elements in understanding our thought, and reinforces the present concern that we proportion our assent wisely—and we keep adjusting that assent as circumstances demand—to each strand of our belief.

Suppose my Aunt Tillie tells me that she loves me. I believe her statement with full confidence because I have a lifetime of warrants for that proposition: she has cared for me well and often over the years, and I cannot think of a single plausible reason she would have maintained what would amount to an extraordinarily elaborate deception otherwise. If my Aunt Tillie tells me on the phone one day, however, that the radius of the star Betelgeuse is 5.5 astronomical units based on something she thinks she heard on a bus that morning, I might accord her statement less than full credibility. And my Aunt Tillie, being a reasonable person, will not take offense at my action in this case. Indeed, she would be the first to admit that perhaps she misheard or misunderstood what was mentioned on the bus—although since my aunt is a professor of astrophysics at Caltech and was talking with her colleague on the bus they take to their lab, I might yet accord her claim rather high likelihood.

Let us be clear about what we can and cannot do in this regard. We are not such masters of our believing that we can ratchet up or down our believings at will. I offer you a million dollars to believe that you are sitting on a Martian mountaintop. Since you could find use for a million dollars, you try hard to believe that you are so poised. You find, however, that despite considerable effort, you cannot. So I up the offer to two million. You redouble your efforts accordingly, but with no greater success. You can *imagine* sitting on a Martian mountaintop. You might even know enough about Martian geography to have a favorite mountain in mind—say, the

---

3. James D. Bratt helps us understand coherence in an appropriately broad context: "a true alignment of our ideas, values, and life-practices, each feeding back on the others through critical reflection, so that genuine coherence might be obtained in our selves and our communities" ("Puritan Schools in a Quaker Age," *Perspectives* [August 1995]: 15).

charmingly named Elysium Mons. But you cannot *believe* that you are actually there. Five million, then? Ten? It doesn't matter. You cannot believe what you do not have adequate grounds—that is, what *to you* are adequate grounds—to believe.[4]

This linkage of belief and warrant demonstrates the foolishness of the common modern antinomy of faith and reason and prompts us to specify the relationship of "knowledge" and "faith." Faith always has its reasons—or, more precisely, its grounds. To put it slightly differently, faith is always based on what we take to be knowledge, whether that knowledge is gained via intuition or reflection. We believe something (to use one sense of the word "believe") and we believe *in* something or someone (to use the other sense) because we possess what we have judged to be good (enough) grounds to do so. I commit my body completely to my bed each night—I just plunk myself down on it without so much as a cursory inspection of its structural integrity—because I know the furniture manufacturer who made it is reputable, because during previous sleeps I detected no disquieting signs of weakness in the bed, and because, so far as I know, nothing has happened between my last enjoyment of the bed and this evening's to suggest that the bed has been compromised in any way. Likewise with believing in a person: I trust my children to this babysitter because I know his parents from church, I have seen him interact with other children in Sunday school, other parents have recommended him, and when I have talked with him he shows the signs of dependability I seek in a sitter. The same is true of a philosophy or religion: Its tenets seem to make sense of the world, its practices help me negotiate the world effectively, and its adherents live a kind of life that I find attractive and compelling.[5]

Faith, therefore, is a disposition toward something or someone, an attitude of trust, an inclination to rely upon it or him or her beyond what I think I know to be the case. This posture then is manifested in action (so James 2:14–26; Hebrews 11). Since I believe in this thing or that person, I shall entrust myself to it or him or her in this case beyond what I can strictly know to be true. I'm confident (*con fide*) that this chair won't give way, that this map will guide me correctly, that this physician will perform the surgery competently, and that this pastor will give me good counsel regarding my marriage—so I will, when the occasion arises, sit in the chair, follow the map, submit to the operation, and do what my counselor said to do. "I know enough to trust" is the way these two connect.[6]

---

4. William Alston goes to some pains to demonstrate how little "will to believe" we actually have: "Deontological Desiderata," chap. in *Beyond "Justification": Dimensions of Epistemic Evaluation* (Ithaca, NY: Cornell University Press, 2006), 58–80.

5. As John Lennox puts it in response to Richard Dawkins, "Where is the evidence that religious faith is not based on evidence? . . . Faith is a response to evidence, not a rejoicing in the absence of evidence. . . . Just as in science, faith, reason and evidence belong together" (John C. Lennox, *God's Undertaker: Has Science Buried God?* [Oxford: Lion, 2009], 16).

6. Nicholas Wolterstorff defines faith similarly, and likewise in an epistemological context, in "Introduction," *Faith and Rationality: Reason and Belief in God*, ed. Alvin Plantinga and Nicholas Wolterstorff (Notre Dame, IN and London: University of Notre Dame Press, 1983), 10–15. So, too, does Richard Swinburne: "The Nature of Faith," chap. in *Faith and Reason* (Oxford: Clarendon, 1981), 104–24.

Conversion from one belief to another—whether "belief *that*" (knowledge) or "belief *in*" (faith)—happens when the warrants have become weak relative to the prospective defeaters I have encountered and the alternative offers a paradigm much more capable of both explaining and helping me cope with the data I now confront. In short, I change my mind when it makes more sense to believe (in) something else. We admire someone continuing to believe a fact or a theory, or believe in a person or an institution, in the teeth of impressive counterevidence *if* that believer holds on because of what he thinks is yet more compelling warrant to do so. C. S. Lewis comments helpfully in this regard:

> I define Faith as the power of continuing to believe what we once honestly thought to be true until cogent reasons for honestly changing our minds are brought before us.... If we wish to be rational, not now and then, but constantly, we must pray for the gift of Faith, for the power to go on believing not in the teeth of reason but in the teeth of lust and terror and jealousy and boredom and indifference that which reason, authority, or experience, or all three, have once delivered to us for truth.[7]

Anyone, Lewis is saying, might be tempted to waver in one's faith in a particular theory when contradicted in public by one's academic superiors, or in a particular person when mocked by one's friends, or in a religion when beguiled by an attractive alternative. No new evidence or arguments have been advanced: one is instead in the grip of emotions. Faith is the proper tenacity to believe even at the risk of incurring shame or forgoing pleasure. Indeed, as Kelly James Clark muses, in the tradition of the "dark night of the soul," dealing well with doubts and doubting can be spiritually edifying: "Perhaps it is through doubt instead of suffering that our faith is being made complete," even as I'm sure Clark would agree that for most of us doubt *is* a kind of suffering.[8]

From a quite different Christian tradition comes the complementary point that our doubts may simply reflect intuitions of our littleness and frailty in the presence of the great truths of the Gospel and of God himself. Thomas Merton writes,

> There are still "doubts," if by that we mean not that we hesitate to accept the truth of revealed doctrine, but that we feel the weakness and instability of our spirit in the presence of the awful mystery of God. This is not so much an objective doubt as a subjective sense of our own helplessness which is perfectly compatible with true faith.[9]

We do not admire someone, however, but rather scorn or pity he who keeps believing when there seem to be decisive grounds to change his mind. We properly judge

---

7. C. S. Lewis, "Religion: Reality or Substitute?" in *Christian Reflections*, ed. Walter Hooper (Grand Rapids, MI: Eerdmans, 1967), 42.

8. Kelly James Clark, *When Faith Is Not Enough* (Grand Rapids, MI: Eerdmans, 1997), 101.

9. Thomas Merton, *New Seeds of Contemplation* (New York: New Directions, 1961), 134.

him to have moved from the noble mode of faithfulness to the ignoble mode of fanaticism, a condition in which critical reason has been abandoned and any contradictory evidence reflexively dismissed. *This* intransigence is "blind faith," a faith that has blinded itself to anything other than what it already believes.

We therefore ought to qualify our assent to our beliefs. We cannot believe merely by an act of will, but we can, and should, analyze our grounds for believing, recognize the strengths and weaknesses of those grounds, and act accordingly. Let us also remember that, in this epistemology, at least, what count as at least *prima facie* "grounds for believing" are all five of the resources in the pentalectic (experience, tradition, scholarship, art, and Scripture) via intuition, imagination, and reason. (There is no brief being offered here, as I trust is obvious by now, for the narrow evidentialism of classical foundationalism.[10]) As I have labored to make plain, much of what we think we know is not grounded in a chain of indubitable evidence and logical inference, but instead arises from basic beliefs, sense impressions, deliverances of authorities, "gut feelings," and more that would be condemned by the severe strictures of modern rationalism or empiricism.[11] We are open to learning however we can learn—all the while submitting everything that seems questionable to good questioning.[12]

It would be well, furthermore, if we applied this principle in our self-representation. Other people should not have to ask us, "How sure are you about that?" because we ought to have told them already (at least, we should have on any subject in which this qualification would matter). We ought not to claim to be certain—at least, not

---

10. Alvin Plantinga advances an early version of his career-long assault on such evidentialism in "Reason and Belief in God," in *Faith and Rationality: Reason and Belief in God*, ed. Alvin Plantinga and Nicholas Wolterstorff (Notre Dame, IN and London: University of Notre Dame Press, 1983), 16–93; see also Nicholas Wolterstorff, *Reason within the Bounds of Religion*, 2nd ed. (Grand Rapids, MI: Eerdmans, 1984 [1976]).

11. Even Immanuel Kant, of all people, speaks of a "transcendental faculty of judgment" that must be relied upon to decide which general principles, rules of thumb, proverbs, and the like are to be applied in this situation or that. Delightfully, the sage of Königsberg identifies this impressively authoritative faculty as "mother wit," and notes that "for the want of [it] no scholastic discipline [or 'school'] can compensate" ("Introduction: Of the Transcendental Faculty of Judgement in General," *Critique of Pure Reason*, 1.2.1.2). Thomas Nagel has aroused the ire of the Darwinist Illuminati by musing similarly: *Mind and Cosmos: Why the Materialist Neo-Darwinian Conception of Nature Is Almost Certainly False* (New York and Oxford: Oxford University Press, 2012). See also Nagel's generally appreciative review of Christian philosopher Alvin Plantinga's more extensive argument along similar lines: "A Philosopher Defends Religion," *New York Review of Books* (September 27, 2012): http://www.nybooks.com/articles/archives/2012/sep/27/philosopher-defends-religion/?pagination=false; accessed 5 April 2013. The book under review is Plantinga's *Where the Conflict Really Lies: Science, Religion, and Naturalism* (New York and Oxford: Oxford University Press, 2011).

12. As Polanyi warns, "objectivism has totally falsified our conception of truth, by exalting what we can know and prove, while covering up with ambiguous utterances all we can know and *cannot* prove, even though the latter knowledge underlies, and must ultimately set its seal to, all that we *can* prove" (*Personal Knowledge*, 286; emphasis in original). See also Wolterstorff, *Reason within the Bounds of Religion*.

in any epistemological sense. Perhaps in a *psychological* sense we might say that we are "certain," by which we mean we are entertaining no doubts but instead have a cloudless mental sky of confidence in this or that. (Some would use the word "certitude" for such a state of mind.) But philosophically, we ought to be careful to say that we humans cannot ever be *certain* of anything more than our own states of mind, such as the state of "feeling pain," and self-evident propositions such as "2 + 2 = 4." For everything else we think is possibly, however remotely, mistaken, or at least not completely correct, and we cannot ever be in a position to know that there is absolutely no possibility that we are anything other than entirely right.

Instead of simply saying we believe or don't believe this or that—or, worse, simply asserting this or that—it would be a good discipline for ourselves and more helpful communication to others to begin more sentences with "It seems to me that..." or "As I understand it...," to indicate our awareness that we are not delivering the simple truth of the matter. Nancey Murphy, moreover, nicely sets out a spectrum of words available to us to qualify our claims: "necessarily—certainly—undoubtedly—presumably—probably—apparently—possibly—perhaps—there is a chance that—it is conceivable that."[13] We would do well, finally, to disclose on precisely what our confidence is based, whether we are affirming that these directions will get you to the next town, or that this wrench is just right for the task, or that your co-worker really is scheming to steal your job. And it would be particularly salubrious, as Locke advised, to apply these principles in our politics: at the national level of parties and parliaments, yes, but also in each significant interaction and transaction of our lives.[14]

QUALIFICATIONS OF PROPORTIONATE ASSENT

We must be aware of just how much doubt we really do have, or at least *ought* to have, especially about the fundamental ideas that shape our lives. One student who encountered these proposals in a course then asked a perceptive question: "What about the case of an *uncertainly tall graduated cylinder*?" The student clearly grasped the limitations of our epistemic situation: We frequently do not know just how much there is to know that is germane to a situation. We might know that there is 1 ml of water in the cylinder, but is the cylinder's capacity 100 ml, 1000 ml, or more? Are we seeing a considerable amount of the available evidence (say, 1/100ml), enough to justify even a tentative generalization, or are we in fact seeing only wildly anomalous bits that a truly comprehensive knowledge would put in perspective as in fact quite misleading?

---

13. Nancey Murphy, *Reasoning and Rhetoric in Religion* (Valley Forge, PA: Trinity, 1994), 32.

14. Neil Postman details many suggestions regarding verbal circumspection in "Alfred Korzybski," chap. in *Conscientious Objections: Stirring Up Trouble about Language, Technology, and Education* (New York: Vintage, 1988), 135–46.

C. S. Lewis sharpens the point as he asserts that

> it is not a question of failing to know everything: it is a question (at least as regards quantity) of knowing next door to nothing. Each of us finds that in his own life every moment of time is completely filled. He is bombarded every second by sensations, emotions, thoughts, which he cannot attend to for multitude, and nine-tenths of which he must simply ignore. A single second of lived time contains more than can be recorded. And every second of past time has been like that for every man that ever lived. The past…was a roaring cataract of billions upon billions of such moments: any one of them too complex to grasp in its entirety, and the aggregate beyond all imagination. By far the greater part of this teeming reality escaped human consciousness almost as soon as it occurred.… [And then Lewis twists the knife:] And if *per impossibile* the whole were known, it would be wholly unmanageable. To know the whole of one minute in Napoleon's life would require a whole minute of your own life. You could not keep up with it.[15]

Therefore we can graduate our assent only in terms of "as far as we know…," and that is a significant, and humbling, qualification indeed.[16] George Steiner asks, "How could the senses, how could the brain impose order and coherence on the kaleidoscope, on the *perpetuum mobile* of swarming existence?"[17] It is particularly important to keep this qualification in mind since, as Daniel Kahneman warns us, we all tend nonetheless very strongly to assume that "what you see is all there is."[18]

Locke himself believed that we had certain knowledge only of our own experiences and, he allowed, of bits of reality of which we might have occasional glimpses, what Locke called "insights." But beyond this very small yield of the rationally or

---

15. C. S. Lewis, "Historicism," in *Christian Reflections*, ed. Walter Hooper (Grand Rapids, MI: Eerdmans, 1967), 107–8. Ernest Zebrowski makes this point at length in the quite different fields of weather and natural disaster forecasting: "We simply don't have a fruitful way of studying complex irreproducible phenomena" (Ernest Zebrowski, Jr., *Perils of a Restless Planet: Scientific Perspectives on Natural Disasters* [Cambridge: Cambridge University Press, 1997] esp. 257–86; the quotation is from p. 285).

16. The most influential work on graduating our assent is the tradition stemming from Thomas Bayes (1702–61). He and his successors have formulated equations to help us arrive at probability theories to describe how people should apportion their assent, even changing their minds, when encountering a particular degree of warrant. This work is not for the mathematically simple or faint of heart, and it frequently arrives at intuitively strange conclusions. Yet, as I say, it is widely regarded as the best theory we have for such considerations.

17. George Steiner, *Errata: An Examined Life* (New Haven, CT, and London: Yale University Press, 1997), 5. Steiner writes elsewhere, "Neither human will nor systematic exploration can attain the final mysteries or any complete grasp of natural phenomena. Frustration is inscribed in reason" (*Lessons of the Masters* [Cambridge, MA and London: Harvard University Press, 2003], 65).

18. Kahneman actually coins an acronym for this phenomenon (WYSIATI) because he refers to it so often in his book: *Thinking, Fast and Slow* (New York: Farrar, Straus and Giroux, 2011), 85.

intuitively certain, we have only belief, opinion, judgment, and the like. Thus, contrary to the stereotype of the Enlightenment thinker subjecting every perception and conception to the gimlet eye of reason, Locke says that one is obligated to undertake such rigorous inquiry only into issues of maximal "concernment" to one. These issues, after all, are the issues that drive people to extremes of belief and action, even to civil war. Locke otherwise does not offer such regulations for thought on anything else.

Instead, as a Christian thinker, Locke says that before God we can humbly do our duty, for God has graciously provided sufficient indications of his will, of the nature of the world and of ourselves, of his salvation, and so on that we can indeed live as Christians and please him thus. We do not have certainty about all these things—so we must not to act as if we do (in, say, religious wars). What we have instead is sufficient for us to humbly believe and obey.

The correct response, therefore, to a properly deep and wide skepticism about our possibility of getting to "the things themselves" is, Locke says, grateful contentment, and thus Locke offers what could be a rebuke to despairing skeptics of our own time:

> We shall not have much reason to complain of the narrowness of our minds, if we will but employ them about what may be of use to us; for of that they are very capable; and it will be an unpardonable as well as childish peevishness, if we undervalue the advantages of our knowledge, and neglect to improve it to the ends for which it was given us, because there are some things that are set out of the reach of it.... The discoveries we can make...ought to satisfy us; and [we ought not] peremptorily or intemperately require demonstration, and demand certainty, where probability only is to be had, and which is sufficient to govern all our concernments. If we will disbelieve everything, because we cannot certainly know all things, we shall do much-what as wisely as he who would not use his legs, but sit still and perish, because he had no wings to fly.[19]

So much, then, for the stereotype of Locke as the Great Modern Knower whose reason magisterially sweeps over the empirical landscape and comes to universal, certain conclusions about it all. Instead, we find a Locke who is fearful precisely of those who are willing to do battle as fanatical believers in this or that—shall we say it?—metanarrative, a fear that would extend into our own time against the ruthless champions of Rationality or Science or Technology or the like. Locke chastens us all with his restricted view of what we can properly claim to know.

As we have seen throughout this volume, skepticism about the accuracy of our perception and conception of things shows up in a variety of analytical modes, from historians and philosophers of science who point to the way scientists actually think, to poststructuralist deconstructions of texts to expose the power relations

---

19. John Locke, *An Essay Concerning Human Understanding*, ed. A. S. Pringle-Pattison (Oxford: Clarendon, 1929), I, i, 5; pp. 12–13.

they both conceal and promote, to postcolonial and feminist critiques of what we might call "mere knowing," to psychologists who probe our penchants for conservatism, quick judgments, and self-interest. Let us consider a sampling of yet more qualifications of the scheme I have advanced so far.

Kahneman sums up much of his Nobel Prize-winning career in his book *Thinking, Fast and Slow*.[20] Kahneman suggests that we typically respond to the world in something very like a reflexive mode, apprehending, comprehending, and responding to what we encounter with as little intellectual effort as possible. We therefore "process" the world, so to speak, along well-worn intellectual pathways, habits of apprehension, comprehension, and response (Kahneman uses the term "heuristics") that have served us well in the past and require little effort to traverse again. Our natural resort to such habits, of course, helps us avoid traffic dangers smoothly, return a tennis serve accurately, and greet a stranger at a party politely.[21]

Our reliance on what Kahneman calls System 1 thinking, however, means that we often miss opportunities to apprehend, comprehend, or respond to reality as well as we might—or ought. For the dark side of System 1 thinking is convention, bias, even prejudice, the very opposites of insightful, creative, and independent thinking. Indeed, System 1 thinking is "a machine for jumping to conclusions," Kahneman says.[22] It is an awfully useful machine—indeed, we could not survive, let alone thrive, without it. But its very speed, general reliability, and relative ease-of-use means that we tend always to resort to it unless we feel we simply have to slow down and think about things in a concentrated way. Then we employ System 2, the mode of complex calculations, critical re-examination of information, and the posing of creative alternatives. Even then, however, we use System 2 only as much and for as long as we feel we need to do so. We are, Kahneman concludes, basically lazy thinkers.

Now, to be sure, one man's laziness might seem to be just another man's efficiency. But Kahneman insists, "Anything that makes it easier for the associative machine to run smoothly will also bias beliefs. A reliable way to make people believe in falsehoods is frequent repetition, because familiarity is not easily distinguished from truth. Authoritarian institutions and marketers have always known this fact."[23] Of course we must become thoroughly familiar with something in order to understand, assess, and respond to it properly. But Kahneman's point is different: *mere* familiarity *feels like* authenticity. What "keeps showing up" in our experience we tend to read as reality, even if in fact what keeps showing up is a function of our own

---

20. Daniel Kahneman, *Thinking, Fast and Slow* (New York: Farrar, Straus and Giroux, 2011).

21. William Hazlitt: "Without the aid of prejudice and custom I should not be able to find my way across the room" (quoted in a review of Duncan Wu, *William Hazlitt: The First Modern Man* [Oxford: Oxford University Press, 2008]: Alan Jacobs, "The English Montaigne," *Books & Culture* [July 2009]: 29).

22. This is the title of chap. 7.

23. Kahneman, 62.

choices (e.g., our choice of news media) or the choices of others seeking to direct us. Indeed, Kahneman's large book bristles with warnings about how we can be nudged or even bamboozled into errors in all sorts of ways by those who capitalize on our habits and particularly our penchant for the easy thought—or, even more basically, the inchoate feeling—over the deliberate, demanding consideration.[24]

Indeed, as Kahneman cautions, "confidence is a feeling which reflects [what appears to us to be] the coherence of the information and the cognitive ease of processing it."[25] Confidence, that is, does not emerge from true mastery of all the relevant data and laborious, skillful effort to interpret it any more than it emerges from a superficial glance at the file and a breezy hop to a conventional conclusion. Confidence itself, as we all know *if we just think about it,* says nothing at all about the actual quality of the thing or concept about which someone, even oneself, is confident.

(Stanford business professor Chip Heath and his Aspen Institute-consultant brother Dan confirm from abundant research that the ideas that make the most immediate and lasting impact on people generally have qualities that have nothing to do with their veracity: simplicity, unexpectedness, concreteness, a measure of credibility, emotional impact, and a vivid exemplifying narrative. Thus contrary ideas that are more complex, banal, abstract, equally credible, dull, and bereft of a fascinating story cannot compete—*even if they have the single quality that matters: truth.*[26])

Careful thinking, moreover, literally makes demands on us, not only of time and effort, but thereby also of glucose, our body's energy reserves. Kahneman makes the point echoed by another eminent psychologist, Roy F. Baumeister, that thinking and self-control draw on the same reserves, since they draw on the same body and particularly the same brain. Thus the more stressed or fatigued we are, the more poorly we think and the more poorly (note the economic metaphor) we decide. Kahneman has found that "people who are cognitively busy are also more likely to make selfish choices, use sexist language, and make superficial judgments in social situations.... A few drinks have the same effect, as does a sleepless night."[27] This insight from social science brings new dimensions to bear on the noetic effects of sin. We literally need power to think well and choose well, and as our limited power is drained, our abilities decline accordingly. We thus again encounter the fundamental fact that our thinking is not done by ghostly intellects, but by bodies that need adequate sleep and nutrition, and appropriate contexts and company, in order to think best.[28]

---

24. Nassim Taleb has become famous for warning most of the rest of us, correctly, about our stupidity in, among other things, economic matters: *The Black Swan: The Impact of the Highly Improbable* (New York: Random House, 2007).

25. Kahneman, 212.

26. Chip Heath and Dan Heath, *Made to Stick: Why Some Ideas Survive and Others Die* (New York: Random House, 2007).

27. Kahneman, 41. See Roy F. Baumeister and John Tierney, *Willpower: Rediscovering the Greatest Human Strength* (New York: Penguin, 2011).

28. I like to think these qualifications are among those Alvin Plantinga has in mind in his well-known definition of "warrant": "A belief has warrant if it is produced by cognitive faculties

One might assume that power to think well and choose well would be abundantly available to those we trust as authorities, but journalist David H. Freedman will keep you awake at night by his account of just how frequently experts have been wrong nonetheless. Let me select just two stories of the many in his entertaining, and thoroughly disconcerting, book.

In 1997 The University of Michigan football team decided to give one of its longtime benchwarmers a shot at a little playing time in his junior year. The young quarterback had at one point been ranked behind six other quarterbacks on the team and, discouraged, had been looking into transferring, but he took advantage of the playing opportunity and shined, eventually going on to set Wolverine records for most pass attempts and completions. Outside Ann Arbor, however, his accomplishments didn't seem to count for much. Not only was he utterly ignored when it came time to consider candidates for the Heisman Trophy but he was passed over for virtually every formal recognition in college football, picking up only an honorable mention with a regional all-star squad. The apparent invisibility of his college passing stats persisted through the NFL draft, where he was selected 199th, and only by a team using an extra pick to make up for the loss of a few players during the off-season. He was promptly assigned the familiar role of watching the games from the bench as the team's fourth-ranked quarterback. But a year later a teammate's injury led to this young player once again getting an unexpected shot, at which point it took him only the rest of that season to become widely considered pro football's most devastatingly effective quarterback. He has since led his team to four Super Bowls, winning three of them, and along the way has grabbed two Super Bowl MVP awards, played in four Pro Bowls, and broken the NFL record for the most touchdown passes in a single season. He also holds the record for the highest single-game completion percentage, the most completions in a single Super Bowl, and the most Super Bowl completions overall. That Wolverine benchwarmer was Tom Brady, now of the New England Patriots, who, while still in the prime of his career, has already nearly assured himself a berth in football's Hall of Fame.[29]

This overlooking of an eventual superstar by a massive industry dedicated to finding such talent is not rare, Freedman points out, as he immediately refers to the career of Curt Warner, another quarterback who is likely destined for the Hall of Fame and who was sent home from his first training camp to stock grocery shelves on his way to athletic immortality.

---

functioning properly (subject to no malfunctioning) in a cognitive environment congenial for those faculties, according to a design plan successfully aimed at truth" (*Warrant and Proper Function* [New York and Oxford: Oxford University Press, 1993], viii–ix).

29. David H. Freedman, *Wrong: Why Experts Keep Failing Us—and How to Know When Not to Trust Them* (New York: Little, Brown, 2010), 18–19. NFL fans will know that Brady added more records in the 2012–13 season, including most postseason wins (surpassing Joe Montana) and the highest percentage of healthy seasons appearing in the NFL's equivalent of the Final Four: fully 64 percent, a record unlikely to be surpassed.

Sports fans, however many of us there are, in our calmer moments recognize that the hunt for the next great athlete is a matter of rather limited consequentiality. The hunt for the cure for a cancer, however, is obviously of the greatest moment. Surely in the realm of medical research, the most important research we conduct, expert knowledge is sure and sound? Meet Dr. John Ioannidis, and never sleep well again.

Ioannidis, an expert in expert medical studies, has impressive credentials. (Yes, the irony is obvious here, but bear with me awhile.) Graduating first in his class from the University of Athens Medical School, he completed a residency at Harvard in internal medicine and then took up a research and clinical appointment at Tufts in infectious diseases. While at Tufts, however, he began to notice that a wide range of medical treatment did not rest on solid scientific evidence. While next at the National Institutes of Health and Johns Hopkins University in the 1990s, Ioannidis noted that two-thirds of hundreds of medical studies he read in the scholarly literature were either fully refuted or pronounced "exaggerated" within a few years of their publication.

This seems troubling. Be more troubled, however.

> [Ioannidis] had been examining only the less than one-tenth of one percent of published medical research that makes it [in]to the most prestigious medical journals. . . . Ioannidis did find one group of studies that more often than not remained unrefuted: randomized controlled studies . . . that appeared in top journals and that were cited in other researchers' papers an extraordinary one thousand times or more. Such studies are extremely rare and represent the absolute tip of the tip of the pyramid of medical research. Yet one-fourth of even these studies were later refuted, and that rate might have been much higher were it not for the fact that no one had ever tried to confirm or refute nearly half of the rest.[30]

Freedman paints a horrifying picture of experts who trust their intuitions over evidence *they have at hand*, let alone evidence they could get but do not bother to obtain.[31] Atul Gawande, himself a medical instructor, writes about his colleagues' frequent refusal to face basic data regarding frequent and preventable medical problems that are attributable to skilled professionals making dumb mistakes ("Unthinkable!") and compares this dangerous attitude with pilot training that early and repeatedly pounds into students' heads that they must *not* trust their instincts but their instruments and their checklists—in other words, the data that

---

30. Freedman, 6; see also Freedman, "Lies, Damned Lies, and Medical Science," *The Atlantic* (November 2010): 76–86. A crucial book in the feminist critique of science as deeply distorted by gendered stereotypes and values is Sandra G. Harding, *The Science Question in Feminism* (Ithaca, NY: Cornell University Press, 1986).

31. Sissela Bok points to a different cluster of problems around physicians who withhold information from patients, or distort it significantly, because of "their own fears (which, according to one study, are much stronger than those of laymen) of facing questions about the meaning of one's life and the inevitability of death" (*Lying: Moral Choice in Public and Private Life* [New York: Vintage, 1989 (1978)], 231).

matter most. You might feel with every nerve in your body that you are flying level and right-side up, but if your instruments say otherwise, it is lethal arrogance to trust your expertise over theirs. You might look around the operating room at your talented and familiar team and believe without a shadow of a doubt that your patient is ready for surgery, but if the scrub nurse cannot confirm it by her checklist, you are culpably foolish to proceed.[32]

To confirm your permanent insomnia, Julian Sher examines the world of forensic science and finds many instances of wrongful convictions. He points to a 2009 study published in the *Virginia Law Review* that surveyed the cases of 137 convicted persons later exonerated by DNA evidence, and found that in more than half of the trials forensic experts gave invalid testimony, "including errors about shoe prints and hair samples."[33] That same year, the National Academy of Sciences published a book-length report warning that even fingerprint matches can be misleading and calling for a drastically improved approach to forensic science. So much, then, for people's fates being determined by the clear, cold, infallible judgment of the scientific expert witness.[34]

As the world begins to shimmer ever more before our eyes and the solid ground beneath our feet threatens to evanesce, along comes historian Alison Winter to offer an entire book about the questionable reliability of memory. What we do not readily comprehend, what does not fit within our set of presuppositions, does not tend to register with us immediately and clearly, if at all, and therefore also not in our memory. Conversely, what we expect to experience, or afterward believe we *must* have experienced, gets written into our memories despite what may have actually happened. Contrary, that is, to the popular notion that somewhere buried in our brains is a perfect recording of everything we have ever experienced, Winter shows through her study of the last century of memory research that our minds instead are constantly coding what we experience as "memorable," "sort of memorable," "not memorable" and the like, according to our understanding of the world and according to our *valuing* of this or that element of the world. Furthermore, our memories are plastic, and remain vulnerable to addition, subtraction, deformation, reformation, confabulation, and other processes as our lives progress and as our beliefs change, rather than being fixed, veracious "imprints" of the external world upon our minds.[35]

---

32. Atul Gawande, *The Checklist Manifesto: How to Get Things Right* (New York: Metropolitan, 2009). See also Rachel Giese, "The Errors of Their Ways," *The Walrus* 9 (April 2012): 24–32: this article details why 24,000 Canadians will die this year from medical error.

33. Julian Sher, "Trials and Error," *The Walrus* (May 2013): 39. The study is Brandon L. Garrett and Peter J. Neufeld, "Invalid Forensic Science Testimony and Wrongful Convictions," 95 Va. L. Rev. 1 (2009).

34. National Academy of Sciences, *Strengthening Forensic Science in the United States: A Path Forward* (Washington, DC: National Academies Press, 2009).

35. For a fascinating analysis of the modern history of memory, its metaphors, related technologies, shifting legal status, and more, see Alison Winter, *Memory: Fragments of a Modern*

What, then, can we possibly trust in our quest for knowledge? Even if we resolve to proportion our assent to what we believe is the strength of the case for, and the importance of, the belief in question, are we not now confronted with giant brackets around all that we claim with the notation, "Of course, we could be entirely wrong about any or all of this"?[36]

A different set of qualifications, spiritual ones, paradoxically make the situation worse and, finally, better.

FURTHER, SPIRITUAL QUALIFICATIONS OF OUR THINKING

According to the Christian religion, the fundamental human problem is not ignorance, a deficiency in the intellect. It isn't even deprivation, a deficiency in our environment. It is sin, a defect in the soul. We are alienated from God, even resistant toward God. Sin—not only the particular wrong actions we commit or the right actions we omit, which are *sins*, but the orientation and pattern and motive of our lives toward evil—corrupts the mind just as it corrupts the heart. For human beings are wholistic entities, in which everything affects everything. Bad digestion, as Scrooge hypothesized, could cause him to see a vision of his expired business partner. Wishful thinking might drive a grieving parent to a glowing vision of a recently dead child. Our skills in making sense of William James's "blooming, buzzing confusion" of the world turn out to lead us astray much more often than we might think.[37] Mere expectation prompts us to see what isn't actually there, or to ignore

---

History (Chicago and London: University of Chicago Press, 2012). Colleague D. Bruce Hindmarsh provides a study of how memories of even such vivid and important experiences as religious conversion can become conventionalized by the tropes of the larger community: *The Evangelical Conversion Narrative: Spiritual Autobiography in Early Modern England* (Oxford: Oxford University Press, 2005). And the eminent military historian John Keegan recites a long list of deficiencies in his field that prevent anyone from reading even the most careful account of a battle or war with anything approaching blithe confidence: *The Face of Battle* (New York and London: Penguin, 1978 [1976]), 25–35.

36. So Pascal: "Man is nothing but a subject full of natural error that cannot be eradicated except through grace. Nothing shows him the truth, everything deceives him. The two principles of truth, reason and senses, are not only both not genuine, but are engaged in mutual deception. The senses deceive reason through false appearances, and, just as they trick the soul, they are tricked by it in their turn: it takes its revenge. The senses are disturbed by passions, which produce false impressions. They both compete in lies and deception.

"But, apart from such accidents, error arising from the failure of these heterogeneous faculties to reach understanding . . . (This is where the chapter on powers of deception must start.)" (*Pensée* 45).

37. I have referred frequently to Daniel Kahneman's work in this regard, among others, but an earlier discussion of these phenomena is still usefully challenging: Thomas Gilovich, *How We Know What Isn't So: The Fallibility of Human Reason in Everyday Life* (New York: Free Press, 1991): "People's preferences influence not only the *kind* of information they consider, but also the *amount* they examine. . . . It is clear that we tend to use different criteria to evaluate propositions or conclusions we desire, and those we abhor" (83). And so on, and so on.

what is. But *sin*—our penchant to put something in the place of God in our lives, whether ourselves, another person, a cause, or an ideal—drives us away from inconvenient truths and toward a view of the world more nicely arrayed according to our fundamental interests.

We tend to see what we *want* to see, to hear what we *want* to hear—or, in some cases, to see and hear what we feel we *ought* to see and hear—and to conclude what we perceive to be advantageous to conclude: in the lab and the library every bit as much as in a lovers' lane or late-night *longueur*.[38] Our once-common academic ideal of "mastering texts" has been exposed as egocentric subjection of others' signs to our own agenda. So Martin Luther, who at the Diet of Worms famously submitted himself to "Scripture and right reason," could also thunder against reason as a "weathermaker" or "Devil's whore" who would serve whoever put down the cash.[39] He similarly spoke of reason as a house beam that, in its original state, nicely played its part in supporting the structure of the cosmos, but has since become cracked and useless on its own. Other Christians, of course, have seen the matter differently, whether medieval Scholastics who sought to mount up to heaven on a ladder of philosophy, or pioneers of the Scientific Revolution who sought to map the heavens using the tools of rationally guided observation and induction. More recently, however, and especially under the radical critiques of postmodernity, reason—that is to say, not *reason* in the abstract, but reason *as we human beings wield it*—has looked less like a pristine priestess of truth and more like Luther's prostitute in the pay of the powerful, less like a sturdy platform from which to observe the world and more like Luther's cracked beam that can support no enterprise at all.[40]

Centuries of western philosophy have warned us of this shadowy reality of our nature and therefore of our thought: Slavoj Zizek and Richard Rorty, Michel Foucault and Jacques Derrida, Jean-Paul Sartre and Simone de Beauvoir, Friedrich

---

38. Once again, John Locke anticipates our point: "Let never so much probability land on one side of a covetous man's reasoning, and money on the other; and it is easy to foresee which will outweigh.... Tell a man passionately in love, that he is jilted; bring a score of witnesses of the falsehood of his mistress; it is ten to one but three kind words of hers shall invalidate all their testimonies. *Quod volumus, facile credimus*; 'What suits our wishes is forwardly believed' is, I suppose, what every one hath more than once experimented [= experienced]" (*An Essay concerning Human Understanding*, IV, xx, 12; p. 367). Michael Polanyi brilliantly skewers Marxism as, indeed, a form of wish-fulfillment: "These supposedly scientific assertions are, of course, accepted only because they satisfy certain moral passions" (*Personal Knowledge*, 230; see "The Magic of Marxism," 227–33).

39. *Martin Luther's Last Sermon in Wittenberg...Second Sunday in Epiphany, 17 January 1546. Dr. Martin Luthers Werke: Kritische Gesamtausgabe* (Weimar: Herman Boehlaus Nachfolger, 1914), Band 51:126. Intriguingly, Nietzsche speaks similarly: "'Reason' in language!—oh, what a deceptive old witch it has been!" (*The Twilight of the Idols*, "Reason in Philosophy," aphorism 5).

40. Richard Weaver acerbically notes, "Not without cause has the devil been called the prince of lawyers, and not by accident are Shakespeare's villains good reasoners" (*Ideas Have Consequences* [Chicago: University of Chicago Press, 1984], 19). Again, for reason as a technology that will serve whoever deploys it as a theme also in the modern anti-Luther, Friedrich Nietzsche: see *The Will to Power*, ed. Walter Kaufmann (New York: Vintage, 1968).

Nietzsche and Arthur Schopenhauer, David Hume and Jonathan Edwards, Thomas Hobbes and Niccolò Machiavelli—back and back the tradition goes to the Stoics and Sophists and Skeptics and Socratics. Christians, grateful as we must be for these warnings, also have their Bibles open in front of them to read the same thing. Indeed, the Bible warns us that reason can be bent not only to our own wills, but to those of evil principalities and powers. Under the force of powerful temptation, whether of pain or pleasure, the grip of our reason on truth can wilt like petals. We will say, and in extreme situations even believe, whatever will make the torture stop or the seduction continue.[41] Less dramatically, but no less consequentially, we are pictured by Jesus as soils in various degrees of receptivity to whatever word comes our way (Matt. 13:3–23).

Paradoxically, moreover, we have seen something of how difficult it is to change our minds in the face of good, solid argument to the contrary—even when the opposing evidence, the qualifiers and defeaters, seem unanswerable. It is hard to let go of what we currently believe even when our own principles suggest we should, even when we truly would like to do so. It is almost impossible for us to change our minds about something important when we fundamentally do not want to change them. Indeed, as we have noted, hermeneutical spirals can as easily head *down* as up, away from reality as toward it. Individuals and groups can reinforce their errors if they have the will to do so—at least, for a considerable time. Some few descend past the warnings offered by confrontations with intractable reality that ought to prompt reconsideration, and protect their views in the impervious sanctuary of insanity. And maybe it is not so few who do so, since avoidance of reality is a mark of mental illness and yet so many continue to dodge and defend against what seem to scientists or prophets to be clear and rationally inescapable truths.[42]

Some Christians, to be sure, have sometimes treated of the noetic effects of sin too starkly. Impressed by the doctrine of total depravity—the doctrine of the magisterial Reformers that every element of human nature was corrupted, and corrupted significantly, by sin, versus the more sanguine understanding of the enduring integrity of reason in, say, Thomas Aquinas—these Christians have emphasized the wretched darkness of the unredeemed intellect.

---

41. C. S. Lewis writes, "Reason may win truths; without Faith she will retain them just so long as Satan pleases. There is nothing we cannot be made to believe or disbelieve. If we wish to be rational, not now and then, but constantly, we must pray for the gift of Faith, for the power to go on believing not in the teeth of reason but in the teeth of lust and terror and jealousy and boredom and indifference that which reason, authority, or experience, or all three, have once delivered to us for truth" (*Christian Reflections*, ed. Walter Hooper [Grand Rapids, MI: Eerdmans, 1967], 43).

42. Regarding mental illnesses as so many strategies for avoiding reality, see M. Scott Peck, *The Road Less Traveled* (New York: Touchstone, 1978). John Hick comments, "Whilst a physical state of affairs imposes its character upon us, a moral state of affairs has to await our free recognition" (*An Interpretation of Religion: Human Responses to the Transcendent* [New Haven, CT: Yale University Press, 1989], 151).

To be sure, these is an important, if commonsensical, point here: If one not only disbelieves in God, but passionately resists even the prospect of believing in (= trusting and obeying) God, then one is in an epistemologically parlous position when it comes to considering even the question of the *existence* of God, let alone the other questions taken seriously by religious and theological inquirers (Rom. 1:18–19). One's preferences clearly interfere with one's processing.[43]

Some of those in the Calvinistic tradition in particular have gone further and denounced non-Christian ways of thinking as by definition *antithetical* to the truth, therefore fundamentally misguided, and therefore untrustworthy. Without putting Jesus and the Gospel in the center, such criticism says, every other worldview spins eccentrically, erratically, erroneously. Only the Christian worldview provides the context for a proper prosecution of theology, yes, but also of philosophy, history, the social sciences, the humanities, the arts, and indeed all of life.[44]

At this climax, however, the listener has to scratch his head for a moment or two. Granted that most of the scientists of the Scientific Revolution were Christians, some of them were quite odd, even heretical, Christians (foremost among those was the foremost among them, Isaac Newton, a unitarian enthusiast of outlandish prophetical interpretations). And most of the leading scientists of the last hundred or so years have not been anything like professing orthodox Christians, from Albert Einstein to Stephen Hawking and from Charles Darwin to E. O. Wilson. How, then, did so much apparent truth emerge under such non-Christian auspices? How, furthermore, do most non-Christians apparently grasp so much of reality that they can conduct their businesses, participate in civic life, raise families in loving marriages, volunteer for charities, make art, and in every other respect than worship in a Christian church succeed rather obviously in negotiating the world?

From the apostolic era until now, of course, Christians have recognized truth in non-Christian intellectual traditions. Paul capitalizes on the measure of truth he recognizes among the philosophers on the Areopagus, while early Apologists, such

---

43. "In the biblical view, we not only sin because we are ignorant but we are also ignorant because we sin, because we find it convenient to misconstrue our place in the universe and to reassign divinity in it" (Cornelius Plantinga, Jr., *Not the Way It's Supposed to Be: A Breviary of Sin* [Grand Rapids, MI/Leicester, UK: Eerdmans/Apollos, 1995], 18). Along with other sources cited in this discussion, see P. Travis Kroeker's erudite demolition of reductionistic positivism in "The Ironic Cage of Positivism and the Nature of Philosophical Theology," *Studies in Religion/ Sciences Religeuses* 22:1 (1993): 93–103.

44. Calvin describes the effects of sin on the mind thus: "That part in which the excellence and nobility of the soul especially shine has not only been wounded, but so corrupted that it needs to be healed and to put on a new nature as well.... The whole man is overwhelmed—as by a deluge—from head to foot, so that no part is immune from sin and all that proceeds from him is to be imputed to sin" (*Institutes* II.ii.12). An overlooked but insightful article sketches out the tensions and agreements between two Reformed intellectual traditions, the Dutch neo-Calvinism of Abraham Kuyper and the Common Sense Realism of Charles Hodge and B. B. Warfield: George Marsden, "The Collapse of American Evangelical Academia," in *Faith and Rationality: Reason and Belief in God*, ed. Alvin Plantinga and Nicholas Wolterstorff (Notre Dame, IN, and London: University of Notre Dame Press, 1983), 219–64.

as Justin Martyr, Athenagoras, and Origen trade on what they see as the undeniable truths of Greek thought, particularly the Platonic tradition. The Logos of all people, they affirm, is the Logos who became Jesus Christ (so John 1).

The answer from traditions that trade in "antithesis" thinking is "common grace," God's gifting of the world such that evil is restrained to a considerable extent and human beings are helped to continue in the basic human calling of making shalom. Antithesis does provide a basis upon which Christian critique of non-Christian views and practices can proceed: after all, if Jesus Christ is indeed the Center of History and Lord of all, and if the gospel is the only satisfactory rendering of the fundamental truth about him, then beliefs and behaviors that make no place, or even an insufficient place, for Christ and his gospel must perforce be awry. But God's common grace evidently is vast, and Christians therefore can be grateful to learn all we can from our non-Christian neighbors who are themselves engaged in the work of making shalom. Even Calvin himself will aver, "We see implanted in human nature some sort of desire to search out the truth."[45]

Even as antithesis provides a cue for critiquing what is non-Christian out there, moreover, it reminds Christians that sin resides still in our hearts and therefore also in our minds. Christians still sin and still are sinners, however grateful we are for the renewing work going on within us by the Holy Spirit. If we take our theology seriously, therefore, we will systematically doubt our own convictions, particularly any that pertain to our self-interest or any other interest that we value highly. Is someone criticizing my denomination or congregation, my school or business, my city or country or ethnic group? Is someone teaching an alternative to what I learned from my favorite professor? Is someone advocating an innovation that is unfamiliar to, and therefore other than, our tradition? Christians manifestly can be as stubbornly, even violently, resistant to alternative hypotheses as anyone as we defend our preferences in the name of the absolute truth of God.

Of course we should be resistant, even to death, about some things. There are truths of Christianity that Christians understand to be both vitally important and overwhelmingly convincing. The noble army of martyrs stands in testimony to the importance of fidelity to the gospel, and the graves of Christian soldiers who fought to preserve what they knew of godly civilization against dark threats inspire us to equivalent faithfulness against God's enemies today, whether flesh and blood or principalities and powers. The characteristic language of the Bible, focused as it is on the core matters of life, is properly binary. The Great Commandment, after all, is to "love the Lord your God with *all* your heart, and with *all* your soul, and with *all* your mind, and with *all* your strength" (Mark 12:30; emphasis added)—not with, say, seventy percent or so.

---

45. Calvin, *Institutes*, II.ii.12. To be sure, Calvin then goes on to describe human beings as stumbling around, addled by sinful vanity, such that they end up in darkness needing the light of revelation and the renewal of salvation. His acknowledgement of the remains of reason in fallen humanity is real, but generally grudging. A fine introduction to the themes of antithesis and common grace is Richard J. Mouw, *He Shines in All That's Fair: Culture and Common Grace* (Grand Rapids, MI: Eerdmans, 2001).

The complementary dangers, then, are obvious. On the one hand, we fail to commit ourselves as we should to God, holding back a measure of allegiance, trust, and obedience that ought to be total. We will not want to claim infallible certainty about our theology, but we should aspire to unflinching faithfulness to our God and the Gospel. On the other hand, we may be inclined to think binarily about *everything*, not only about what is Christian versus what is not, as we have been discussing, but even within the complex of Christian belief. Jesus keeps offering us examples in the Gospel of not regarding every moral stricture as absolutely inviolable, as he not only heals on the Sabbath but allows his disciples to break off snacks as they pass through a wheatfield during one. Paul warns Christians repeatedly that they must be willing to set aside a range of both scruples and freedoms in the supreme interest of fostering faith in others. Some things matter more than others, and lesser values sometimes must be sacrificed for greater ones. And these are *religious* matters, let alone questions of science, history, business, politics, and the like. No, a binary approach to everything is inconsistent with Scripture, incongruous with our lived experience, ungrateful for the manifest gifts of God on all human beings, and disruptive to our cooperation with our neighbors in making shalom.

Good theology and healthy spiritual disciplines can aid us greatly in our thinking.[46] Good theology teaches us to make distinctions among matters of primary, secondary, and tertiary importance. Good theology teaches us about the Christian Story, God's work in it, and what we can and cannot therefore expect from God, from ourselves, and from others as we make our way through it. Good theology teaches us about sin and sanctification, about antithesis and common grace, about God's work in the church and God's work beyond it, about those things to which we ought to aspire and those things that are ever beyond our grasp. And good theology reminds us that God is ever with us, before us, above us, in us, under us, and for us in all we do, including in our thinking.

Good theology also helps us recognize both the value and the danger in other modes of thinking. Some Christians have been so worried particularly about the rise of scientific and technological thinking, with themes of "autonomy," "mastery," "hubris," and the like, that they denounce all "worldly" thinking as antagonistic to the gospel and proper Christian living. Whether these fears—understandable as they are—are enunciated in the blunt terms of fundamentalism, the opacities of certain so-called radical or postliberal theologians, or the lofty categorical denunciations of Karl Barth particularly in his feisty earlier years, they are all overreactions.[47]

---

46. Sarah Coakley has been working out the implications of these two spheres in what she calls her *théologie totale*: see, for a brief example, "Is There a Future for Gender and Theology? On Gender, Contemplation, and the Systematic Task," *Criterion* (Spring 2009): 2–11.

47. To such people, I am tempted to respond with just two words: "David Martin." If that is not enough, I have four more: "Robert Wuthnow, Peter Berger." Such sweeping denunciations of fields that Christians have cultivated so well seems almost willful, a reckless sort of second naïveté.

Of course it is true that the social sciences can be, and customarily are, conducted in terms of rival narratives to Scripture. From Auguste Comte to Pierre Bourdieu, social sciences have proceeded and declaimed from a variety of essentially atheistic perspectives and it is the foolish Christian who adopts their methods without critically examining their methodologies according to the Christian worldview and in prayerful attention to the guidance of the Holy Spirit. Critical appropriation of the worthy work of other human beings, however, ought to be the normal mode for the Christian who believes the Bible's account of God's calling upon all human beings to make shalom. For that calling implies, even downstream of the Fall, that much of what even ungodly people find out about the world, if they undertake that work with appropriate intellectual rigor, will be true and helpful for anyone else to consider. And good theology helps the Christian social scientist—or film critic, or political philosopher, or musicologist—practice her craft with the advantage of a basically correct orientation to reality given by Christianity while she then refines her thought in creative tension with the best minds of her field, Christian or otherwise. Good theology, resting on the Christian Story and the fundamental mandates given to human beings in general and to Christians in particular, lets Christians enjoy the whole world of scholarship, yes, and of experience, art, and tradition while maintaining healthy and necessary critical filters to screen out what is genuinely antithetical to the truth.

Spiritual disciplines, for their part, keep us walking with God aright. They keep us connected with God, conversant with God, compliant with God, and confident in God. Through prayer, corporate worship, the sacraments, Bible reading, confession, fasting, and the other ways in which Christians habituate ourselves to holiness, we gradually shed the distortions of sin and gain the clarities of righteousness; we lose evil, sick appetites and develop good, healthy ones. We genuinely hunger for the truth, however painful or humiliating or costly it might be. There is a profound sense of happy humility in any serious thinking: a compelling desire for the knowledge to be gained in a particular domain, an eager willingness to submit one's conceptualization to whatever realities one discovers, a joyful devotion to the challenges and delights of a discourse. This, more than particular intellectual skills, requisite as they are, is what we mean by someone having a scientific cast of mind, or a philosophical or musical one. We have to be the right sort of person, with the right sort of values and drives, in order to be the right sort of thinkers. And Christian thinkers need, first and foremost, to love setting ourselves before God if our thinking is to be conducted aright. "The fear of Yhwh is the beginning of wisdom," the Psalms and Proverbs remind us, and spiritual disciplines cultivate that posture of awed respect for, and reliance upon, God.[48]

---

48. Ps. 111:10; Prov. 1:7; 4:7; 9:10. Along with other sources mentioned here, see the following influential modern exhortations to the Christian thinker regarding character (particularly, in these cases, theologians, but with obvious application to Christians in other fields): Karl Barth, *Evangelical Theology: An Introduction* (Grand Rapids, MI: Eerdmans, 1992 [1962]);

Prayer in particular—heartfelt, comprehensive, continual, and hopeful prayer—is obviously basic to Christian thought when we construe that work, as we ought, as depending entirely on God's gracious provision from first to last.[49] Prayer as invocation obviously is entailed, but so is prayer in a number of other respects:

- as condition (without prayer, how can one expect God to respond?);
- as attitude (trusting in God as gracious provider and regarding oneself as thankful child and agent);
- as confession (removing motives and memories that impede one's responsiveness to God);
- as compass (remembering to regard the goal of knowledge as an element in the love of God and service to God's kingdom);
- as both brake ("Avoid this!") and motive ("Seek that!");
- as celebration when things seem to go well;
- and as consolation that God is yet at work in us when the project of thinking seems to stall or fail.

Regular attendance at church helps us epistemologically in exactly the way it helps inquirers. Church life, when it is not hopelessly dysfunctional, renders the gospel *plausible*, even *credible*, for one more week. Christianity is fraught with tenets that cannot even be fully and coherently expressed, let alone readily believed: a creation *ex nihilo* by a triune God, a cataclysmic Fall by original human parents, an incarnate Savior, a victorious Cross, a bodily Resurrection, an Ascension to glory, an indwelling Holy Spirit, efficacious sacraments, a Second Coming in judgment. Who could possibly believe this welter of mind-breaking proposals? Only those convinced to do so by the power of God.[50] As Jesus exclaims, upon Peter's uncharacteristically correct

---

Richard B. Hays, *The Moral Vision of the New Testament: Community, Cross, New Creation* (San Francisco: HarperSanFrancisco, 1996); and Helmut Thielicke, *A Little Exercise for Young Theologians* (Grand Rapids, MI: Eerdmans, 1962 [1959]).

49. "The Christian is bound to perform many good works, but before all else what he ought to do is pray, for without prayer no other good work whatever can be accomplished. Without prayer he cannot find the way to the Lord, *he cannot understand the truth*, he cannot crucify the flesh with its passions and lusts, his heart cannot be enlightened with the light of Christ, he cannot be savingly united to God" (*The Way of a Pilgrim*, trans. R. M. French [San Francisco: HarperOne, 1965], 8; emphasis added.

50. Richard Niebuhr speaks of this phenomenon from the human side, as a Kierkegaardian "leap of faith." I trust Niebuhr would agree that such a leap is justified, however, only at the impulse of the Holy Spirit: "If we begin with the spectator's knowledge of events, we cannot proceed to the participant's apprehension. There is no continuous movement from an objective inquiry into the life of Jesus to a knowledge of him as the Christ who is our Lord. Only a decision of the self, a leap of faith, a *metanoia* or revolution of the mind can lead form observation to participation and from observed to lived history" (H. Richard Niebuhr, "The Story of Our Life," from his *The Meaning of Revelation* [New York: Macmillan, 1941], 78; anthologized in *Why Narrative? Readings in Narrative Theology*, ed. Stanley Hauerwas and L. Gregory Jones [Grand Rapids, MI: Eerdmans, 1989], 41).

answer to the question, "Who do people say that I am?": "Blessed are you, Simon son of Jonah! For flesh and blood has not revealed this to you [you didn't just figure this out by a chain of reasoning], but my Father in heaven" (Matt. 16:17). To believe that this old book is The Book and to believe that this crucified carpenter is the Lord of Glory requires Spiritual assistance.[51] No one believes such things on the basis of evidences and arguments alone, nor can faith in them be sustained thereby—important as such are in commending and defending faith.[52]

Christians encounter the daily winds of doubt that any person does, let alone the occasional tornadoes of disaster, and God provides the means to deal with those doubts. Such means include inward assurance wrought directly by the Holy Spirit, yes, and also outward reassurance by fellow believers, filled with the Spirit, who manifest reassuring integrity and encouraging intelligence. (This assurance is what many modern Christians seem to mean when they say that, contrary to the deliverances of reason, which are necessarily qualified by human fallibility, faith provides certainty. Trying to keep on believing the strange doctrines of Christianity in the face of the constant whirlwind of ideological alternatives without the comfort of the Comforter and the fortification of the church—for all its faults—is to implicitly demand from God a psychological miracle, and God rarely honors demands for miracles. "Use the means I have given you" is God's customary reply to those who would prefer to go it alone.)

Spiritual disciplines—undertaken in, and assisted by, the creative power of the Holy Spirit of God—thus form us into properly functioning human beings in right relationship to God, ourselves, each other, and the rest of Creation. As such, and

---

51. I am indebted to my sometime colleague Gordon Fee for assuring me that many, even most, of the New Testament uses of "spiritual" ought to be capitalized as they refer to the Holy Spirit. See Gordon D. Fee, *God's Empowering Presence: The Holy Spirit in the Letters of Paul* (Peabody, MA: Hendrickson, 1994).

52. This theme of the necessity of the Holy Spirit supplying assurance that cannot be gained by even the most rigorous reasoning about religious matters is a constant theme in the testimonies of front-rank Christian philosophers: See Kelly James Clark, ed., *Philosophers Who Believe: The Spiritual Journeys of 11 Leading Thinkers* (Downers Grove, IL: InterVarsity, 1993); and Thomas V. Morris, ed., *God and the Philosophers: The Reconciliation of Faith and Reason* (New York and Oxford: Oxford UP, 1994).
See also John Dryden's exhortation:

"Thus Man by his own strength to Heaven would soar:
And would not be obliged to God for more.
Vain, wretched creature, how art thou misled
To think thy Wit these God-like notions bred!
These truths are not the product of thy mind,
But dropped from Heaven, and of a nobler kind.
Revealed religion first informed thy sight,
And *Reason* saw not till *Faith* sprung the light.
Hence all thy *Natural Worship* takes the *Source*:
'Tis *Revelation* what thou thinkst *Discourse*."
   (From *Religio Laici*, lines 67–76, [1682]; emphasis in original; I have modernized the spellings.)

unless God has a reason to direct us otherwise, we think better—of course we do.[53] The cognitive, moral, aesthetic, practical, and spiritual receptivity to all that God has to show us is the attitude of deferential acceptance and trust, the gift of the Holy Spirit known to all believers as *faith*. This entire epistemology, of course, rests on trusting God to show us what we need to know in order to fulfill our vocations. We cannot expect God to be gracious to us if we practice indifference (which is manifest in any sort of autonomy), let alone disobedience or resistance, to him. "There are things," Rodney Clapp observes with ironic mildness, "we can't actually know or see until we change our lives and adopt the appropriate perspective."[54]

If we lack wisdom, we ought to ask for it from God, who, the first chapter of the Epistle of James promises us, gives generously and never rebukes anyone for asking. But, James also warns, we must ask in faith. If we really want to learn something beyond what we already know, if we genuinely want God to show us new, unexpected truths and to form new, unexpected habits of mind, then we have to expect God will answer. And then we must receive what God subsequently sends us with grateful acceptance, to be truly willing to adapt our thinking to what God teaches us next. If, instead, we ask without being confident God will deliver on the promise of wisdom, we will remain conservatively resistant to anything that challenges our thinking, that directs us to any distinctly new way of thinking. We will especially shy away

---

53. So-called virtue epistemology has arisen of late as a way of offering a sort of assurance to interpreters: if you are the (morally, as well as intellectually) right sort of person performing the (morally, as well as intellectually) right sorts of interpretative tasks, then—well, then what? It cannot follow that you will come to certain knowledge. Virtue epistemology properly emphasizes the moral and spiritual dimensions of knowing in line with the typical deontological requirements of epistemology—and, indeed, in line with some of the recommendations made here—but I don't yet see what it adds to the conversation that ought not always to have been there. The logic of virtue epistemology also seems not to account for God's mysterious providence that sometimes, for a season and for an overriding good purpose, does not reward the faithful immediately with truth. For introductions to virtue epistemology, see W. Jay Wood, *Epistemology: Becoming Intellectually Virtuous* (Downers Grove, IL: InterVarsity, 1998) and Linda Trinkhaus Zagzebski, *Virtues of the Mind: An Inquiry into the Nature of Virtue and the Ethical Foundations of Knowledge* (Cambridge: Cambridge University Press, 1996). See also Alasdair McIntyre, *Dependent Rational Animals: Why Human Beings Need the Virtues* (Chicago: Open Court, 1999). William Alston happens to share my lack of enthusiasm: *Beyond "Justification,"* 3–4.

One more reason I prefer vocational framing of epistemology to virtue epistemology is as follows. Striving, as we ought, to be morally right persons performing morally right tasks is a useful approximation of what it means to be vocationally faithful—so long as we do not isolate "moral rightness" from "discipleship to Jesus Christ," as Bonhoeffer would warn we must not. Alas, virtue epistemology is easily construed as heroically moralistic, à la Kant. Thus virtue epistemology can—I certainly am not saying that it must; only that it can—miss the crucial element of existential reliance on the Holy Spirit to guide one's thinking in every moment. So Bonhoeffer's warning is of fundamental importance.

Virtue epistemology's concerns, therefore, coincide with mine, but the category of vocation seems to me to be much the preferable one in which to understand our work of thinking, since vocation, rather than virtue, is much the preferable way to understand Christian life.

54. Rodney Clapp, *Families at the Crossroads: Beyond Traditional and Modern Options* (Downers Grove, IL: InterVarsity, 1993), 121.

from anything that we find unpleasant or frustrating, let alone anything that calls us to repentance. Thus we will remain closed to God's gift, the gift for which we prayed. James is telling us the way creative thinking works: go to the source, open yourself to it, and receive what it gives.

Of course James doesn't expect us to dispense with all critical filters and to make ourselves vulnerable thereby to any of our own dark imaginings, let alone demonic counterfeits. He does, however, teach us a basic truth: attitude toward wisdom determines acquisition of wisdom. Those whose filters are set too high, so to speak, will receive nothing but slight modifications of their current ideas.[55] How could they receive anything else? They do not trust much, so they cannot learn much, just as Augustine warned: *nisi credideritis non intelligitis*.[56] The principle holds for the skier following her instructor down a mountain, or for the counselee facing some hard truth rendered by a psychologist, just as it does for the disciple following Jesus over one. Too much critical resistance to a person seeking to bless us with revelation of what he knows that we don't results in frustration and, at last, withdrawal. Thus Christian thinking really is "faith seeking understanding," as disciples of Jesus seek to become more and more aware of the cosmos so as to enjoy and obey God in it, and thus we proceed with an attitude of trustful expectation that God will, indeed, teach us all we need to know.

The Apostle Paul sets out a striking causal line of rightly ordered love prompting knowledge, insight, and discernment that blossoms in the shalom-making of our God-given vocation. Repeatedly in this discussion we have noted the intertwining of the affective and the evaluative with the cognitive. So does Paul. If our loves are oriented rightly, we are thereby disposed to see the world with increasing acuity and to act in it with increasing fitness.

> And this is my prayer: that your love may abound more and more in knowledge and depth of insight, so that you may be able to discern what is best and may be pure and blameless until the day of Christ, filled with the fruit of righteousness that comes through Jesus Christ—to the glory and praise of God.
>
> (Phil. 1:9–11)

Similarly, Thomas Dubay queries,

> If we were asked: "Who in this world (aside from God and his saints) understands you best?" most of us would designate the person who, in our judgment, loves us most deeply. The keener the love, the deeper the penetration.[57]

---

55. This is a theme in Søren Kierkegaard's reflections on 1 Corinthians 13 in *Works of Love* (1847).

56. Augustine, *City of God*, xii, 17. So Prov. 14:6: "The mocker seeks wisdom and finds none, but knowledge comes easily to the discerning" (TNIV).

57. Thomas Dubay, *The Evidential Power of Beauty: Science and Theology Meet* (San Francisco: Ignatius, 1999), 78.

"Love is blind," we say, but we refer to infatuation. Mature, deep, sustained love sees quite clearly, taking in all of the beloved because all is loved. (That is why Paul tells us that love must "endure all things" [1 Cor. 13:7], for love sees all things.) Hatred urges distortion, while indifference prompts sloppiness. Only caring deeply for a subject will bring one clarity about the subject.

Dietrich Bonhoeffer sounds a relevant pastoral—and epistemological— warning as he links the inner life with the outer, belief with action, faith with works:

> You complain that you cannot believe? No one should be surprised that they cannot come to believe so long as, in deliberate disobedience, they flee or reject some aspect of Jesus' commandment. You do not want to subject some sinful passion, and enmity, a hope, your life plans, or your reason to Jesus' commandment? Do not be surprised that you do not receive the Holy Spirit, that you cannot pray, that your prayer for faith remains empty! Instead, go and be reconciled with your sister or brother; let go of the sin which keeps you captive; and you will be able to believe again! If you reject God's commanding word, you will not receive God's gracious word. How would you expect to find community while you intentionally withdraw from it at some point? The disobedient cannot believe; only the obedient believe.[58]

Finally, it is generic human experience, not specifically Christian, to experience particularly the highest forms of thought as blessings from somewhere/someone else. In his masterful study of *Creativity*, Mihaly Csikszentmihalyi quotes innovator after innovator describing the emergence of a great idea in his or her imagination as the receiving of a gift, as the opening of a package in one's mind.[59] Whether believers in God or not, the predominant image of creativity was of receptivity. This receptivity was prepared by the acquisition of great learning, refined skill, and habits conducive to discovery, to be sure. There is much we can do, as we have seen throughout this book, to position ourselves in the best possible epistemic situation with the best possible skills and attitude. But good ideas remain a matter of *receptivity* rather than *manufacture*. Christians, who "praise God from whom all blessings flow," therefore will place a high priority on prayer and on all the other spiritual disciplines in order to position and condition ourselves, with the help of the Holy Spirit and our fellow believers, to be as receptive and responsible to God as possible.

---

58. Dietrich Bonhoeffer, *Discipleship*, ed. Geoffrey B. Kelly and John D. Godsey, trans. Barbara Green and Reinhard Krauss (Minneapolis: Fortress, 2001 [1937]), 66.

59. Csikszentmihalyi, *Creativity*. Margaret Atwood, not known for traditional Christian piety, testifies similarly: "It comes from the realm of gift....It can't be expected or demanded; rather it is granted, or else not. In theological terms it's a grace, proceeding from the fullness of being. One can pray for it, but one's prayer will not therefore be answered. If this were not so, there would never be any writer's block. The composition of a novel may be one part inspiration and nine parts perspiration, but that one part inspiration is essential if the work is to live as art" (*Negotiating with the Dead: A Writer on Writing* [Cambridge: Cambridge University Press, 2002], 69–70).

It is good to consider the work of the Holy Spirit in our lives. Yet in the wake of all this skepticism about how even experts—sometimes *especially* experts—make up their minds, how are *we*, whoever we might be, to make up our minds? Invoking the Holy Spirit doesn't obviously release us from what might appear to be our helpless incarceration in intellectual prisons constructed by the various layers of our successive and overlapping social contexts. We might *think* God's Spirit is helping us think aright, but we might also be deluding ourselves. So many people—including good people, smart people, admirable people—believe so many different things. Can we be sure, then, of nothing except the obvious and the self-referential? Can we really know whether we are butterflies dreaming we are humans, deluded victims of Cartesian evil demons, hallucinating brains in jars, or livestock-cum-batteries dreaming in the Matrix?

Alvin Plantinga shrugs off this storm of frightening doubt with the robust common sense of his Frisian forebears:

> Such Christian thinkers as Pascal, Kierkegaard, and Kuyper...recognize that there aren't any certain foundations of the sort Descartes sought—or, if there are, they are exceedingly slim, and there is no way to transfer their certainty to our important non-foundational beliefs about material objects, the past, other persons, and the like. This is a stance that requires a certain epistemic hardihood: there is, indeed, such a thing as truth; the stakes are, indeed, very high (it matters greatly whether you believe the truth); but there is no way to be sure that you have the truth; there is no sure and certain method of attaining truth by starting from beliefs about which you can't be mistaken and moving infallibly to the rest of your beliefs. Furthermore, many others reject what seems to you to be most important. This is life under uncertainty, life under epistemic risk and fallibility. I believe a thousand things, and many of them are things others—others of great acuity and seriousness—do not believe. Indeed, many of the beliefs that mean the most to me are of that sort. I realize I can be seriously, dreadfully, fatally wrong, and wrong about what it is enormously important to be right. That is simply the human condition: my response must be finally, "Here I stand; this is the way the world looks to me."[60]

In this attitude Plantinga follows in the cheerful train of Thomas Reid, the great Scottish philosopher who arguably stands with Kant among the most influential philosophers of modernity after Descartes. Interestingly, both Kant and Reid dwell at length on questions of skepticism, both of them having David Hume in mind.[61]

---

60. Plantinga, *Warranted Christian Belief*, 436–37.

61. In this interpretation of Reid, as in so much else, I follow Nicholas Wolterstorff: *Thomas Reid and the Story of Epistemology* (Cambridge: Cambridge University Press, 2001). In fairness to Hume, we must note that he himself dismisses radical (what he calls "Cartesian") doubt as

Reid, not unlike his Scottish counterpart, devotes a great deal of energy to demolishing what he sees to be a misguided approach to knowledge, which he terms the "Way of Ideas." Unfortunately for standard-brand modern philosophy, the Way of Ideas is not merely some odd little branch but the main trunk of epistemology from Descartes (and Locke) forward to Kant. The Way of Ideas, roughly speaking, is the basic scheme of perception by which the things "out there" somehow cause us to have ideas of them in our minds, and thus we form appropriate beliefs about them. Reid contends, startlingly, that this scheme fails to illuminate what is happening. In fact, Reid pulverizes this scheme as simply incoherent—an understanding so basic that most of us take it for granted, even if we could not actually explain it if asked. The "problem of the external world" remains intractable: We just don't know how we reliably get "in here" (in our minds) what is "out there" (in the world).[62]

Having set aside the Way of Ideas, Reid then stuns the reader again with this declaration: "I do not attempt to substitute any other theory in [its] place."[63] Reid asserts instead that it is a "mystery" how we form beliefs about the world that

---

intellectually intolerable: "It recommends a universal doubt, not only of all our former opinions and principles, but also of our very faculties, of whose veracity, say they, we must assure ourselves by a chain of reasoning deduced from some original principle which cannot possibly be fallacious or deceitful. But neither is there any such original principle which has a prerogative above others that are self-evident and convincing. Or if there were, could we advance a step beyond it but by the use of those very faculties of which we are supposed to be already diffident? The Cartesian doubt, therefore, were it ever possible to be attained by any human creature (as it plainly is not), would be entirely incurable, and no reasoning could ever bring us to a state of assurance and conviction upon any subject" (*An Inquiry concerning Human Understanding*, XII.1).

62. Dallas Willard manfully exposits difficult themes in Edmund Husserl's phenomenology in this regard on the question of the correspondence theory of truth, but, in my view, without overcoming Reid's fundamental skepticism regarding any such project of identifying a solid chain of phenomena from object to perception to conception. See "Toward a Phenomenology for the Correspondence Theory of Truth," which appears in print only in an Italian translation, "Verso una teoria fenomenologica della verita come corrispondenza," *Discipline Filosofiche* (Bologna) (I: 1991): 125–47; available online in English at http://www.dwillard.org/articles/artview.asp?artID=61; accessed on 1 February 2013. In fact, as C. S. Lewis and Philip Yancey argue, the problem for us is twofold: we encounter the world via our bodies and each experience must then be rendered into code (rendered as nerve impulses) that the brain must then assemble into meaning. Problems can attend, of course, either of those processes. See C. S. Lewis, "Transposition," in *The Weight of Glory and Other Addresses* (Grand Rapids, MI: Eerdmans, 1949), 18–19; Philip Yancey, *Disappointment with God: Three Questions No One Asks Aloud* (Grand Rapids, MI: Zondervan, 1988), 222–24.

63. Thomas Reid, *Essays on the Intellectual and Active Powers of Man*, 3 vols. (Dublin: P. Byrne & J. Milliken, 1790), vol. 1, 268 (I have modernized the punctuation): "I believe no man is able to explain how we perceive external objects, any more than how we are conscious of those that are internal. Perception, consciousness, memory, and imagination are all original and simple powers of the mind and parts of its constitution. For this reason, though I have endeavored to show that the theories of philosophers on this subject are ill grounded and insufficient, I do not attempt to substitute any other theory in their place."

actually do seem to correspond to the world as it is. (Our beliefs do seem to have the virtue of helping us negotiate that world pretty well.)

The epistemologist who has followed Reid to this point now might well be aghast. "What?" she might sputter. "You have destroyed the main scheme of modern Western epistemology only to say that you don't have anything better to offer in its place? What kind of philosopher are you?"

"A Christian one," Reid might reply. For Reid takes great comfort (as, we should recall, did Locke) in trusting God for creating the world such that human beings seem eminently well equipped to apprehend and live in it. Reid encourages readers therefore to thank God for this provision, this "bounty of heaven," and to obey God in confidence that God continues to provide the means (including the epistemic means) to do so.[64] Furthermore, Reid affirms, any other position than grateful acceptance of the fact that we believe the way we do just because that is the way we are is not just intellectually untenable, but (almost Biblically) foolish.[65]

Thus Thomas Reid dispenses with modern hubris on the one side and postmodern despair on the other. To those who would say, "I am certain I now sit upon this chair," Reid would reply, "Good luck proving that." To those who would say, "You just think you're sitting in a chair now, but in fact you could be anyone, anywhere, just imagining you are you sitting in a chair," he would simply snort and perhaps chastise them for their ingratitude for the knowledge they have gained so effortlessly by the grace of God.[66]

---

64. Reid, *Intellectual and Active Powers of Man*, vol. 3, 55: "That degree of power which we have received from the bounty of Heaven, is one of the noblest gifts of God to man; of which we ought not to be insensible, that we may not be ungrateful, and that we may be excited to make the proper use of it. The extent of human power is perfectly suited to the state of man, as a state of improvement and discipline."

65. Strikingly, at the end of his *magnum opus*, Michael Polanyi sounds a similar note: "I have arrived at the opening of this last chapter without having suggested any definite theory concerning the nature of things; and I shall finish this chapter without having presented any such theory. This book tries to serve a different and in a sense perhaps more ambitious purpose. Its aim is to re-equip men with the faculties which centuries of critical thought have taught them to distrust. The reader has been invited to use these faculties and contemplate thus a picture of things restored to their fairly obvious nature. This is all the book was meant to do" (*Personal Knowledge*, 381). For an even more recent rigorously commonsensical riposte to modern/postmodern agnosticism from another scientist-cum-epistemologist, see Stanley L. Jaki, *Means to Message: A Treatise on Truth* (Grand Rapids, MI: Eerdmans, 1999). Curiously, a detailed argument for extreme skepticism shares some of Jaki's premises regarding the fundamental commitment our language has to the reality of *things*, but then argues at length that we cannot make coherent sense of such language, ergo radical doubt is the only logical conclusion: Peter Unger, *Ignorance: A Case for Skepticism* (Oxford: Clarendon, 1975). Since Unger has also argued that he himself does not exist, on the basis of mereological nihilism ("I Do Not Exist," in *Perception and Identity*, ed. G. F. Macdonald [London: Macmillan, 1979]), I shall not pause to refute him. For a robust defense of realism from a quite different perspective, see Edward Pols, *Radical Realism: Direct Knowing in Science and Philosophy* (Ithaca, NY: Cornell University Press, 1992).

66. Pascal takes a similar line: "We know the truth not only through our reason but also through our hearts. It is through the latter that we know first principles, and reason, which has nothing to do with it, tries in vain to refute them. The skeptics have no other object than that,

The burden of proof, then, is put where it belongs: on the radical skeptic who has to show why we should doubt what seems so immediately evident, rather than on the believer who has to show why one ought to believe what seems effortless to believe.[67] Indeed, the burden of proof is also upon Locke to demonstrate why he is so confident of reason's ability to illuminate even the restricted territory he assigns it. Reid is dubious about all claims to such knowledge, even those as circumspect as Locke's. Darkness, Reid writes, is heavy upon all such investigations. We know through our own action that we are efficient causes of things; we know God is, too. More than this, however, we cannot say, since we cannot peer into the essences of things. Reid commends to us all sorts of inquiries, including scientific ones, but we will always be stymied at some level by the four-year-old's incessant question: "Yes, but why?" Such explanations always come back to questions of efficient causation, and human reason simply cannot lay bare the way things are in themselves so as to see how things do cause each other to be this or that way.

David Hume therefore was right on this score, Reid allows. But unlike Hume— very much unlike Hume—Reid is cheerful about us carrying on anyway with the practically reliable beliefs we generally do form, as God wants us to do. Far from being paralyzed by epistemological doubt, therefore, and far also from being inflamed by any epistemological chauvinism (as in "We men/women/whites/ blacks/heterosexuals/homosexuals see things better than you do"), Reid offers all of us a thankful epistemology of trust and obedience.

Let us consider, then, an awkward question. If, on the one hand, there is precious little certainty to be had and if, on the other hand, God can be relied upon to show us what he wants us to know, then why go to all the trouble of serious intellectual effort? Why read challenging books, and industriously seek out more? Why engage in rigorous conversation about difficult subjects? Why go to seminars, attend expensive schools, support Christian education in the church? Why work so hard at Christian thought?

---

and they work at it to no purpose. We know that we are not dreaming, but, however unable we may be to prove it rationally, our inability proves nothing but the weakness of our reason, and not the uncertainty of our knowledge, as they maintain. For knowledge of first principles, like space, time, motion, number, is as solid as any derived through reason, and it is on such knowledge, coming from the heart and instinct, that reason has to depend and base all its argument" (*Pensée* 110).

67. This approach is what William Alston claims should be meant by the term "naturalized epistemology" and "not the extreme version put on the map, unfortunately, by Quine in his too well known essay 'Epistemology Naturalized.'" Naturalized epistemology, Alston goes on, "is distinguished precisely by avoiding the temptation to play the skeptic's game. One declines to pursue epistemology as 'first philosophy,' an attempt to get conclusions as to what we know or how we know before we address ourselves to getting any knowledge about anything else. Instead, one approaches epistemology in the same 'natural' spirit as any other problem area— by working with any of our knowledge, beliefs, or assumptions that seem to be of relevance to the problems at hand; remembering, of course, that any of them can be called into question at a further stage of inquiry" (*Beyond "Justification,"* 8; see also Alston's impressive response to various forms of skepticism in the same volume, 191–229).

Christian tradition through the years has formulated the category of a "means of grace." This phrase denotes some vehicle, some instrument by which God conveys good things to his people. For most Christians a means of grace has been the Lord's Supper, in which Christ blesses his church as they worship in this way. For all Christians, the Bible has been a medium through which Christ nourishes his people. Preaching, music, prayer—all of these and many more have been recognized by Christians as means of grace.[68]

None of these means, however, are infallible guides to certain truth. People can receive communion and exit the church with hearts of stone. Bibles can be read only to be dissected into bits that confirm my prejudices and preferences or exhibited as inane and offensive elements of an atrocious religion.[69] Preaching can be ignored or mocked; hymns can be ridiculed as misguided or enjoyed merely as art; and prayer can be reduced to selfish begging or derided as psychotic babblings to an empty room. Even when undertaken in genuine faith, moreover, Bibles can still be misunderstood and misapplied, preaching can yet miss the mark, music can merely whip up emotion or reinforce misshapen piety—yet these means of grace have shown through the centuries that they are generally reliable sources of blessing. Despite our great capability to subvert and pervert even the finest of God's gifts, God continues to bless through the means he has ordained to do so, and we therefore rightly rely on them.

Could God not give us the results of these means more directly, bypassing them entirely? Perhaps he could—although in at least some cases it would be difficult to imagine just how things would work. Maybe, in fact, he cannot. Maybe we are such creatures as to benefit best, or at all, only by God blessing us through various intermediaries. Instant revision of our minds or souls might be too violent for us, or inauthentic, or *something* bad such that God must take, as God obviously generally does, the longer, indirect route.

Christian thought, I suggest, can be considered helpfully in this way. Responsible Christian thought gladly responds to the resources God has made available to it, and uses them well. We cannot choose what to believe, but we do in fact choose what resources we will consult, how rigorously we will consult them, how we will interpret their deliverances to us, and how we will connect that knowledge with what else we think we know. For that entire process we are entirely responsible.[70]

---

68. I have found suggestive this illuminating guide to the sacramental nature of the Word of God in Calvin: B. A. Gerrish, "The New Heir and the Sacramental Word," chap. in *Grace and Gratitude: The Eucharistic Theology of John Calvin* (Minneapolis: Fortress, 1993), 50–86.

69. We can note in passing that William Abraham uses the notion of "means of grace" in regard to Scripture in *Canon and Criterion in Christian Theology: From the Fathers to Feminism* (Oxford: Clarendon, 1998); John Webster briefly critiques this usage in *Holy Scripture: A Dogmatic Sketch* (Cambridge: Cambridge University Press, 2003), even as he later speaks of reading Scripture as "analogous" to receiving the sacraments (24–25; cf. 87).

70. My Regent College colleague Paul Helm has reflected fruitfully and far more subtly than I on such matters. See his *Belief Policies* (Cambridge: Cambridge University Press, 1994).

It certainly is not for us to dismiss these resources and disciplines because they do not work the way we might wish they would, either as media of instant knowledge or as purveyors of certain knowledge. Indeed, we might reconsider our wish for "instant knowledge" when we recognize that any direct "download" of knowledge would leave no traces to analyze for authenticity. (Think of those who have indeed claimed "instant messages" from God: Without the normal patterns and resources of Christian thinking by which to assess them, their validity would be literally invisible and unverifiable.)

More importantly, God simply "dropping" knowledge onto us would teach us nothing of faith: nothing of the fundamental lesson of the Christian life, which is to walk with God in continual dependence and cooperation. As Glenn Tinder avers, "When those who hope for salvation confess their objective uncertainty they are not confessing their cosmic peril but rather their entire dependence on God."[71] Of course God can tell us anything he wants us to know directly. He can use the telephone or e-mail as well as anyone else can. The fact that he rarely does send us such a direct message indicates that he is trying to accomplish more than the relaying of information in the process of our training. We need to remember that basic point, especially when we feel we are in crisis: If the need of the moment were for us to know something from God immediately, God would tell us immediately. God will not fail to enable us to fulfill our calling. When he doesn't, it mustn't be that God is unable or unwilling to help. God's overarching purpose with us includes teaching us how to be, as well as what to do. Thus the disciplines of responsible Christian thought really are means of grace, and not just intellectual grace, but person-shaping grace in much broader dimensions than the cognitive.

Likewise, in reckoning with the fact that these means of grace do not work infallibly and cannot deliver to us the certainty we might prefer they did, we also recognize gratefully that what the intellectual means of grace are supposed to do, they do well. They help us fulfill our vocations by reliably negotiating reality: predicting future events; confirming the rhythms of sowing and reaping; helping us reach destinations and other objectives; giving advice to others that seems genuinely to help them also; and so on. Indeed, one of the checks we can run on our decisions is to note their implications, actual or foreseen. If I conclude *A* rather than *B*, what follows? What will I then be obliged to feel or to do? Does this implication make sense, does it cohere well with what else I believe? If *A* seems instead to entail absurdity or, worse, evil, then I had better revisit my analysis, recheck my inferences, reexamine my heart, reflect on my circumstances, and resume my prayers. Thus do intuition and imagination once again come into service alongside reason: If what follows from my carefully considered conclusion seems nonetheless bad, then of course I must suspect myself of some bad thinking and reconsider.

Therefore it is not for us to recline in a lazy stupor or to retreat fearfully from the rigors of serious thought and expect God simply to hand us truth, as some Christian

---

71. Glenn Tinder, *The Fabric of Hope: An Essay* (Atlanta, GA: Scholars Press, 1999), 38.

dogmatists or mystics seem to expect.[72] These expectations reflect infantile attitudes: all receptivity, no activity, because no responsibility. Nor are we to act like clever adolescents, misusing our rational powers to mount radically skeptical attacks on all attempts to sort out truth from error, right from wrong, and the aesthetically valuable from junk, kitsch, or propaganda.[73] It is not for us to remain immature when God calls us to maturity through these disciplines. It is not for us to disobey God by ignoring or avoiding divinely sanctioned means. And it is especially odious to avoid the rigors of responsible Christian thinking in the name of piety. We trust God, yes, to do what God alone can do. But as God trains us in the glorious dignity of partnership, we do our part. And what is up to us to do is to position ourselves to look—*really* look—at the warrants we have in order to be persuaded by them; acquire the skills necessary to interpret them; locate ourselves in environments conducive to exploring and evaluating them; qualify our conclusions accordingly; and proceed gratefully into appropriate action.

The category of vocation returns to help us apply this model now to any reader's situation. For God expects of each of us what each of us can do in order to accomplish what God has called each of us to accomplish. Take, for example, Carolyn. She is responsible to know whatever she needs to know, and therefore to become the sort of person in the right set of circumstances to seek out the resources to learn what she needs to learn and decide what she needs to decide in order to fulfill her distinctive vocation. If her job is chemical engineering, guess what? She needs to learn chemical engineering and pursue that profession—in its ethical as well as its scientific implications—with a Christian mind. She is also, of course, someone's daughter, likely someone's sister, maybe someone's spouse or mother, and certainly the neighbor and colleague of many others. She is responsible then to learn what she needs to learn according to the resources available to her in order to think as she needs to think so that she can fulfill her calling among these people in that patch of the globe: to cultivate all the shalom she can and to make disciples of Jesus Christ as effectively as she can.

---

72. As Galileo writes, "I do not think one has to believe that the same God who has given us senses, language, and intellect would want to set aside the use of these and give us by other means the information we can acquire with them, so that we would deny our senses and reason even in the case of those physical conclusions which are placed before our eyes and intellect by our sensory experiences or by necessary demonstrations" ("Letter to the Grand Duchess Christina [1615]," in *The Galileo Affair: A Documentary History*, ed. Maurice Finocchiaro [Berkeley and Los Angeles: University of California Press, 1989], 94). Calvin anticipates him brusquely in his commentary on Genesis: "He who would learn astronomy, and other recondite arts, let him go elsewhere [than the Bible]" (John Calvin, *Commentaries on the First Book of Moses Called Genesis*, trans. John King [Edinburgh: Banner of Truth, 1975], 42).

73. For another contemporary Christian philosophical defense of critical realism against radical skepticism, see William Alston's discussion of valid "doxastic practices" as he follows in the train of Thomas Reid against Descartes and Hume: "A 'Doxastic Practice' Approach to Epistemology," chap. in *Perceiving God: The Epistemology of Religious Experience* (Ithaca, NY: Cornell University Press, 1991), 146–83.

Another example: Gordon is an Ottawa schoolteacher, a single dad, a hockey coach, a Neighborhood Watch block captain, a taxpayer, a voter, a golf buddy, a Bible study participant, and the only child of aging parents. He does not need to know what is happening on Broadway this season. He might enjoy following New York theater, but he obviously is not obliged by his calling to do so. He does not need to understand the latest trends in Milanese fashion, or the Mayo Clinic's preferred treatment course for myocardial infarction, or Monaco's odds on the next Grand Prix, or Mozambique's political situation. In fact, his calling—matched to his strengths and weaknesses, opportunities and limitations—actually requires him to know nothing about, and contribute nothing toward, most of what happens across the globe. Moreover, he must guard against the vague sense that he is somehow obliged to "know what's going on in the world" if it compels him to watch a lot of news on TV or to spend hours surfing the Web in place of learning and deciding about what is indeed part of his vocation, whether new methods of teaching, the next phase of his daughters' social development, the best assignment of roles to this year's team, and so on.

Christians sometimes endure their particular versions of such misplaced "obligation" to know literally more than they actually need to know. So, for example, Gordon does not have to undertake the Herculean task of learning about all of the world's religions and philosophies in order to be ready to share the Gospel with any person who crosses his path. Nor must he have resolved every oddity in the Bible or developed a dazzling reply to every atheist's challenge. He is instead obliged to know, yes, *what he needs to know* in order to do what he (particularly) needs to do: share the life and light of Christ with the people who actually do cross his path. And since he cannot possibly be a walking encyclopedia of the world's ideological options—even friends of mine who have written textbooks of the world's religions do not consider themselves experts on them all—God will not waste Gordon's time or the other person's by bringing Gordon together with someone he does not understand for what cannot help but be a frustrating or trivial conversation. No, God equips us, and works with us as we equip ourselves, for what God has shown us to be our vocation. To be sure, God might well place us in a surprising conversation for which we feel unprepared, but either we have indeed been prepared to play the particular role intended for us to play (perhaps we have been placed there to be kind or sympathetic or humble, rather than merely knowledgeable about the other person's religion!) or God is introducing us through that encounter into a new zone of learning and service. Either way, however, we trust God to guide us and we prepare ourselves according to that guidance. What else, as I have asked before, can we reasonably and responsibly do?

Experts, therefore, are properly held to the standards of their particular brand and level of expertise. The rest of us, however, and all of us outside our narrow zones of expertise, must use the resources available to us to tackle the problems presented to us according to our abilities and limitations. Yes, maybe we need to stretch more than we do, making use of resources that truly are available to us that we have heretofore underutilized, whether local libraries, acquaintances with relevant expertise, websites, books, and so on that have always been there while we have been insufficiently motivated to consult them. But one of the key characteristics of this vocational model of epistemology is that it expands and shrinks according to the person using it—in her particular circumstances, according to her particular gifts, in the light of her particular vocation. Since the objective is to fulfill as best we can God's generic call to human beings to maximize shalom and God's specific call to make disciples, and since God has equipped and deployed each of us quite intentionally to be and to do what each of us particularly can be and do, then each of us uses the resources we can obtain, as responsibly as we can, in order to do God's will—trusting God thereby never to under-resource any of us. We each need to know, that is, whatever we particularly need to know. And God can be relied upon fully to teach us—but on a "need to know" basis.[74]

Dietrich Bonhoeffer emphasizes the profoundly existential nature of our reliance on God's guidance, God's direction, God's commandment:

> The commandment of God is not, in distinction from the ethical, the most general summation of all ethical rules. It is not timeless and generally valid as opposed to being historical and temporal. It is not the principle as opposed to its application, not the abstract as opposed to the concrete, not the indeterminate as opposed to the determinate. If it were anything of the kind, it would have ceased to be the commandment of *God*. For each case would then be up to us to turn the indeterminate into the determinate, the principle into the application, the timeless into the temporal. At precisely the crucial point it would no longer be the commandment that is decisive, but instead our understanding, our interpretation, our application. Then the commandment of God would again have become our own choice.... Does this mean that in every moment of our lives we could come to know the will of God through some kind of special, direct divine inspiration, that in every moment God would unmistakably and unambiguously mark a specific action, as willed by God, with the "accent of eternity"? No, this is not what it means. For the concreteness of the divine commandment consists in its historicity; it encounters us in historical form. Does this now mean that we are after all, with a final uncertainty, at the mercy of all sorts of claims that historical powers place on us, that with regard to God's commandments we actually grope around in the dark? No, this is not what it means, precisely because God makes the commandment heard in a specific, historical form.[75]

---

74. I have come to the conclusion that every good idea I have ever had has been anticipated by C. S. Lewis. The particular point at hand, many readers will recognize, is portrayed frequently in *The Chronicles of Narnia*, as Aslan reveals to particular characters aspects of their own life stories while refusing pointedly and explicitly to discuss any other character's story.

75. Dietrich Bonhoeffer, *Ethics*, ed. Clifford J. Green, trans. Reinhard Krauss, Charles C. West, and Douglas W. Stott (Minneapolis: Fortress, 2005 [1949]), 378–79.

So what does it mean? Bonhoeffer adds the following advice:

> Intellect, cognitive ability, and attentive perception of the context come into lively play here. All of this discerning will be encompassed and pervaded by the commandment. Prior experiences will raise encouraging or cautionary notes. Under no circumstances must one count on or wait for unmediated inspirations, lest all too easily one fall prey to self-deception. Given the matter at hand, an intensely sober attitude will govern the discerning. Possibilities and consequences will be considered carefully. In short, in order to discern what the will of God may be, the entire array of human abilities will be employed. But in all of this there will be no place for the torment of being confronted with insoluble conflicts, nor the arrogance of being able to master any conflict, nor also the enthusiastic expectation and claim of direct inspirations. There will be faith that, to those who humbly ask, God will surely make the divine will known.[76]

As a corollary of what we have seen about God making that divine will known, moreover, we develop the humble habit of *hesitation* in what Glenn Tinder calls "the prophetic stance." Instead of self-confidently, even self-righteously, leaping into the fray with the false certainty of our own prejudices, intuitions, or cogitations, we practice a posture of receptivity and expectancy, waiting upon God—not as a way of avoiding decision and action, but as the way of enjoying God's assistance in both.[77]

As a modest exercise in imagination, we might consider our epistemic situation thus. The data we are considering in a given instance are multicolored stars we view out the various ports and monitors of a spaceship. We can go in any direction; we just need to know in which direction to go. Green stars mean "come here"; red stars mean "stay away"; yellow stars mean "be careful of this"; and white stars are neutral. In a complex and ambiguous situation, the starscape is varied, with stars of each color in each sector of the sky. Moreover, we can see only the stars we can see—we cannot account for the unimaginably large number of stars beyond our view. So what do we do?

Some people would see our epistemic situation as one in which we scan for a singular sector in which there are nothing but bright green stars thickly grouped with only black empty space around it. Ambiguity disturbs such people; only certainty (or, at least, certitude) will do. So they look and look for that single, clearly correct option. Perhaps they find it. Or perhaps they squint so hard that they don't see the yellow and red stars nearby or mixed in, and they congratulate themselves on finding nothing but green.

I suggest instead that our *modus operandi* be to seek a *preponderance* of green stars in a particular direction. If we are in the happy circumstance of seeing nothing but green, then, of course, off we go. Normally, however, we have only *mostly* green lights ahead of us even in optimal situations, and maybe not all that many of them.

---

76. Bonhoeffer, *Ethics*, 323–24.

77. Glenn Tinder, *The Political Meaning of Christianity: An Interpretation* (Baton Rouge: Louisiana State University Press, 1989), esp. 68–80.

Yet that is all we need for now. Once we have those in sight, we head for them while keeping our eyes open for changes in the pattern that might prompt us to alter course.[78]

If we don't see yet a nice field of green, at least we steer well away from banks of red stars and keep our distance from clusters of yellow ones. And if we simply have no sense of direction, we wisely stop. We may be able to stop for quite a while—we may have plenty of provisions, other things to do, and no urgent need to arrive at a decision. It would be more intelligent not to decide than to proceed to a wrong decision such that we will later have the trouble of extricating ourselves and making our way more laboriously to a better option. Often, in fact, the wisest position to take on a matter is to remain in doubt.[79] (So much time has been wasted, and so much anguish has been endured, in trying to harmonize a particular scientific consensus with a particular interpretation of the Bible, only for one view, or both, later to be discarded. History gives one perspective on the unwisdom of hurrying to a conclusion in matters on which the relevant knowledge is not, in fact, yet available.)[80]

Often, however, we cannot enjoy the luxury of suspending our decision, and we must move. Circumstances compel us onward. We can do, therefore, only what we can do. We don't demand that the universe arrange itself in utterly clear patterns. We don't insist that any option we elect be warranted beyond doubt by abundant and unambiguous evidence. We look at the options available to us and pick what seems to be the best one. All we can responsibly do is steer by the stars we have.

In so steering, we trust God, recognizing that God recognizes us: our limitations, our tendencies, our drives, our fears. God guides us accordingly, and works with and beyond our limitations so as to bring us from place to place according to the beneficent divine plan revealed, piecemeal but adequately, in the data God sets before us. Most of the time, God helps us simply to do well what we would ordinarily do: head for the green and away from the red. Sometimes, however, God knows that the best way forward is actually to head for that peculiar range of yellow over there instead, the one dangerously

---

78. Despite the "space age" conceit I am using, this emphasis on "preponderance," or what what we might also call "probability," is commended in Christian thought at least as far back as Joseph Butler, *The Analogy of Religion* (1736).

79. Lady Reason cautions her acolyte thus: "Can you not remain in doubt?"

"I don't know that I have ever tried."

"You must learn to, if you are to come far with me" (C. S. Lewis, *The Pilgrim's Regress: An Allegorical Apology for Christianity, Reason and Romanticism* (San Francisco: Fount, 1998 [1953]), 76.

80. I recognize that this deferring could be used as an excuse for avoiding the hard work of reconciling apparently conflicting resources in one's mind and particularly for holding, say, to Christian faith in the teeth of powerful arguments to the contrary. I have already averred, however, that one is obliged to respond to apparent defeaters of one's views, religious or otherwise, as competently as one can. The range of competent responses yet does include deferral, of coming to the considered judgment that there are not yet strong enough grounds to resolve the apparent conflict and that the cost of forcing a conclusion is unwarrantedly high. One would be obliged to make a valid argument for *that* response, of course, on pain of being guilty of merely dodging the question. But in at least some situations one surely could, and should, do so.

close to the frightening red patch. Since we would not make that decision in the natural course of things, God intervenes supernaturally, adding information to the system whether by way of a sudden report from another ship that has just traversed that route successfully; or by a last-minute upgrade of our scanners that helps us see the wealth of green stars beyond the closer yellow ones; or by some other unexpected means. Other times, of course, the problem lies not in any ambiguity of data or interpretation, but in ambivalence of will. We might know all too well where the truth seems to lie, but we hesitate because we recognize, consciously or unconsciously, that to accede to that truth will entail sacrifice. We thus need moral assistance from God to embrace what we would strongly prefer to ignore or abhor. Christians believe in a personal deity who loves us, so God can be counted upon to provide guidance and power whenever and however necessary to help us—each of us, as distinct individuals and communities—get where we are supposed to go and do what we are supposed to do along the way.[81]

I recognize that this proposal seems a long way from the popular Christian sentiment, "The Bible says it; I believe it; that settles it." It also has moved away from more sophisticated forms of Christian thought, rooted as they are in the Enlightenment and modernity's epistemological confidence. To be sure, much of this confidence arose out of sincere Christian convictions about a rational God who made an orderly world and equipped human reason to understand what he had made. And this proposal shares some of that confidence in that it values reason and experience as genuine means of grace.

This proposal, however, takes other things more radically into account, whether the realities of intellectual pluralism and postmodernity in the culture at large, or sin in the hearts *and minds* of us all. It tries to keep, from a faithfully Christian point of view, first things first.[82] It does not promise certain knowledge. Following this scheme will not, I say one last time, render Christian thinking infallible. But this epistemology does promise God's sufficient provision for the basic calling of every Christian.[83] It trades fundamentally on faith, hope, and love. And that is enough.

---

81. Polanyi himself concludes, "I accept these accidents of personal existence as the concrete opportunities for exercising our personal responsibility. *This acceptance is the sense of my calling*" (*Personal Knowledge*, 322; emphasis in original). And David Ford adds this word of encouragement: "The root activity of all Christian life is calling out: 'Come, Holy Spirit!' The trust is that God will always give sufficient power for what he wants done: the loving that we are called to do this minute" (David F. Ford, *The Shape of Living* [London: HarperCollins, 1997], 57). And, I suppose, this passage in particular is my reply to William James, "The Will to Believe," in *The Will to Believe and Other Essays in Popular Philosophy* (New York: Dover, 1956 [1896]), 1–31.

82. As Emil Brunner puts it, "The being of man as person depends not on his thought but on his responsibility, upon the fact that a supreme Self calls to him and communicates Himself to him" (*Truth as Encounter*, trans. Amandus W. Loos and David Cairns [London: SCM, 1964 (1938)], 19). And Peter L. Berger argues magisterially for a vulnerable but effective nexus of faith, knowledge, community, institutions, and action in "Protestantism and the Quest for Certainty," *The Christian Century* 115 (August 26, 1998): 782–96.

83. Thomas Merton reminds us, "You must trust in God, who 'writes straight on crooked lines' and brings great good out of evil. What matters . . . is not for you . . . to be always infallibly

For on that great day, no sensible person will hope to hear from our Master a commendation such as, "Good for you! You figured it out. Aren't you clever."[84]

Instead, we will yearn to hear the strong, soft music of this blessing: "Well done, thou good and faithful servant. Enter thou into the joy of thy Lord."

---

right, but for you to be heroically faithful to grace and to love. If God calls you to Him, then He implicitly promises you all the graces you need to reach Him" (Thomas Merton, *New Seeds of Contemplation* [New York: New Directions, 1961], 244).

84. Søren Kierkegaard writes, "What I really lack is to be clear in my mind *what I am to do*, not what I am to know, except in so far as a certain understanding must precede every action. The thing is to understand myself, to see what God really wishes *me* to do; the thing is to find a truth which is true *for me*, to find *the idea for which I can live and die*. What would be the use of discovering so-called objective truth, of working through all the systems of philosophy and of being able, if required, to review them all and show up the inconsistencies of each system... [and] what good would it do me to be able to explain the meaning of Christianity if it had *no* deeper significance *for me and for my life*...?" (*The Journals of Søren Kierkegaard*, trans. and ed. Alexander Dru [London: Oxford University Press, 1959], 14–15).

Appendix

A SKETCH OF THE MODEL AT WORK

I have detailed elsewhere both my understanding of gender and how I arrived at it. Here I would like to use it briefly as an example of this epistemology at work.[1]

I begin with the five resources: experience, tradition, scholarship, art, and Scripture. I was raised in a family in which gender roles were typical of middle-class, white Canadians of the 1960s. My father was a busy physician whose non-medical time was spent largely at church as an elder of our small congregation, in sports, and at home with us. My mother was at least as busy as a full-time homemaker mothering four children while also pursuing, as the years went on, both university education and extensive volunteer work at church and on civic artistic and educational boards. By the time of my early adulthood, I was being taught by very few women: almost all of my teachers in my last two years of high school were male, and I did not have a single female professor in my entire formal educational experience. Yet I had experienced female leadership in the ecclesial and spiritual sectors of my life: an unusually assertive and capable mother, yes, but also an impressive group of aunts, an able sponsor to my high school Christian club, wise and articulate staff members in my university Christian organization, and a growing number of women writing persuasive books and articles about gender. I also, of course, had become friends with, and occasionally fallen in love with, some young women who were easily the equal of any man I knew in terms of intelligence, insight, prudence, creativity, and initiative.

Meanwhile, Western culture in the 1970s and 1980s was replete with women who gave the lie to the old gender stereotypes, not least British prime minister Margaret Thatcher. Feminism was *de rigueur* among the university people I most admired. Women were breaking through glass ceilings all around me. In the category of experience, therefore, I had increasing grounds to think that whatever

---

1. *Finally Feminist: A Pragmatic Christian Understanding of Gender* (Grand Rapids, MI: Baker Academic, 2005); "How to Produce an Egalitarian Man," chap. in *How I Changed My Mind about Women in Leadership: Compelling Stories from Prominent Evangelicals*, ed. Alan F. Johnson (Grand Rapids, MI: Zondervan, 2010), 235–43.

real differences might differentiate men and women, women ought not to be excluded from positions of influence and authority because of their sex.

Tradition, of course, was generally against gender equality—both social tradition and church tradition. My own family was clearly—which is to say, officially—headed by my father. To be sure, my mother ran the household, and by the time I was an adolescent it was obvious how she could and did direct my father on various matters. Still, the party line in our family was patriarchy, and it was a line echoed in my church's teaching and practice and in Canadian society at large, however much the old norms were changing before our eyes.

Tradition, however, always presented an ambiguous category to me. Our church reflexively observed its own traditions, of course, but among those traditions was a radical break with mainstream ecclesiastical patterns. We had no ordained clergy. We had an extremely low view of the sacraments, with just any group of Christians encouraged to "break bread" as they felt led by the Spirit to do so. We had a dim view of the spiritual validity and vitality of most other denominations. And we differed conspicuously on such cultural norms as playing card games or attending school dances. Thus among our most basic traditions was a Biblicism that stood ready to challenge any tradition—even, at least in theory, our own. That tradition would stand me in good stead, ironically enough, as I later decided to break with that group regarding gender precisely once I became convinced that the Bible warranted such a break.

Scholarship on gender was increasingly available to me in the later 1970s and 1980s, and particularly from the evangelical community I was most willing to trust. When I began doctoral studies at the Divinity School of the University of Chicago in the mid-1980s, I entered an intellectual environment in which feminism was taken quite definitively for granted. Indeed, it was here that I encountered for the first time the proposal that lesbianism was the logical outcome of a consistent feminism in which heterosexual relations were construed as just one more way in which men sought to subjugate women to their (that is, our) own nefarious purposes. Such debatable extrapolations notwithstanding, it seemed merely obvious in the culture of first-rank universities that women were demonstrably just as "smart" as men, just as able to lead, and so on, in whatever scholarly discourse one cared to enter. (A woman, university President Hanna Holborn Gray, handed me my doctoral diploma at the end of my studies.) Still, most of the evangelical theological literature available by the mid-1980s was patriarchalist, so evangelical feminism had to make its way academically against a strong tribal counter-current.

I remember art functioning for me in this regard mainly at a popular level, generally ignorant as I was of higher culture. (I could not have distinguished Isadora Duncan from Georgia O'Keeffe, much less Simone de Beauvoir.) Movies and television programs were shifting to portrayals of women as independently capable and no longer confined to the responsive, collateral, even decorative roles typical of even the recent past. Spunky but still deferential Mary Richards of *The Mary Tyler Moore Show* had given way to tough female detectives on *Cagney and Lacey*, although it would be another decade before leading ladies even as strong as Jodie

Foster and Meryl Streep would emerge into roles of powerful female agency. Authors Margaret Atwood and Margaret Laurence, however, had figured prominently in my courses in Canadian literature, and these displayed minds not to be trifled with. So my limited exposure to art at the time was nudging me out of patriarchy little by little, even as men still utterly dominated both the production and the substance of most of the art I had taken in by then.

Finally, Scripture. Two crucial considerations made a difference for me in moving from a patriarchalist view to a feminist one. First, I recognized that some Scriptures, including some at the very center of the gender debate, seemed impossible to explain easily *by anyone*. Paul's command to women to veil themselves when they pray and prophesy seemed difficult, to say the least, to square with his command a few chapters later in the same epistle to be silent in church (1 Corinthians 11 and 14). Paul's rationale(s) for women's subordination appeared almost bizarre in the *locus classicus* of 1 Timothy 2:11–15, which is likely why the passage has provoked such a wide range of ingenious explanations.

I had not previously encountered this sort of irreducible hermeneutical complexity. I began to think, then, that the theological task ought to be reframed: from getting it all right, with every item finding its comfortable place in a seamless array of nicely fitted elements to selecting the best construal, the one that seems to deal with the most elements, and particularly those that seem most important, in the way that makes the most sense of everything I know and particularly of what the Scripture says. Instead of stopping dead whenever I was faced with a Scriptural phrase I could not readily fit into my scheme, I was charged instead with the responsibility of selecting the best interpretative option of those available if one of those options seemed clearly superior to the others and made good sense of the preponderance of data, and especially of the key data, available.

The second crucial consideration about Scripture was provoked by the phrase "the whole counsel of God" (Acts 20:27). Instead of depending on a few key passages in Paul's epistles, important as they were, the responsible interpreter was charged with making sense of the whole canon of Scripture in regard to gender. That meant that not only apostolic commands, but law, prophecy, wisdom, gospel, history, and apocalyptic needed to be taken into account as well. And when the frame of reference broadened to include even just Paul's treatment of women, rather than just a selection of his commands about or to them, the questions shifted. Why would Paul speak as he did to, and about, prominent women in the early church, treating them as if they were leaders and colleagues? Why did Jesus, who was himself male and appointed only males to the Twelve, say and do what he said and did in regard to women, frequently transgressing gender lines to the scandal of onlookers? Why did Leviticus, of all books of the Bible, seem to render a strangely double view of women: as both subordinate to, and even lesser than, men, as one would expect in an ancient near eastern law code, but also as fully equal to men?

Intuitively, I was disquieted by patriarchy, not least because I had married a woman who I felt was certainly my equal at the very least and who had made her own decisive break with patriarchy on the basis of strong spiritual and moral convictions, even as she couldn't satisfy my exegetical questions. And I did have exegetical questions, investigation on behalf of which led to the intuition that something was wrong with the state of the debate as late as the 1990s: the traditionalists were simply refining their views while the egalitarians seemed to be trying to explain (away) one apparently restrictive Bible passage at a time (here an interpolation, there a mistranslation).

Scholarship in terms of church history and the theology of providence arose alongside my Biblical studies. How to make sense of the church's general endorsement of patriarchy over two thousand years, a pattern that yet was studded with exceptions to the rule, and especially in situations of maximum spiritual heat in which traditions were rendered fluid—as in missionary expansion and revival? How to respect our ecclesial forebears as themselves attentive to the Holy Spirit, the Spirit who seemed now to be telling us to set aside patriarchy but seemed not to be saying it to the vast majority of Christians in almost all of the Christian past? What model of gender would make sense of this experience of the church and of God's wise providence over it?

Imaginatively, then, I wondered what the church would look like if women were encouraged to preach, to lead in worship, to serve in pastoral work, and so on. While fellow church members would routinely declaim, "I just can't imagine a women preaching," I certainly could. And it seemed increasingly to be only right that they should. I also wondered imaginatively: what would the theological data look like if everyone involved were somehow right? Instead of trying to prove one side or another alone faithful and true, especially since I knew people of manifestly good will and intelligence on every side of the debate, what construal of gender would make sense of all the good arguments being rendered in the conversation?

My social location also inclined me strongly to such an agenda, teaching as I now was (by 1998) at an evangelical theological school that harbored both professors and students across the spectrum of views. A model of gender that would treat all reasonable participants in the debate with respect would certainly be better accepted at Regent College than would an all-or-nothing model of a kind undoubtedly socially advantageous for someone teaching at a school at one or the other end of the theological spectrum. And as I worked away at the lectures that would eventually become my book on the subject, my mind's eye constantly would visualize good friends and colleagues of this or that conviction, and I would temper my writing accordingly to be sure to give them their due.

The best available model at the time was something called a "redemptive movement hermeneutic" that saw an upward trajectory in Scripture toward the ever-more-equal status of women.[2] It was coupled with intensive work on various texts problematic to a feminist reading by Biblical scholars who seemed to be pursuing a

---

2. See William J. Webb, *Slaves, Women and Homosexuals* (Downers Grove, IL: InterVarsity, 2001).

strategy of reinterpreting them one by one in order to render them unproblematic at least, and actually supportive at best, to an egalitarian reading.[3]

I continued to find this approach problematic, however, as it seemed to me that (a) the upward movement in Scripture wasn't all that upward, as Jesus and Paul seemed yet to manifest decidedly patriarchalist patterns; (b) if it took a Ph.D. in classical or Biblical studies to decode what a New Testament author meant in this or that passage, the Holy Spirit had been strangely obscure in the work of inspiration; and (c) the Church for two thousand years had been reading the Bible generally in a patriarchalist way, so why was this generation suddenly enlightened as to the Bible's single trajectory regarding gender, especially when perhaps our views could be explained by the oft-advanced charge of sheer capitulation to liberal culture?

I needed, then, a conceptual alternative, and when it occurred to me that the Bible might in fact be saying what everyone was saying—both patriarchalist and egalitarian (to simplify a complex situation)—I found it. I posited a *double* message in Scripture, a pattern that did indeed validate women as originally and ultimately equal in dignity and ability with men while conceding to the universal patriarchy of human societies—ameliorating that patriarchy, to be sure, even as it also complied with it rather than pressing too hard, too fast, on this social norm. Scripture included many clues as to the quality of women, that is, even as God did not press ancient Israel nor the early church to what would have been a social revolution of a highly disruptive sort. In the modern era, however, as activists (many of them motivated by Biblical principles) advanced the cause of women and society responded, the reasons to comply with patriarchy (e.g., women were refused the same education as men; laws didn't protect women in regard to divorce, property, or even standing before the courts; people generally harbored views of women's capacities that prevented them from accepting a female authority) fell away. Pushing too early and too much for women's equality, which would have scandalized society and thereby drastically reduced its openness to the gospel message—a situation in which women's rights would have been the focus of attention, rather than the good news of salvation—had become in the present era the scandal of refusing to recognize women's rights that were everywhere else acknowledged.

This paradigm seemed to make better sense of the Bible—of the whole Bible—than any other I had encountered. It seemed to make better sense of church history: At the bright, blazing edge of renewal, gender roles melted away, only to be restored when each movement had to "cool off" and make its way in the social mainstream. It seemed to explain why egalitarianism made sense in this society while it had not in others: We were not more spiritual or more intelligent than our forebears; rather, the modern social situation positioned us to see more fully the Biblical teaching regarding women's equality. It seemed to make better sense of our current social

---

3. See Ronald W. Pierce, Rebecca Merrill Groothuis, and Gordon D. Fee, eds., *Discovering Biblical Equality: Complementarity without Hierarchy* (Downers Grove, IL: InterVarsity, 2004).

experience of leadership teams being enriched by the presence of women alongside men, as well as the more obvious benefits of opening leadership positions to individual women and avoiding the scandal of refusing opportunities to serve merely on the basis of sex.

I tried out the model on well-informed friends of various viewpoints, including theological experts of a complementarian outlook, as well as in public lectures before audiences of diverse views of gender. Such interaction helped me refine the model, and while none of the theologically expert complementarians immediately converted to my view (!), I was encouraged by their reception of the model as both respectful of the arguments they were making and not easily amenable to refutation. The model has since been tested in the field, so to speak, and has met with some success as both individuals and entire congregations have communicated with me that reading the resulting book convinced them to make a decisive move to egalitarianism. Not every reader has been so convinced, of course. But many have found the model to do what it is supposed to do: provide grounds for those who *want* to remove gender barriers to women in churches, families, and society at large, and who want to do so with confidence that they *can* do so as responsible Christian thinkers. (To be completely explicit, I do not think that many people can be argued out of or into a view of something as personally involving as gender, but at best can only be given grounds on which to make a move they already intuitively want to make.)

The model, to be sure, remains vulnerable to criticism. A particular exegetical sticking point is that the argument from creation order *as advanced by the Apostle Paul* seems to militate against egalitarianism. Paul still seems to me to be saying that women's subordination to men arises out of the story of pristine creation in Genesis 2 (which does not seem to me to teach anything like subordination), as well as the story of the fall in Genesis 3 (1 Tim. 2:13–14). So I cannot claim that all the stars are green, so to speak, in the direction of my model. But I do claim that the preponderance of green indicators—including the rest of the Pauline corpus regarding gender—lie in this direction, so it is in this direction that I continue to steer.

INDEX OF SUBJECTS

charismatic, 8, 13, 45, 180n79
Christendom, 42, 64–5
Church, 62, 187–89, 226–27
   and authority, 10–11
   and biblical interpretation, 6–7, 126
   and canon formation, 113
   congregations, 174
   ecumenicity, 176
   mission of the, 75–80
   and patriarchy, 83
   and theology, 175, 184–85
   tradition of the, 18, 102, 104–6
communism, 28, 189
compartmentalization, 4–5, 14, 18n21
confidence, 16, 18, 21, 28, 30, 32, 165–66,
     170–71, 196, 204–5
   and certainty, 210–11
   Christian, 71–72, 81, 149, 233,
     242, 250
   definition of, 215
   and modernity, 39–41, 55, 71
   and postmodernity, 41, 43–44, 46
   of Romanticism, 35, 40
   in science, 40
conflict, 150–51, 159, 192, 240, 241n80
   among intellectuals, 137
   between faith and reason, 107–8, 127
   between Scripture and theology,
     149n18
conservatism, 5–16, 29, 53n41, 55, 135
conversion, 31–32, 84, 161–62, 171–72,
     179, 209
   and community, 218–19n35
   and evangelism, 81
   and syncretism, 159
councils, 6, 8n8, 11, 106n31
creation, 67, 73, 226–27, 250
   in Biblical narrative, 58, 61, 66, 85n34
   and evolution, 15, 37
   and Genesis, 147
   and humanity, 68–71
   and the sciences, 107
Creation Commandments, 76–77, 79–80
creeds, 105, 123, 174, 178n73
   Apostle's Creed, 104
   Athanasian Creed, 104
   Nicene Creed, 89–90n6, 104
culture, 18, 27–30, 42–46, 54–55, 192
   capitulation to, 14
   definition of, 194n106

deconstruction, 12n12, 50–51, 53n41,
     189–90, 213
   and Derrida, 45–46n27
denominations, 7, 111, 185
   and authority, 126, 199
   and tradition, 15, 223, 246
deontology, 228n53
dichotomy, 16, 113n38
discernment, 9, 13, 195, 229, 240
   spiritual, 56, 137
discipleship, 27, 56, 61–62, 122, 228n53
   political, 65
disciplines, academic. See scholarship
disciplines, spiritual, 79, 224–25, 227, 230
doctrine. See theology
doubt, 7, 20, 28, 34, 95, 146–47, 170n58, 209,
     223, 227, 231–32, 241
   benefits of, 205, 209
   and burden of proof, 234
   and the Fall, 58–59
   and intuition, 130n68
   and mystical experience, 99
   and postmodernity, 38, 43–44, 51, 55, 87
   and science, 178n75

economics, 36–37, 139, 172, 178n75, 180n79,
     182, 195, 199, 215
   and Biblical interpretation, 17
   economic pluralism, 23, 54,
   and the Enlightenment, 32
   and heaven, 65–66
elitism, 198
embodiment, 9n10, 136, 173
Enlightenment, 31–33
entertainment, 5, 81, 173, 186
entertainers, 5, 19
epistemology, 18–21, 64–65, 72, 137, 156,
     182, 195
   and the church, 185, 226
   and fallenness, 89–90
   and metaphysics, 158
   "naturalized epistemology," 234n67
   Reformed, 129
   virtue, 228n53
eternal life, 66, 73, 74, 78, 129n64
ethics, 13, 74, 117, 133, 182n85, 237, 239
   and the Bible, 60, 125
   Christian, 4, 62, 63n6, 67, 68n16
   and the Fall, 59–60
   and pluralism, 26–27

evangelicalism, 6, 14
  anti–intellectualism of, 92n10, 106
  and the Christian mission, 76–77
  Evangelical Revivals, 15
  and Scripture, 115–24
  and special revelation, 89–90n6
evangelism, 68, 80–81
evil, 81, 89, 102, 176, 221, 225
  good and, 9, 26, 28, 59, 84–85n33,
    242–43n83
  natural, 74
  problem of, 73–75, 83, 130
"evil demon," 95, 99, 231
evolution, 15, 37
exegesis, 13, 120, 122, 124, 127
existentialism, 50, 53n41
experience, 10–13, 77, 92–101
  and interpretation of reality, 144–45, 158,
    157–58n36
  mystical, 7–10, 129–30, 149n17
  practical, 163–64n45

faith, 129n64, 146n14, 208–9, 242
fanaticism, 204–5, 210, 213
feeling, 47, 56, 77, 98n18, 210–11, 215
  in process thought, 37
  in Romanticism, 33, 36
  and sense experience, 88, 96–98
feminism, 13, 52, 83, 245–46
feminist epistemology, 135, 167, 193n103, 194
foundationalism, 135, 168, 210
freedom, 68n16, 135, 180–81, 224
  from authorities, 14–15
  false, 13
  and Romanticism, 34, 35
fruitfulness, 20, 69
fundamentalism, 45, 116n42, 224

gender, 41, 51, 147, 245–50
  stereotypes, 217n30
  and women, 26–27
general revelation, 15
generosity, 78n27, 183
genocide, 28
good. See evil
gospel. See evangelism; narrative, of the Bible
grace, 143n7, 219n36, 230n59, 233
  "common grace," 223–24
  means of, 235–36, 242
Great Commandment, 56, 138, 223

Great Commission, 79
Great Story, 43–44, 57–67, 79, 85n34

heaven, 58, 65–66, 74, 7598, 144, 220, 233
  kingdom of, 185n89
hell, 66, 80, 104
heresy, 11, 126, 178n75
hermeneutics, 17, 87–88n4, 117, 128, 189
  hermeneutical circle, 105, 121, 148
  hermeneutical spiral, 152, 176, 221
history, 36–37, 43–44, 50–51, 154, 176–77
  the discipline of, 4n3, 88–89n5, 108, 222
  and Scripture, 57, 63, 112, 113n38, 119–25, 161
  and values/ethics, 27, 84–85n33, 106n31
holiness, 17, 225
Holy Spirit, 3–4, 20n23, 65, 75, 78–79, 83,
    98, 114n41, 119n46, 227n52, 228n53
  baptism of, 13
  and Biblical interpretation, 10, 122–23, 149
  and doubt, 226–27, 231
  and inspiration, 10, 63, 89–90n6
hope, 57, 73–74, 78, 195n89, 242
  and modernity, 39–40
  of shalom, 66
hospitality, 185–86, 192
humanism, 26, 28, 173
human nature, 81, 221, 223
humility, 57, 133, 155n31, 165n47, 205, 225
  of God, 78–79n28

identity, 19, 62, 155
  Christian, 12
  human, 70, 102
ideology, 5, 14, 24, 43, 159, 181
  of multiculturalism, 54
idolatry, 118–19n44
ignorance, 10, 72, 83, 171n60, 219
illumination, 9n10, 34, 89, 119
  by the Holy Spirit, 89–90n6, 98n18,
    113n38, 114n41
imagination, 66, 111, 123, 131–34, 169n54, 230
  limits of, 186, 207–8
Incarnation, 61, 70, 98, 114n40
  of God, 89–90n6
  of the savior, 226
individualism, 40, 175, 185n89
infallibility, 20, 83
inner light, 8
inspiration, 10, 63, 114n41, 117, 121, 127
  definition of, 113

interior life, 92–93
interpretation. *See* hermeneutics
intuition, 36, 83, 91, 127–31, 217–18
   and cognitive dissonance, 157–58n36
   in mysticism, 135, 149n17
   in Romanticism, 33, 128
   "women's intuition," 128

Jesus, 61–63, 70–71, 76
judgment, 24, 26–28, 56, 88–89n5, 165,
     195, 198, 202n116, 210n11
   eternal, 14, 79, 226
   private, 185n89
justice, 24, 43, 65, 68, 89, 120, 176, 183
   and evil, 74–75
   and social constructivism, 172–73

Kingdom of God, 5, 62, 77–79, 198
knowledge, definition of, 145, 162n44,
     169, 209. *See also* certainty

liberalism, 11–16, 27, 55, 173
Liberal Triangle, 11, 13
liberation theology, 12–13, 180n79, 183
linguistics, 13, 108
liturgy, 89–90n6, 103, 120
logos, 9n10, 28, 70, 222–23
Lord's Supper, 4, 235
Lutherans, 15

masters of suspicion, 3, 49
mastery, 41, 137, 140, 215, 224
Mennonites, 6, 15
mentality, 6–8, 37, 136
metanarrative, 43, 46, 57, 154, 213
metaphysics, 28, 36, 43, 87, 108, 158
   in Christian theology, 117, 123
   and morality, 71n20
   and postmodernity, 48
Methodists, 15
middle ages, 15, 38
miracles, 89, 108, 127, 147–48n16, 227
mission, 56, 61–62, 69–71, 81–82, 93, 116,
     120–21, 123
   as temporary Christian vocation,
     75–80
modernity, 4, 14, 45–46, 52, 126
   definition of, 39–40
   and individualism, 185
   postmodern critique of, 42–43

morality, 50, 59, 118, 125
   and Scripture, 150n22
   as a social construction, 27
mysticism, 7–11, 16, 33, 65–66, 73, 79,
     97–98, 129, 149n17
   Eastern, 37
   in the Enlightenment, 33
   and reason, 99–101, 135–36, 236–37
   in Romanticism, 33, 36
myth, 178n75, 196

narrative, 91, 130n66, 136, 186, 215
   of the Bible, 56–67, 69, 72, 155n31
   "grand narratives," 45–46, 123
   and hypotheses, 153, 156
   metanarrative, 43, 46, 57, 154, 213
   and science, 154n29, 176–77, 225
naturalism, 19n22, 165n47, 196
nature. *See* creation
nihilism, 28, 52, 233n65
nominalism, 38

ontology, 12, 117
oppression, 12–13, 15, 35, 62
ordination, 13
Orthodox Church, 6–7, 10–11, 67–68,
     114n41

paradigm shift, 177–78n72
paradox, 80, 83, 87, 145–46, 193, 219, 221
   of the gospel, 145n12
   of providence, 84–85n33
   and tradition, 130–4
Pentalectic, 139–48, 152, 157, 210
Pentecostalism, 7, 13, 45, 89–90n6
   and mysticism, 8, 36
perception, 12n12, 16, 48, 111, 130n67,
     141n3, 157–58, 170n58, 232nn62–63
   extra–sensory, 99, 127, 161n41
   mystical, 8n8, 36, 99
   sensory, 96–97, 154
   and skepticism, 213
   and subjectivity, 41
physics, 17, 28, 32, 52, 87, 127, 135, 147,
     166n50, 176
   and causation, 19n22
   and elegance, 91–92
   Theory of Everything, 87, 96
pluralism, 22–29, 45n25, 87, 90, 205
   and postmodernism, 52, 54–55, 159, 242

politics, 4, 25, 54, 147, 182n85, 183, 224
  and Locke, 38, 204, 211
  and sin, 20n23, 81
postliberalism, 58n2, 194n107, 224
postmodernity, 38–55
  hypermodernity, 30, 43, 45n25, 50
poststructuralism, 51, 184, 213–14
power, 44, 51–55, 65, 76, 78–79, 84, 89, 102,
    174, 183, 191, 193, 197, 213–14
  of God and of reason, 136–38, 226
  and pluralism, 24, 37
  and sense experience, 96–97
  supernatural, 32
pragmatism, 39, 91, 142–43, 151, 192–93, 207
  and God, 84
  and politics, 53–54
prayer, 56, 225–26, 230
predestination, 12, 82n31
process theology, 12
process, 36–38
progress, 37, 44, 91–92n9
providence, 73, 84, 89–90n6, 138, 194, 204,
    228n53, 248
  and Bonhoeffer, 84–85n33
  definition of, 69
  in the Enlightenment, 31
  and false beliefs, 20n23
psychology, 37–38, 89, 168, 171n60, 187,
    203, 214–15
  and certainty, 146–47, 211
  and intuition, 130
  and Scripture, 149n17
  and sin, 72
psychosis, 8, 99–100

realism, 38, 71–72, 87–88, 90, 96, 171
  critical, 86, 172, 193, 237n73
  and postmodernism, 52
  and relativism, 169
reality, 36, 42, 44, 49–50, 84–85n33, 91, 110,
    134–35, 141–48, 214–15
  approximations of, 40, 97
  avoidance of, 221
  definition of, 140–41
  as socially constructed, 172–73
  ultimate, 25, 158
reason, 12, 36, 42–43, 56, 59, 87, 134–38,
    146n14, 150n22, 159, 196
  definition of, 134
  and faith, 208

limitations of, 98, 129–30, 213, 219–221,
    233–34n67
  and priors, 165–66
  and science, 97
recreation, 107
redemption, 136
  in the Biblical narrative, 58, 60–62, 67, 80,
    83–84, 85n34, 119, 121
  of the earth, 5
Redemption Commandments, 79. *See also*
    Salvation Commandments
Reformation, 15, 31, 68, 89–90n6, 104n27
  and the Bible, 126
  and individualism, 185
reincarnation, 14
relativism, 24–29, 42, 51, 194
  antirealistic, 169
  and multiculturalism, 55
  and pragmatism, 142–43
reliability, 18, 87, 95n15, 143n8, 145, 154,
    170, 178, 199, 203, 214
  of experience, 18, 94, 99
  of memory, 154, 218
  of testimony, 198
religion, 35, 54, 86–87, 108, 162n43, 208
  and mysticism, 7, 9n10
  New Religions, 23
  and particularity, 77, 118
  and pluralism, 23–25
  "religion à la carte," 14, 54
  and science, 143n9, 162n43
remythologizing, 12n12
Renaissance, 31, 126, 173
responsibility, 18, 100–101, 105, 124, 149,
    169, 181, 202, 235, 237
  and calling, 242nn81–82
  in the Creation Commandments, 71
  in earthly matters, 65
  in Scripture, 64
Restorationists, 15
revelation, 5, 13, 17n20, 31, 74–75, 82n31, 83,
    86n3, 98n18, 106n31, 136–38
  general, 15, 89–90n6
  light of, 223n45
  media of, 75, 114n41
  propositional, 89–90n6
  in Scripture, 14–15, 113n38, 121n50, 149,
    150n22
  special, 15, 89, 89–90n6
  verbal, 123

revolution, 44, 51, 52, 73, 179, 249
French Revolution, 33
and communism, 36–37
Scientific Revolution, 30–32, 177,
177–78n72, 220, 222
rights, 13, 173, 249
Roman Catholicism, 105, 106n31, 126,
159, 201
and conservative thinking, 6–7, 10–11,
13, 15
and special revelation, 89–90n6
and vocation, 67
Romanticism, 33–36

salvation, 60–61, 73–74, 83
Salvation Commandments, 79–80. *See also*
Redemption Commandments
sanctification, 20n23, 32, 113n38, 136, 224
scholarship, 12, 105–8, 122, 124, 147–48n16
science, 17n20, 31–32, 37, 40–41, 96–97, 107,
162–72, 169–70
and authority, 195, 218
and faith, 208n5
historical, 154, 176–79
and the medieval mind, 92n10
and myth, 178n75
scientific method, 43, 49, 167
and Scripture, 149n17
and theology, 151n24
and truth, 143, 162n44, 222
Scientific Revolution. *See* revolution
Scripture, 7–16, 32, 57–67, 70, 111–27, 98n18,
148–52
inerrancy of, 114–16, 117–18
infallibility of, 119
inspiration of, 113–14
interpretation of, 16–17, 62–64, 104–5,
106n31, 123–27
nature of, 118–19
perspicuity of, 126
privileging of, 89–90n6, 105, 150–51
secularism, 28, 67–68, 125, 161, 169
methodological secularity, 147–48n16
sex, 54, 73, 198, 245–46, 249–50
sexism, 27, 194n106, 215
sexual experience, 31
sexuality, 51, 180, 234, 246
sexual purity, 14
shalom, 66–67, 71, 74, 79–80, 84,
90, 107

and the Christian vocation, 76–77, 237
definition of, 20
sin, 10, 59–60, 68n16, 83 219–20
and the human vocation, 73–78
noetic effects of, 20n23, 72, 93,
183n87, 215, 221, 222nn43–44
and spiritual disciplines, 225
skepticism, 38, 43, 45, 57, 90–91, 99, 213,
231–34
definition of, 28
radical, 52, 96, 170n58, 234, 237
and subjectivism, 42
slavery, 15, 26
social science, 15, 32, 53, 98, 184, 222
and Marxism, 37
and naturalism, 165n47
Society of Friends (Quakers), 8, 116
sociology, 13–14, 72, 133, 147,
154n30, 171
and the Enlightenment, 32
and pluralism, 22, 23
and Scripture, 225
sola scriptura, 6, 89–90n6, 105
sovereignty
of God, 12, 121
of the individual self, 14, 54, 126, 178,
184n88
special revelation, 89–90
statements of faith. *See* creeds
stereotypes, 29, 33, 213, 217, 245
story. *See* narrative
suffering, 74, 78, 168, 183, 209
superstition, 30

tabula rasa, 38
taxonomy, 6, 53n41
testimony, 196n109, 198, 218, 223
Christian, 77, 78n26, 80
of Scripture, 113n38
of the Spirit, 8, 98n18
theology, 11–15, 105, 134, 222–25, 247
and community, 175–76
and the Holy Spirit, 227
and science, 151n24
and Scripture, 32, 123–24, 149–51
and the *via negativa*, 86n3
and "the whole counsel of God," 115, 117
theory of everything, 38. *See also* physics
tolerance, 205
tongues, speaking in, 13

tradition, 101–6
  authority of, 10–11, 13
  definition of, 6
  and modernity, 29
truth, definitions of, 13, 32, 44, 52,
  141–43

Ultimate Reality, 25

vocation, definition of, 67–68

Wesleyan Quadrilateral, 9–10
  Christian version, 16, 18
  Protestant version, 10–11, 16
will of God, 9, 60n4, 85, 239–240
women. *See* feminism

work, definition of, 58, 62, 67–68. *See also*
  vocation
worldview, 14, 90, 108, 144n11, 157n35,
  160–62, 169, 171, 201–2
  Christian, 222, 225
  and metanarratives, 154
  modern, 166n50
  of Scripture, 10
  of skepticism, 99
World Wars, 8n9, 23, 44
worship, 5, 56, 77, 116, 138, 222,
  225, 235
  and the Bible, 123n53
  effect on epistemology of, 18
  and heaven, 56
  and women, 248

INDEX OF AUTHORS AND NAMES

Michaelangelo, 139
Middleton, J. Richard, 39n19
Milton, Michael, 17n20
Mitchell, Mark T., 127–28n60, 143n9
Moltke, Konrad von, 128n62
Mondrian, Piet, 46
Monmonier, Mark, 142, 188n93
Montana, Joe, 216n29
Morris, Thomas V., 91n8, 131, 134, 227n52
Mouw, Richard J., 66n10, 175–76n68, 198n112, 223n45
Muhammad, 114
Murphy, Nancey, 177–78n72, 211
Murphy, Terrence, 23n2

Nagel, Thomas, 95n15, 210n11
Navasky, Victor, 40n20, 202n115
Netland, Harold, 175–76n68
Neufeld, Peter J., 218n33
Neurath, Otto, 177–78n72
Newton, Isaac, 33, 40, 53, 87, 143, 222
Niebuhr, H. Richard, 186, 226n50
Niebuhr, Reinhold, 176
Nielsen, Kai, 163–64n45
Nietzsche, Friedrich, 28, 40, 43, 160, 220–21n40
Nijenhuis, W., 104n27
Noll, Mark A., 4n2, 91n10, 106, 112n37, 113n39, 116n42, 176n70
Numbers, Ronald L., 97n17

Oakeshott, Michael, 192
Oden, Thomas C., 10n11
O'Donovan, Oliver, 65–66
O'Keeffe, Georgia, 246
Okholm, Dennis L., 194n107
Origen, 223
Orr, James, 118–19n44
Ott, Craig, 175–76n68
Otto, Rudolph, 7
Outler, Albert C., 10n10
Owen, John, 121n48
Ozment, Steven, 30n6

Padgett, Alan G., 30n6
Pascal, 87, 130, 219n36, 231, 233–34n66
Pasteur, Louis, 163
Pauls, Jerry, 56n1
Payne, Peter, 91n8
Peck, M. Scott, 221n42

Pelikan, Jaroslav, 103n24
Perlin, Robert, 23n2
Philips, Timothy R., 194n107
Picasso, 111, 140, 173
Pierce, Ronald W., 249n3
Pinnock, Clark H., 6, 21n24
Placher, William C., 52n37, 163–64n45, 194n107
Planck, 87, 143
Plantinga, Alvin, 36, 53n43, 71–72n21, 95n15, 98n19, 124n56, 129, 150n22, 159–60n39, 165n48, 168n53, 169n54, 194n106, 196n109, 208n6, 210n10, 210n11, 215–16n28, 222n44, 231
Plantinga, Cornelius, 73–74, 222n43
Plato, 31, 141
Polanyi, Michael, 91n11, 127–28n60, 130n66, 140n2, 143n9, 143n10, 161n41, 163–64n45, 165n47, 167–71, 173, 175n67, 178n73, 195, 196, 197n111, 206n2, 210n12, 221n38, 233n65, 242n81
Polkinghorne, John, 132n72, 143n8
Pols, Edward, 233n65
Pope, Alexander, 33
Postman, Neil, 45, 211n14
Potter, Elizabeth, 103n23, 181n83, 182n84
Prior, Barry, 178–79n76
Provan, Iain, 125n58
Pushkin, Alexander, 33

Quine, W. v. O., 177–78n72, 234n67

Rambo, Lewis R., 171n61
Ranke, Leopold von, 128, 133n75
Raphael, 42
Reid, Thomas, 95n15, 231–34, 237n73
Rhine, J. B., 161n41
Richardson, W. Mark, 33n11, 164n46, 169
Ricoeur, Paul, 39
Rorty, Richard, 13, 53n41, 71n20, 176n70, 220–21
Rosen, Christine, 176n70
Ruether, Rosemary, 7
Russell, Jeffrey Burton, 166n50
Rybczynski, Witold, 47n28, 47n29
Ryken, Leland, 12n13

Sacks, Oliver, 157–58
Sanneh, Lamin, 116n43
Sartre, Jean-Paul, 28, 50, 220–21

Sayers, Dorothey L., 110n35
Scarry, Elaine, 130n65
Scheiermacher, Friedrich D. E., 11,
    106n31, 128, 175, 185
Schiffrin, Deborah, 141n4
Schlink, Basilea, 8–9n9
Schopenhauer, Arthur, 28, 220–21
Schreiner, Susan E., 147n15
Schreiter, Robert, 175–76n68
Schwartz, Hans, 74n24
Scorgie, Glen G., 118–19n44
Scott, Sir Walter, 42
Seitz, Christopher R., 124n56
Shakespeare, William, 180, 220n40
Shankara, 102
Sheldon, Charles, 61n5
Sher, Julian, 218
Sillars, Les, 13n15
Simons, Menno, 6
Smith, Myles, 116n42
Snyder, Howard A., 187n91
Socrates, 31
Sokal, Alan, 51n36
Soskice, Janet Martine, 156n33
Stark, Rodney, 119n46
Steiner, George, 21n24, 39n19,
    50n34, 87–88n4, 120, 140n1,
    141n4, 212
Stevens, Wallace, 48, 49n32
Streep, Meryl, 246–47
Stromberg, Roland N., 30n6
Sullivan, William M., 4n3
Swinburne, Richard, 165n48, 208n6
Swindler, Ann, 4n3

Taleb, Nassim, 215n24
Tannen, Deborah, 141n4
Tanner, Kathryn, 175n66
Tanner, Kenneth, 175–76n68
Tarule, Jill, 193n103
Taylor, Charles, 5n4, 14n18, 55n46
Tentler, Leslie Woodcock, 4n3
Teresa of Ávila, 102
Thatcher, Margaret, 245
Thielicke, Helmut, 225–26n48
Thiselton, Anthony C., 43n24, 155–56,
    191n96
Thomas á Kempis, 61
Thornton, John F., 179n77
Thorsen, Donald A. D., 10n11

Thucydides, 102
Thuesen, Peter J., 116n42
Tierney, John, 215n27
Tillich, Paul, 7, 141n3, 156
Tinder, Glenn, 236, 240
Tipton, Stephen M., 4n3
Tolkien, J. R. R., 109
Tolle, Eckhard, 25–26n3
Torrance, T. F., 92n10
Treier, Daniel J., 123n55, 175–76n68
Trible, Phyllis, 125n57
Trueblood, Elton, 42–43
Turner, Frank, 106n31

Unger, Peter, 233n65

Vanhoozer, Kevin J., 120
Van Inwagen, Peter, 124n56
Vinci, Leonardo da, 31
Volf, Miroslav, 58n2, 150n21
Voltaire, 31, 41, 98–99n20

Walls, Andrew, 145n12, 179, 194n105
Walsh, Brian J., 39n19, 51n35, 66n9
Waltke, Bruce, 56n1, 121n48
Warfield, B. B., 112n37, 113, 222n44
Warner, Curt, 216
Washburn, Katharine, 179n77
Weaver, Richard, 220n40
Webb, William J., 248n2
Webber, Robert E., 175–76n68
Weber, Max, 138n80
Webster, John, 104, 113n38, 114n40,
    114n41, 118–19n44, 123n53, 127,
    235n69
Wells, David F., 185
Wesley, Charles, 102–3
Wesley, John, 10–11, 31, 103, 106n31
Westphal, Merold, 150n20, 183n87
Whitehead, Alfred North, 12, 97n17
Wildman, Wesley J., 33n11, 164n46, 169
Wilken, Robert L., 78n26
Wilkens, Steve, 30n6
Wilkinson, Loren, 97n17
Willard, Dallas, 70–71n19, 232n62
William of Ockham, 38
Wilson, Edward O., 90n7, 222
Winch, Peter, 163–64n45
Winter, Alison, 218, 218–219n35
Wolfe, David L., 169